MAN AND HIS MUSIC

VOLUME TWO

This book is published also as Part II in a one-volume, illustrated, bound edition containing all four volumes. The cross-references to page numbers, Parts, and Plates, refer to that edition and should be disregarded here.

MAN AND HIS MUSIC

THE STORY OF MUSICAL EXPERIENCE IN THE WEST

ALEC HARMAN
with Anthony Milner

VOLUME TWO

LONDON
BARRIE AND JENKINS

First published in paperback 1969 by
Barrie & Rockliff (Barrie Books Ltd.)
Reprinted 1973 by Barrie & Jenkins Ltd.
24 Highbury Crescent, London N5 1RX

I.S.B.N. 0.214.66581.X

Made and printed in Great Britain by
J. W. Arrowsmith Ltd., Bristol 3

CONTENTS

VOLUME II

LATE RENAISSANCE AND BAROQUE MUSIC (*c.1525–c.1750*)

PREFACE

In the Preface to a later volume of this history Wilfrid Mellers remarks that a music historian should approach his task with both "circumspection and humility". He is undoubtedly right, for when one considers what is involved in such an undertaking one should be extremely chary of adding to what has already been achieved in this sphere; indeed, it is doubtful whether the attempt should ever be made unless one is convinced that the kind of history one has in mind is sufficiently distinctive to justify the writing of yet another.

In this series the authors have been guided by three chief aims, and we believe that it is in the combination of these aims that the distinctiveness of this particular history lies.

To begin with, we have tried to convey something of the feelings aroused in us by the music we write about and to give as many aesthetic judgments on individual works and composers as is possible in a work of this size and scope, for although we realize that such feelings and judgments are purely personal and that therefore it is hardly likely that everyone will agree with them, we believe that a history which does not seek to arouse a critical enthusiasm for each and every period and in which there are few or no aesthetic judgments to guide the taste of those less familiar with the music in question is not fulfilling one of its functions.

Our second aim has been to write a history that would be of use in both schools and universities, and while conscious that there is a marked difference in ability and attainment between those studying music in their last two or three years at school and those specializing in the subject at university level, and that hence this history will provide more for the one and less for the other than is needed, we hope that both will find something of value.

But a history of music should do more than stimulate enthusiasm, or assess greatness, or pass aesthetic judgments; it should do more than present facts and reasonable deductions, or include well-chosen examples and quotations, or give accurate analyses of styles and techniques, important as all these are; it should also (to quote *The New Oxford History of Music*) "present music not as an isolated phenomenon or the work of a few outstanding composers, but as an art developing in constant association with every form of human culture and activity". This has been our third aim, and in pursuing it we have tried, by giving what we hope is sufficient relevant information of a general nature, to set the stage, as it were, for each successive scene and (to continue the analogy) by outlining the principal characters involved (religion, painting, literature, etc.), to show in what ways and to what extent they influenced or were influenced by music.

This attempt to present music as an integral part of western civilization is essential, we believe, because all creative artists are influenced by the spiritual and intellectual environment in which they live, and so it follows that the more we know about a particular period the more we can enter into the creative minds of that period and hence appreciate more fully their aims and achievements. This may appear, and indeed is, obvious enough, but it is all too often forgotten, because each of us can enjoy and even be profoundly moved by a work of art knowing little or nothing about its creator or general background. Nevertheless, it remains true that every creative artist gains in significance when his work is related to the conditions in which it was created, whether he be someone whose name is a household word, like Mozart, or a comparatively obscure mediaeval composer, like Pérotin. Thus, knowing something of the rationalism, the sophisticated sentimentality, the polished elegance of society in the latter half of the eighteenth century, of the delicate sensuousness and exquisite refinement of Watteau's and Boucher's paintings, we marvel more than if we knew nothing of all this, not so much at the utter perfection of Mozart's style and sense of structure as at the undercurrents of emotion that pervade his work and which at times amount almost to romantic passion.

Compared to Mozart, Pérotin gains in significance to a much greater extent when we know something about his background because the time at which he lived and the style in which he wrote have far fewer points of contact for us today than is the case with the eighteenth century. At first hearing, his music may well sound bare, monotonous, and meaningless, but when it is realized that the systematization and reiteration of rhythmic patterns, which are the main features of Pérotin's style, not only represented a new development in music, but also reflected, as did the solutions to the structural problems of Gothic architecture, the intellectual awakening of the twelfth and thirteenth centuries, an awakening that was stimulated by the discovery, through Arab philosophers, of the works of Aristotle, and which led men like Peter Abelard and St. Thomas Aquinas to believe and teach that faith can only be wholly assured when founded on reason; when it is further realized that, apart from the octave, the fourth and fifth were the basic intervals because they were as satisfyingly sonorous to ears accustomed to unison singing and playing as thirds and sixths are to us; and, lastly, that the music was intended to be performed as an act of devotion in a cathedral rather than listened to as an aesthetic experience in a concert hall—then the significance of the man becomes apparent and, after adjusting our ears and minds in the light of what we have learnt, we can begin to understand, assess, and (because he was in fact a fine composer) enjoy his music, with its marked contrast between the lively, bouncy rhythmic figures in one part and the sustained or slower-moving notes in another.

But writing alone cannot give an adequate account of any period, especially with regard to the fine arts, and if there had been no considerations as to cost this history would have included many more reproductions, some of them coloured, of buildings, paintings, sculpture, etc. Nevertheless, we hope that all those who read it will want to discover more of the achievements in other fields and that some will wish to pursue in greater detail the development of the music itself.

It is obvious, however, that the greatest value from knowing something about the background of a particular art can only be obtained if one has experienced or has the opportunity of experiencing that art, and so, because it has been impossible, for financial reasons, to include more than a very few complete examples in the text I have therefore given a number of references to Vol. I of *The Historical Anthology of Music* (*H.A.M.*).

This volume is deliberately less well balanced than Vol. I because late Renaissance music, and particularly Baroque opera are likely to be more unfamiliar to the student than Baroque instrumental and vocal music.

R. Alec Harman

I

THE LATE RENAISSANCE: SECULAR MUSIC

THE most important type of composition in the late Renaissance was undoubtedly the madrigal, for not only did it exert a greater influence than any other type, but it eventually foreshadowed more clearly the advent of baroque music. Despite its name, there is no connexion whatever with the fourteenth-century type (which was probably completely unknown in the Renaissance, anyway), except, of course, that both were written in the 'mother tongue', not in Latin.

The sixteenth-century madrigal sprang from a fusion of the Italian frottola, the French chanson, and the polyphonic imitative style of the north European composers, who were mostly Netherlanders or Flemings.

From about 1510 onwards the frottola texts grew more serious in content and the music more 'learned' in style, but the lighter side was kept alive and eventually developed into the less sophisticated, racy villanesca (see p. 245). The most important of the serious frottola types was the canzona, in which the poetic text varies considerably in structure (a feature of the later madrigal), the music is mildly polyphonic, and the beginnings and ends of phrases are clear-cut.

The brilliance of the late Renaissance in Italy not only attracted men from all over the Continent, but exerted a powerful influence on aristocratic society, arts, and letters everywhere, particularly in France, Spain, and, towards the end of the century, England. Of all the European countries France had had the longest and most distinctive and distinguished musical tradition, and while she absorbed some of the characteristics of the early frottola—the only kind of music that was purely Italian—she produced a type of composition, the chanson, that was different in many respects and which had little connexion with the fifteenth-century Burgundian type. Its main features are a lightness, simplicity, and beauty achieved through the frequent use of rapid repeated notes, dance-like rhythms, and a predominantly chordal texture; these, together with clear-cut phrases and melodic and sectional repetitions, provide a sharp contrast with the Burgundian chanson, and while the chordal texture and phrasing show Italian influence, the frottola on the whole had never placed such a premium on melody (how could it, coming from Italy?), nor had it been so rhythmically precise. This does not mean that the chansons are tuneless, but that in most cases their appeal depends to a greater extent on their harmonic and rhythmic qualities and on the words to which they are set than on the attractiveness or expressiveness of their melodies.

The first two leading masters of the French chanson were Clément Janequin [d. *c.* 1560] and Claudin de Sermisy [*c.* 1490–1562]. The former was by far the more popular, and not only was he the first 'Composer in Ordinary' to any French king, but he also set the fashion for the 'programme-chanson', which became all the rage. These pieces carried the Renaissance delight in realistic word-painting a stage further than hitherto, and titles such as *Les chants des oiseaux* and *Le caquet des femmes* ('Women's chatter') are typical. By far his most celebrated piece, a positive smash-hit, in fact, was *La Guerre*, written to celebrate the French victory at the Battle of Marignano (1515). This was imitated more widely and arranged for instruments more frequently than any of his other songs, and its vivid word-painting in which trumpet fanfares, drum-beats, war-cries, and other battle noises are imitated in the music represents an extreme example of the programme-chanson. (Ex. 1,* see p. 241. Notice the cross-accents which, in bars 2–5, result in a stress on each crochet in one part or another, and so add to the general confusion.)

By far the greater number of chansons, however, both by Janequin himself and others, are characterized by a text, usually expressive of unrequited love, that is set more conventionally but with a greater regard for purely musical qualities. It was this type that Claudin favoured, and among his examples are some that tell a story—the 'narrative-chanson'. Most of these begin with three repeated notes in the rhythm 𝅗𝅥 ♩ ♩, a feature of some frottole, but why it became

* From *Clément Janequin: Chansons* (*Attaignant, 1529*) (*Les Maîtres musiciens de la Renaissance française*), ed. H. Expert, Vol. VII, p. 31.

Ex. 1 From the programme chanson - *La Guerre* (1529) Janequin

(as it did) a hall-mark of all narrative-chansons is not clear. Despite Janequin's fame, his work is no better than Claudin's, though the lively if naïve realism of his descriptive pieces will probably always be more immediately attractive than the delicate charm of those of his contemporary (Ex. 2*, p. 242).

The Janequin-Claudin chanson, like the frottola, did not last against the invincible tide of polyphony that continued to sweep from the north, and imitation and through-composition rather than counterpoint and repetition were favoured by the next generation of composers, especially, as we would expect, those born in the Netherlands or of Flemish stock. Even the leading French chanson writers, Jean Richafort [*c.* 1480–1548] and Thomas Crecquillon [d. *c.* 1557], were affected, but not so

* Adapted from *Chansons au luth* . . ., ed. Laurencie, Mairy, and Thibaut, p. 14. Accompaniment omitted.

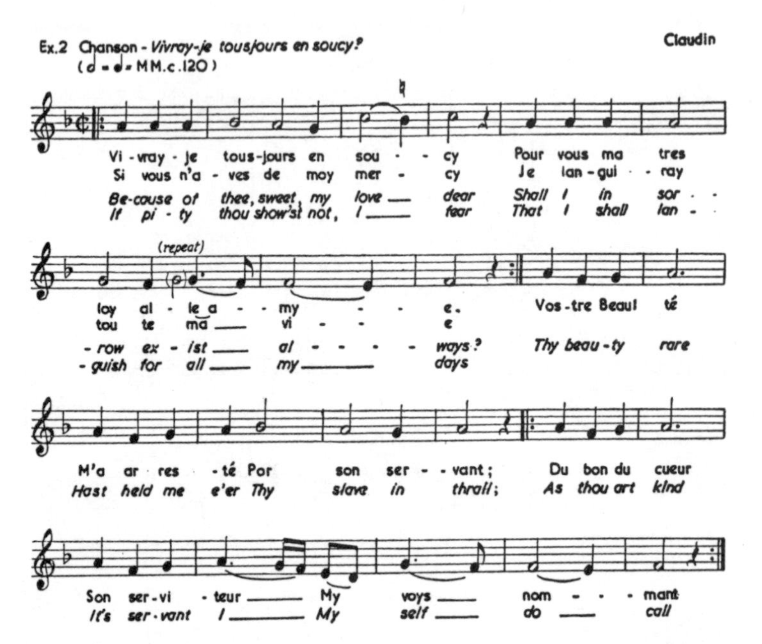

markedly as the northerners, Clemens non Papa [1510–*c.* 1557/8], Nicolas Gombert [d. after 1556], Adrian Willaert [*c.* 1490–1562], and Jacques Arcadelt [*c.* 1504–after 1567].

The popularity of the French chanson throughout the sixteenth century is attested by the number that were printed by the leading music publishers, particularly those outside Italy. The chief of these were Pierre Attaignant [d. 1552], who issued nearly seventy collections, Adrian le Roy [d. *c.* 1589] and Robert Ballard [d. 1606], Jacques Moderne [*c.* 1500–*c.* 1567], and Nicolas du Chemin [*c.* 1510–1576] in France, and Tielman Susato [d. *c.* 1561], and Pierre Phalèse [*c.* 1510–*c.* 1573] in the Low Countries. All used the single impression method (see Part I, pp. 210-11), and Moderne seems to have been the first to arrange the parts on opposite pages so that they can be read by people sitting on opposite sides of a table (Ex. 3, see p. 243).

Arcadelt and Willaert were not only important chanson composers, but also played a considerable part in the development of the early madrigal, though they were preceded by the Frenchman Philippe Verdelot [d. *c.* 1540] and the Italian Constanzo Festa [d. 1545]. The works of these last show the

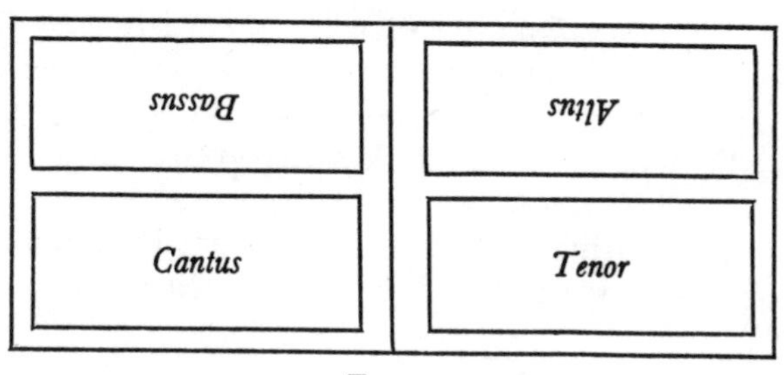

Ex 3.

opposing styles of imitative polyphony and counterpoint which in some of their madrigals are fused into an essentially chordal texture, but with the parts enlivened by short snatches of imitation or rhythmic independence. The main difference between the two men is that while Verdelot, being a northerner, preferred the richness of five or six parts, Festa favoured the greater simplicity and clarity of writing *a*3. The latter was also more 'modern' in sometimes employing a kind of notation called 'note nere' in which the mensuration sign is 'c' and in which the semiminim (our crotchet) is the harmonic unit (the tactus therefore being the minim); hence most of the notes are 'black'. In Part I we stated that from Josquin onwards most compositions were written in ¢, with the minim as the harmonic unit, the semibreve being the tactus ('note bianche', because most of the notes are 'white'), but from *c.* 1540 on note nere was increasingly used in madrigals and other secular pieces, while masses and motets continued to use note bianche. Now although the minim in ¢ ranged from M.M. 120–160, the crotchet therefore ranging from M.M. 240–320, there is some doubt as to the speed of the crotchet in c; occasionally it might be as fast as M.M. 240, as in some of the more frivolous French chansons, but in general it probably fluctuated between M.M. 120 and 160, thus equalling the range of the minim in ¢. From 1550 onwards many vocal pieces were written, in effect, in both c and ¢, in the sense that either the crotchet or the minim was the harmonic unit of a particular section, the choice usually depending on the text. Thus, for example, if the words 'joy' or 'quickly' occur in a line, the harmonic movement is usually in crotchets at, say, M.M. 180, but if 'grief' or 'slowly' occur this would change to minims, the speed of which would now be M.M. 90 (see pp. 292f.).

Of the chanson composers mentioned earlier, only Arcadelt and Willaert are important as madrigalists. The former achieved fame from the very start, and his first book of madrigals (1538?) was reprinted no less than thirty-three times by 1654. Most of his madrigals are *a*4 and are characterized by clear, diatonic harmony, smooth lyrical melody, and a classical approach that rejects undue expressiveness or emotion. (Ex. 4*):

* From *Trésor musical: Musique profane*, ed. Maldeghem, Vol. XXV, p. 9.

This is, deservedly, his most famous madrigal. Note the simple but most expressive slip to the flat side of the key on '*piangendo*' ('weeping'), and the ending with its held note in the top part. We call this an 'inverted pedal'; if the held note is in a middle part it is called an 'inner pedal', and if in the lowest part (the usual place) it is called simply a 'pedal', from the held tonic or dominant pedal note so common in the final bars of organ extemporisations and compositions. It was a favourite ending in both instrumental and vocal music during the late Renaissance. The last point of imitation ('*di mille mort' il dì*'), with its initial upward leap followed by a stepwise descent, became the most hackneyed of all such points during the same period. Most of Arcadelt's madrigals were written in Rome, but in 1553 he settled in France and adopted the chanson instead.

Rome was also the scene of Festa's activity, while Verdelot spent most of his life in Florence and Venice. These three cities were the main centres of madrigal writing, especially the last, owing to the pre-eminence of Willaert, one of the greatest composers, and certainly the most influential, of the sixteenth century. In 1527 he was appointed *maestro di capella* ('chapel master') of the famous Romanesque basilica of St. Mark, and apart from occasional short visits abroad he remained there till his death. Willaert's genius is equalled by his versatility, and his enormous output includes masses, motets, madrigals, chansons, and frivolous pieces, such as villanescas. These last (sometimes called 'villanelle') originated in Naples and developed from the lighter kind of frottola, becoming popular mainly through the attractive, simple, and often humorous examples of one Giovane Domenico da Nola [*c.* 1520–1592] who, while not the earliest, was certainly the first important master of this type. The main characteristics are animated rhythm, chordal texture (usually *a*3), $\frac{4}{4}$ time (note nere), and a fair sprinkling of consecutive fifths in the part writing, this last being deliberate. The texts range from the plaints of lovesick swains through caricatures of famous madrigals to scurrilous and obscene verse. The opinion commonly held that sixteenth-century music is 'proper' is due to the 'quaintness' of its style and to the shadow of sanctity cast by its most famous representative, Palestrina, but many of the madrigals, chansons, and other secular types reflect more or less bluntly the full-bloodedness of the period. This is especially true of the 'mascherata' sung during 'masked' balls and processions, and the 'moresca', in which the singers represent 'Moorish' girls of doubtful reputation.

Willaert's early madrigals, like those of Arcadelt and Festa, show the influence of the chanson and frottola in their simple polyphony, clear-cut phrases, and melodic importance of the highest voice, but his later ones reveal his northern origin in their greater complexity, use of imitation, equality of voices, and overlapping cadences. Although chromaticism is a far less significant feature of his work than is often made out, it seems likely that he was in fact more than usually interested in this aspect of composition, judging by his pupils at any rate, especially the Italian Nicolo Vicentino [1511–1572].

Vicentino attempted to present in modern notation the ancient Greek diatonic, chromatic, and enharmonic divisions of the scale (see Part I, p. 17), and by placing dots over notes and laying down certain rules as to the meaning of sharps, flats, and naturals in conjunction with the dots, he composed pieces in which the whole-tone was divided into five parts. Such music is impossible to sing—though Vicentino is supposed to have trained a choir for this express purpose—and of more practical value are his 'normal' madrigals, which are chromatically very advanced for their time in their use of such rare notes as are included in the major chords of D♯ and D♭, and in intervals such as the augmented third, e.g. E♭–G♯. The most important aspect of these pieces is that they show a desire for a melodic and harmonic expressiveness which the modal system could not possibly give, even though the latter had expanded during the fifteenth century and now included four other modes in addition to the eight discussed in Part I. These were the Aeolian (A–A, our descending melodic minor scale), Hypoaeolian (E–E, final A), Ionian (C–C, our major scale), and Hypoionian (G–G, final C), and the first theorist to give these new modes an independent status was the Swiss Heinrich Loris or, as he is generally known, Henricus Glareanus [1488–1563], in his famous *Dodecachordon* (1547) (literally 'twelve strings'). In this treatise Glareanus demonstrates from examples by Josquin and others that a melody ending in F with a B♭ in the signature had a quite different flavour and character if there was no flat. Formerly, both had been regarded as Lydian (see Part I, Chapter 5, p. 131), but Glareanus called only the second Lydian, the first being Ionian transposed, which of course it is. In actual fact, by Glareanus's day the genuine Lydian was hardly ever used, and the Phrygian too became less common as the century progressed, leaving the Dorian, Mixolydian, Aeolian, and Ionian modes, and of these only the last two have survived to the present day.

Vicentino's experiments were strongly attacked by a number of theorists, including one of the greatest, his fellow pupil and countryman, Gioseffe Zarlino [1517–1590]. Zarlino spent most of his life in Venice, and his three main treatises, which were published in one volume in 1589, contain a great deal of valuable information, such as the statement that the two beats of the tactus are equal to the rate of a human pulse (this averages about M.M. 70, hence our calculations earlier). More important is his realization and convincing demonstration of just intonation, a system of intervals that had already been discovered to all intents and purposes by the Spaniard Ramos (see Part I, Chapter 6, p. 231) and also by the Italian theorists Pietro Aron [*c.* 1490–1545] and more especially by Ludovico Fogliano [d. 1539].

Just intonation is a scale made up of certain intervals that occur naturally. If, for instance, a flexible string of uniform diameter, weight, and tension (e.g. a piano or violin string) is hit, plucked, or bowed it not only vibrates as a whole but in fractions of its length as well. The vibrations of the complete string give the fundamental note or first partial, and those of the various fractions of the string give the upper partials, the total sound of the string consisting of some or all of these partials, the number audible depending on the way the string is excited, the pitch of the fundamental, its loudness, and the sensitivity of the ear. Thus if we take the bottom string of the 'cello as our fundamental note or first partial the next fifteen partials are (Ex. 5):

Ex. 5

1 2 3 4 5 6 7 8 9 10 11 12 13 14 15 16

C c g c' e' g' c'' d'' e'' g'' c'''

(The black semibreves indicate notes that cannot be correctly represented on the stave, e.g. the eleventh partial (*f''*) is not a perfect fourth above *c″*; they are therefore omitted from the discussion that follows. This succession of notes is called 'the harmonic series'.) The interval between any one note in the harmonic series and any other can be expressed by a ratio consisting of the partial 'number' of the notes. Thus (reckoning downwards) the ratio of *c*–*C* (octave) is $\frac{2}{1}$; of *g*–*c* (fifth) $\frac{3}{2}$; of *c″*–*g′* (fourth) $\frac{4}{3}$, and so on. Furthermore, the ratio of any interval can be found by either multiplying the ratios of its constituent intervals or else dividing the ratio of a larger interval by the ratio of the remaining smaller interval. For instance, a major sixth is made up of a fourth and major third (ratio $\frac{5}{4}$, e.g. *e′*–*c′*), so that $\frac{4}{3} \cdot \frac{5}{4} = \frac{5}{3}$ (e.g. *e′*–*g*); again, an octave minus a minor third (ratio $\frac{6}{5}$, e.g. *g′*–*e′*) also leaves a major sixth $\frac{2}{1} \div \frac{6}{5}$ or $\frac{2}{1} \cdot \frac{5}{6} = \frac{5}{3}$.

All the first six partial notes are, and were to sixteenth-century ears, concordant with each other, and they can be used to construct a complete major scale. The most important notes are, and were, the tonic, dominant, and subdominant, and the first step is obviously to build major triads on each of these three notes. Taking C as our 'keynote' the tonic triad, C, E, G, already exists; the dominant chord consists of G, B (ratio $\frac{5}{4}$ to G) and D (ratio $\frac{3}{2}$ to G), and the subdominant chord F, A (ratio $\frac{5}{4}$ to F), and C. But before we can play or sing this scale we must place each note in relation to C; we already know the ratio of C–E, C–F, C–G, and C–C, and the others can be found; thus the major seventh C–B = C–G plus G–B, or $\frac{3}{2} \cdot \frac{5}{4} = \frac{15}{8}$; the major sixth C–A must be $\frac{5}{3}$ (C–F plus F–A, or $\frac{4}{3} \cdot \frac{5}{4} = \frac{5}{3}$); C–D = C–G minus D–G, or $\frac{3}{2} \cdot \frac{3}{4} = \frac{9}{8}$. We can now draw a diagram of the just intonation scale showing the ratios between each note and the lower tonic (Ex. 6):

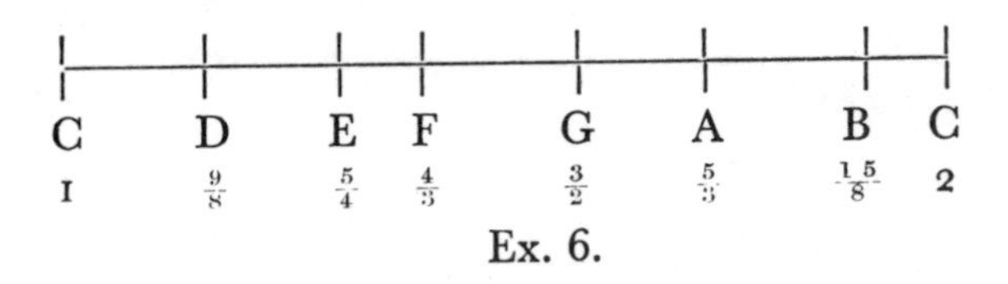

Ex. 6.

In this diagram the semitones look the same size, but the whole tones do not, and this is indeed the case, because whereas C–D, F–G, and A–B are all of ratio $\frac{9}{8}$, D–E and G–A are both $\frac{10}{9}$ (i.e. $\frac{5}{4} \cdot \frac{8}{9}$ and $\frac{5}{3} \cdot \frac{2}{3}$ respectively). Moreover, while the fifths

C–G, E–B, F–C, and G–D are all of ratio $\frac{3}{2}$, D–A is $\frac{40}{27}$ (i.e. $\frac{5}{3} \cdot \frac{8}{9}$.) Similarly, there are two kinds of fourth and minor seventh. The whole trouble arises from the fact that there are two different whole tones, the greater tone, $\frac{9}{8}$, and the lesser tone, $\frac{10}{9}$; this severely limits the possibilities of this particular scale, especially if harmony is involved, in that not only does the super-tonic chord (D minor in the key of C) sound false, but the scale of the relative minor has two notes out of tune. The chief merit of just intonation is the purity of the three main chords, tonic, dominant, and subdominant, with their true thirds and fifths, and although this scale was not recognized theoretically until the sixteenth century it is most probable that in practice competent singers and string players of part-music had always rendered sustained fifths and complete triads in just intonation, as, indeed, they should do today, the false fifth being made true by flattening the super-tonic note when necessary.

Voices and stringed instruments are capable of flexible intonation, but keyboard instruments are not, and up to *c.* 1500 organs and harpsichords must either have sounded vilely out of tune sometimes, or else some of the notes must have been slightly and inoffensively mistuned. Mistuning, in fact, is inevitable in normal keyboard instruments, and the first person to tackle this problem seriously was the German organist mentioned in Part I, p. 216, Arnolt Schlick, who advocated making most of the fifths a little flatter than the true fifth. Not until Zarlino, however, and more especially the great Spanish theorist, Francisco de Salinas [1513–1590], was a system of tuning called 'mean-tone' temperament fully worked out.

The difference between a greater tone and a lesser tone is known as the 'comma of Didymus' [b. 63 B.C.], a Greek theorist who had realized that the Pythagorean major third was not the 'natural' one, being too sharp by a small interval of ratio, $\frac{81}{80}$, which is the same as that between the lesser tone and the greater tone, i.e. $\frac{9}{8} \cdot \frac{9}{10} = \frac{81}{80}$. In mean-tone temperament half of this 'comma' is added to the lesser tone and the other half is subtracted from the greater tone, the result being two equal 'mean' tones. This tampering with or 'tempering' the notes leads to a true octave and major third (with its complement, the minor sixth), all the other intervals being slightly out of tune compared to just intonation; but the important thing is that although the fifths are half a comma flatter than the true fifth, the 'wrong 'un', D–A, has disappeared, for they are all equally mistuned and therefore all sound the same.

Chromatic notes in the upper octaves had been introduced on some organs as early as the late fourteenth century, and by the middle of the fifteenth century the keyboard was completely chromatic, except for the lowest octave. In mean-tone tuning the five 'black' keys represented those notes most commonly used—namely, C♯, F♯, G♯, B♭, and E♭, the first three being tuned a true major third above A, D, and E respectively, and the last two a true major third below D and G. On the harpsichord G♯ was sometimes retuned as A♭, a major third below C, and in the latter half of the sixteenth century E♭ was occasionally retuned as D♯, a major third above B. On our modern pianos G♯ and A♭ are the same, but in mean-tone temperament G♯ is appreciably flatter than A♭, and a true G♯ would sound horrible in an A♭ major or F minor chord. Similarly with E♭ and D♯. There were thus two kinds of semitone, the greater, e.g. G♯-A, and the lesser, e.g. G-G♯.

To overcome this difficulty, some organs were built during the early sixteenth century and later with separate pipes for A♭ and D♯ and therefore with two extra keys in each octave. Zarlino went further and in 1548 had a harpsichord built containing the greater and lesser semitone between each whole tone, which meant seventeen keys to the octave, seven 'white' and ten 'black', but Vicentino capped this in 1555 with a harpsichord in which the octave was divided into thirty intervals spread over six manuals, each manual being tuned to one of the six Greek scales (see Part I, p. 17). It was, of course, too cumbersome to be of much practical value, unlike Zarlino's, but both showed dissatisfaction with the limited harmonic range of the modal system, a dissatisfaction that rapidly increased during the latter part of the century and which resulted in a greater degree of chromaticism and modulation.

Neither Vicentino nor Zarlino were composers of the first rank, and it was left to yet another pupil of Willaert to embody the new chromaticism in madrigals that are among the greatest ever written. The pupil was the northerner, Cipriano de Rore [1516–1565], who succeeded his master as *maestro di cappella* at St. Mark's for a few years and who, after his resignation, was in turn succeeded by Zarlino. Rore was a man of serious even austere outlook, who set no frivolous texts, and whose preoccupation with mood-expression marks the beginning of a fundamental change in madrigal writing. Word-painting, both in sacred and secular pieces, had been common for some time, but this was usually a naïve and often flippant procedure; mood-expression, on the other hand, is concerned with the predominant emotion of a particular line or lines of a poem or even of a complete verse, and is thus more truly musical, for, as we observed in Part I (p. 226), music is essentially ill-suited to realism but can portray a general mood with complete success. In his striving for this kind of expression Rore employs not only chromaticism, but all the standard procedures of his time as well, e.g. imitation, polyphonic and contrapuntal textures, note nere, chains of $^6_3$ chords, etc., but everything is subject to the emotions suggested by the text, and it is these that now govern the unity of the music, not the poetic structure or rhyme endings of the verse, nor purely musical devices such as the repetition of a phrase to different words at the end of a piece, as commonly occurs in the French chanson. This treatment of the madrigal, which is chiefly to be found in Rore's mature work, set the fashion for nearly all later madrigalists, though few of them matched the intensity of his personal expression; it also sowed the seeds of destruction, for by stressing the fact that music can greatly enhance the emotional content of the written word Rore unwittingly initiated the movement which placed this ideal above all others and which, as a result, rejected polyphony in pursuit of its goal (Ex. 7)*.

The skill, sensitivity, and originality with which Rore wedded music to text, as in the superb example quoted above, makes him one of the outstanding composers of the sixteenth century, an estimation shared by his contemporaries, for not only were his madrigals reprinted many times, but an edition of all those he wrote for four voices was published in score in 1577; this, apart from being one of the earliest printed scores in existence, can only have been used for study purposes—a rare tribute to any composer.

Despite Rore's popularity and influence, two leading composers remained virtually untouched by the prevailing trend in madrigal writing—Giovanni Pierluigi [1524/5–1594], who later added the name of his native town, Palestrina, and

* Adapted from A. Einstein, *The Italian Madrigal*, Vol. III, p. 114.

Ex.7 Madrigal - *Crudele acerba inesorabil morte* (1557) (Petrarch) de Rore

Ex.7 (contd.)

- nar tut-ta mia vi-ta in pian - - - - to
pass my wretched life in weep - - - - ing,
Ma di me - nar tut - - ta mia vi-ta in pian - - - - to
But bid me pass my wretch-ed life in weep - - - - ing,
- nar, ma di me-nar tut-ta mia vi-ta in pian - - - - to
pass, but bid me pass my wretch-ed life in weep - - - - ing,
Ma di me-nar tut - - - ta mia vi - - - - ta in pian - - - - - to
But bid me pass my wretch - - ed life in weep - - - - - ing,
E i gior-ni o-scu - - ri e le do-glio - - se not - - - - - - -
My days in dark - - ness, and all my nights in tra - - - - - - -
E i gior-ni o-scu - - - - ri, e i gior-ni o-scu - - ri, e le do-
My days in dark - - - - ness, my days in dark - ness, and my
E i gior-ni o-scu - - ri e le do-glio - - se not - - - - - -
My days in dark - - ness, and all my nights in tra - - - - - -
E i gior-ni o-scu - - - - - - - ri e le do-
My days in dark - - - - - ness, and all my
- - ti. I miei gra-vi so-spir non van-no in
- vail. My deep sighs of des-pair rhyme not I
- glio - - se not - - - - - - - ti. I miei gra-vi so-spir non van-no in
nights in tra - - - - - - vail. My deep sighs of des-pair rhyme not I
- ti. I miei gra - vi so - spir non van-no in
- vail. My deep sighs of des - pair rhyme not I
- glio - se not - - - ti. I miei gra - vi so - spir non
nights in tra - - - vail. My deep sighs of des - pair rhyme

Ex.7 (contd.)

ri - - - - me E'l mio du - - ro mar - - tir, e'l
fear me, And my mer - - ci - less fate, and
ri - - - - me E'l mio du - - - ro mar - tir,
fear me, And my mer - - ci - less fate,
ri - - - - me E'l mio du - - ro mar -
fear me, And my mer - - ci - less
van-no in ri - - - - - - me E'l mio du - -
not I fear me, And my mer -
mio du - - - ro mar - tir vin - ce o-gni sti - - - - - le, e'l
my mer - - ci - less fate all styles doth con - - - - - quer, and
e'l mio du - - - ro mar - tir vin-ce o-gni sti - - le,
and my mer - - - ci - less fate all styles doth con - - quer,
- tir, e'l mio du - - ro mar - tir vin - - ce o - gni sti - - - -
fate, and my mer - - ci - less fate all styles doth con - - - -
- ro mar - tir vin - - - ce o-gni sti - -
- ci - less fate all styles doth con - -
mio du - - - ro mar - tir, e'l mio du - - - ro mar - tir
my mer - ci - less fate, and my mer - - - ci - less fate
e'l mio du - - ro mar-tir, e'l mio du - - ro mar-
and my mer - - - ci - - less fate, and my mer - - ci - less
- le, e'l mio du - - - ro mar - tir, e'l mio du - ro mar -
- quer, and my mer - - - ci - less fate, and my mer - ci - less
- le, e'l mio du - ro mar - tir
- quer, and my mer - ci - less fate

Ex. 7 (concln.)

Roland de Lassus [1532–1594]. The former, who spent most of his life in Rome, found the natural outlet for his genius in liturgical music (see pp. 307f.), and his undramatic, emotionally balanced approach, in which word-painting is very discreetly used and chromaticism practically non-existent, harks back to the classically poised madrigals of Festa and Arcadelt, both of whom were working in Rome during the composer's early manhood; indeed, Arcadelt may have been his teacher for a time. While many of Palestrina's madrigals are fine compositions showing impeccable style and sensitive, if limited treatment of the text, they contributed nothing to the general development of the type, with one exception, *Vestiva i colli* (1566), a narrative madrigal which borrows the traditional opening formula of the French chanson (see p. 240) and which was so popular that literally hundreds of similar pieces were composed during the next fifty years or so.

Lassus shows Rore's influence far more than does Palestrina, and he was more versatile than the earlier master; in fact, he was the greatest international composer of the Renaissance, writing French chansons and German Lieder with as much ease and brilliance as madrigals and villanelle. Towards the end of his life he was profoundly affected by the Counter-Reformation (see Chapter 2, p. 310), and his 'spiritual madrigals' are based on texts with a strong religious and moral flavour; the musical treatment, however, only differs from his earlier style in the less frequent use of chromaticism. Although Lassus contributed little to the development of the madrigal, his superb craftsmanship, inventive genius, and powerful personality created works that are, on the whole, superior to Palestrina's, and that have stood the test of time more successfully than many more progressive pieces of his day.

Rore wrote nearly 100 madrigals, Palestrina about 150, and Lassus over 270, but these numbers pale before the astonishing output of Philippe de Monte [1521–1603], another northerner, who produced over 1,100. More important, however, is the fact that their quality is equal to their quantity, this being achieved through a completely assured technique which handles word-painting, chromaticism, voice-grouping, rhythmic interplay, and contrasts in texture (polyphony *versus* counterpoint) in a masterly fashion, together with an extraordinarily high standard of sheer musical beauty. Like Rore, he had a serious cast of mind, writing no villanelle, etc., and only a few chansons, and this partly explains why his treatment of the text, while less conservative than Lassus's, is not so progressive as his compatriot, Giaches de Wert [1535–1596], a composer greatly esteemed by his contemporaries and successors. If Monte is Rore's emotional successor, Wert is his stylistic one, and his later madrigals are typical of the late sixteenth-century trend in their detailed and vivid word-painting (e.g. Ex. 8b, at the words "*E i giorni oscuri*", where all the voices are in their 'darkest' register), striking chromaticism (e.g. Ex. 8b), increased voice range, greater tonal feeling, declamation (i.e. rapid notes syllabically underlaid, e.g. Ex. 8a), and—of particular importance, as we shall see—the tendency to make the lower voices accompany the upper. (Ex. 8,* p. 257. For a translation of (b) see Ex. 7, pp. 252-5.)

Monte and Wert were the last of the great madrigal composers who invaded Italy from the north; from now on the leading men are all Italian, and it is no coincidence that in their hands the madrigal finally merged into the accompanied monody of the early baroque, for the Italian genius naturally favours sensuous melody, clear-cut harmony and rhythm, and colourful

* (a) Adapted from A. Einstein, *The Italian Madrigal*, Vol. III, p. 221.
(b) Adapted from ibid., p. 208.

Ex. 8(a) From the madrigal - Giunto a la tomba ove al suo spirto vivo (1581)
(Tasso: La Gerusalemme liberata)
Wert
(♩ = ♩ = MM. c.72)
Di co - lor di ca - lor di mo - - - to pri - - vo Già
Di co - lor di ca - lor di mo - - - - - - to pri - - vo
mar-mo in vis - - ta al mar-mo il vi-so af-fis - - - se
(etc.)
(Of colour, of heat, of move ment deprived, yea marble in appearance to the marble [tomb] the face gazes)
Ex. 8(b) From the madrigal - Crudele acerba inesorabil morte (1588) (Petrarch)
Wert
(♩ = ♩ = MM. c.60)
Ma di me - nar tut - - ta mia vi - ta in pian - to, in pian - - to,
Ma..
Ma.
Ma.
Ei..
Ei..
E i gior- ni o - scu - ri
Ei.
Ei..
(etc.)

expression. Thus polyphonic texture in general and imitation in particular were increasingly superseded by a marked melodic superiority of the upper part or parts, predominantly chordal writing, dramatic contrasts between groups of voices, and a treatment of the text which for detailed realism is unsurpassed in any vocal music before or since.

The earliest Italian composer who shows the new approach is Andrea Gabrieli [*c.* 1520–1586], who, like his teacher Willaert and his co-pupils Rore and Zarlino, was associated with the Chapel of St. Mark, becoming second organist in 1564 and first organist in 1585. Like Willaert also, but not Rore, he was one of the most versatile composers of the century, excelling in all branches of his art and being particularly important and influential in the instrumental field (see Chapter 2, p. 354).

The fact that there were two organs and two organists at St. Mark's obviously encouraged the idea of polychoral writing, i.e. writing for two or more choral groups, and Willaert, though not the inventor of this technique, as is so often claimed, certainly played a leading part in its development. For some reason or other, he restricted its use to his motets, and it was left to Andrea Gabrieli to introduce it into the madrigal. This he did with great brilliance, and the resultant dramatic contrasts together with the sonorous climaxes when both choirs unite, the expressive chromaticism, and hammering rhythm achieved through declamation, give both power and colour to his music. In contrast to the splendour of these pieces he also composed madrigals which show the increasing pre-occupation already noted with detailed word-painting, and it is this aspect that is carried to its extreme by the greatest madrigal composer of the late Renaissance, Luca Marenzio [1553–1599].

Marenzio is the summation of practically all the previous trends in the madrigal, polychoral writing being the only exception. He can be as vivacious as Nola, as classically restrained and limpid in texture as Arcadelt, as serious and complex as Rore and almost as passionate, as declamatory as Monte, and as sonorous and colourful as Andrea Gabrieli. Moreover, he developed that feature of Wert's style which made the upper part or parts melodically superior to the lower and thus advanced a stage nearer to baroque monody; but his most outstanding characteristic, in which he outstrips all his predecessors and contemporaries, is his word-painting, and the care with which practically every word is treated that represents a sound or an object, an idea or a mood is matched only by an inventiveness that turns a technique that had been largely trivial before and, in the hands of less gifted composers, became mechanical during his time and later into something live and fascinating, and by a sensitive feeling for the whole that prevented this detailed realism from disintegrating the entire composition.

In order to give some idea of the variety of means used by Marenzio and others, here are some typical examples of word-painting; 'sea'—a wavy melodic line; 'sigh'—short rest like a catch of the breath, either after the first syllable of the word ('*so-spiro*') or else separating the word from the previous one; 'arch'—an ascending and descending 'curved' melody; 'night' —black notation; 'day'—long 'white' note values; 'suffering'— chromatic changes or major chords in which the roots usually lie a third apart, or have at least one note in common, e.g. C major to E major or G major to E♭ major. These examples, while only constituting a fraction of those that can be found, were inevitably duplicated; thus black notes are also used when the Devil or Hell is mentioned, slowness or length of time is also indicated by long notes, and undulating lines represent 'flying' as well. (Ex. 9,* p. 260. Note the ravishing effects—in their essentially diatonic contexts—of the C major–E major progression on '*sospira*', and of the held B♭ major chord on '*dolce*men*te*'. Note too the rising scales of anger ('*adira*') and the broken rhythm of the phrase for '*romper*').

The important thing about nearly all these devices used by Marenzio and others is that they are not only seen on paper but are actually heard. The chief exception is the use of black notation, for whereas the shape of a melody or the switch from quick to slow movement, or an abrupt chord change are all perfectly intelligible aurally, the insertion of, say, a group of black semibreves at the word 'darkness' only makes sense to the eye, in other words to the performer (eye-music). This, together with remarks by contemporary theorists, makes it quite clear that the normal madrigal was largely concerned with providing entertainment (in its widest sense) for the singers,

* From A. Einstein, *A Short History of Music* (1948), p. 232.

Ex. 9 From the madrigal - *Io piango* (1581) (Petrarch) Marenzio
(o = 𝅗𝅥 = MM. c. 60)

and that it was sung with *one voice to each part*, as indeed we might expect, judging from the size of the printed editions. The madrigal is essentially chamber music, intimate, subtle, refined, and performances, alas only too common today, in which each part is sung by six or more voices are as indefensible as playing a Mozart quartet on the strings of a symphony orchestra, for in doubling a vocal or instrumental part purity of intonation is lost, tone becomes rougher, and the gradations of nuance and expression coarsen. There was, however, a class of madrigal in which part-doubling did occur—namely, those written for a particular ceremony, such as a wedding or a birthday. On such occasions, of course, there was an audience, either in a largish room or else out of doors; in any case, a greater volume of sound would be preferred or even required than one singer per part could give. These madrigals, which fulfilled the same function as the 'occasional' secular motets of earlier times, are invariably much simpler in texture and less detailed in expression than the normal type, a fact which supports what we have already said concerning the performance of the latter. In addition to such pieces, it is likely that many of Andrea Gabrieli's polychoral madrigals, in which sheer sonority plays an important part, were intended for a larger choral body than usual. This applies particularly to his nephew and pupil, Giovanni Gabrieli [1557–1612], who represents the peak of the Venetian School, and who is, moreover, a most important link between the Renaissance and baroque eras, as we shall see in later chapters.

Giovanni, while naturally owing much to his uncle's style and teaching, surpassed him in the brilliance of his voice groupings and dramatic choral contrasts, in the rich colour of his harmony with its greater use of chromaticism, and in the power of his rhythmic drive. Colour and sonority meant far more to him than to any other composer of his generation or earlier, and by relegating imitation and, indeed, polyphony as a whole, to a very subordinate position, and revelling in the sheer delight of chord progressions as such, particularly those whose roots lie a fourth or fifth apart, he anticipated the basically harmonic approach of baroque music.

Both Gabrielis, of course, wrote normal polyphonic madrigals in which word-painting is a marked feature, and it was this aspect, not dramatic brilliance, that dominated the late sixteenth-century Italian madrigal, and while the general trend, represented to perfection by Marenzio, can be described as a balance between graphic and emotional word-painting, the latter became the main objective of one of the most extraordinary composers in the history of music, Carlo Gesualdo, Prince of Venosa [*c.* 1560–1613]. This nobleman, whose private life reads like a nineteenth-century melodrama, concentrated on the expression of mood and feeling of a line or phrase of the text rather than on the detailed description of individual words. In this respect he is Rore's and Monte's successor, but in his obsession with the emotional he went far beyond them, and by a quite astonishing use of chromaticism and violent changes in movement he all but destroyed the musical fabric of the madrigal. Indeed, the boldness and originality of his chromaticism, in which chords totally unconnected with each other are juxtaposed, e.g. A minor–F♯ major, or C minor–E major, remained unequalled until Wagner. Never before had music so depended on the words to give it meaning and unity, for without them the sudden alterations in harmony, melody, and rhythm would be largely incomprehensible. (Ex. 10,* p. 263). (Note in (d) not only the unprepared seventh in bar 2, but more especially the way the chord B♭–D–F–A♭ is resolved in bar 3; it is in fact what we now call an augmented sixth chord (the so-called 'German sixth'), because the augmented sixth (A♭—which should strictly be written as G♯) rises a semitone to A, while the root (B♭) falls a semitone to A. This is the commonest form of the German sixth, i.e. in root position, but it is found very rarely in the music of the period. A much rarer form occurs in bars 5–6, where the German sixth on F is given in its last inversion, i.e. the augmented sixth (E♭—really D♯) is the bass note. With regard to (c) it might be mentioned that the haunting effect of the minor-major ending of the first movement of Walton's Viola Concerto is here anticipated by Gesualdo nearly 350 years earlier.)

The importance of the text had been growing steadily from the end of the fifteenth century on. Before Josquin vocal compositions are largely abstract in conception, for most of them would sound just as well to other words. From Josquin on, however, not only are the syllables set with increasing regard for their

* (a), (b) From *Gesualdo: Madrigale,* ed. Weismann, p. 30. (c) From ibid., p. 6. (d) From *H.A.M.*, 161.

Ex.10(a) From the madrigal - Moro lasso al mio duolo (1611)
Gesualdo
(♩= MM.c.72)
Mo - ro las - so al mio duo - lo
I die from grief so wretch-ed
(etc.)
Ex.10(b) (ibid.)
O... do-lo - ro - - sa sor - te, O..
O...
(etc.)
(O grievous fate)
Ex.10(c) The end of the madrigal - Luci serene e chiare (1596)
Gesualdo
(♩= MM.c.72)
mor' e non lan - - - - - - gue.
e...
mor'...
mor'...
(You die and languish not)
Ex.10(d) From the madrigal - Io pur respiro (1613)
Gesualdo
(♩= MM.c.72)
Deh mor - - - - te
Deh...
deh...
(etc.)
(Then death)

natural accents, but the words begin to be more closely linked with the music, and in Janequin's programme-chansons they form an integral part of the whole. These latter profoundly influenced the Italian madrigal and eventually led, as we have seen, to a style in which the text is the *raison d'être* of the music. This being so, it is clearly important for us to see in what ways poetry influenced the madrigal and vice versa.

In Part I, Chapter 6 (p. 209), we stated that the practice of reciting poems to simple improvised melodies and accompaniments was widespread. Most of the melodies were simple variations on standard types which fitted all verses with identical structure, and the most common poetic form was 'ottava rime', that is verses of 'eight' lines with the 'rhyme' scheme *ab ab ab cc*. It was in this form that Ludovico Ariosto [1474–1533], one of the greatest of all Italian poets, wrote his epic masterpiece, *Orlando furioso* (1516), which has been described as "the noblest literary glorification of the Renaissance", and which swept the length and breadth of Italy. Several standard melodies were used in reciting this poem, but the most popular was called 'ruggiero', the name of one of the characters in the epic, which deals with the fight between Christian and Saracen in the days of Charlemagne. This melody was used in part-music also, but was more important in instrumental compositions.

The popularity of *Orlando furioso* among all classes of society shows that a change in literary standards had occurred during the early sixteenth century. While the early frottola texts are mostly trivial, the later ones include an increasing number of first-rate poems; this reflects the general trend of the times, and the man most responsible for the improvement was Cardinal Pietro Bembo [1470–1547], whose scholarly ideals, prestige, and, to a lesser extent, published work restored the dignity and expressiveness of the Italian language, which had sadly lapsed after Dante and Petrarch. The latter poet was in fact Bembo's model, and partly as a result of this Petrarch's collection of lyric poems, the *Canzoniere*, not only went through nearly 130 editions during the century, but were set so frequently (some of the poems exist in as many as twenty different musical versions) that no other poet, not even Shakespeare or Goethe, has inspired so much music.

But no man's reputation and influence in the literary sphere, no matter how great, can dictate which poet is best suited to a particular musical type, and although Bembo clearly prepared the way for the greater seriousness of the early madrigal compared to the early frottola, it was the character of Petrarch's verse which was the decisive factor, for it provided well-nigh perfect madrigalian texts. Each verse is short enough to permit imitative interplay between the voices without making the piece too long, the clarity and conciseness with which each mood is expressed almost dictates the musical treatment, and the emotional contrasts give the composer full scope for varying his rhythm, melody, and harmony.

Petrarch's popularity led inevitably to shoals of imitations which, as usually happens, are distinctly inferior to their model. Apart from Bembo, the earliest imitator of any importance was an otherwise obscure poet, Luigi Cassola, most of whose output was clearly intended to be set to music, not to be read as poetry. This is an important distinction and one that applies to a tremendous number of sixteenth-century poems all over Europe, and it is as unfair and as unscholarly to judge madrigal texts from a purely poetical standpoint as it is to compare opera libretti with contemporary drama.

Cassola's poems are typical of a great many madrigal texts in their freedom of rhyme and metre, their sentimentality, their contrasts of mood, and the provision of a neat conclusion. Two examples from English madrigals will make this clearer than any description. The first contrasts the opening four lines with the last two, which provide a neat conclusion; the second shows the structural freedom possible.

> So light is love in matchless beauty shining,
> When she revisits Cypris' hallowed bowers,
> Two feeble doves, harnessed in silken twining,
> Can draw her chariot midst the Paphian flowers.
> Lightness to Love, how ill it fitteth,
> So heavy on my heart she sitteth!*
>
> Come life, come death, I care not,
> If I may only see my lovely fere [=companion]
> But further, ah, I dare not!
> When she but spies me,
> She flies me,
> She fools me,
> She cools my desire!†

* *English Madrigal Verse*, ed. Fellowes, p. 239. † Ibid., p. 82.

The two main poetic types, epic and lyric, represented by Ariosto and Petrarch respectively, were cultivated throughout the century with the lyric in the ascendant. From *c.* 1550 on this became increasingly pastoral in character, and idealized and sentimentalized shepherds and shepherdesses, the Amaryllises, Floras, Clorises, and Phyllises vied with Petrarch's Laura. The first important pastoral poet was Jacopo Sannazaro [1455/6–1530], whose *Arcadia*, published in 1502, eventually became so popular that it gave rise to a spate of pastoral poems and madrigals that outnumbered all other types. In this it truly reflected one aspect of the Renaissance—the romantic longing for the past—and in the hands of Torquato Tasso [1544–95] and Giovanni Battista Guarini [1538–1612] it reached its peak; Guarini's *Pastor Fido* ('The Faithful Shepherd') (1581–90), though inferior poetically to Tasso's *Aminta* (1573), was more frequently set to music because its use of words and contrasting emotions is more virtuosic than in the simpler earlier poem. Tasso, however, was both a lyric and an epic poet and his *Gerusalemme liberata* ('Jerusalem liberated') (1581) virtually replaced Ariosto's great work because its more obvious darker emotional qualities suited the age of the Counter-Reformation better than the rather detached, ironic, even capricious treatment of Christianity *versus* Mohammedanism in *Orlando furioso*.

The delight in Arcadia and in the amours of the rustic characters who populated it spread to the stage, and many pastoral poems, or 'pastorales' as they were called, were intended to be either read or acted; indeed, the pastorale was the most important dramatic form in Italy during the late Renaissance, and because the lyricism of its verse was so well suited to and frequently received musical treatment it was one of the forerunners of opera, as we shall see in Chapter 3.

Music played an important part too in the only other significant drama of the Italian Renaissance, the classical tragedy and its imitations. The sixteenth-century author and producer knew that the Greeks and Romans included musical performance of some kind in their dramatic presentations, and this prompted them to insert between the acts of the plot, and often as prologue and epilogue as well, short scenes called 'intermedii', which consisted of songs, instrumental pieces, and sometimes dances. On especially festive occasions these intermedii were staged with great splendour, foreshadowing the elaborate scenic settings of seventeenth-century opera, but on all occasions they were greatly enjoyed and eventually became far more popular than the serious drama of which they were originally only appendages. Like the pastorale, the intermedio is also a forerunner of opera.

Both Tasso and Guarini spent most of their lives at Ferrara, the home of one of the oldest and most brilliant Italian families. From Hercules I [reigned 1472–1505], an outstanding patron of the arts, especially music, and the father of Isabella (see Part I, Chapter 6, p. 209) and her almost equally famous sister, Beatrice, to Alfonso II [1558–1597], the Ferrarese Court was one of the main cultural centres of Italy. Alfonso employed both Tasso and Guarini, as well as one of the leading composers of the time, Luzzasco Luzzaschi [d. 1607], who had been a pupil of Rore's. This man, who certainly knew and probably influenced Gesualdo, published in 1601 a remarkable collection of madrigals for one, two, and three sopranos, with a written-out keyboard part (the first of its kind), and with the vocal lines highly ornamented (Ex. 11,* p. 268).

We know from contemporary theorists that both instrumental accompaniment and vocal embellishment were common, and that therefore once again the music printed or in manuscript does not completely represent actual practice. Unaccompanied or 'a capella' performance, as it is often called, was certainly more widespread in the sixteenth century than in preceding centuries, but the use of instruments and the improvised ornamentation of the vocal line were typical features in certain circumstances. Thus at courtly festivities, when, as we have seen, the number of voices per part was increased, an 'orchestra' would accompany which might include a positive organ, harpsichord, viols, recorders, trombones, lutes, and cornets. On more intimate and less auspicious occasions a positive, harpsichord, lute, or viols might be used, and sometimes the lower or even all the parts were performed instrumentally. A keyboard player or lutanist (who was not, of course, restricted to pieces in tablature) would improvise chords from the lowest part, according to certain rules which were fairly simple, owing to the restricted harmony of the period. The violists would each play a separate part and, if the singer was absent

* Adapted from *Geschichte de Musik in Beispielen*, ed. Schering, p. 176.

Ex. 11 The end of the madrigal *O primavera* (1601) (Guarini *Pastor Fido*)
Luzzaschi
(𝅗𝅥 = 𝅘𝅥 = MM. c. 60)
Soprano
Keyboard
Ma non son' io già quel' ch'un tem-po fu - - - i, Si ca - ro a gl'oc-chi al - tru - i, si ca-ro a gl'oc - - - ch'al - - tru - i, ma ca - - ro a gl'oc-chi — al - - tru - i.
But I no more am he who once was lo - - ved By eyes with pas-sion mo-ved, by eyes with pas - - - sion mo - ved, but eyes with pas-sion — so mo - ved.
1.
2.

or unskilled, very likely embellish it. This was called playing 'divisions', as the original notes were 'divided' into smaller ornamental ones.

As regards vocal embellishment, this too was mostly improvised and only occurred, ideally at any rate, when there was one singer per part, otherwise confusion would have reigned. The same applies, but less strictly, to written-out ornamentation. Taken as a whole, it is unlikely that improvised vocal embellishment was applied indiscriminately, and those madrigals or sections of madrigals in which the rhythmic movement is quick, or the music is wedded to the words, or the polyphony is complex, were almost certainly sung as they stand. In the more straightforward pieces and simpler passages, the choice of normal or elaborate rendering was doubtless dictated by the vocal dexterity and musicianship of the singer. Much the same considerations probably applied to instrumental accompaniment also.

The fact that the voices in Luzzaschi's print are sopranos illustrates the tendency already noted (pp. 256, 258)—namely, the increasing domination of the lower parts by the upper. This tendency was undoubtedly stimulated at Ferrara by the presence at various times of three highly talented ladies, Lucrezia Bendidio, Laura Peperara, and Tarquinia Molza. Tasso worshipped the first two, and Wert's passion for the third, which was returned, ended disastrously in her banishment from court. The fame of these three spread far beyond Ferrara and even beyond Italy, and Alfonso, fully aware of this and knowing that attempts had been made to find out what kind of music they sang and how they sang it, forbade the publication of their repertoire. Thus many, if not all, of Luzzaschi's madrigals of 1601 were written several years earlier.

Among the numerous composers who paid homage to the three ladies was Claudio Monteverdi [1567–1643], who spent the last thirty years of his life as 'master of the chapel' at St. Mark's, Venice. Although he is definitely more a man of the early baroque than the late Renaissance, much of his finest music stems from the older tradition. His first madrigal book (1587) already shows his dramatic feeling, and this increases in his later publications, together with an expressive use of dissonance unmatched by any contemporary. Rapid repeated notes and contrapuntal texture result in a choral recitative style that clearly aims at making the text fully intelligible (see Ex. 12b), and shows that the pieces were intended for an audience and not just for performers as in the classical madrigal. (Ex. 12.* This madrigal is an arrangement of the famous lament from the composer's opera, *Arianna* (see Chapter 3, p. 376). The opening (a) was as remarkable and memorable in its day as that of Wagner's *Tristan und Isolde* some 250 years later):

Ex. 12(a) The beginning of the madrigal - *Lamento d'Arianna* Pt. I: *Lasciatemi morire* (1614)
(𝅗𝅥 = ♩ = MM. c. 60) Monteverdi

Ex. 12(b) From the same madrigal Pt. IV: *Ahi ch'ei non pur risponde*

(And with foul limbs fill the deep pit)

* From *Claudio Monteverdi: Tutte le Opere*, ed. Malipiero, Vol. VI, p. 3.

Monteverdi's madrigal books of 1605 and 1614 contain a separate instrumental bass part which in some cases is essential to the harmonic structure of the whole, and which thus departs from earlier practice (see p. 318).

The dramatic element in Monteverdi's madrigals was not new, for once again musical dialogues anticipated future development, but whereas the tenth- and eleventh-century Easter and Christmas tropes led directly to the mediaeval church opera and ultimately to European drama, the polyphonic 'dialogue madrigal' of the latter half of the sixteenth century, in which the 'actors' were frequently shepherds and shepherdesses and the scene 'Arcadia', only indicated a general trend and did not of itself give birth to baroque opera. This type of madrigal became immensely popular, and eventually gave rise to the so-called 'madrigal comedies', an unfortunate name, for 'comedy' smacks of the theatre and these works were neither intended nor are they suitable for stage performance. Moreover, they are more than just comic, and many of the items are not madrigals at all! However, as the name distinguishes works of this kind from the madrigal proper and also intimates that plot is an important constituent, we shall continue to use it. The greatest composer of this quasi-dramatic choral music was Orazio Vecchi [1550–1605], and his most outstanding work is *L'Amfiparnasso* (1594), in which are combined tragedy and comedy representing the twin peaks of the sacred mountain of the ancient Greeks, Parnassus. The 'cast' includes shepherds and shepherdesses as well as the traditional characters, Harlequin, Columbine, Pantaloon, Pierrot, etc., of the immensely popular, satirical, sentimental, and largely improvised type of drama known as the *Commedia dell' Arte* ('comedy of the arts'). Although *L'Amfiparnasso* is grouped into a prologue and three acts and there is some sort of a plot, it was definitely *not* meant to be acted, for in the Preface Vecchi expressly states that the work should be "seen through the mind, into which it enters through the ears, not through the eyes".

This madrigal comedy and the three others by Vecchi, together with similar works by Alessandro Striggio [*c.* 1535–before 1596], Giovanni Croce [*c.* 1557–1609], an important composer of church music, and Adriano Banchieri [1567–1634), who also wrote in the new style of the early baroque, give a fascinating cross-section of secular vocal music at the end of the century. Serious, sentimental, and lighthearted madrigals mix with comic, satirical, and nonsensical villanelle, mascherate, moresche, villote, and balletti. The villota usually includes one or more well-known street cries with a certain amount of gibberish and, like the balletto, is dance-like. The latter, in the hands of its most famous composer, Giovanni Giacomo Gastoldi [*c.* 1550–1622?], vied with and possibly surpassed the madrigal in popularity, not only in Italy, but all over Europe, and in its chordal texture, strong rhythm, and regular phrase construction it shows the strong influence of dance music, particularly that of France, where the ballet was first cultivated (*H.A.M.*, 158).

Banchieri, in his madrigal comedies, directs that the outline of the plot be told before the work is sung; they were thus clearly intended for an audience, and the same is probably also true of other madrigal comedies. The audience before which such compositions were given might well have been one of the many 'academies' which sprang up all over Italy during the latter part of the century and at which professionals and amateurs alike met to discuss literature, philosophy, archaeology, and even mathematics. The earliest important musical academy was founded in Verona in 1543 and included painters and poets as well as musicians, one of whom was actually employed by the academy and who, among other duties, was obliged to set to music anything a member requested! The atmosphere of these academies, in which compositions were not only performed and listened to but also criticized, and where the arts as a whole were discussed, was quite different from either the intimate music-making of a few friends or the festive performance at court, for in the first the singers and instrumentalists were their own audience, and in the second most of those who listened were there for reasons other than musical.

There is no doubt that the number and artistic standard of the academies in Italy contributed greatly to the development of the madrigal, for whether they sang and played at their meetings or in smaller groups at home, their members provided nuclei of intelligence and culture which were receptive to both the conventional and the experimental; indeed, some of these nuclei contributed directly through discussion and criticism to new ways of expression (see p. 366). Such a state of affairs was only possible in Italy, where the light of learning and artistic activity burnt more brightly than anywhere else; this at a time when she was politically defeated and economically exhausted, for although the French invasion of 1494 failed, it was followed by Spanish and German troops who succeeded, particularly the former. Ferdinand of Spain saw his opportunity, and from 1503, when he captured Naples, to 1700 almost the whole of Italy was under Spanish rule, the only notable exception being, significantly enough, Venice. But although she was subjugated territorially and poverty-stricken through constant war and heavy taxation, the power and richness of her civilization conquered the rest of Europe.

The improved literary standards and greater importance of the text in the late sixteenth-century Italian madrigal is also found in the secular music of France, but the French, who have always tended to place literary considerations above purely musical ones, went much further than the Italians in this respect, and a group of poets who called themselves 'Le Pléiade' aimed at restoring the greatness of French poetry through the imitation of Greek and Roman dramatic and lyric verse, which, unlike the epic, were invariably associated with music. The most famous member of this group was Pierre de Ronsard [1524–1585], the greatest French poet of the Renaissance, who stressed the desirability, not only of emulating the nobleness and expressiveness of the greatest classical authors, such as Homer, Virgil, Horace, Pindar, and indeed later writers, such as Petrarch, but also of fashioning poetry so as to make it suitable for polyphonic composition. He and most other members of Le Pléiade realized that classical verse, unlike French verse, consisted of long and short syllables, and made no attempt to imitate this; but one member did, Jean Antoine de Baïf [1532–1589], who in his enthusiasm founded in 1570 the 'Académie de poésie et musique'. One of the aims of the Academy was to provide instruction, not only in music and poetry, but in such subjects as languages, geography, mathematics, military history, and even gardening and gastronomy. The breadth of the curriculum was fully in keeping with the Renaissance ideal of the 'complete man', but it seems that it did not in fact materialize. At any rate, the only definite information we have is solely concerned with the musical settings of French verse similar to that of Le Pléiade, except that it is written in classical metres of long and short syllables. This was called 'vers mesurés' by Baïf, and although he claimed to have invented it similar attempts had been made in the late fifteenth century in France and Germany, and, more successfully, towards the middle of the sixteenth century in Italy, and it is from Italy, which he visited *c.* 1563, that Baïf probably received the idea of 'measured verse', and possibly the idea of an academy also.

Unlike Ronsard, who desired his poems to be set polyphonically, Baïf insisted that all the voices should sing the words at the same time, and this, together with the shackling of the music to poetic form and metre, resulted in a largely sterile art. In Claude le Jeune [*c.* 1525–1600], however, Baïf found a composer whose melodic and harmonic gifts were sufficient to overcome the rigidity of the rules and who produced some wholly delightful songs in what was called 'musique mesurée'. Admittedly, the strict application of long (= 𝅗𝅥 or 𝅝) and short (= 𝅗𝅥 or ♩) is relieved by breaking the basic notes into shorter ones, but the essential metre is kept, and its irregularity provides one of the main attractions of these pieces (Ex. 13*):

* Adapted from *Geschichte de Musik in Beispielen*, ed. Schering, p. 142.

Le Jeune, who achieved a considerable reputation in Paris and who, *c.* 1598, was appointed 'compositeur de la musique de la chambre' to Henry IV [reigned 1589–1610], also wrote 'normal' polyphonic chansons which show the influence of the Italian madrigal in their word-painting and use of chromaticism, and these differ markedly from Arcadelt's, which parallel the harmonic and textural simplicity of the early madrigal. Other composers who wrote both musique mesurée and ordinary chansons include Claude Goudimel [d. 1572], Guillaume Costeley [*c.* 1531–1606], and Jacques Mauduit [1557–1627], the last-named being an important member of Baïf's Academy towards the end of its existence (*c.* 1585). But, taken as a whole, the finest chansons were composed by Lassus, whose catholicity in general is reflected in the choice and treatment of his texts, and he is equally at home in the light-hearted contrapuntal type as in the serious or sentimental polyphonic one. His chansons became so popular that some were reprinted with new, even religious texts ('contrafacta'), a procedure that was much more common in the sixteenth than in earlier centuries (see Part I, p. 83), especially in Germany.

De Baïf's Academy also aimed at creating a unified spectacle in which music, poetry, dancing, and scenic display all played an equal part, an aim that was realized in *Circe, ou le ballet comique de le Royne* [=Reine], performed with sumptuous splendour at Paris by the lords and ladies of the court during the wedding festivities of Margaret of Lorraine and the Duke of Joyeuse in 1581 (see Plate XVIII).

Entertainments in which dancing occupied a prominent place had been popular with the French aristocracy from the late fifteenth century and remained so until the Revolution. With but few exceptions, of which *Circe* is the most outstanding, all the ballets produced before *c.* 1650 lacked dramatic unity, being composed of a more or less haphazard succession of scenes; moreover, the actual dances themselves were, until the latter part of the sixteenth century, less varied and less skilfully executed than in Italy. During the third quarter of the century, however, there arrived at the courts of Henry II [reigned 1547–1559], Francis II [reigned 1559–1560] (husband of Mary Stuart), and Charles IX [reigned 1560–1574], a number of Milanese dancing masters, who came as a direct or indirect result of the delight in this kind of entertainment of Catherine de' Medici [1519–1589], wife of Henry and mother of Francis and Charles. In 1573 Catherine presented *Le Ballet des Polonais* in honour of the Polish Ambassadors, who had that year elected her third son, who later became Henry III of France [reigned 1574–1589], as King of Poland. The choreography of this ballet, to music by Lassus, was more complex than that of any previous dance spectacle either in France or abroad, and if we take as true Arnold Haskell's statement that "Ballet as we know it was born when the acrobatics of the professional and the aristocratic grace of the courtier were united"* then the year of birth was 1573. But Haskell's definition is incomplete, for ballet as we know it is also a unified dramatic spectacle, and this *Le Ballet des Polonais* was not.

The first real ballet, or 'ballet de cour', as this kind of entertainment came to be called, and the first also of which the music has been preserved intact, was *Circe*, because it combined unity of plot—in this instance based on the legend of the mythological witch-goddess—with dances that exemplified Haskell's definition. These dances can be classified into two groups, the 'ballet à entrées', which were 'character' dances expressive of the principal characters in the story and often very dramatic, being the forerunners of the modern dramatic ballet, e.g. Stravinsky's *Petrouchka*, and the final 'grand ballet', which consisted of stylized dances, i.e. those fashionable at the time, such as the gaillarde and courante, and in which ladies of the court always and royalty frequently took part; from this stemmed the classical ballet of later times. The dances were accompanied by a string band of violins, violas, and 'cellos to which lutes were sometimes added, or choruses, sometimes a cappella, or solo songs with lute ('airs de cour'); the air de cour, indeed, became the most popular musical item of the late sixteenth- and early seventeenth-century ballet, and a great number were published separately in collections by Le Roy and Ballard. Its popularity extended abroad and it undoubtedly influenced the English ayre (see p. 48), though its essential lightness of subject (often pastoral), its invariable strophic verse, and almost invariable lute accompaniment compares unfavourably with the range of mood, subtlety of construction, and variety of performance of the ayre.

* A. Haskell, *Ballet*, Pelican Special, 1938, p. 20.

As we mentioned above, the character dancers in *Circe* were courtiers, the principals as usual being male, while the *corps de ballet* included, for the first time, some of the ladies of the court, and this innovation created a fashion for most of the ballets performed at court before the Revolution. Elsewhere in the ballet female characters were impersonated by suitably masked male dancers. The action of the story was unfolded by means of verses or 'récits', which were usually spoken and which contained much fulsome flattery of the king.

So far as the general purpose (i.e. a social entertainment which glorified king and country), overall plan, and function and layout of the music are concerned, all ballets during the next twenty-five years or so were modelled on *Circe*, but this ballet remained unique in its dramatic unity and the careful integration of the various components. The man who was responsible for all this and who, doubtless influenced by de Baïf's aims, supervised the writing of the verse, the composition of the music, the *décor*, and the choreography, was an eminent Italian violinist named Baldasar da Belgioioso, who later changed his name to Balthasar de Beaujoyeulx [d. *c.* 1587]. Balthasar arrived at the French court *c.* 1555 as leader of an Italian string band sent to Catherine by one of Henry II's marshals. Thus while ballet can be said to have originated in France, the seeds were sown by Italians—namely, Catherine, the Milanese dancing masters, and Balthasar.

If French taste and French talent had been so inclined, *Circe* could have led to the birth of French opera, but it was not to be. Nevertheless, this ballet, like the pastorale and intermedio, is one of the forerunners of opera in that it too consists of singing, dancing, scenic display, and unity of plot.

German secular songs, or Lieder, during the first half of the century are, on the whole, written in the same tradition as those by Isaac; in other words, they are predominantly imitative in style and are based on borrowed melodies. They reached their peak in the compositions of Ludwig Senfl [*c.* 1490–*c.* 1556], a pupil of Isaac, who shows a complete mastery of polyphonic technique combined with a new melodic gracefulness. The bulk of these songs appeared in a number of collections, the most important of which are Johann Ott's *121 neue Lieder* (1534), which includes twenty of his own songs and over eighty by Senfl, and his *115 guter neuer Liedlein* (1544), which is more cosmopolitan than the first set, including pieces by Verdelot, Richafort, Gombert, and Crecquillon, as well as by Senfl, Isaac, Stoltzer, etc. The largest collection is the *Frische teutsche Liedlein*, by Georg Forster [*c.* 1510–1568], which appeared in five parts between 1539 and 1556, and contains 380 songs, mostly by Germanic writers, including Kaspar Othmayr [1515–1553], the composer of probably the first song-cycle.

In the latter half of the century Italian influence is increasingly apparent, beginning with *Il primo delle Canzone Napoletane* (1566) by Antonio Scandello [1517–1580], an Italian at the Dresden court, which was the first exclusively Italian collection of vocal music to be published in Germany. In 1567 appeared *Newe Teutsche Liedlein mit fünff Stimmen* (including a fine five-part setting, based on the traditional tune, of Luther's hymn *Vater unser*), the first of a large number of Lieder by Lassus in which, as we should expect, the influence of the madrigal and villanella is unmistakable, although they are not so varied in expression or technique as his Italian and French compositions. (All his published Lieder, incidentally, were intended for vocal and/or instrumental performance.) The success of Lassus's and Scandello's collections (the latter also brought out some Lieder in 1568) prompted a number of German and Netherlandish composers to follow suit, notably Leonhard Lechner [1553–1606], Jakob Regnart [d. *c.* 1600], and Hans Leo Hassler [1564–1612], a pupil of Andrea Gabrieli. Lechner's Lieder show him to be thoroughly conversant with Italian vocal styles and equally successful in both gay and sombre moods. His songs are superior to Regnart's, though the latter's were the most popular of all Leider during the last third of the century (e.g. *Venus du und dein kind* that later became the well-known chorale *Auf neinen lieben Gott*) and were only superseded by Hassler's, especially those in his *Lustgarten neuer teutscher Gesäng, Balletti, Galliarden und Intraden* (1601). Hassler had already published a set of Italian canzonettes in 1590 and, in 1596, a book of madrigals that are among the finest of the century. His Lieder of 1601 are superbly written and cover a wide range of expressions, from the delightfully gay balletto, *Tantzen und springen*, to the very moving *Ach weh des Leiden*.

Taken as a whole, German secular compositions of the late Renaissance, even those written after the middle of the century, cannot compare with their Italian counterparts. The same is true of England, except that when, in the 1580s, Italian influence finally broke through the innate conservatism of English composers there resulted a spate of secular music superior to that produced in any other country save Italy. Indeed a few, a very few, English madrigals can hold their own with the best of the Italian, while many balletti surpass their models. But for sheer quantity of excellence as well as for range of expression and technique, both within the madrigal itself and in secular music as a whole, Italy holds the palm, which is not surprising when one considers the wealth of composers who worked within her boundaries and the fact that she had been actively cultivating secular music for nearly a century before England. What is surprising is the enormous difference in quality, quantity, technique, and variety between English secular compositions before and after *c.* 1590.

For most of the sixteenth century, as in the previous one, English secular song lagged far behind that on the Continent, and the comparatively few pieces that have come down to us are written in an out-of-date style and show inferior technique. This state of affairs cannot be explained by the forces of time and destruction, for this applies to every country, nor was it due to lack of competent composers, as we shall see when we deal with the Church music of the period. The reason probably lies in the widespread and ancient practice of adding parts extempore to a popular song (discanting) rather than composing them, together with the almost complete lack of lyric poets, for, apart from the satiric verses of John Skelton [*c.* 1460–1529], a few of which were in fact set to music, hardly a poet worthy of the name lived between Chaucer and Sir Thomas Wyatt [1503–1542]. Wyatt and Henry Howard, Earl of Surrey [1517–1547], introduced the sonnet into English poetry, but were at their best in the freer forms. Their poetry was very popular in court circles, but was not published until 1557. Both men were primarily experimenters and breakers of new ground, and they were the first to show the influence of Italian poetry to any marked extent, but their talent was small compared to the genius of Edmund Spenser [*c.* 1552–1599], whose work set a new standard, especially the *Shepheardes Calendar* (1579), which perhaps reveals the influence of Sannazaro and Guarini, and *The Faerie Queene* (1590–6), which has distinct affinities with Ariosto, whom, with Tasso, Spenser much admired. Spenser had many followers, both during his lifetime and in the succeeding century, the most notable of the former being Sir Walter Raleigh [*c.* 1552–1618] and Sir Philip Sydney [1554–1586].

The extent of English lyricism in the late Renaissance cannot be judged by the number of known writers, for the considerable body of verse that exists only in the secular music of the period and which has been disregarded by almost every literary historian is, unlike that of Italy, largely anonymous, but, as in Italy, much of it was undoubtedly written with a musical setting in mind. In view of the fact that secular vocal music must always be more dependent on the state of contemporary poetry than liturgical music, in which the majority of the texts have changed but little, being excerpts, translations, or adaptations from the Bible, and considering especially the close links between the words and music in the sixteenth century, it is no coincidence that the flowering of the lyric art in England occurred at the same time as that of the madrigal.

The only secular music printed between 1530 (see Part I, Chapter 6, p. 213) and 1588 was a collection of seventy-six songs for from three to five voices by Thomas Whythorne 'Gentleman' [b. 1528?], published in 1571. Although he states that he had visited Italy, one would not have guessed as much from the music, for while some of the songs have a certain charm, they reveal hardly any of the madrigalian characteristics discussed earlier and are often technically clumsy. The texts are mostly moralistic in tone, and this feature is the only link between him and the first great English composer of secular music in the late Renaissance—indeed, one of the greatest composers of all time—William Byrd [1543–1623].

In 1588 Byrd issued his *Psalmes, Sonets & songs of sadness and pietie*, and initiated a spate of secular composition that lasted for a brief but glorious period of forty years. None of the pieces in the above collection are madrigals, for they were "originally made for instruments [viols] to expresse the harmonie, and one voice to pronounce the dittie", and have, as a result, an abstract quality quite different from the realistic or emotional approach of the normal late sixteenth-century madrigal. The religious or moralistic tone which permeates the book (many of the items are in fact anthems) can be likened to the spiritual madrigals of Lassus, but the musical treatment of these is not greatly different from Lassus's purely secular examples, i.e. is thoroughly modern, whereas in Byrd's pieces the main madrigalian features of word-painting and strong rhythmic contrasts are rare, and the harmonic idiom is of the simplest. His two later books of 1589 ("fit for all companies and voyces") and 1611, especially the latter, in which the music is significantly enough "framed to the life of the words", show Italian influence to a greater extent; more of the texts are secular than in the 1588 set, and their treatment is more up-to-date, but if one had only these three collections to judge from one would unhesitatingly say that Byrd was more inspired by words of a serious than a flippant nature; in fact, it is largely true that the most moving and most brilliant songs are those that either petition or praise God, and, paradoxically, he is more madrigalesque in his Catholic Church music than in his secular output.

In addition to his published work, nearly forty songs with sacred or secular words remained in manuscript. These are for the same ensemble as the original settings of the 1588 book—namely, solo voice accompanied by a consort (group) of viols—and this fact, together with a similarity in style, makes it probable that they are early pieces. Nevertheless, they show, as do those in the 1588 set, a mastery of smooth-flowing, imitative polyphony combined with a subtle rhythmic sense that produces on occasion a perfect gem, as, for example, *My little sweet darling*, and the well-known *Lullaby*.

Byrd's resistance to Italian influence was partly due to the native conservatism in general of English composers, but mainly to the view he took of his art; this is clearly expressed in his 1588 publication, where he states that "The better the voyce is, the meeter it is to honour and serve God there-with: and the voyce of man is chiefely to be imployed to that ende". At the time when this was written, Byrd was acknowledged as the foremost English composer, but his rather severe conception of the purpose of music, while plainly influencing some of his contemporaries, fortunately did not affect the most gifted of them, with the possible exception of Orlando Gibbons and Thomas Tomkins.

The youngest of Byrd's gifted contemporaries and the first genuine madrigalist was Thomas Morley [1557–1603?], who more than anyone else laid the foundations of what is now called the English Madrigal School. But Morley was no lone torch-bearer who single-handed brought the light of Italian secular music to this country, for from the time of Henry VIII [reigned 1509–1547] onwards an increasing number of foreign musicians, particularly from the Netherlands and Italy, visited or settled in England. The most important of these was the Italian, Alfonso Ferrabosco (i) [1543–1588], who lived in London *c.* 1560–78 and who was so admired by Elizabeth I [reigned 1558–1603] that when he was only twenty-six years old she granted him a pension of £100 a year (the equivalent of about £1,500 today), provided he bound himself to her service for life. This he promised to do, but broke his word, spending the last years of his life in the employ of an Italian duke. Elizabeth was not alone in her admiration, for Morley calls him "a great musician famous and admired for his works amongst the best", and he was a personal friend of Byrd. Ferrabosco's reputation undoubtedly did much to stimulate interest in the secular music of his own country, for it is from *c.* 1560 on that a growing number of Italian madrigals, chiefly in manuscript, began to circulate in English musical society, and the popularity of these eventually induced a certain Nicholas Yonge to publish a selection of them under the title *Musica Transalpina* (1588). This was patently a success, and two years later Thomas Watson, a minor poet, brought out a similar book, *Italian Madrigals Englished.* The increase in home production in the 1590s probably accounts for the fact that not until 1597 did a second volume of *Musica Transalpina* appear, together with selections of Italian madrigals edited by Morley himself in 1597 and 1598. Morley had clearly steeped himself in this art, but he was no slavish imitator, and the bulk of his secular output—the canzonets *a*3 (really madrigals) (1593), the madrigals *a*4 (1594), the two-part canzonets, and five-part balletts (both 1595)—all of which appeared before any other English madrigal print, show that although he had fully grasped the technique of madrigal writing he selected, on the whole, only the pastoral and narrative types, but infused them with a greater tunefulness and sense of tonality. The former had been a characteristic of English composers for centuries, but Morley's melodies have a consistent freshness that not only mark them off from Continental pieces, but from those of his countrymen also, though to a lesser extent. This and his harmonic clarity, his tendency to stress a tonal centre by well-planned modulations to the dominant and subdominant, and his strong feeling for dance rhythms, introduced a more frankly popular element into the madrigal and set the fashion for most of his compatriots. The dance-like features of his music are most marked in his balletts, and he surpasses his models, Gastoldi's balletti, in the length and polyphonic brilliance of his 'fa la' refrains (*H.A.M.*, 139).

In 1601 Morley edited a collection of English madrigals by English composers entitled *The Triumphes of Oriana*, which was modelled on an earlier Italian collection, *Il Trionfo di Dori* (1592). It has always been assumed that Oriana was Elizabeth I, but this has recently been queried owing to the apparent fact that (a) the Collection was not sold until 1603, i.e. after Elizabeth's death, and (b) she objected to the name Oriana. However, it has now been convincingly shewn that the evidence for the latter is wholly inconclusive and misleading, and, moreover, that copies of the work were on sale by at least December 1601. (See R. C. Strong, *Studies in the Renaissance*, Vol. VI.) All the leading composers contributed to *The Triumphs of Oriana* except Byrd and Giles Farnaby [*c.* 1565–1640]. It is often assumed that Byrd, because he had published no book of madrigals and was out of sympathy with the type, was not asked, but this is unlikely, considering his prestige and that he was Morley's teacher, and it is more probable that he declined the invitation. Actually, Farnaby's omission is more curious because he had already produced an excellent book of canzonets in 1598.

As Vesta was from Latmos hill descending, by Thomas Weelkes [*c.* 1575–1623] is usually regarded as the finest of the *Oriana* collection, and is typical of much of the composer's work in its detailed and vivid word-painting. In this as in other respects he is more Italianate than Morley, and while the latter is essentially an exquisite miniaturist with a somewhat limited range of feeling, Weelkes is at his best when he is portraying a dramatic or passionate subject on a large canvas—for example, the wonderful five-part madrigal, *O Care, thou wilt despatch me*, with its equally fine second part, *Hence Care; thou art too cruel*; even so, he was more successful in shorter, fewer-voiced pieces than most of his contemporaries (his *Cease sorrows now* is the most outstanding three-part madrigal ever written). His versatility is shown by delightful settings of nonsense verse, balletts that are sometimes even more brilliant than Morley's, and madrigals that range from the conventionally amorous to the profoundly emotional and highly dramatic. In these last he was undoubtedly influenced by Marenzio (who is represented more often than any other composer in the second book of *Musica Transalpina*), and in his use of chromaticism and dissonance he is the boldest and most experimental of the English madrigalists.

The high spot of Weelkes's secular output is reached in his *Madrigals of 5. and 6. parts, apt for the viols and voices* (1600), which contains pieces unsurpassed in emotional intensity and unequalled in brilliance by any other English madrigalist. The expression "apt for the viols and voices", or something similar, was included in nearly every later madrigal print, but Weelkes was not the first Englishman to suggest that instruments should accompany or replace voices in the performance of vocal music, for not only does Byrd mention this possibility in 'The Epistle to the Reader' of his 1588 book, but a psalter of 1563 specifically states in its title that the contents "may be song to al musicall instrumentes", and another (1599) not only specifies which instruments, but actually includes in tablature a reduction of the three lowest vocal parts (see Chapter 2, p. 329).

It is a fact greatly to be regretted that Weelkes wrote no full-scale madrigals after his set of 1600, apart from the six-part elegy on Morley's death included in his *Ayeres or Phantasticke Spirites for three voices* (1608); had he done so he would almost certainly have reached a more refined style without detracting from his vivid imagination, and laid claim to be regarded as the greatest native madrigalist. As it is, however, the palm falls to John Wilbye [1574–1638], whose two sets, printed in 1597 and 1609, represent the high-water mark of the English madrigal. In the quality of his inspiration, his sensitivity to the rhythm of the text, his realistic but always musical approach to word-painting, his poetic taste, and his well-nigh impeccable technique he might well be called the English Marenzio, although he lacked the latter's versatility both in his harmonic variety and his expressive range. His *Draw on, sweet night* is not only the finest of all English madrigals, but one of the most beautiful short vocal pieces of all time.

Among the many other lesser madrigalists, Orlando Gibbons [1583–1625], John Ward, and Thomas Tomkins [1572–1656] must be mentioned. Each published only one set of madrigals, in 1613, 1614, and 1622 respectively. Ward rarely chose flippant texts and is at his best when writing for six voices, where his bold dissonances (he was unusually fond of double suspensions), breadth of phrase, and detailed word-painting have full scope.

Gibbons, like Byrd, produced his greatest music for the Church and is, together with the older man, the least affected by Italian influence of all his fellow madrigalists. Like Byrd, too, he took a serious view of his art, and it is perhaps no coincidence that the words of the second madrigal of the set run as follows:

> O that the learned poets of this time,
> Who in a Love-sick line so well can speak,
> Would not consume good wit in hateful rhyme,
> But with deep care some better subject find.
> For if their music please in earthly things
> How would it sound if strung with heavenly strings?

At any rate, the moralistic tone of his deservedly famous *The Silver Swan* is typical of most of the others. This piece has distinct affinities with Byrd's secular work in the clear, melodic superiority of the top voice, and even in the more purely madrigalian examples there is an abstract, almost instrumental quality about the music—which a discreet use of word-painting does not lessen—that is reminiscent of Byrd's style.

Tomkins, too, has certain affinities with Byrd (who was his teacher) in that the greater part of his vocal music was composed for the Church. Even his one 'secular' publication, which, significantly enough, is entitled *Songs*, not 'Madrigals', includes some anthems, just as Byrd's three sets had done. But Tomkins is much more madrigalian in his technique and choice of texts than either Byrd or Gibbons, and is equally at home when writing a ballett or setting a short conventional lyric, as in *Sure there is no God of love*, as when he is clothing a longer and more complex text with almost the entire range of madrigalian devices, as in *Weep no more thou sorry Boy*.

Although, as we have seen, instruments could and undoubtedly did on occasion take part in the performance of secular music on the Continent, their participation seems to have been much more frequent in England, doubtless owing to a tradition of which Byrd's unpublished secular pieces and those in his 1588 set (in their original layout) were the first notable examples. This traditional fondness for accompanied song is strikingly shown in the ayre, which, from *c.* 1600 on, gradually displaced the madrigal in popularity. The ayre was often so arranged that it could be performed in three different ways: by unaccompanied voices, by accompanied voices, and by a solo voice supported (usually) by a lute with a bass viol playing the lowest voice part. The solo part and the lute tablature are placed on one page, the other voices on the opposite page; hence all can perform from one book (see Plate XIX). Sometimes the lute accompaniment clashes with the inner vocal parts, so that presumably in these ayres the voices are not meant to be accompanied, only the solo voice. This provision of alternative methods of performance in the same volume is a distinctive feature of the ayre, as is the fact that it is almost without exception an original composition, whereas a tremendous number of Continental songs are simply transcriptions of vocal part-songs and were published separately from the latter.

Two other noteworthy features of the ayre in general are a much stronger sense of key and, through the use of a few pervading motifs, a more closely knit melodic line than existed abroad. The former is very apparent in the work of John Dowland [1563–1626], a fine singer, a lute virtuoso of international repute, and the greatest of the ayre composers. His fame, both as a lutanist and as a composer, led to several appointments abroad, where he spent much of his life, and where he met and was admired by many distinguished musicians, including Marenzio, but all his printed music was first issued in England, and his *First Booke of Songes or Ayres . . . with Tableture for the Lute* (1597) was the earliest and most popular of its kind (it was the only music-book by any composer that went through four editions during the composer's lifetime). The esteem in which his music was held on the Continent can be gauged from the fact that, as he himself says in his Preface to his last published work, *A Pilgrimes Solace* (1612), "some part of my poore labours have found favour in the greatest part of Europe, and been printed in eight most famous Cities beyond the seas, viz.: Paris, Antwerpe, Collein [Cologne], Nurenberge,

Franckfort, Leipsig, Amsterdam, and Hamburge". No other English composer and few foreign ones could claim as much.

Dowland's *First Booke of Songes* has the voice and lute parts arranged in the manner described above, and it set the fashion for most succeeding ayre prints. Indeed, its extraordinary popularity may be partly accounted for by the fact that it provided, for the first time, three alternative methods of performance, but the chief reason was undoubtedly the quality of the songs themselves. In his wide range of expressiveness, Dowland resembles Weelkes, and, like the latter, he is at his best when dealing with an emotional subject, as, for example, *Flow, my teares* from his *Second Booke of Songes or Ayres* (1600), which he had previously arranged for the lute under the title *Lachrimae* (1596). This song became enormously popular—a household word, in fact; references to it occur in many poems and plays of the early seventeenth century, and it was the basis of numerous instrumental pieces, including 'Seaven Passionate Pavans', by Dowland himself.

Although Dowland's emotionalism is akin to Weelkes's, he is more intense that the madrigalist, and a number of his songs show a passion and a sense of the dramatic which are unsurpassed by any other contemporary composer, with the possible exception of Gesualdo and Monteverdi. The fluctuating rhythms and wonderful expressiveness of his melody, the sensitive appreciation of the accentual and emotional qualities of the words, the daring use of chromaticism and dissonance, the utter perfection and variety of his lute accompaniments make him one of the finest song-writers of all time. Compared to him, most of the other ayre-composers are emotionally restricted and harmonically and melodically conventional, but this did not prevent them from producing a considerable number of charming and occasionally exquisite pieces. The chief exceptions are Thomas Campian [1567–1620] and John Danyel [*c.* 1565–*c.* 1630]. Campian, apart from being a poet of some repute, possessed a lyric gift of a high order, and his ayres, most of which are settings of his own verse, frequently show the second feature mentioned earlier—a closely knit melodic line. Danyel's ayres are uneven in quality, but the best of the twenty he published in 1606 come very near to Dowland's in their passionate intensity, and his rhythmic changes and use of dissonance are often most telling. Other notable ayre-composers are Robert Jones [fl. 1600], Philip Rosseter [1568–1623], and Michael Cavendish [*c.* 1565–1628], of whom the first and last also published madrigals.

Campian is also an important figure in the history of the masque, his two most notable essays in this sphere being the *Masque in honour of Lord Hayes* (1607) and *The Lord's Masque* (1613), for both of which, as for his other masques, he wrote the text and some of the music.

The masque was an offshoot of the late fifteenth-century 'mascherate', or masquerades, that formed part of the carnivals held before and after Lent in many Italian cities, notably Florence (see Part I, Chapter 6, p. 208), but in England it eventually developed into a musico-dramatic entertainment far more artistic and complex than its parent. So far as we know, the first masque took place in 1513, for a contemporary writer tells us that on Twelfth Night of that year Henry VIII and eleven others disguised themselves "after the maner of Italie, called a maske, a thyng not seen afore in Englande . . .". The masquers, wearing voluminous garments embroidered in gold, as well as gold masks and capes, appeared after the banquet and requested some of the ladies to dance. Information as to how the masque developed during the next ninety years or so is scanty, but from the end of the sixteenth century to the Civil War (1642) it was considerably influenced by the French ballet de cour, although in general it was more dramatically unified than its model.

The leading light of the Jacobean masque—that is, up to the death of James I [reigned 1603–1625]—was the famous dramatist and Poet Laureate, Ben Jonson, who, apart from writing a number of brilliantly satirical plays, of which *Volpone, or the Fox* (1606), *The Alchemist* (1610), and *Bartholomew Fair* (1614) are the best, and still performed, also produced a series of 'entertainments' from 1603 on which were commissioned by James and his successor, Charles I. In 1605 Jonson wrote the *Masque of Blackness*, and the man appointed by James to design the settings and devise the scenic effects was Inigo Jones [1573–1652], who became Royal Surveyor in 1615, and was the first great English architect. Jones probably visited Italy in 1601 and 1609, was certainly in Paris in the latter year, and in Italy and Germany in 1613–14. His study of Renaissance architecture in both France and Italy bore fruit in the classical designs of his buildings, notably the west portico of St. Paul's, the banqueting house of Whitehall Palace (now the United Services Museum), and the Queen's house at Greenwich, and also in the planning of certain small areas, such as Lincoln's Inn Fields and Covent Garden—the first instance of regulated planning in England. His studies abroad bore fruit too in his stage designs and use of stage machinery (see Plate XX), and he clearly learnt much from the Italian and French theatre. But Jones did not make his reputation as an architect, a reputation that eventually extended to the Continent, until some ten years after his successful début as a designer of masques, and in this capacity he was almost continuously employed by the Crown until the outbreak of the Civil War; indeed, he became so popular that when, in 1631, after much friction, the Jones-Jonson collaboration finally broke down, Jones was able to prevent Jonson from receiving any more commissions.

But we anticipate, for we shall here only deal with the Jacobean masque, leaving the Caroline masques, i.e. those written in Charles I's reign, to Chapter 3.

The best of Jonson's Jacobean masques are the *Masque of Queens* (1609), *Oberon* (1611), and *The Vision of Delight* (1617), which last we shall return to in Chapter 3, as the music reflects the vocal style of the Italian early baroque. While none of his masques can compare as a whole with the best of his plays, all of them contain passages that reveal the quality of his skill, learning, and wit.

Jonson and Campian were not the only writers of masques, and even if we omit Shakespeare's *The Tempest* (1611), which can be regarded as the finest masque ever written, there exist a number of excellent examples by other men, notably the *Inner Temple Masque* (1615), by the poet William Browne [*c.* 1591–*c.* 1645], and the *Masque of the Inner Temple and Gray's Inn* (1613), by the popular dramatist Francis Beaumont [1584/5–1616], whose collaboration with John Fletcher [1579–1625] provides one of the landmarks in the history of English drama.

The typical masque was very similar to the ballet de cour in that (1) its general layout consisted of dances accompanied instrumentally, or vocally, or both, and interspersed with prose and poetry, the latter spoken or set for one or more voices with or without instruments; (2) the presentation relied to a great extent on spectacular stage settings, devices, and costumes, including, of course, masks; (3) it was essentially an aristocratic entertainment containing much adulation of royalty and realm. This similarity became even more marked after 1609, when Jonson, in direct imitation of the ballet à entrées, introduced antimasques into his *Masque of Queens*. These, with their stress on characterization and dramatic expressiveness, which ranged from slap-stick to the macabre, were inserted between the 'scenes' of the masque proper and were usually so striking in their effect that they became, like the intermezzi of Italian opera (see Chapter 4), more popular than the main work. From 1609 on there were thus three groups of dances, those for the semi-professional masquers and antimasquers, and those in which the ladies of the audience joined—the final 'revels', equivalent to the French 'grand ballet', these last being the only occasions on which ladies danced on the stage, for in the remainder of the entertainment female characters were impersonated by male dancers wearing appropriate masks, as in the ballet de cour.

Apart from Campian, the chief composers of the Jacobean masque were Coperario, Alfonso Ferrabosco (ii) [*c.*1575–1628], whose father we mentioned earlier in this chapter, and Robert Johnson [*c.* 1583–1633]. Coperario and Ferrabosco were also important composers of consort music (see Chapter 2, p. 345), while Johnson established a considerable and well-deserved reputation in the spheres of instrumental music and songs with lute accompaniment; most of the best of these he wrote for Jonson's masques, and in general his masque music is superior, both melodically and in its sense of the dramatic, to that by Coperario or Ferrabosco, though the latter was ranked first by Jonson, an estimation that did not prevent the playwright's violent temper ending their association after 1610.

Although few of these early masques have survived with their music complete, some of it can be found scattered throughout various manuscripts or in published collections of instrumental and vocal pieces. Thus, apart from such obvious titles as *A Maske*, a number of dances which are linked with a high-ranking name, e.g. *Corranto Lady Riche* from the *Fitzwilliam Virginal Book* (see Chapter 2, p. 336), may have originally been part of a masque in honour of or presented by the individual concerned. Again, a piece such as Johnson's *The Pretty Wanton* very likely comes from a masque of that title (which in this case has been lost), or else is descriptive of the character that danced to it in (most probably) an antimasque. Similarly with vocal music; for example, *See, O see, who comes here a-maying?*, a four-part piece for two voices and two stringed instruments by Martin Peerson [*c.* 1572–1650], which was composed for Jonson's *Entertainment of the King and Queen* (1604) and published sixteen years later in the composer's *Private Musicke*. Jonson's favourite composer, Ferrabosco, also published some of his masque music several years after its first performance, and his *Ayres* (1609) include one for voice and lute from Jonson's *Masque of Blackness*.

The madrigal and its allied types, together with the ayre and masque-songs, did not cover the whole field of English secular vocal music, for all these demanded a fair degree of musical skill, and the stock melodies to which Italian poetry was sung (e.g. *ruggiero*) were paralleled by the ballads—that is, traditional tunes such as *Greensleeves*, to which a varying number of texts were adapted. In addition, Weelkes and Gibbons each wrote a piece for voices and instruments based on street cries, an idea similar to the villota, but more learnedly executed, particularly that by Gibbons, which is in fact an In nomine (see Chapter 2, p. 335), though one would never guess as much from the delightful way in which the cries are shared between the voices. More important are the three collections of Thomas Ravenscroft [*c.* 1590–*c.* 1633], *Pammelia* (1609), *Deuteromelia* (1609), and *Melismata* (1611), the first of their kind printed in England. They are definitely popular in appeal and consist in the main of simple part-songs, canons, and rounds—for example, *Three Blind Mice*, printed for the first time in *Deuteromelia*. This round and some of the other pieces may well go back to the early years of the sixteenth century.

Ravenscroft's three publications fall into line with the general trend of the English madrigal and ayre, for in general these last are, with their melodic freshness and harmonic clarity, more frankly popular than Italian madrigals and allied types. That the technical and expressive range of secular music in England fell below that of Italy was partly due to the inferior quality of the texts chosen, but mainly to the fact that, unlike Italy, with her teeming generations of composers, native and foreign, and her great musical centres at Venice, Florence, Rome, Bologna, Ferrara, Mantua, Milan, Naples, and Verona, each with their discerning patrons, knowledgeable amateurs, highly trained professional performers, and academies, English musical culture was largely amateur and, apart from a few aristocratic establishments, such as Hengrave Hall, the seat of the Kytson family, where Wilbye was employed, was centred in London. Moreover, there were no academies, and a composer was therefore denied both the stimulus of composing for and the benefits of criticism by a keen intelligent group.

But if English secular music is surpassed by Italian, it can certainly compare with French and is undoubtedly superior to German and Spanish, especially the latter, and it is a curious coincidence that its late flowering occurred immediately after the defeat of the Spanish Armada in 1588, when the period of tension and uncertainty was ended. Some people think that this naval victory, by ushering in an era of peace and prosperity, was the main cause for the sudden surge of creation, but it should be remembered that Italy produced one of the most brilliant chapters in the history of civilization while suffering far more and for a longer period than England.

Spanish domination in Italy did not make her immune from cultural invasion, and the Italian madrigal was cultivated by a number of native composers together with the purely national villancico. But the difference in quantity and quality between sacred and secular music in Spain was far greater than in any other country, and all the leading composers of vocal polyphony concentrated almost entirely on the mass and motet. The reason for this takes us into the realm of sacred music and the next chapter.

PERFORMANCE

(*See also pp.* 243, 249, 261, 267 269, 284, 286)

The most notable trend in late Renaissance music—particularly evident in the madrigal and chanson—is the change from the classical poise and restraint of the early part of the period, when music and text were of roughly equal importance, to the vivid word-painting and franker emotionalism of the late sixteenth and early seventeenth centuries, when the music was dictated by and in extreme cases depended on the nature of the text. The remarkable difference in approach between, say, the madrigals of Arcadelt and Gesualdo, or (though to a lesser extent) the chansons of Claudin and Lassus should therefore be reflected in performance. Details of speed, expression, the number of voices per part, and the use of instruments will depend to some extent on personal taste, but more especially on one or other of the following considerations: the period in which the piece was written, the nature of the words, the texture of the music, and, in certain instances, the personality of the composer, but, broadly speaking, the ensuing remarks hold good.

1. *Madrigals*

(*a*) In those written before Rore's first book *a*4 (1550) the tactus (semibreve in ȼ, minim in c) should be between M.M. 60–80, the choice depending on the texture and the poem; thus a mainly contrapuntal and rhythmically simple piece should be sung faster than a polyphonic and rhythmically complex one, unless the character of the poem as a whole contradicts this and/or there is a significant amount of syllabic underlay in minims (in ȼ) or crotchets (in c), especially if this is allied to extended harmonic movement in minims or crotchets respectively. It should be noted in this connexion that, although in ȼ and c the harmonic units are almost invariably the minim and crotchet respectively, in that they represent the longest dissonance and the shortest rate of harmonic change, the normal harmonic change occurs on the tactus; hence a piece in which changes of chord at twice the normal rate are at all frequent should be sung at or near the speed of tactus=M.M. 60. Once the speed has been decided on it should remain invariable. Dynamic contrasts should be abrupt (i.e. only occur between phrases) and gentle (e.g. *p* to *mf*, not *pp* to *ff*); in other words, while rising and falling lines within an individual vocal phrase will naturally increase and decrease in sound to a greater or lesser degree, there should be no overall crescendos, and only cadential diminuendos. Ornaments should not be extemporized, as this involves specialized knowledge.

(*b*) In those by Rore or written between 1550 and Marenzio's first book *a*5 (1580) the expressive range widens, though one mood is generally dominant throughout a single composition. Hence while dynamic contrasts, which should still be abrupt, may cover a bigger range, the tempo decided on should remain invariable, otherwise the unity of mood will tend to be disrupted. When a piece fluctuates between semibreve and minim tacti (see p. 243) then the choice of speed should lie between minim = M.M. 60–90, the exact speed depending on the same factors as in (*a*). The individual vocal lines should be sung with a keen sense of the text, and especially of the more emotional words.

(*c*) In those written after 1580 in which detailed word-painting and mood-change are the dominant factors, abrupt changes not only of dynamics (which may cover an even wider range than before), but also of speed may occur, as may restrained diminuendos (other than cadential) and even crescendos. The exact speed will depend on the same factors as in (*a*), and if there are changes in speed within a piece these must be abrupt, except as in (*a*), and should lie between minim = M.M. 60–90. Where the text demands it, the voices may range from staccato to legato in manner and from lightness to sombreness in timbre. In general, the more varied the musical treatment of the text, the more varied the performance. (*N.B.*—Clearly not all madrigals written between 1550 and 1580 are like Rore's, nor were all Marenzio's contemporaries so concerned with word-painting as he was; 'classical' madrigals continued to be written long after Arcadelt. The deciding factor is the nature of the piece, and it is seldom difficult to decide which period it belongs to stylistically and hence how it should be performed. For example, all English madrigals were written after 1580, but some (e.g. Morley's) are often more reminiscent of Arcadelt than Rore or Marenzio. The main difference between English and contemporary Italian madrigals in performance is that the former may be partially or wholly rendered on instruments with less ill-effect than the latter because the association between text and music is not nearly so close.)

2. *Chansons*

The importance attached to intelligibility of text, the simpler part-writing that resulted, the lightness and clarity of the language, and the natural refinement of feeling made the chanson less emotionally expressive than the madrigal, but the same dynamic changes should occur during roughly the same periods and, where the words warrant it, an even greater variety of speed (depending on the same factors as for the madrigal), the minim ranging from M.M. 60 to as much as 120. As in the madrigal, the later chansons (e.g. by Lassus) may demand much more varied performance than the earlier (e.g. by Claudin), though the programme- and narrative-chansons by Janequin and others should be more freely treated.

3. *Lieder*

Instrumental participation in vocal music was much commoner in Germany than in France or Italy because of a strong instrumental tradition (see Part I, p. 216). Thus while the practice of doubling or replacing some of the voices undoubtedly occurred in both France and Italy, the French stress on intelligibility of text and the close links between word, mood, and music in most late Renaissance Italian madrigals discouraged wholly instrumental performance. Apart from this, and the fact that the language is less sonorous than Italian and heavier than French, and the range of speed should therefore not exceed tactus = M.M. 60–90, the relevant remarks concerning the chanson apply also to the Lied. The most suitable instruments for taking part in Lieder (and madrigals and chansons for that matter) are strings and woodwind, including recorders.

4. *Balletti, Villanelle, etc.*

The clear texture, dance-like rhythms, and light character of the balletti call for a quick tempo of tactus = M.M. 80–100. The range of expression is limited. They are almost as effective when played on instruments. Villanelle and the other frivolous kinds mentioned in the chapter may range in speed from tactus = M.M. 60–100, the choice depending on factors already discussed under the madrigal. The expressive range, particularly in the villanelle, is wider than in the balletti. Instruments may double the voices.

5. *Lute Songs*

Ideally, of course, the lute should provide the accompaniment or, failing this, the guitar, but as competent players of either instrument are comparatively rare, the piano may be substituted, provided that the sustaining pedal is very discreetly used. In any case, a 'cello should play the bass of the accompaniment when the original demands a gamba. The range of expression is considerable and so speeds may lie between tactus=M.M. 60–100. As variations in tone and timbre are much more telling when sung by a solo voice than by a group of voices, they should occur more often, particularly in those songs (e.g. by Dowland) that are deeply expressive; in these slight changes of speed are often effective.

2

THE LATE RENAISSANCE: SACRED MUSIC—INSTRUMENTAL MUSIC

THE fact that Spanish composers in the late Renaissance were far more concerned with sacred than with secular music was undoubtedly due to the powerful combination of passion and mysticism that is such a marked characteristic of the Spanish people, and it was this characteristic that made Spain the spearhead of the movement known as the Counter-Reformation. We have already used this term several times, but before we can define it and describe its effects on art in general and music in particular, we must find out what Reformation it countered or opposed.

In Part I we saw how the Church during the fourteenth and fifteenth centuries had become disrupted within and discredited without, and how she later attempted to put her house in order. She was not on the whole averse to reform, for she had on several occasions in the past adapted herself to new ideas—the Franciscan movement for one, and Thomism for another—but the Great Schism had seriously weakened her authority, and in order to recover at least a part of this she withdrew within herself, becoming more rigid in her orthodoxy, fearful lest change should bring chaos. This explains but does not altogether condone the often violent persecution of those sects which disagreed with her, but neither the swords of her hired soldiers nor the torture chambers and burning stakes of her zealots could annihilate the growing belief that the soul of man can establish a direct relationship with God without the mediation of a priest.

On 31st October 1517, Martin Luther [1483–1546] nailed his famous ninety-five indictments on the sale of indulgences to the door of the castle church at Wittenberg, and it is usual and convenient to date the beginning of the Reformation from this act. The practice of receiving pardon for sins by paying certain sums of money had become an outrageous scandal during the early years of the century, when funds were needed to rebuild

St. Peter's Church in Rome, and Luther's condemnation of it was the result of a growing dissatisfaction with the Church of which he was an ordained priest, for he maintained that ecclesiastical penalties and pardons can never remove guilt or divine punishment, a view which the Church herself eventually adopted. In 1520 he published three treatises which represent the kernel of the Lutheran movement, and make it clear that he did not want separation from the Church, but simply that it should be reformed. In his belief, however, of "the priesthood of all believers", in his rejection of the Pope's supremacy, and in several other respects he cut right across some of the fundamentals of Catholicism, and his defiance of the Papal Bull of excommunication, which he burnt in public, caused a tremendous stir all over Europe.

Lutheranism swept through Germany like wild-fire, finding adherents among the common folk and aristocracy alike, for Luther, by showing an indifference to secular government, had been careful not to tread on the toes of traditional authority. In 1521 Charles V [1500–1558], at the famous Diet of Worms, banned the movement from his Empire, but five years later the German princes decreed that Lutherans should be allowed to preach and worship unhindered. In 1529, however, under intense pressure from Rome, this decree was revoked, and as a result a number of princes 'protested'—the origin of the term 'Protestant', the one now used to cover all reformed Churches. Finally, in 1555 Charles was forced to grant full religious equality to the reformed Church, and in the same year abdicated in favour of his brother, Ferdinand I [1501–1564].

Luther's stress on reformation rather than separation is clearly shown in his regulations concerning the place and practice of music in the service, for the early Lutheran mass differed little from that of the Catholic Church, and even his later German mass, which, in general, conformed to his aim of making the words intelligible to the ordinary man (hence his translation of the Bible), permitted the use of Latin if so desired, though some of the traditional mass movements were omitted altogether or replaced by German songs, and the Credo was sung in German. The Lutheran mass was thus a very fluid affair, but through its predominant use of the vernacular it did encourage the congregation to take part, though to what exact extent we do not know.

As for the music itself, most of it was adapted from Gregorian chants or, more especially, from pre-Reformation religious songs, mainly of German origin. In the first group the chant was either taken over intact or else altered, the texts in any case being translated. In the second group the sources range from Geisserlieder and Minnesäng to Latin and German part-songs. In addition, a number of new songs were written expressly for the Lutheran service; some of these were composed by Luther himself, who was a competent musician and a great admirer of Josquin, but the first notable Lutheran composer was his friend and musical adviser, Johann Walter [1496–1570]. Although Walter's publications include settings of both German and Latin texts, his most popular and important work is the *Geystliche Gesangk Buchleyn* ('Little Book of Spiritual Songs'), first printed in 1524 and almost entirely made up of German Lieder for three, four, and five voices. Almost half of these are written in much the same polyphonic style as Isaac's, with the principal melody in long notes, sometimes broken, in the tenor part, the other parts being free, with occasional imitation. The rest of the pieces anticipate the later chorale in their contrapuntal 'hymn tune' texture, but the tenor still carries the main melody. As the contents of the book are all part-songs, they could only have been performed by musically educated people, and to ensure that there were sufficient of these, choral societies for both children and adults were started at which the rudiments of music were taught and the repertoire practised. Thus uneducated members of the congregation presumably sang the tunes (borrowed or newly composed) that were not treated polyphonically or contrapuntally, and possibly also sang the tenor melodies in the chorale-like settings, the choir adding the other parts. In any case, the choir and congregation were unaccompanied, as the organ did not act as a support until the following century.

Walter's 1524 publication—the first Protestant hymnbook, in fact—was followed by many others and, towards the end of the century, by numerous simple settings of the psalms. But the tradition of northern polyphony was not only too powerful to be overthrown all at once, but also gave composers far greater scope for their talents than the simple congregational hymn or psalm. Even the use of Latin, which Luther after all had permitted, died hard, and Bach's Mass in B minor is simply the greatest among a host of others composed during the sixteenth, seventeenth, and eighteenth centuries. The Protestant motet, too, is very little different in style from its Catholic counterpart, except that, unlike the Protestant mass, the text is invariably in German. Moreover, several Protestant composers wrote Latin motets and a number of Catholic composers, including Stoltzer, Senfl, and Lassus, contributed to Protestant hymnbooks or set Lutheran texts independently. But their contributions, together with a number of fine hymns, motets, and masses by the leading Lutheran composers, Walter, Hassler, and Johann Eccard [1553–1611], simply cannot match in quantity or quality the output of the numerous Catholic composers who mostly centred round the Hapsburg court at Vienna, and of whom the chief were Senfl, Lassus, Kerle, and Monte, but we shall leave discussion of their works until we deal with the whole field of Latin liturgical music (see below).

The rapid spread of Lutheranism in Germany, and similar movements in Switzerland, France, England, and the Netherlands, caused great and growing concern in the Catholic Church, and resulted in the revival known as the Counter-Reformation. The first important outcome of this was the Council of Trent, at which leading Catholics met for a total period of about seven years between 1545 and 1563 and reconsidered and where necessary revised the Church's doctrine. On the whole the Council was a success, for while certain thorny theological problems were left unsolved, its deliberations undeniably strengthened the Church's position by restating more clearly her fundamental beliefs, advocating more strongly her responsibilities towards society, and cleaning up the abuses that were staining her reputation. Some of these abuses concerned music, and the Council spent over a year in deciding what reforms to adopt. The result can be summarized under two headings: the music itself and its performers. As regards the first, it was laid down that the prime aim of liturgical music is to promote a greater sense of worship in the congregation, and from this it naturally followed that no secular material may be introduced and the style of composition should allow the words to be clearly heard, this last being undoubtedly inspired by Luther. As to performance, it was decided, though largely by implication, that only the organ was to be used either in accompanying voices or playing solos, and that virtuoso or theatrical vocal and instrumental displays were to be prohibited.

These reforms give us some idea of the state of Catholic music in the 1560s, but to get a clearer picture we must trace its development after Josquin, and in so doing we shall not take each nation separately, but cover the entire field, for, unlike secular composition, which varied in language and to some extent in style from country to country, music for the Roman rite, no matter where it was written, continued to use a common language, and its style was virtually international.

Ockeghem wrote twelve masses, including a Requiem, and about ten motets; Josquin nineteen masses and about 100 motets. The difference is striking and important, as it reflects the general tendency throughout the sixteenth century whereby composers (with notable exceptions) increasingly favoured the motet rather than the mass. The reason for this was partly the composer's growing consciousness of his individuality—one of the main characteristics of the Renaissance outlook—and partly his purely artistic desire to give full rein to his talents, and, because the motet, unlike the mass, could be based on any sacred text written in Latin, it gave the composer not only freedom to choose those texts that especially appealed to his temperament, but also greater opportunities for technical experiments and expressive treatment. This tendency was not arrested by the Counter-Reformation, for the Council of Trent had been primarily concerned with the mass, the words of which, being the largely unchanging core of the service, were of far greater spiritual importance than any motet text. In a sense, then, the Council's reforms underlined and widened the distinction that already existed between mass and motet composition. Even in the second half of the fifteenth century, and especially with Josquin, the mass was more dependent than the motet on purely musical devices, such as canon and cantus firmi; in the vast majority of cases canon was introduced as a *tour de force* or for climactic purposes, and the cantus firmi, which rarely have any connexion with the text of the mass, although they may connect it with a particular feast, were generally employed as a means of providing unity or as a compliment to a patron (see Part I, p. 203). This use of canon and cantus firmus thus differs on the one hand from the earlier Italian caccie, in which canon was originally and usually a natural outcome of the subject, as in Ex. 59, Part I, p. 162, and on the other from the fourteenth- and fifteenth-century motet, where the word or words of the borrowed chant frequently have a connexion with those of the upper parts, as in Ex. 52, Part I, p. 132.

The various types of sixteenth-century mass are much the same as in Josquin's day, but it will be as well to describe the most important ones again, beginning with the 'parody mass'. In this all the parts of a previously composed piece (motet, chanson, madrigal), either by the composer himself or someone else, are used as a basis; sometimes only the opening bars are selected and placed at the beginning of each movement of the mass, but more often the original is divided into sections and these, often altered, are spread throughout the mass, each being separated by passages of free composition. About three-quarters of the masses by Lassus and nearly half of those by Palestrina are parody masses, and this preponderance is typical of the century.

Almost as common as the parody technique is that which uses a single borrowed melody or cantus firmus. This is frequently paraphrased and usually placed in the tenor, but is sometimes shared by all the voices; the paraphrase is often so elaborate that the original melody is unrecognizable in performance. Another type has the cantus firmus in long notes in one voice in each movement, the other voices being quite independent; if the borrowed melody is a chant, the voice that sings it sometimes has the original words, which naturally results in bi-textualism, as in Palestrina's *Ecce sacerdos magnus* ('Behold the High Priest'), where, for example, in Kyrie I the treble sings the entire melody and words of the antiphon on which the mass is based, while at the same time the alto, tenor, and bass sing 'Kyrie eleison'. A number of masses of this simple cantus-firmus type are based on invented melodies, such as the notes of the hexachord (e.g. C, D, E, F, G, A), ascending and descending in various rhythmic guises, or solmisation syllables derived from a laudatory address to a patron, as in Josquin's *Missa Hercules Dux Ferrariae* (see Part I, Chapter 6, p. 203). Yet another type of cantus-firmus mass, where the melody may be paraphrased or simple, is that in which each movement is based on a different chant. Except for the type of mass in which the cantus firmus is invented, all the main melodies are either chants or secular songs, but the use of the latter became much less frequent in the latter part of the sixteenth century than in the fifteenth century, due mainly to the influence of the Counter-Reformation.

Thirdly, there are the comparatively small number of masses that are, as far as we can tell, freely invented, but it is likely that some of these are in fact based on secular pieces or tunes which composers, especially after the Council of Trent, did not want to divulge. For example, Palestrina's *Missa Quarta*, published in 1582, actually paraphrases the famous old secular song, *L'Homme armé*.

Lastly, there is the 'missa brevis' or 'short mass', which, as its name implies, takes less time to perform than the normal mass owing to its simpler, more contrapuntal style and predominantly syllabic underlay. In the cathedrals and larger churches it was sung on those days that were not feast days, the elaborate polyphonic mass being reserved for the latter occasions, but in the more modest establishments it was performed much more frequently. The missa brevis, in fact, increasingly tended to replace Gregorian chant, which in earlier centuries had always been sung on 'ordinary' days, and thus reflected the general decline of the traditional chant throughout the entire Catholic Church. Because of its simplicity, the missa brevis was greatly favoured during the Counter-Reformation.

All the above types of mass composition, except the parody, can be found in the motets of the period, but they play a far less important part. The reason is not so much that composers felt that the motet, being shorter and sung all of a piece, needed a unifying device less than the mass, in which all but the Kyrie and Gloria are separated by other sung or spoken items during the service, but that the latter with its greater length and division into five separate movements gave more scope for their skill in ornamenting or varying pre-existent material. The practice of basing a composition on a borrowed melody or a complete piece has sometimes been criticized on the grounds that it shows lack of melodic originality and inventive power, but as we observed in Part I (p. 38), this attitude is comparatively modern, and in any case cannot be used to distinguish, for example, the symphonies of Mozart or the fugues of Bach from those of their contemporaries, for both are largely composed of the melodic and harmonic clichés of their time, and what makes them superior is the way these clichés are placed in their context and developed. In fact, the history of music shows that, as a rule, it is not the distinctiveness of basic material, but the way it is handled that provides the yard-stick by which a composer is measured.

Another reason why the various cantus-firmus techniques were seldom used in the motet is that its length and the comparatively free choice of texts made it more susceptible to the influence of secular music, in which the expression of the words provide both variety and unity. Thus not only was there a growing tendency to choose texts of an emotional and dramatic nature, but word-painting, chromaticism, and other elements from the madrigal and chanson became increasingly used and, during the last quarter of the century, produced a class of composition, the 'spiritual madrigal', which in its religious sentiments, vernacular texts, and musical treatment is halfway between the purely sacred and the wholly secular.

The infiltration of secular elements into the motet naturally affected its style, and the distinction between mass and motet, in this respect already present to some extent with Josquin, grew more marked as the century progressed; thus the stylistic differences between masses and motets by any one composer who died before or shortly after the Council of Trent are less than in the case of most later composers.

Although Italy, through the brilliant development of the madrigal, was undeniably the greatest centre of secular music, despite the long tradition and excellent quality of the chanson in France, she was by no means so pre-eminent in the field of Catholic composition except, as we would expect, in sheer quantity. This sharing of the honours, so to speak, by Europe as a whole was a direct result of the international character of Catholicism, which enabled a composer of masses and motets to receive fame within his own country and outside it, whereas his reputation as a composer of secular music was, in most cases, a purely national one.

Of the first six leading composers of Catholic music after Josquin only one, Willaert, spent most of his life in Italy. The others were the Netherlanders Gombert and Clemens non Papa, both of whom worked mainly in France; the Spaniard Cristobal de Morales [*c.* 1500–1553], who lived in the land of his birth, apart from ten or eleven years at Rome; Senfl, a Swiss who, from the time he became a pupil of Isaac to his death, never moved outside Germany (though biographical details are sketchy); and, finally, the Englishman John Taverner [*c.* 1495–1545], who remained in his native country all his life.

Taverner's music, like that of his predecessors since Dunstable, is fifty years or so behind his Continental contemporaries in its infrequent use of imitation, long florid melismas, and strong modal flavour, but it is up-to-date in the predeliction for writing *a*5 and *a*6. Although he wrote some charming motets for smaller groups and in a simpler contrapuntal style, he is essentially a master of flowing line and complex texture, and the richness of his five- and six-part polyphony, admirably set off by contrasting sections for fewer voices, represents the culmination of a tradition stretching back to the Old Hall MS. Like most English composers before him, his masses include no Kyrie (for probably the same reason as that given in Part I, Chapter 6, p. 189) and omit certain passages in the Credo.

Compared to Taverner, all the other five composers mentioned above are 'progressive', but not all of them are superior in craftsmanship or musicianship. Gombert, for instance, who used pervading imitation as a structural principle far more consistently than did Josquin, and most of whose masses are based on the parody technique, which Taverner uses only once, is reminiscent of Ockeghem in his dislike of clear-cut phrases and contrasting groups of voices, but, like the latter, he avoids monotony by the wonderful variety of his rhythms. Artistically, however, he is no greater than Taverner, and the same applies to Clemens, whose style is much less interesting rhythmically than Gombert's, though it is more varied in its texture and expressive of the text; in fact, Clemens is one of the earliest composers in whose motets we can see the beginnings of secular influence, which is not surprising when we remember that he, together with Gombert, was one of the chief composers of French chansons. In this respect these two men differ markedly from Morales, who, like Taverner, wrote almost entirely sacred music, but the Spaniard is even more old-fashioned than the Englishman in his liking for bi-textualism, especially in his motets, and in the rigid way in which he usually treats his Gregorian cantus firmi. He is more 'modern', however, in that he does not restrict the cantus firmus to one voice at a time, as Taverner does, but shares it between all the voices. He also uses parody and pervading imitation. There is a somewhat austere flavour to much of Morales' music, and also a strength and power which give it a character quite distinct from and on the whole superior to the liturgical compositions of Taverner, Gombert, and Clemens. In complete contrast are the motets and masses of Senfl, in which the technical mastery imparted by his great teacher, Isaac, is frequently allied to a lyricism reminiscent of the south, a lyricism that may, indeed, have stemmed from Isaac's Italian pieces.

The greatest composer of this early group is Willaert, whose fame both as a creative artist and as a teacher enabled him to exert an influence far more potent than any of his contemporaries or indeed any other Renaissance composer. By grafting the imitative polyphony of northern Europe on to the chordal texture of Italy, and by stressing the importance of accurate word-setting, Willaert laid the stylistic foundations of almost the entire Catholic repertoire of the late Renaissance. As with the other composers discussed above, except Taverner, pervading imitation is the essential feature of Willaert's style, but he shows Italian influence in his greater harmonic clarity. This is particularly noticeable in his polychoral writing, a technique that, we repeat, he did not invent, for it was practised in Italy, where it may have originated, during the latter part of the fifteenth century, and in France during the early years of the sixteenth; but Willaert undoubtedly gave it a new lease of life and was thus largely responsible for its magnificent development by the Gabrielis, the elder of whom, it will be remembered, was his pupil.

The colour and brilliance achieved through the dramatic contrasts inherent in polychoral writing and the fact that a predominantly chordal texture is the most effective one in this style of composition, admirably suited the Italian genius, and at the same time satisfied the Council of Trent's demands for intelligibility of text. It also suited the emotional fervour of the Counter-Reformation, and all the leading composers of the Catholic revival favoured it to a greater or lesser extent, notably the man whose liturgical music is officially regarded by Catholics as second to none—Palestrina.

On Good Friday, 1555, Pope Marcellus II, who only reigned for three weeks, summoned the musicians of the Papal Choir; after criticizing the casual and even flippant way in which they sang the service, he instructed them to perform in future "with properly modulated voices, and so that everything could be both heard and understood properly".* This sentence implies what we already know from other sources, that the singers indulged in a certain amount of vocal improvisation, and also that the complexity of the music itself made the words unintelligible. Among the members of the Choir was the newly-elected Palestrina, who was so impressed by the Pope's earnestness and ideals that he renamed a mass written at least ten years earlier, the now famous *Missa Papae Marcelli*. The style of this fine work, in which counterpoint and syllabic underlay predominate much more than was usual for the period, happened to fit in with Marcellus' objective, but, contrary to popular belief, it was not inspired by the Pope, nor was it composed in order to prevent the Council of Trent from banning all music but Gregorian chant in the performance of the mass, though Palestrina, along with Lassus, Kerle, and others, did in fact write 'demonstration' masses for the Council. If anyone deserves to be called the 'saviour of Catholic Church music' (a title once given to Palestrina owing to the erroneous belief mentioned above) it is the Fleming, Jacobus de Kerle [*c.* 1532–1591], who dedicated a collection of 'preces' or 'prayers' to the Council which were probably sung at the opening of each session during the last year the Council met, and undoubtedly influenced its decisions on liturgical music. In these pieces the style, while predominantly imitative and employing discreet chromaticism and word-painting, is essentially simple, and the words come through clearly. It is indeed typical of most of Kerle's output, whether composed in Italy or (later) in Germany and Prague, and he did much to spread its influence in the two latter places.

In many respects Kerle's style is similar to Palestrina's, but as the latter was regarded by most people of his own time and since as the greatest writer of Church music, whether Catholic or Protestant, the main features of his mature style must be mentioned. Virtually all these features are the result of the composer's attempts to achieve a perfect poise, to let nothing

* Quoted from H. Coates, *Palestrina*, p. 41.

obtrude or be given undue importance, whether in rhythm, melody, or harmony. Thus a run of crotchets is balanced by a succession of longer notes; the usual range of a melody is restricted to a tenth and is often no more than an octave; a movement upwards or downwards, whether by one or two leaps or by a series of steps, is followed by a movement in the opposite direction; a weak crotchet, i.e. the second one in a minim, is rarely approached or quitted by more than a step above its neighbours, for this would make too prominent a note that rhythmically is very unimportant; leaps of augmented or diminished intervals are avoided, as are major sixths, all sevenths, and ninths; no dissonance is longer than a minim, and this is nearly always prepared, suspended, and resolved, the resolution being a step down; the most common passing dissonance is an unaccented crotchet approached and quitted by a step; remote modulations or chromatic changes of chord are avoided. These details of Palestrina's technique, while not invariable, are typical of his mature style, and, compared to that of Josquin, they represent the culmination of a refining process that had been going on in the intervening years, and one that can be seen, for instance, in the style of Gombert and Clemens. No one, however, carried this process quite so far as Palestrina, and it must always be remembered that in this he was not typical of his generation, for although he could not fully escape the influence of the madrigal, he did so to a greater extent than any of his contemporaries. Neither is he typical in the numerical relationship between his masses on the one hand and his motets and other allied works on the other, and the fact that he is at his greatest in the former is not surprising, because, as we have already seen, the mass by its very nature—and particularly after the Council of Trent—was a much more suitable mould in which to pour music so restricted in style and emotion. But this does not mean that his music lacks emotion; Palestrina was no ascetic who shut himself off from his fellow-men and composed in an aura of holiness, for he combined a warm heart and affectionate nature with a shrewd business head. Furthermore, he composed a sizeable number of madrigals which differ little in style from his liturgical pieces, and he was quite capable of a little hypocrisy if it suited his book, as when, in dedicating some masses to a Pope, he bewails the popularity of secular music, but produces another book of madrigals shortly afterwards. He even flouted the Council by using secular models for several of his masses, one of the last being based on his own famous madrigal, *Vestiva i colli.*

Whether or not he was and still is, as many people think, the greatest composer of Church music depends on what you demand from such music; if you believe that the composer should become as impersonal in this particular branch of his art as the priest at the altar, then Palestrina takes the palm, but if you believe that, given the same sincerity and a comparable technical mastery, individuality, however striking, has a place in worship, then other composers will appeal more. But whatever your view, it must be admitted that his style, while occasionally resulting in a monotony due to the limitations that were an integral part of his artistic outlook, at its best produced music which, because of these very limitations, is unique in the flawlessness of its execution, the perfect poise of its rhythmic and melodic elements, and the delicate sensuousness of its harmony. In rhythm, melody, and harmony Palestrina was conservative, but in his feeling for and delight in pure sound (abundantly evident in his part-writing, which is frequently adjusted so as to produce full triads), in his vocal orchestration, and in the number of his polychoral pieces with their predominantly chordal texture, he was a 'modern'.

In placing purely musical considerations before those of the words he was setting, Palestrina, even in his motets, is much closer to the north European tradition than is his Netherlandish contemporary, Lassus, who spent the last thirty-eight years of his life at Munich and who, to complete the paradox, was the more Italianate of the two. This being so, we should expect the latter to favour and excel in motet composition, which is indeed the case, and although his masses do not compare with Palestrina's, his motets are quite definitely superior. The versatility that he shows in general is also evident in the treatment and selection of his motet texts. Detailed word-painting, abrupt changes of rhythm, declamatory passages, and chromaticism all show the influence of the madrigal and to a lesser extent the chanson. But these by themselves are merely means to an end, and it is in the superb quality and richness of his imagination that Lassus' greatness lies, an imagination that constantly needed new texts, preferably of an emotional or dramatic nature, to set it fully alight, and although he ranged successfully over the entire field of sacred and secular vocal music, it is in the motet and its allied type, the spiritual madrigal, that we find him at his greatest. This is particularly true of his later works, for the missionary zeal of the Counter-Reformation appealed to the introspective side of his personality and affected him more profoundly perhaps than any of his contemporaries. The result was a series of works of a predominantly penitent character of which the best, in their superb technique, emotional depth, and rich expressiveness, are among the greatest contributions to our musical treasure house, notably the 'Penitential Psalms' (1563–70), the 'Lamentations' (1585), and the two books of 'Spiritual Madrigals' (1585 and 1587).

Comparing the merits of two composers is often a profitless occupation, but when one has received less than his due share, both in literature and performance, it becomes necessary, and although this is clearly not the place to give a detailed critical assessment of Palestrina and Lassus, it must be pointed out that the centuries-old veneration accorded to the former, especially and quite rightly in view of his masses, by the Catholic Church, should not blind us to the greatness of the latter. The flawless execution of worthwhile ideas will always rank high in any art, but the ideas themselves, man being what he is, will always be somewhat limited in their extent and depth. Conversely, a wide and profound emotional range will never be presented with the same utter perfection, for although practice may indeed make perfect, that which is practised must be restricted in scope. Of the perfection of Palestrina's music there is no question, and the mere versatility and increased range of expression of Lassus's output cannot of itself equal this, but when to this versatility and expressive range is added Lassus's superb technique, then there can be little, if any, doubt that he is at least equal in stature to his great Italian contemporary.

Byrd has sometimes been called 'the English Palestrina', but this is a complete misnomer, for he is much more akin to Lassus in his style, in his preference for the motet rather than the mass, and in his versatility, and while he cannot compete with the Netherlander in the variety of his secular music, he far outstrips him in the instrumental field. But Byrd's versatile artistic temperament was almost certainly not the only reason why he wrote only three masses and over 230 motets (a higher ratio than any other major Catholic composer) for he could hardly help being profoundly affected by the Reformation in England (see p. 312). This can be conveniently dated as beginning in 1529, when Henry VIII summoned the so-called 'Reformation Parliament' which five years later dutifully passed the Act of Supremacy establishing Henry as the supreme head of the English Church and putting the final seal on his break with Rome. But the Church itself remained much the same as before because Henry was suspicious of the democratic character of Lutheranism and, being a dictator, disliked its deliberate dissociation from politics, but he could not prevent the infiltration of Lutheran ideas which, during the reign of Edward VI [1547–1553], became clearly evident in the first Book of Common Prayer (1549), but much more so in the second (1552). The changes in the service, notably the replacing of Latin by English, which these Prayer Books introduced did not reflect the temper of the country as a whole, and when Catholicism reasserted itself under Mary [reigned 1553–1558] there was no violent protest. Mary, however, went too far, and by condemning to the stake some of the leading reformers she fanned the embers of a reaction against Catholicism—embers that were already aglow as a result of her unpopular marriage to the fanatical papist Philip II of Spain [reigned 1556–1598]. This reaction increased sharply on the accession of Elizabeth I, mainly owing to the return of those who, in order to escape 'Bloody Mary', had fled to the Continent and had there come under the influence of Calvinism. This, a much stricter and simpler form of Protestantism than Lutheranism, was founded at Geneva by a Frenchman, Jean Calvin [1509–1564], who viewed liturgical ceremony with suspicion, banned elaborate ritual, and replaced, as did Luther, the infallibility of the Pope by the infallibility of the Bible. To the returning English exiles from Geneva the Prayer Book (which was and still is largely a translated adaptation of the Catholic service) reeked of popery, and anti-Catholic feeling, gathering force throughout the succeeding eighty years and aggravated by the tactlessness and arrogance of James I and the stubborness and incompetence of Charles I, eventually burst into the flames of civil war.

But, despite the Puritans, as they were called, not only was the Prayer Book accepted by the majority of Englishmen during Elizabeth's reign, but even Catholics suffered little persecution;

indeed, Byrd, who remained a Catholic all his life, spent the whole of his adulthood in the service of the Anglican Church, being appointed organist at Lincoln Cathedral when he was only twenty and remaining there until, in 1572, he left to share a similar post at the Chapel Royal with his renowned teacher, Thomas Tallis [*c.* 1505–1585]. In 1575 Tallis and Byrd were granted a virtual monopoly of all music-printing for twenty-one years; later, after a gap of two years, the monopoly transferred to Morley for a similar period. In the same year the two men jointly published a collection of motets, other collections by Byrd alone following in 1589, 1591, 1605, and 1607. All these have the printer's name and date on the title-page, but the three masses, *a*3, *a*4, and *a*5, have not, and we can only guess their dates of composition (*c.* 1600) from stylistic features and one or two other clues. They are all similar in style, are freely composed, contain the normal five movements, and use the old 'head motive' technique as a means of binding together some of the movements. That Byrd wrote and published no more than three masses, that the printer's name is omitted from these, that he composed and published no Latin music at all during the last sixteen years of his life (the forty-four motets that remained in manuscript were all written before *c.* 1590), may well be explained by the growing influence of Puritanism, for while the motets were probably composed for those who still privately practised their old faith, though necessarily in a much restricted manner, and could only have been objected to on the grounds that their texts are in Latin, and that some of them are addressed to the Virgin Mary or the saints, the mass, apart from needing full ceremonial for its performance, also represents the very core of the Catholic liturgy, and would therefore have been much more offensive to the authorities and hence riskier to publish.

In his motets, and indeed in his vocal output as a whole, Byrd is the exact opposite of Lassus in one rather interesting respect, for while the latter increasingly favoured texts of a penitential, meditative nature in his sacred music, and of a serious, even religious bias in his secular, Byrd became progressively more cheerful in both. Furthermore, his later works, i.e. those issued in 1605, 1607, and 1611, reveal some important differences compared to his earlier ones. Between 1591 and 1605 Byrd published nothing, but during this period over half the total output of the English Madrigal School was published. Byrd could hardly have escaped being influenced by this rush of native secular composition; at any rate, the important differences mentioned above can most satisfactorily be explained as being due to secular influence. Thus, compared to his earlier works, his later are scored for higher voices, with the soprano part usually doubled instead of the alto or tenor in five- and six-part pieces, reflecting the trend in Italian music noted earlier. Similarly, the phrases are shorter, words are repeated less often, and word-painting is more frequent, and it is worth noting in this connexion the similarity in approach between the quotation from the title-page of his 1611 book (see p. 281) and the following excerpt from his Latin dedication of 1605: "there is a certain hidden power, as I learnt by experience, in the thoughts underlying the words themselves; so that, as one meditates upon the sacred words, the right notes, in some inexplicable manner, suggest themselves quite spontaneously".* Another distinction between his earlier and later works is the fact that nearly all the motets constructed on the old plan of a cantus firmus in long notes in one of the parts were written before 1591. In all these respects Byrd was a 'modern', but in his tonal feeling he was not, and in his treatment of discord he was often unorthodox. As regards the first, a point of imitation, say in the 'key' of F, which begins with a leap up from the tonic to the dominant (F–C), is more likely to be answered with another fifth (C–G) than with the fourth (C–F). The former is called a 'real' answer because it imitates exactly, and the latter is called a 'tonal' answer because it helps to define the tonality of the piece.

Byrd's treatment of discord is more difficult to place in perspective because in the latter half of the sixteenth century there were two opposing trends, especially in Italy, one contracting, the other expanding, as it were. The first, more typical of sacred than secular music, shows an increasing refinement in the use of discord and reached perfection in Palestrina's mature work; it also reached a dead-end, for perfection cannot be developed. The second, starting from the same point as the first—namely, the careful approach to and departure from a discord—shows a growing freedom of treatment for expressive purposes and reached its peak in the

* E. H. Fellowes, *William Byrd*, 1936, p. 83.

madrigals of Gesualdo and Monteverdi and the motets of Giovanni Gabrieli. Now, Byrd's use of discord, while much freer than Palestrina's, is not in the main employed as a means of greater expression, but is usually the result of either exuberant part-writing, where the individual lines matter more than their combination, or else of a definite liking for the actual sound of the discords.

That Byrd was fully aware of the unusual sound of some of the passages he wrote we can be sure, for in 'The Epistle to the Reader' of his 1588 book he particularly draws attention to the fact that "if ther happen to be any jarre or dissonance, blame not the Printer, who (I doe assure thee) through his great paines and diligence doth heere deliver to thee a perfect and true Coppie". If his unorthodox use of dissonance was deliberate in 1588, it was obviously intentional in his later works. Thus in Ex. 14 the exposed weak quaver (crotchet in the original) of the point of imitation, e.g. the second quaver in bar 1—which in itself is very untypical of Palestrina style—is sometimes concordant, but sometimes, owing to the melodic line of the other parts and also to chordal considerations, is treated as a freely quitted discord (bars 2, 3, 4; this treatment of a discord is now called 'échappée'). In the tenor part in bar 3 and, more strikingly because the point is augmented, in bar 6 the discord is the dominant seventh; Byrd, in fact, was very fond of the unprepared (usually dominant) seventh, and at cadences often leaps up to it from the fifth of the dominant chord. In the penultimate bar is one form of the so-called 'English cadence' in which the essential feature is a normal suspension coupled with false-relation; in this case F♮ in one part followed immediately by F♯ in another. Byrd clearly liked false-relations, and they occur in his work more frequently than in any of his compatriots, not only successively, as in the above cadence, but simultaneously, e.g. *g″–f♯″–g″* in the soprano against *e′–f♮′–e′* in the alto. It must be remembered, however, that such clashes sound more dissonant when played on the piano than when sung, for not only are voices non-percussive instruments, but the actual interval is different, being larger and less harsh owing to the fact that, in the instance given above, the *f♯″* is, or should be much nearer to *g″* and the *f♮′* much nearer to *e′* than on the equally tempered piano (Ex. 14,* opposite).

* From *The Collected Vocal Works of William Byrd*, ed. Fellowes, Vol. V, p. 18.

It may well be that Byrd's treatment of discord was the result of his fondness for instrumental composition, because not only was he much more versatile and prolific in this field than any other major composer of vocal music, either of his time or before it, but by far the greater proportion of his pieces are for the virginal or spinet, a name originally given to a small harpsichord but, which by Byrd's day often included the normal-sized instrument as well. Now, it is a fact that every composer of keyboard music (excluding that for the organ, but including the piano repertoire) uses discords with greater freedom than when he is writing for voices, and while Byrd's virginal pieces, compared to those by other composers of his day, are not exceptional in their freer use of discord, it is more than likely that, because they occupy such a comparatively large place in his total output, this particular feature affected his vocal music to a greater extent than with other composers. This is truer of his Catholic than of his Anglican works as many of the latter are chordal in texture and this is less naturally suited to discord than polyphony (see pp. 314, 331).

The expressive range and technical mastery of Byrd's Latin Church music reveal him as an outstanding creative artist, and the quality and variety of his inspiration is as apparent in his Mass for Three Voices and his three-part motets as it is in his Mass *a*5 and his motets for five and six voices. Indeed, if he had written nothing else, his compositions for the Catholic liturgy would place him high in the ranks of late Renaissance composers.

There was in fact one great composer of the late Renaissance who wrote nothing else but liturgical music, the Spaniard Tomás Luis de Victoria [1548–1611]. That he was an ordained priest of the Catholic Church does not explain his exclusive preoccupation with sacred music, for a number of clerics (like Cardinal Bembo) wrote madrigal texts, or (like Gastoldi) composed secular music. The explanation lies partly in the man's make-up and partly in the religious atmosphere of Spain, the country least affected by the secular humanistic influence of the Renaissance or the heresies of the Reformation. Moreover, as we mentioned earlier, it was Spanish fervour rather than the decisions of the Council of Trent that gave to the Counter-Reformation something of the old Crusading spirit, and in the missionary zeal, high intelligence, and devotion to duty of the Jesuits, a religious society founded in 1534 by the Spaniard Ignatius Loyola [1495?–1536] and predominantly Spanish in its early years, the Church found a powerful weapon with which to combat her enemies.

It was Spanish fervour too that revived the ecclesiastical court known as the Inquisition during the reign of Ferdinand and Isabella in order to put a check on the number of Jews and Moors who were adopting Christianity for purely social and political reasons. This institution was first organized in 1231 as a means of converting or, failing this, punishing heretics, but by the early fifteenth century it had almost entirely ceased to function, and while Ferdinand and Isabella's use of it was perfectly orthodox and correct, it was disgracefully abused later on, particularly under the fanatical Philip II, who married Mary Tudor, and whose 'crusade' against Protestant England in 1588 failed so completely and ignominiously. Philip's religious fanaticism, the largely Spanish Jesuit movement, and the new monastic flowering initiated by Teresa of Avila [1515–1582]—one of the most remarkable women in history—and her younger disciple, John of the Cross [1542–1591]—one of the greatest of Christian mystics—all contributed to make Spain the spiritual centre of the Counter-Reformation. Small wonder that Protestantism could gain no foothold nor secular music flourish in such an atmosphere; small wonder also that Victoria more than any of his countrymen reflected this in his output, for while his devotion to Catholicism was a national characteristic, it was more strongly developed in him than usual because, firstly, he was, like St. Teresa, a Castilian, a race whose pride, tenacity, and passion made them the most powerful in the Peninsula, and, secondly, he was not only probably influenced by Teresa's monastic order (the first convent of which was founded at Avila in 1562), but certainly affected by the Jesuit movement, for during most of the period he spent in Rome between 1565 and 1584 (where he may well have studied under Palestrina) he was a member and later chapel master of the Collegium Germanicum, an institution founded by Loyola to combat Lutheranism.

Whether or no Victoria was taught by Palestrina, he could hardly have helped being influenced by so famous a master, but while the high proportion of masses to motets is common to both men, this was also typical of Spanish but not of Italian Church composers in general, and reflects the different religious outlook of the two countries; so does the fact that not one of Victoria's masses is based on secular material. Moreover, his style, while lying closer to that of the great Italian than does Byrd's, is distinctive in its emotional and dramatic, even ecstatic, qualities, his melodic line is freer, the contrasts of rhythm and texture more pronounced, and there is a greater preoccupation with the purely chordal side. This last feature, indeed, may well have influenced the older man, whose later works show an increasing delight in homophony as opposed to polyphony; if this is true, then Palestrina was like Haydn, for both gave to and received from their younger and more emotionally profound contemporary.

Despite the fact that Victoria composed no secular or instrumental music and to this extent was not of his time, he is completely 'modern' in both his style and in his fondness for polychoral writing, and of his comparatively small output nearly a sixth (excluding the masses) are for two or three choirs. A few of these, published in 1600, have a written-out organ accompaniment which is simply a reduction of the music for Chorus I, and when that chorus rests so does the instrument. This feature was not essentially new, for although the provision of a complete accompaniment was rare at the time the practice of extemporizing on the organ from a bass part was fairly common. This bass part, called 'basso seguente' ('following bass'), was not necessarily the same as the vocal bass, but consisted of the lowest note at any given point, which in fact might be sung by a tenor or even an alto. A new step, and one which provides a link with baroque practice, was taken by an Italian, Ludovico Grossi da Viadana [1564–1627], who, in 1602, published a collection of motets with an organ bass (later called 'basso continuo') that is frequently different from the lowest given part and is hence, unlike the basso seguente, essential from the harmonic point of view.

Independent instrumental accompaniments in fact were coming increasingly to the fore. We have already mentioned, in the previous chapter, the elaborate keyboard parts of Luzzaschi's madrigals for the three ladies of Mantua, but these pale before Giovanni Gabrieli's sumptuous polychoral motets, some of which have an orchestral accompaniment. Giovanni learnt much from his uncle Andrea, but he surpassed the older man, and indeed all others of his time or before it, in the brilliance of his tonal colours achieved through the blending of many voices and instruments, and in his dramatic handling of vocal groups, with or without instrumental accompaniment. It was natural that the full splendour of Giovanni's style should be revealed in his motets rather than his madrigals, because most of the latter, with their word-painting, intimate character, and basically polyphonic texture, did not favour the broad, clearly defined washes of sound and the essentially contrapuntal texture which are so typical of his mature work. Moreover, such music, especially when the voices are divided into two, three, or even four separate choirs, is only fully effective in a large hall, which in those days generally meant a church.

It is in his later motets, probably composed after 1600, that Giovanni's genius is shown at its height. Polychoral compositions abound, ranging from two choirs *a*4 to four choirs *a*4, as well as 'normal' pieces written for anything up to twenty voices. In some of these, contrary to general practice, the accompanying instruments are specifically mentioned, and include violini piccolo (violins), violini (violas), bass viols, cornetts (see Part I, p. 68), bassoons, and trombones. In one piece, *Suscipe clementissime*, a six-part chorus is contrasted with an ensemble of six trombones; another, *In Ecclesiis*, his most brilliant work, calls for two four-part choirs, a quartet of soloists, an organ, and an orchestra scored for violas, three cornetts, and two trombones. Only the bass of the organ part is given, and most of the time it is accompanying one or more solo voices, thus providing the harmonic foundation (basso continuo); the other instrumental parts are either quite different from the vocal solos or choruses they support, or else double the voices at the octave, a completely new idea and one doubtless suggested by those organ stops which combine the principal note with its octave or double octave, above or below. Particularly noteworthy is the distinction in style between orchestral and vocal writing, and also that between soloists and chorus.

With Giovanni Gabrieli, as with Viadana, we are on the threshold of baroque style, and although the greater of the two, Gabrieli, considerably enriched the expressive technique of his age, what he expressed in his sacred works does not rank him much, if at all, above some of his more orthodox contemporaries, for it must be remembered that almost every composer of any consequence, whether Protestant or Catholic, wrote fine music for his Church. Apart from those already mentioned, the chief figures in Catholic music were Monte, whose motets rank near to those of Lassus; Felice Anerio [*c.* 1564–1614], who most closely approaches Palestrina in purity of style; Andrea Gabrieli; the Spaniard, Francisco Guerrero [1528–1599], whose gentle lyricism found its natural inspiration in texts praising or supplicating the Virgin Mary; the Englishman, Thomas Tallis, who, despite a formidable technique that enabled him to write a fine motet for eight five-part choirs (*Spem in alium*) and a number of other pieces which are magnificent in their rich sonority and rhythmic interplay, is old-fashioned stylistically, but who could on occasion compose in a charmingly simple vein; Giovanni Animuccia [d. 1571], chiefly famous for his spiritual songs written for the Congregation of the Oratory, an organization founded by a priest, Filippo Neri [1515–1595], in 1544, who, in his desire to make religion attractive to the young, combined sermons and Bible readings with suitable musical and theatrical entertainments, an idea that eventually developed into the oratorio; Jan Pieterzoon Sweelinck [1562–1621], the last of the Netherlanders, who set in motet style the complete French Psalter in addition to writing Latin motets and chansons, but whose keyboard music, which we shall discuss later, is of greater importance; and, lastly, the Frenchman, Claude Goudimel, whose works are typically French in their simplicity, melodic brevity, clear-cut phrases, and predominantly syllabic underlay.

Goudimel is more famous, however, for his settings of the psalm-tunes in the Genevan Psalter. The tunes themselves were so popular that they were sung not only by Protestants, but by Catholics as well, until forbidden by Papal decree, and Goudimel's settings were written both before and after his conversion to Protestantism, *c.* 1560. The texts of the Psalter are in French metrical verse, selected and, in a few cases, translated by Calvin, the majority being translated by the most fashionable poet of the time, Clément Marot [1497–1544]. In accord with his strict religious outlook, already mentioned, Calvin, unlike Luther, insisted on the psalms being sung to simple, unharmonized tunes of a devout character, and it is ironical therefore to find that far more of these are based on secular models than is the case with Lutheran melodies. The man most responsible for these unadorned settings was Louis Bourgeois [*c.* 1510–*c.* 1561], who, although dying before the complete Psalter was published in 1562, composed or adapted two-thirds of the total of 125 psalm-tunes.

But even Calvin could not prevent the widespread popularity of part-music from invading psalm-singing, and while Bourgeois himself set some of the tunes for four voices, and a number of other composers, including Janequin, le Jeune, and Mauduit, did likewise, it was Goudimel who really established the practice, for he not only published, between 1551 and 1566, a number of fairly elaborate polyphonic settings of the psalm-tunes, but in 1564 and 1565 issued two harmonizations of the complete Genevan Psalter. The 1564 book is in simple motet style, while that of 1565 is in hymn-tune style; in the former most of the tunes are, for the first time in any psalter, placed in the soprano rather than in the usual tenor voice, but in the 1565 edition the traditional role of the tenor is re-established. This latter edition, which Goudimel specifically intended for home use, became so popular that it was reissued many times during the next 200 years; moreover, practically every psalter during this period, no matter what the language, included a generous selection of his settings.

Although the Reformation quickly found a foothold in France, it was far more bitterly contested than in Germany, and persecution under Francis I [reigned 1515–1547] and Henry II was severe, the latter monarch ordaining in the year he died that heretics should be executed. This was revoked three years later, but was followed almost immediately by the massacre of Vassy in 1562, and from this date until the accession of Henry IV in 1589 religious war was more or less continuous, the worst incident occurring on St. Bartholomew's Day (24th August) 1572, when about 3,000 French Protestants, or Huguenots, as they were called, were murdered. But persecution, as usually happens, only served to increase the ardour and influence of the persecuted, and Henry IV, who had reverted to Catholicism in order to be crowned, was obliged in 1598 to sign the Edict of Nantes, which gave his former co-religionists freedom to worship as they pleased and admission to all employment.

In the Netherlands the Reformation had an even longer and bloodier struggle to establish itself than in France, for while they, like Germany, were affected by the imperial ban of Charles V, they alone had to suffer the domination of Spanish fanaticism, particularly during the reign of Charles' son, Philip II, to whom his father left this part of his Empire, the rest going to his brother Ferdinand. For nearly 100 years from Philip's accession the Netherlands were torn by civil war between Catholics and Protestants or by bitter strife against Spanish imperialism. These terrible years probably explain the dearth of native psalters, for, apart from the monophonic *Souterliedekens* ('Little Psalter Songs'), published at Antwerp in 1540, which Clemens later set for three voices, virtually no Protestant music was produced. The 1540 print, however, became so popular that over thirty editions appeared during the next seventy years. It differs from the Genevan Psalter in that the Dutch texts are anonymous verse translations, probably by an amateur or amateurs, which were more or less forced to fit popular tunes and folk songs, and, moreover, was intended for use in the home, not in church. Clemens' settings, like Goudimel's 1565 edition, place the main melody in the tenor far more often than in the soprano.

Compared with Germany, France, and the Netherlands, England had an almost bloodless religious revolution, partly because her two most influential rulers, Henry VIII and Elizabeth

I, pursued a course somewhere between Lutheranism and Catholicism, Henry veering more closely to the latter than his daughter, and partly because of the geographical position and natural conservatism to new ideas of the English, who have always been less extremist on the whole than other nations. So far as the Reformation is concerned, the English genius for compromise resulted in a way of worship that retained the general structure of the Catholic liturgy on the one hand (which that of the Calvinists and Huguenots did not) and on the other expressly forbade, from 1549 on, the use of Latin (optional in the Lutheran Church). Thus the English Church, in replacing the mass by the Anglican service and the motet by the anthem, encouraged Protestant musical composition more than anywhere else except Germany, but the restriction to the English language, while it led to a more unified and, possibly because of this, a finer body of music than in the latter country, also presented composers with a problem of style.

The chief distinction in sound, and therefore the one that most affects music, between Latin and English is that in the former vowels are more frequent and more important than consonants. In other words, Latin is the more sonorous language and, as a result, is more suitable for melismatic writing, and it is tempting to speculate how Catholic music, from chant to polyphony, would have been affected if it had been based on a less sonorous language. Admittedly, French and German also stress consonants more than vowels, and this is reflected in the greater degree of syllabic underlay in the Protestant music of these two countries, but in neither country were composers urged to set "as near as may be for every syllable a note", as were their English brethren. The quotation comes from a letter to Henry VIII by the Archbishop of Canterbury, Thomas Cranmer [1489–1556], and was written in 1545, the year after the first English Litany appeared. It does not, as is sometimes claimed, refer to the Litany (although this too was Cranmer's work), but to the translations of certain special chants sung in procession on Sundays and feast days. In these, and in the Litany, the traditional Gregorian chant is so adapted that there is only one note to each syllable, and though in the letter there is no suggestion of enforcing this on all compositions for the Church, there most certainly is in the Royal Injunctions of Edward VI to Lincoln Cathedral issued three years later which, among other things, order that the service must be sung in English and that settings must be to a "plain and distinct note, for every syllable one". The same document also forbids the singing of anthems to the Virgin Mary or to the saints, and recommends that the best Latin motets be adapted to English use with their texts translated or, if unsuitable, replaced. A number of such adaptations dating from the 1540s or earlier, some by the composers themselves, have fortunately survived; these include masses as well as motets and make it clear that several years before the first Prayer Book of 1549—indeed, probably before 1536, when each church had to have a copy of the 'Great Bible', as this particular translation was called—the service was being said and sung in the vernacular, though the precise details of its performance must have varied from place to place, as those who opposed the Reformation would continue to use Latin. This lack of uniformity ended with the publication of the first Prayer Book, for which Cranmer was responsible; with it the Anglican Church became Protestant and a new order of service was laid down which has remained essentially unaltered to this day.

The Anglican service is divided into three main parts, Morning Prayer, Evening Prayer, and Communion. The first two parts are condensed from the Catholic offices or Canonical Hours and the third from the Catholic mass, the Latin titles of the various sections within each part being retained. (In the following discussion only those portions of the service which may properly be set to music are mentioned.) In 1549 Morning Prayer consisted of 'Venite exultemus Domino' ('O come, let us sing unto the Lord'), 'Te Deum laudamus' ('We praise Thee, O God'), and 'Benedictus es Dominus Deus Israel' ('Blessed be the Lord God of Israel'); Evening Prayer of 'Magnificat anima mea Dominus' ('My soul doth magnify the Lord') and 'Nunc dimittis servum tuum Domine . . . in pace' ('Lord, now lettest Thou thy servant depart in peace'); Communion of 'Kyrie eleison, Christe eleison, Kyrie eleison', 'Gloria', 'Credo', 'Sanctus', 'Benedictus qui venit in nomine Domini' ('Blessed is he that cometh in the name of the Lord'), 'Agnus Dei', and various passages from the Bible called 'post-Communions'. Apart from these last, the Communion service was identical in structure with that of the mass, as can be seen by comparing the above with Part I, p. 9. (Note that the Benedictus in the mass is not a separate movement, but is the second part of the Sanctus.) In the following year (1550) the parts of the Prayer Book given above were adapted by John Marbeck [*c.* 1510–*c.* 1585] to various chants drawn from the Gregorian repertoire, pruned so that there is only one note to a syllable, and published under the title, *The Booke of Common Praier noted*—the first musical setting of the English liturgy (see Plate XXI). Apart from the chants to the versicles and responses in Morning and Evening Prayer, which were used in most later harmonized versions from Tallis's famous set onwards, the music was soon forgotten because this version of the Prayer Book became obsolete with the introduction of the second Prayer Book in 1552, and in any case there was a growing demand for part-music. The 1552 Prayer Book reflects the growing influence of Continental Protestantism on the Anglican leaders, especially Cranmer, and the chief alterations occur, as we should expect, in the Communion service, for in the 1549 book this part of the liturgy most closely resembles its Catholic counterpart, the mass. Thus the three-fold Kyrie is replaced by the response, 'Lord have mercy upon us . . . ., to each of the Ten Commandments, the Gloria, Credo, and Sanctus are kept intact, but the first is placed much later in the service, while the Benedictus, Agnus Dei, and 'post-Communions' disappear entirely. In Morning and Evening Prayer no changes were made, except to add alternatives to the Te Deum, Benedictus, Magnificat, and Nunc Dimittis—namely, 'Benedicite omnia opera Domini Domino' ('O all ye works of the Lord, bless ye the Lord'), 'Jubilate Deo' ('O be joyful in the Lord'), 'Cantate Domino' ('O sing unto the Lord'), and 'Deus misereatur nostri' ('God be merciful unto us') respectively.

From the musical point of view the arrangement of the 1552 Prayer Book is retained in the later versions of 1559 and 1662, but the treatment of individual items varied considerably. For example, up to the Restoration (1660) the Venite was usually set, but the alternatives in Morning and Evening Prayer and the Sanctus and Gloria in the Communion service were almost invariably chanted, while from the Restoration on the Venite was usually chanted and all or some of the Morning and Evening Prayer, together with the Sanctus, was composed.

The effect of all these changes on mid-sixteenth-century composers was naturally very disturbing, for they had to contend not only with the switch from the Catholic mass to the Anglican Service,* but also with the differences between the first two Prayer Books. Moreover, the recommendation, which later became law, that only English be used, and that the flowing melismas and pervading imitation typical of the motet and mass be replaced by predominantly syllabic underlay and chordal texture, necessitated a far more abrupt change of style than that required by either the Counter-Reformation or Luther. It is not surprising, therefore, to find that most of the music composed for the new Church during its early years is distinctly inferior to previous or contemporary Latin compositions, nor that the anthem was preferred to the Service, for although the latter had a much greater chance of frequent performance than the former because the words were sung daily, its strong Catholic flavour probably proved embarrassing to those who still had leanings towards the older faith and objectionable to the Protestant-minded, whereas the anthem was more specifically Anglican in that its text rejected all references to the Virgin Mary and the saints and, moreover, like the motet, reflected the general tendency already noted by providing a greater freedom of choice in the words to be set compared to the invariable texts of the Service. The anthem in fact was, and is, the most characteristic musical feature of the Anglican Service, for nothing like it developed on the Continent.

Of the leading composers before Byrd who are represented either by original contributions or adaptations, the earliest is Taverner, two of whose masses, rather unskilfully adapted to English words, are found in the so-called 'Wanley MS.' This manuscript contains eight other masses in addition to Taverner's two, a few items for Morning and Evening Prayer, and almost 100 anthems, all to English words; the masses could, therefore, have been used for the full Communion service of 1549, and were almost certainly used after 1552, pruned of the altered or rejected items. Two of the anthems in this MS. are original pieces by Tallis, whose output for the Anglican Church includes fifteen similar compositions, together with nine adapted from his motets, several psalms, an isolated Te Deum (*c.* 1547), and two Services, of which the only one to survive complete, entitled 'short', follows the order of the

* Service with a capital 'S' denotes the setting to part-music of all or some of the appropriate items from Morning and Evening Prayer and the Communion Service.

second Prayer Book, but the fact that it includes settings of the Sanctus and Gloria makes it fairly certain that it, like the Te Deum, was composed before 1552. The term 'short' was frequently used by composers up to the early seventeenth century to indicate a mainly syllabic setting of the text as opposed to 'great' or occasionally 'high', in which the music is more elaborate, as in Tallis's Te Deum, for the mere preference of authority (Cranmer) for a syllable per note was clearly not sufficient cause for composers to abandon entirely the riches of polyphony—the subtle interplay of contrasting rhythms, the complex imitative web, the flowing melodic lines—and during the latter half of the century not only Services but anthems too became increasingly more elaborate, though because of the nature of the language they never became as florid as their Catholic counterparts.

Three of Tallis's anthems were included in the first printed collection of part-music for the Anglican service, i.e. *Certaine notes set forthe in foure and three partes, to be sung at the Mornyng Communion and Evenyng Praier*, by John Day [1522–1584], one of the earliest and most important printers of music in England. The first edition appeared in 1560 and contains twenty anthems and two Services, both the latter including settings of the Sanctus and Gloria. This, together with the fact that a number of the anthems were certainly written prior to Mary's reign, makes it likely that the remainder of the pieces were also. The book was evidently popular enough to warrant a second edition in 1565, and this remained the only printed collection intended specifically for the Anglican service for nearly eighty years. Even if we include Byrd's publications of 1588 and 1589 and a few other similar works, the number of printed anthems (which, like motets, are, strictly speaking, non-liturgical) was extremely small. We shall give the probable reason for this when we discuss the English Psalter.

To the ordinary church-goer Tallis is best known through his Preces and Responses, and the two tunes associated with the hymns 'Glory to Thee, my God, this night' and 'O Holy Spirit, Lord of Grace'. The Responses, like those of later composers, are based on the melodies to which they are set in *The Booke of Common Praier noted*, while the 'hymn-tunes' are two of nine originally written for *The whole Psalter translated into English metre* (1567), by Matthew Parker [1504–1575],

Elizabeth's first Archbishop of Canterbury. This was not the first metrical psalter in English nor even the first complete one; indeed, the fact that it never came into general use is probably explained by the enormous popularity of an earlier publication, *The Whole Booke of Psalmes* (1562), based mainly on the metrical translations of Thomas Sternhold [*c.* 1500–1549] and John Hopkins [d. 1570] and printed, as was Parker's version, by John Day. Even before this a complete metrical translation by the printer Robert Crowley entitled *The Psalter of David* had appeared in 1549. This contains a simple four-part setting to which all the psalms were to be sung, and is not only the first complete metrical psalter in English, but also the first of its kind in England that includes part-music, for all the earlier examples are simply selections from the psalms, and only one of these, the *Goostly psalmes and spirituall songes* (1539–1540) of Miles Coverdale [*c.* 1488–1568], the translator of the Great Bible, has any music, and this consists only of melodies.

It was probably in the year of Crowley's publication and Sternhold's death that the latter's Psalter first appeared. This contains nineteen psalms, but in the second edition published later in the year eighteen more by Sternhold were added, together with seven by Hopkins, and from this time on all psalters that use these forty-four metrical psalms as a nucleus are called 'Sternhold and Hopkins'. Both the first two editions are without music, but this did not prevent the second from becoming a best-seller, and during the next four years it was reprinted three times. In 1556, during Mary's reign, it was slightly enlarged and published in Geneva for the English Protestant refugees there; this edition is particularly important in that it was the first Sternhold and Hopkins's Psalter to contain music, this consisting of fifty-one tunes, one for each of the fifty-one selected psalms—a unique feature because in all later editions many of the tunes serve two or more psalms. In 1558 a larger collection was issued, also at Geneva, in which over half the original tunes are replaced by new ones. In the same year Elizabeth became Queen, and the tunes of the 1558 Psalter, introduced into England by the returning refugees, became so popular that in 1559 congregational psalm-singing was officially permitted in church. There followed a spate of psalters, most of them expanded editions of Sternhold and Hopkins, the number of translations and tunes growing until

The Whole Booke of [*150*] *Psalmes*, together with sixty-five tunes, was published in 1562 (see Plate XXII). This went through innumerable editions and, despite several attempts to replace it, continued to be printed until the early nineteenth century; during the latter part of this period a new translation by Nahum Tate [1652–1715] and Nicholas Brady [1659–1726], published in 1696, gradually ousted but did not long survive the earlier version.

The enormous popularity of Sternhold and Hopkins's Psalter cannot be explained by the quality of the verse nor the faithfulness of the translation, as the former is often crude and the latter misleading, though a number of the more offensive lines and words were improved in the eighteenth century. In these respects Parker's version is much better, but at the same time it is less straightforward, and this, together with the general high quality of the tunes in the earlier Psalter and in its later editions—so admirably suited to congregational use, which the artistically superior four-part settings by Tallis are not—probably provides the explanation.

The psalm-tunes themselves were either adapted from Continental models, especially those of Bourgeois, or else newly composed in imitation of these models, and, as on the Continent, their popularity resulted in their being sung at home as well as in church. This led to a demand for harmonized versions, for in middle- and upper-class families singing in parts had received a new impetus from the influx into secular society of the monk musicians, who, owing to the dissolution of the monasteries by Henry VIII, had had to find employment elsewhere, and some of whom found permanent posts as secretaries or music tutors in the wealthier aristocratic and merchant households. It was clearly to meet this demand that John Day, only one year after he had published *The Whole Booke of Psalmes*, issued a companion volume entitled *The Whole Psalmes in four partes*, for not only does he state that instruments may be used if desired (the earliest printed indication of such alternative performance), but also that the purpose of the book is to supplant "other vain and trifling ballads". This publication contains over 140 compositions based on the sixty-five tunes of *The Whole Booke* with thirty new ones, and though the music does not equal Tallis's in artistic merit, it set the fashion for a spate of similar works, all based on Sternhold and Hopkins's Psalter. The three best of these are by the printer-composer Thomas East [d. 1609], Richard Alison, and William Leighton [d. *c.* 1616]. East's Psalter (1592) consists of harmonizations by ten of his contemporaries (including John Dowland and Giles Farnaby) of most of the tunes in *The Whole Booke*, plus a few that were either completely new or had become current since 1562. Of these last, three (now known as 'Canterbury', 'Cambridge', and 'Oxford') were clearly great favourites, as over half of the psalms are directed to be sung to one or other of them. The Psalter of Alison (who also contributed to East's collection), published in 1599, is unique in that the four-part settings (and very fine ones they are too) are all his own, important in that the tune is always placed in the soprano part instead of the customary tenor, and interesting in that it contains an arrangement of the three lowest parts, for lute, orpharion, and cittern (both of the guitar family), either separately or all together, with or without a bass viol, when the tune is sung by a solo soprano or tenor. Leighton's Psalter (1614) is a collection of fifty-four psalm-settings, some with lute accompaniment, by most of the leading composers of his day, with the affecting title of *The Teares or Lamentacions of a Sorrowfull Soule*.

A number of the psalm-tunes in these early psalters are sung as hymns today, among them the Old Hundredth, Old 124th (both French melodies originally), and Winchester Old, in addition to the three mentioned above.

Most of the pieces in Leighton's collection are anthems, the distinction between these and psalm-settings being that the former are through-composed and select only certain verses of the psalm, while the latter, like present-day versions, are simpler and shorter, with every verse repeated to the same music.

As we pointed out earlier, very few anthems compared to the number of psalm-settings and not a single Service after Day's *Certaine notes* were printed before the middle of the seventeenth century; as regards the Service, the probable reason is that it, like the mass, is liturgical, and hence its proper place is the church, but the number of churches in which part-settings of the Service were sung every day or even on most days was very small compared to the number of Catholic churches abroad that performed polyphonic masses, and whereas it was worth an Italian printer's trouble and expense to issue masses that would be bought and performed in the greater part of Europe, it was simply uneconomic for an English printer to do likewise with Anglican Services. The case of the anthem is somewhat similar, for while it too was primarily associated with the Church and so the same line of reasoning can be applied as to the Service, the fact that it was not part of the actual liturgy, was shorter, and, most important of all, was usually based on that mainstay of Protestant and particularly Calvinist music—the psalms—made it more acceptable to the average Englishman and resulted in a certain number being printed. Furthermore, not only was the tradition of copying music still powerful and, of course, much cheaper than printing, but also every organist and choirmaster was expected to compose music for his own church, and hence relied less on the work of others than is the case today.

The most important composers of Anglican music were Christopher Tye [*c.* 1500–1575], Tallis, Byrd, Weelkes, Gibbons, and Thomas Tomkins. The differences between the simplicity of Tye's Services and anthems and the complexity of his masses and motets is typical of Anglican and Catholic music as a whole, for while imitation is still used in the former, the points are shorter and syllabic underlay has replaced melismatic. The result in Tye's case is a deliberately popular hymn-like style, most clearly shown in his *The Actes of the Apostles translated into Englyshe Metre* (1553), dedicated to Edward VI, in which the verse is appalling, but the music often charming in its simple melodiousness. This work was clearly meant for home consumption, as the author states that the music could be either sung or played on the lute, although the part-book arrangements makes the latter impossible. Tye only completed fourteen chapters of *The Actes*, but the music proved a veritable mine for later adaptors, who replaced the original words with new texts and published them as anthems (e.g. 'O come, ye servants of the Lord'), or hymns (e.g. Winchester Old). Tallis's services and anthems are more numerous than and superior to Tye's, his greater technical mastery being revealed in his preference for composing *a*5 as opposed to the almost invariable four-part writing of the older man. But the output of both these composers pales before that of Byrd, who contributed some of the finest examples in the entire Anglican repertoire. Byrd's English Church music reflects more markedly than Tallis's the tendency in the latter half of the century towards greater elaboration, for, as we have remarked elsewhere (Part I, p. 191), a new style or idea is usually applied more strictly at first than later, and Byrd was writing when the severity of "for every syllable a note" was largely a thing of the past, and composers were beginning to enrich the simple counterpoint typical of mid-century settings. This enrichment and elaboration applies particularly to Byrd's anthems that remained in manuscript, and which include some of the most brilliant and expressive music he ever wrote. These were probably composed after 1600, for they are far more polyphonic in style and madrigalian in treatment than almost all those in the 1588 and 1589 books; indeed, apart from the language, some of them are no different from his motets.

The majority of Byrd's anthems are 'full' anthems—that is, the vocal parts are complete in themselves—but he also wrote a number of 'verse' anthems in which one or two solo voices are accompanied by an organ or a consort of viols, while a chorus, usually echoing a previous solo phrase, interrupts at various points. Byrd was certainly among the earliest to compose such pieces and may well have been the first, considering his fondness for instrumentally accompanied solo song. Although he introduced the verse idea into one of his Services, these are, on the whole, more restrained than his anthems in their predominantly contrapuntal texture and discreet use of imitation. This is undoubtedly due to the fact that the Service, unlike the anthem, is an essential part of the liturgy, and hence the words are of prime importance, but in Byrd's hands the simplicity of texture is offset by a remarkable rhythmic power and flexibility derived from a vivid appreciation of the verbal accents, together with a most effective use of tonal contrasts achieved through the customary division of the choir into decani and cantoris, the former being placed on the same side as the 'dean', the latter on that of the 'cantor' or 'precentor'. Earlier composers—for example, Tallis—had used this polychoral technique to some extent, but with nothing like the skill and variety shown in Byrd's 'Great' Service.

Weelkes's contributions to the Anglican repertoire were almost certainly written after his appointments to the post of organist at Winchester College (*c.* 1598) and Chichester Cathedral (1602), and the majority are therefore later than his madrigals, in comparison with which they are more conservative. While he was more prolific than Byrd in this field, his anthems, some of which are extremely fine, cannot compare as a whole to those of the older man. It is a major misfortune that none of his ten Services (six of which are verse) has survived complete, because the four that have been reconstructed, together with the skeletons of the others, show that he was second only to Byrd in his liturgical compositions.

The verse Service and anthem became increasingly popular from the turn of the century on, as is revealed not only by Weelkes's output, but also by that of Gibbons and Tomkins, whose best work, however, lies in their full anthems, despite some very fine examples of the other type. Unlike most of their compatriots, neither Gibbons nor Tomkins composed any music to Latin words, and while the latter wrote more for the Anglican Church than any previous composer, his work is uneven in quality and below that of Gibbons. Although both were major pioneers in the verse anthem, both were rooted in the older polyphonic tradition, but Tomkins, who was composing twenty-five years after Gibbons's death, was naturally more affected by the 'New Music' from Italy that slowly found its way into England, and hence his style is less pure. With these two composers the anthem was even more favoured than before, not only because, like the motet, it allowed greater freedom in the choice of texts, but also because it could and did reflect the new surge of Puritanism that swept the country when the stabilizing influence of Elizabeth's policy of religious compromise ended with her death.

In comparing English music with that of the Continent during the latter part of the sixteenth and early seventeenth centuries, two things stand out: the fondness for independent and therefore essential instrumental accompaniment, and the greater versatility of most of her leading composers. The former is clearly shown in the secular and sacred chamber songs for voice and viols (particularly Byrd's), the verse Services and anthems, and the ayres. The first of these types was practically non-existent abroad, and the second, with its combination of vocal solos, chorus, and instruments, was only used by a few foreign musicians, such as G. Gabrieli. Gabrieli, however, with his predominantly chordal style, was primarily interested in the dramatic colour contrasts that could be obtained by combining voices and instruments, and hence preferred the louder and more brilliant cornetts and trombones to the softer, even-toned viols favoured by English composers, whose polyphonic, imitative style was best served by such instruments. As for the ayres, they too were more prominent in England than anywhere else, not only because the ayre is almost without exception an original composition, whereas most of the lute songs abroad are transcriptions, but also because it occupied a larger place in the total output of English music than did the lute song in any other country.

That the majority of leading English composers of the period were more versatile than their Continental brethren is apparent in the fact that they not only contributed to most of the various vocal types and styles which were common all over Europe, e.g. mass, motet, madrigal, ballett, lute song, but also to those that were the result of the Reformation, e.g. the Service (great, short, and verse), the anthem (full and verse), and the hymn-like settings of psalm-tunes; moreover the Service and anthem were peculiar to England, as was the solo song with string ensemble accompaniment. Admittedly the full anthem can be likened to the motet, and the great and short Services to the normal mass and missa brevis respectively, but Catholic composers elsewhere were not faced with the problem of switching from Latin to another language, let alone one so markedly different as English. English versatility is also shown in the fact that instrumental music occupied a far more prominent position in England than in any other country. This is not surprising when we consider the part played by instruments in vocal music, and it underlines an attitude that seems to have persisted longer in England than elsewhere, and provides, in addition to inborn English conservatism, an explanation not only of the continued use in most compositions written in Latin, *c.* 1475–*c.* 1575, of a style long abandoned abroad, which with its long, flowing melismas and 'abstract' quality virtually treats voices as instruments, but also of the fondness for instrumental accompaniment itself, and indeed of the comparative lack of realism in the English madrigal, for it is the abstract quality of instrumental music that is one of the main distinctions between it and vocal music in that the use of words, quite apart from their treatment (e.g. word-painting), inevitably introduces an element of realism.

The most versatile of the leading English composers were Tallis, Byrd, Morley, Weelkes, Gibbons, and Tomkins, all of whom wrote successfully and often with distinction a great variety of both vocal and instrumental pieces. Of these six composers Byrd is the most outstanding in the range and quality of his work, for he not only excelled in the mass and motet, great, short, and verse service, full and verse anthem, and accompanied song, but also in music for keyboard and for viols. Tallis is less versatile, but he made notable contributions to the mass, motet, great and short service, full anthem, and the keyboard repertoire. The other four are well represented in the above types and styles, excluding the accompanied song, except that Morley and Weelkes wrote no masses, and Gibbons and Tomkins no motets either, but they were, unlike Byrd, fine madrigalists. The achievements of these men over such a wide field was not matched by any Continental musician, except possibly G. Gabrieli; indeed, if greatness is measured by versatility allied to excellence, then Byrd was the greatest composer of his time or before it.

Instrumental music in the late Renaissance can be divided into three main classes, keyboard, lute, and ensemble, and it is in the first of these that English composers were pre-eminent. From Aston to John Bull [1563–1628], the greatest virtuoso of them all, they show a far clearer and more imaginative grasp of keyboard technique and style than any of their contemporaries abroad, and a greater feeling for the distinctive characteristics of stringed keyboard as opposed to organ music. Thus while most keyboard music of the sixteenth and seventeenth centuries was played indiscriminately on either organ, harpsichord, or clavichord, those pieces, far commoner in England than elsewhere, in which very rapid scale passages and, more especially, broken chord figures, arpeggios, and brilliant ornamentation occur, are much more effective and were clearly intended for the latter two instruments, while pieces containing a melody in long notes with elaborate figuration above or below, or in which the style is basically vocal, are more suitable for the organ. These last predominate in the earlier sources of English keyboard music, not only because most of the composers represented were organists, but also because it is simpler and usually wiser to proceed from the known (in this case vocal techniques) to the unknown (characteristic keyboard style). The vocal technique that occurs most frequently in the early keyboard sources stems from the cantus-firmus mass and motet; in other words, a Gregorian chant is either written in long notes with a florid accompaniment or else paraphrased and shared between three or four equally important parts. For example, in the *Mulliner Book*, compiled by an organist, Thomas Mulliner, between *c.* 1545 and *c.* 1585 and the most important of the earlier collections of keyboard music, over half of the 121 pieces are based on chants, and nearly all the remaining ones are vocal in style, even when they are not simple transcriptions of actual part-songs and anthems. Nearly one quarter are by John Redford [d. 1547]; Tallis and William Blitheman [d. 1591] have considerably fewer, while Taverner and Tye have only one each.

The chant most widely used in the *Mulliner Book* is 'Gloria tibi Trinitas', an antiphon for second vespers on Trinity Sunday. This melody became more popular than any other as the cantus firmus of a whole class of compositions, unique to England, written for lute and strings as well as keyboard, and called 'In nomines'. The explanation of this title has only recently been discovered, and is as follows: one of Taverner's masses is based on the above chant, and in the Benedictus section, at the words 'in nomine Domini', it is presented complete and unelaborated in notes of equal value in the alto part, while the other voices weave points of imitation above and below. This is a particularly beautiful passage, and doubtless Taverner was as anxious to make the most of it as many later composers have been with pieces they have regarded as more than usually attractive, and so he arranged it for the organ. But Taverner was not alone in thinking highly of this passage, for not only is his organ arrangement included in the *Mulliner Book*, but it was also transcribed for both lute and string ensemble and, moreover, twice adapted to English words and sung as an anthem, one of these adaptations being printed in Day's *Certaine notes*. The enormous popularity of the piece itself led other composers to set the same cantus firmus, and during the succeeding 150 years or so literally hundreds of In nomines were written, the last and among the finest examples being Purcell's two settings in six and seven parts. It is worth noting, in view of the claim made earlier concerning the exceptionally prominent position of instrumental music in

England, that the In nomine for strings was the only type of composition in Europe in which a beginner could participate with experts, for the vast majority of these, by presenting the chant melody in long notes and placing it in one part throughout, make this part extremely easy to play.

About a fifth of the *Mulliner Book* consists of arrangements of secular vocal pieces, but this does not mean that they were not played on the organ, for while this was probably the case with the great organ (used exclusively in churches and chapels) it was certainly not true of the positive or the regal, as both these instruments were used as much outside the church as in. (The portative had fallen into disuse during the fifteenth century because it was virtually impossible to play part-music on it.)

The most striking thing about the *Mulliner Book* is that there are only two dances and no variations—the two most popular types of keyboard composition with later composers, as is shown by the contents of the *Fitzwilliam Virginal Book*, the most important source of English keyboard music in the late Renaissance. This was compiled by a Catholic Cornishman, Francis Tregian, during a term of imprisonment between 1609 and his death in 1619, and of its nigh on 300 pieces, which include every type of English keyboard composition of the time, nearly half are dances and almost an eighth are variations. This latter fraction, however, does not take into account the widespread application of variation technique, for almost all the dances are made up of several sections, each of which is followed by a varied and often elaborate repeat.

The sixteenth century has well been called the 'century of the dance', for just as society in the fourteenth century rebelled against the suppression of dancing by the Church in the previous century, so did that of the late Renaissance after ecclesiastical authority had reinforced its ban during the fifteenth century. The result was a whole host of new dances, of which the most important were the 'pavane' (the first printed example appearing in 1508), a slow dance in duple time almost certainly of Spanish origin, which virtually replaced the earlier French basse danse in European esteem; the 'gaillarde' (English 'galliard'), a fairly quick dance in triple time first printed in 1530; and the 'passamezzo' or 'step and a half', an Italian dance in duple time and slightly quicker than the pavane, which it replaced in Italy during the second half of the century. The passamezzo, like the basse danse, is constructed on a simple series of notes that are repeated a number of times and placed in the lowest part (in England this was called a 'ground'); unlike the earlier dance, however, which is based on one of several grounds, the passamezzo had only a choice of two (see p. 353). The use of a ground as the basis for a set of variations was later applied to many pavanes and galliards after *c.* 1560, and represents the earliest and one of the most popular types of variation writing in the late Renaissance. In addition there was the Italian saltarello, a quicker dance than in the fourteenth century, but not so quick as the modern type, as exemplified, for instance, in the last movement of Mendelssohn's 'Italian' Symphony; it is in triple time, and in Italy was sometimes used as an alternative for the galliard. The allemande, of German origin, was a moderately slow dance in duple time that became popular after *c.* 1550, as did the French courante—a quick dance in triple time.

Examples of all the above dances except the saltarello are in the *Fitzwilliam Virginal Book*, and nearly two-thirds of these are pavanes and galliards, many of them based on the passamezzo technique of variations on a ground. In addition, there are a handful of dances not mentioned above, including the English jig.

As already stated, the earliest type of keyboard variation is that constructed on a ground bass, and the oldest example we have is a piece entitled *My Lady Carey's Dompe*, contained in the same manuscript as Aston's *Hornpype* (see Part I, p. 215). 'Dompe' or 'dump' most likely means a composition written in memory of someone—at any rate, most of the dumps that have survived are associated with some usually high-ranking personage, as in the example mentioned, where the lady in question is probably the sister of Anne Boleyn and wife of Henry Carey; she died in 1543. The bass 'themes' of the dumps, like most other grounds, are extremely simple and sometimes consist of two notes only—tonic and dominant.

Other types of variation are those in which the tune is kept in the top part all through, often being considerably elaborated, while the accompaniment changes, or in which the tune wanders from part to part rather like the old cantus-firmus mass technique, or in which the figuration, which may elaborate the tune itself or provide an ornamental accompaniment, is placed, usually alternately, in either bass or treble.

The rest of the *Fitzwilliam Virginal Book* is made up, in order of frequency, of fantasias, cantus-firmus pieces, pieces with descriptive titles, and transcriptions of vocal part-music. The fantasias, with their successive points of imitation and essentially strict part-writing, are the most closely allied to vocal style of all the keyboard types of composition, and are as effective, if not more so, on the organ as on the virginal. This also applies to most of those pieces based on a cantus firmus, among which are two by Tallis based on the chant *Felix namque* and dated 1562 and 1564 respectively. In both the cantus firmus is repeated a number of times, switched from part to part, and accompanied by figuration which becomes increasingly complex; indeed, some of the figuration is not only unique among contemporary English pieces, but quite astonishing in its complexity and sense of keyboard style, and may, in part at any rate, have been inspired by the Spanish composer Cabezón (see p. 348). The cantus-firmus pieces also include a number of In nomines, and several which use part or whole of the hexachord scale. Byrd, for example, constructed an entire composition on *ut*, *mi*, *re*, which, in terms of actual notes, becomes G B A, or C E D, or F A G, but he does not keep strictly to these three note groups, as he starts the motif and its inversion on various degrees of the scale. Byrd also wrote a piece using all six notes of the hexachord in which *ut* is not only G, C, and F, as in Guido's system, but also D, A, and B♭, and in which the notes G♯ and A♭, D♯ and E♭ occur, thus requiring a virginal with separate keys for each of these notes (see Chapter 1, p. 250). Bull went much further than this in a now famous piece in the *Fitzwilliam Virginal Book* also based on the hexachord, for the *ut* is placed on each step of the complete chromatic scale arranged in this order, G, A, B, D♭, E♭, F, A♭, B♭, C, D, E, and F♯, and includes the additional chromatic notes of C♭, C♯, D♯, G♭, G♯, and A♯. Such a piece could only have been played on a keyboard tuned to something like our present system of equal temperament, in which the octave is divided into twelve equal semitones, and all the intervals except the octave are slightly mistuned compared to the natural scale. Most of the chromatic notes in the above pieces had been recognized theoretically since the beginning of the fifteenth century, but only a limited number were used in practice, and even by Bull's time no other keyboard work contained such a wide range, although a few sixteenth-century lute and viol pieces employed even more out-of-the-way notes (see page 345).

The widespread practice of word-painting in vocal music was reflected in keyboard compositions with descriptive and fanciful titles. These were particularly popular in England and range from delightfully whimsical little pieces, such as Giles Farnaby's *Dreame*, *His Rest*, and *His Humour* [Farnaby, d. 1640], to more elaborate and frankly programmatic works, such as the fantasia by John Mundy [d. 1630], which describes a succession of thunderstorms ending with 'A Cleare Day', Byrd's charming and most skilfully written *The Bells*, and the same composer's suite, *The Battell*. This last may well have been inspired by Janequin's famous chanson, *La Guerre* (see Chapter 1, p. 240). Such arrangements of vocal music, however, were comparatively rare in England, and most of these are by the Catholic Peter Philips [d. after 1633], a fine composer of motets and to a lesser extent madrigals, who left England *c.* 1590 and spent the rest of his life abroad, mostly in the Netherlands, and who, as a result, was considerably more influenced by Continental practices than his compatriots.

Another Englishman who spent much of his creative life abroad was Bull, and such was the reputation he made as a keyboard player and composer during his visits to the Netherlands, France, and Germany in 1601 that he was recalled by Elizabeth, who feared he might accept a position at one of the foreign courts. Twelve years later, however, he left England for good, and in 1617 was appointed organist of Antwerp Cathedral, a post he held till his death. Bull was the most virtuosic of all the Renaissance writers for the keyboard, and played the leading part in transmitting English keyboard style to Continental musicians. In fact, there is a direct line of succession from him to Bach, as we shall see later. Much of his music, while fascinating to the student of keyboard technique, is rather dry, even downright dull, but occasionally, as in the well-known *The King's Hunt*, usually ascribed to him, or in the *Walsingham* variations, the music is both brilliant and attractive, and some of his simpler pieces are perfectly exquisite in their strangely delicate harmony and melody.

That Bull's reputation as a keyboard composer exceeded Byrd's was undoubtedly due to his virtuosity as a performer and the technical difficulty of much of his music (he has, indeed, been called the Liszt of his age), for neither in quantity nor quality does it equal that of the older man. Admittedly, there are many pieces by Byrd which are tedious or commonplace harmonically, or in which stock rhythmic and melodic figures are used mechanically, but in most of these there are movements of beauty, and a greater number than in Bull's output show a high level of inspiration. Other important writers for the keyboard were Giles Farnaby, Orlando Gibbons, Tomkins, Morley, and Peter Philips; all of them, while composing far fewer works than either Byrd or Bull, contributed many fine pieces, some of which are perfect gems.

The two most outstanding features of English keyboard music, apart from its advanced technique, are melodic freshness and harmonic clarity. Both have already been mentioned in connexion with the madrigal and ayre, but, compared to Continental examples, they are much more distinctive in compositions for the virginal than in any other sphere. Another feature (and one that applies to other countries as well) is the inevitable intrusion of imitative part-writing, even though the instrument does not take kindly to polyphony, and the vast majority of keyboard pieces are shot through with brief and often telling rhythmic or melodic motives which are passed from part to part. As we should expect, this feature is particularly evident in Byrd's output, much less so in Bull's, and as a result, when inspiration flags, Byrd's polyphonic skill keeps our interest alive, whereas with Bull we tend to tire of mere brilliance. The combination of this imitative by-play with the melodic, harmonic, and technical characteristics mentioned above result at its best in music that is ravishing to the ear and fascinating to the mind, and which in general ranks higher than any other instrumental music of the time, either English or Continental.

Most of this music was played on the virginal rather than the clavichord, for the latter was never as popular as the former either in England or abroad, and only in Germany during the seventeenth and eighteenth centuries did it in any way rival the virginal; while the delicate, sensuous beauty of clavichord tone and its expressive subtlety is superior to that of the harpsichord, its lack of volume is probably the main reason why it was overshadowed by the latter instrument. Another reason may well have been the impossibility of re-tuning easily certain notes, e.g. A♭ for G♯, because to alter the position of the tangent would be a major operation; moreover, if the pair of strings was tightened in order to sound, say, A♭, then the other note or notes produced from the same pair would be thrown out of tune.

During the latter part of the sixteenth century another set of strings tuned an octave higher than the original unison sets was added to Italian harpsichords, and slightly later another row of jacks was so placed that the plectra plucked one of the unison sets near the end, producing a hard but brilliant tone (lute stop). There were thus four rows of jacks, two for the unison strings and one each for the octave set and lute stop, and as these could be operated either alone or with any of the others a number of variations of both timbre and volume were possible.

This large harpsichord does not seem to have been made in England, but it is certain that the English definition of virginal included it as well as the simple type with only two unison sets of strings, because many of the pieces by the later virginalists were undoubtedly written for the larger instrument, this being imported from abroad, especially from Antwerp, where the most famous family of harpsichord-makers, the Ruckers, whose instruments have never been surpassed in purity and beauty of tone, flourished from *c.* 1550 to *c.* 1670 (see Plate XXIII).

Almost the entire corpus of English keyboard composition remained in manuscript, the only exceptions being *Parthenia, or the Maydenhead of the First Musicke that ever was printed for the Virginalles* (1611) (see Plate XXIV), containing twenty-one pieces by Byrd, Bull, and Gibbons, and its sequel, *Parthenia In-violata or Mayden-Musicke for the Virginalls and Bass-Viol* (*c.* 1614), containing twenty anonymous pieces. The chief reason why so little was published was almost certainly the difficulty of setting up movable type so that clusters of short notes, particularly semiquavers and demisemiquavers, were accurately aligned with the longer ones, and although this difficulty could be partially overcome by engraving, as in the two prints mentioned above (though even here the notes are very badly spaced), this was a much more costly process. Contributory reasons, already referred to in connexion with Anglican music, were the widespread habit of copying and the likelihood of a small sale, the number of people who could afford or play a virginal being small.

The difficulty of aligning the notes on two staves did not arise with lute or ensemble music, the former being set in tablature and the latter being printed in part-books, as in vocal music. We should therefore expect more publications in these two fields, and so indeed there are, and during the thirty years or so from Whythorne's *Duos, or Songs for two voices* (1590)—the first print of English instrumental music, as all the items were intended to be either played or sung—a number of pieces for ensemble were published, some of them in madrigal books, like Morley's nine two-part fantasias contained in his *Canzonets for Two Voyces*, and some of them as separate collections, like Gibbons' nine three-part fantasias (*c.* 1610), his first published work and the earliest example in England of music engraved on copper.

The instrumental ensembles of the late sixteenth and early seventeenth centuries were called 'consorts', a misspelling of 'concert' which, like 'concerto', probably comes from the Latin verb *conserere* with its past participle *consertus*, meaning 'to combine together'. Consorts were either 'whole' or 'broken', the former and by far the most popular consisting of members of the same family, as 'consort of viols' or 'consort of recorders', and the latter of various instruments, as in Morley's *Booke of Consort Lessons* (1599), which is 'scored' for treble and bass viols, flute (=recorder), lute, cittern, and pandora (for descriptions of the last two, see below). In Part I, Chapter 6, p. 220, we stated that the practice of playing in 'whole consort' began in the latter part of the fifteenth century, but this did not become widespread until the following century. Most consort music is for treble, alto, tenor, and bass viols, and the two main types of composition are the fantasia, and that based on a cantus firmus. Of the latter the In nomines easily exceed not only other cantus firmus pieces, but also the number of In nomines written for the keyboard or lute, the reason being that this type of composition is a fundamentally polyphonic one, and hence lends itself more naturally to, and indeed sounds better on, a group of strings than on a single instrument, even an organ. Polyphony, in fact, is a far more essential constituent of extended string writing (as Haydn discovered after he had written a number of string quartets) than any other class of vocal or instrumental composition, because, being completely abstract (i.e. no words) and with only a limited range of timbre, the ear requires more than just accompanied melody, although this is perfectly satisfactory in short pieces, such as dance movements. This fact also explains the greater number of fantasias for strings than for keyboard or lute, because the fantasia consists, in the main, of imitative polyphony and, like the cantus-firmus type, usually differs little in technique and style from the contemporary motet or madrigal. In some of the later fantasias, however, especially those of Gibbons—the greatest master of this type of composition—the writing is decidedly instrumental in character, with rapid, repeated notes and wide leaps, and with more complex cross-rhythms and frequent use of sequence than in any vocal music of the time (Ex. 15*):

* From *Nine Fantasies . . .*, ed. Fellowes.

Ex. 15(c) From Fantasy No.4 (c.1610)
(𝅗𝅥 = ♩ = MM.c.72)

(etc.)

Several of Gibbons's fantasias are divided into two or more contrasting sections; for instance, an imitative first section in duple time will be followed by a simple, minuet-like second section in triple time, and a final imitative section in duple time, sometimes thematically related to the first section. Thematic relationship between different parts of an instrumental work, which occurs in fantasias by composers other than Gibbons, may well have developed from the practice of pairing pavanes and galliards, many of which are linked by similarity of melody and harmony. Another much rarer, but very important, feature of the fantasia, and one almost certainly derived from Italy, is the use of only one theme throughout a piece instead of a succession of imitative points, the theme being inverted, augmented, diminished, and rhythmically varied, a type that, in the hands of Sweelinck (see below, p. 352), led eventually to the fugue.

Dance pieces for consorts are few compared either to the number of fantasia and cantus-firmus compositions or to the number written for the virginal (the organ can be counted out for this kind of music), probably because viols lack the rhythmic 'bite' which the plucking action of the virginal gives, even though it is less capable of producing strong and weak accents. Admittedly, much of the dance music from the late sixteenth century onwards, because of its melodic, rhythmic, and polyphonic complexity, was not meant to be danced to, just as in the suites of Bach or the symphonic minuets of Haydn and Mozart, but its fundamentally rhythmic nature was still felt, and rightly so, to be more effective on a plucked or hit stringed instrument than on one that was bowed, hence the enormous number of dance suites for the harpsichord in the seventeenth and eighteenth centuries.

The leading composers of consort music, apart from Gibbons, were Byrd, Morley, Coperario, Thomas Lupo [d. 1628], an Italian who settled in England, and Alfonso Ferrabosco (ii). Coperario, the most prolific writer of fantasias, visited Italy *c.* 1604 and acquired a lyricism and lightness that influenced his compatriots on his return home, and it is noteworthy and typical of Continental influence that, compared to their output, a far higher proportion of his pieces are arrangements of vocal compositions. Ferrabosco, a better composer than Coperario, has left us some exquisite dances and extremely fine fantasias, two being of exceptional interest, one for four and the other for five viols. The one *a*4 has the notes of the hexachord in ascending order placed in the top part and repeated eight times, starting on C, C♯, D, E♭, E, F, F♯, and G respectively, and employing all the chromatic notes of Bull's hexachord piece plus E♯ and F♭. In the fantasia *a*5 the hexachord notes, placed in the next to highest part, are in descending order, starting on E (i.e. E, D, C, B, A, G), and also repeated eight times, each repeat being a semitone lower than the previous one, i.e. D♯, D, C♯, C, B, B♭, and A. All the chromatic notes of the fantasia *a*4 are used except F♭, but in addition there occur the extremely rare notes of F double-sharp and C double-sharp. In both pieces Ferrabosco manages his modulations more smoothly than does Bull.

The intimate polyphonic nature of music for viol consort gives much greater pleasure to the performers for whom, as in the normal madrigal, it was primarily intended than to the listener, for although the viol is, within a limited range, a most expressive instrument, the lack of brilliance and resonance and the fact that the beauty and structure of the music are only fully revealed to those who commune together in performing it make it less acceptable to the 'outsider' than the less sensitive but more brilliant virginal.

In addition to the four viols mentioned earlier and the violone (see Part I, Chapter 6, p. 220), there were two solo instruments, a small bass called the 'division viol' because it was chiefly used to play divisions (i.e. variations) on a ground, and the 'lyra viol', an even smaller bass which, with its flatter bridge that decreases the difference in level between the strings and its slacker bow, is capable of playing several strings simultaneously, and hence can perform part-music more effectively than can the other viols.

Despite the fact that more lute than keyboard pieces were published, several of them in song-books, there seems little doubt that the instrument was not so popular in England as abroad, even though in Dowland she possessed one of the leading lute virtuosi of the time. Thus the first four books of instruction, published between 1563 and 1596, are all translations of the whole or a part of a well-known work by the Frenchman, Adrian le Roy, and not until 1603 was an original work produced with similar aims—Thomas Robinson's *Schoole of Musicke*.

Apart from Dowland, who, surprisingly enough, issued no collections of lute solos and the bulk of whose output remained in manuscript, apart from a few pieces in other men's publications, the chief lutanist-composers were his son Robert [*c.* 1586–1641], Anthony Holborne [d. 1602], John Johnson [*c.* 1540–1595], Francis Cutting, Daniel Batchelor, Richard Alison, Philip Rosseter [1568–1623], and Francis Pilkington [d. 1638]. Dowland's output consists mainly of dances and is typical of the English lutanist school as a whole, contrasting markedly with Continental production, which, as already pointed out, preferred arrangements of vocal pieces. A strong sense of rhythm and a flair for fresh-sounding melodies—the latter a general characteristic of English music of the time—are abundantly apparent in his lute music and in that of his compatriots, but his melancholic nature is revealed in a number of fine compositions that employ chromaticism to a greater degree than do other English lutanists. Apart from dances, the lute repertoire consists of In nomines, fantasias, and transcriptions of both sacred and secular vocal music, including some of complete masses. In this last category Byrd is drawn upon more frequently than any other composer, a further indication of the esteem in which he was held.

English music for the lute or for its near relations, the theorbo, guitar, cittern, and pandora, like keyboard and secular vocal music, but not like music for consort, enjoyed but a brief flowering compared to the Continent, where during the whole of the sixteenth century and much of the seventeenth these instruments, especially the lute, were enormously popular. The theorbo, which emerged *c.* 1560 in Italy, can be described as a bass lute; it had single strings at first, but by the middle of the seventeenth century was double-strung, the number of strings being either fourteen or sixteen, the lowest eight or ten tuned to the diatonic notes lying immediately below one or other of the lute tunings given in Part I, Chapter 6, p. 217. These bass strings necessitated not only a larger body than the lute, but also frets spaced at wider intervals, thus making it more difficult to play normal lute music, with the result that the theorbo became more of an accompanying instrument, and as such found a place in ensembles and even the opera orchestra as late as the eighteenth century (see p. 382).

The cittern, which has been aptly called 'the poor man's guitar', was very popular with amateurs of all classes. It has the guitar's flat back, but the lute's rounded sides. It is double-strung and ranges in size from a small one with four pairs of strings (courses) to one with twelve courses. The pandora was the popular substitute for the theorbo.

In point of time, Spain was the first European country to adopt the lute from the Moors, but during the sixteenth century and later she virtually rejected the instrument in favour of the vihuela, a name which denoted both the viol and (more especially) the guitar family. The vihuela has a flat back and slightly incurved sides, and is double-strung with either six courses tuned like the lute, or four, the lowest and highest strings of the six-course vihuela being omitted; this last was very popular with amateurs, while the six-course vihuelas were played by professionals. Why the Spaniards forsook the lute for the vihuela is not clear, but it may have been because it is easier to play and is a more resonant instrument, thus suiting the more rhapsodic, emotional nature of Spanish music. (The Renaissance guitar is very similar to the vihuela, except that it has five courses.)

The leading Spanish vihuelists were Luis Milán, Luis de Narváez, Alonso de Mudarra, Enriquez de Valderabano, and Miguel de Fuenllana, the first four living in the earlier part of the sixteenth century, the last during the middle of the century. Whilst most of Milán's pieces are fantasias, he also wrote dances, arrangements of vocal compositions, and variations, many of the latter taking the form of a varied accompaniment to a popular song with the original melody and words placed above the tablature, a unique feature of the Spanish School. The other vihuelists also wrote mostly fantasias; those by Narváez are more purely instrumental than those of his compatriots, and his variations are remarkable for their subtlety, artistry, and the way they exploit the technical resources of the instrument. Fuenllana's fantasias show a more vocal approach in their essentially polyphonic texture, and it is amazing how he manages to achieve such 'correct' and full part-writing on an instrument anything but suited to such a style.

Compared to the amount of English and Italian lute music actually written down, there is very little for the vihuela, possibly because extemporization played a bigger part than elsewhere. This dearth is even more acute as regards ensemble music, the chief composer of which was Diego Ortiz [fl. mid-century], though literary references are common. It even applies to keyboard composition, most of what there is being written for the organ. The outstanding composer for this instrument was Antonio de Cabezón [1510–1566], whose fantasias, 'diferencias' (=variations), vocal transcriptions, and settings of psalms and hymns surpass all other Spanish instrumental composers in the richness of their texture, the quality of their themes, and the exquisiteness of their craftsmanship. Furthermore, the ornateness and variety of his figuration exceeds those of his compatriots, and in some of his diferencias he achieves a greater degree of unity by dove-tailing the variations together instead of making a distinct break between each. In 1554 he accompanied Philip II to England for his marriage to Mary, and it is a moot point whether or no his keyboard technique and variation-writing opened the eyes of English composers. The latter may have developed their keyboard style from a purely native tradition stemming from Aston, but the astonishing advance in figuration shown by Tallis in his two settings of *Felix namque*, which were written only a few years after Cabezón's arrival, i.e. 1562 and 1564 respectively, make it likely that the English learned something at any rate from the Spaniard. As regards the variation, it is much more likely that Cabezón's diferencias did indeed have a marked effect on English keyboard composition, for in both style and structure they were greatly in advance of anything written outside Spain, and only after his visit did this type of composition become popular in England. Indeed, the variation was favoured far more in those two countries than anywhere else. Cabezón is undoubtedly one of the greatest instrumental composers of the Renaissance, ranking with the best that England or Italy could produce and superior to those of France and Germany.

Germany, after her notable composer-performers of the fifteenth century, rather tailed off in the sixteenth, much of her keyboard music (and there is a great deal compared to Spain) consisting of grossly ornate arrangements of vocal works. Her lute music, while roughly equal in quantity to her keyboard music, is superior in quality, using ornamentation more discreetly and being fresher and more melodious, the outcome possibly of the enormous popularity of the instrument with amateurs. The leading lute composers were Hans Judenkünig [d. 1526], Hans Gerle [fl. early sixteenth century], Wolf Heckel [fl. mid-sixteenth century], Melchior Neusiedler [1507–1590], and his brother Hans [*c.* 1509–1563], Matthaeus Waisselius, and Sixtus Kangel, the two last living in the second half of the century. Although the majority of their compositions, like those for keyboard, are vocal transcriptions, they also wrote a number of dances, the most interesting of which was a specifically German type, the 'Tanz', usually in duple time, which was followed by a 'Nachtanz' or 'after dance', usually a variation in triple time of the Tanz. We shall be returning to these two dances when we deal with the dance suite in Chapter 6. Of ensemble music very little remains, but there are numerous pictorial and literary references to wind bands, of which the Germans were specially fond, and which resulted in an international reputation in the making and playing of wind instruments, a reputation that lasted until well into the nineteenth century.

France produced more ensemble music than Germany, the bulk of it consisting of dances which, unlike the mainly elaborate ones in other countries, are melodically and rhythmically simple and, in keeping with the French love of this kind of entertainment, were clearly meant to be danced to. Apart from these, a number of fantasias exist, mostly by Eustache du Caurroy [1549–1609], many of which are based on secular or sacred tunes. As in other countries, French lute and keyboard music outstrips that for ensemble, a host of pieces for both types of instrument being published and a great many more remaining in manuscript. As we might expect from the nation that gave birth to the ballet, dances occupy a more prominent position in music for the lute than in any other country. Sometimes two or three contrasting dances were grouped together, such as pavane–salterello–piva, the last being in triple time, like the salterello, but quicker, both dances occasionally being variations of the pavane. By the middle of the century the salterello and piva were replaced by the gaillarde. Most of these dances, like those for ensemble, are simple and could easily have been danced to at some intimate gathering, but hardly at a court ball, where the sound of the instrument would have been drowned by rustling skirts and chattering voices. The chief lute composers were Antoine Francisque [*c.* 1570–1605], Adrian le Roy, author of the textbook already mentioned (p. 346) on how to compose for and play on the lute, Guillaume Morlaye, and the Mantuan Albert de Rippe, the last two living in the middle years of the century.

French keyboard music was more 'learned' than that for lute and ensemble, as much of it consists of transcriptions of both sacred and secular vocal works which demand a fairly high degree of technical competence. As elsewhere, except England, there is little or no distinction between organ and stringed-keyboard styles, and most of the pieces are taken up with rather mechanical repetitions of ornamental figures, scale passages, and broken chords that are effective on both types of keyboard. Only one man deserves special mention, Jean Titelouze [1563–1633], an organist who was not only a gifted composer, but who knew a good deal about organ construction, and who advocated the use of two manuals and a pedal keyboard, the latter being virtually unknown outside Germany.

Sweelinck, the last of the great line of composers from the Netherlands, was also important in the development of the organ as an instrument, for while he was greatly indebted to the keyboard figuration and variations of the English virginalists (largely through Bull, with whom he was probably on intimate terms), and was thoroughly acquainted with the Italian fantasia and toccata (see below, p. 355), his variations on psalm- and hymn-tunes (chorales) call for sharply differentiated registration that permits the chorale to stand out, because, unlike the borrowed melodies in English virginal variations which are usually absorbed into the general figuration, Sweelinck keeps the chorale cantus firmus virtually intact and aloof, as it were, from the lively other parts. (The same characteristic is found, though to a lesser extent, in his harpsichord variations on secular themes.)

The instrument that Sweelinck's chorale variations demand we now call the baroque organ, although its main features had been incorporated into the German Renaissance organ. The Renaissance organ outside the Germanic countries had a soft tonal structure, its mixture stops (i.e. those which reinforce two or more upper partials of the fundamental note) lacked brilliance and penetration, solo stops were rare, the flute being the most popular, and the pedal keyboard, on the few organs that possessed one, was merely a very short lower extension of the manual. (Two-manual organs were also exceptional.) This type of organ remained popular, especially in England and Italy, until the eighteenth century. In contrast to this, the German organ of the late Renaissance and baroque had not only an increased range of solo stops, particularly reeds, together with mixture stops that were more brilliant and penetrating, but not excessively so owing to light wind pressure, but also a large number of mutation stops (which strengthen a particular upper partial), and a pedal keyboard that was a more extensive continuation of the (usually) two manuals and which, moreover, was capable of carrying both a supporting bass and, by means of two-foot and four-foot stops, an independent melody on equal terms with the manuals. Such an organ provided both a clear, ringing ensemble and a number of delightfully varied solo stops, on one of which the chorale theme would be played.

Sweelinck's chorale variations were the first of a whole series of distinguished and sometimes profound examples that reached its highest point, but not its end, in those by J. S. Bach. They are essentially organ pieces, which his fantasias are not, but many of them sound just as effective on the harpsichord. In his fantasias Sweelinck laid the foundation of the fugue by reducing the succession of imitative points to one, unlike the typical polythematic fantasia of England and elsewhere. More important, however, and again unlike the few English and Italian monothematic examples, it is not the theme that is altered, but its accompanying counterpoints.

Sweelinck enjoyed considerable fame as a keyboard composer, and manuscript copies of his organ and harpsichord pieces were widely circulated all over Europe. He was also an outstanding teacher, and his pupils included Scheidt and Scheidemann, the latter of whom taught Reinken, who in turn considerably influenced Bach. In view of all this, it is astonishing that none of Sweelinck's keyboard works was printed during his lifetime, and in this respect his Italian contemporaries were very much better served.

Compared to the rest of Europe, excluding England, Italian instrumental music of the late Renaissance is, on the whole, superior in both quantity and quality, and a far higher proportion of it was printed than anywhere else. Indeed, from the lute books issued by Petrucci, the first of which appeared in 1507, until the latter half of the eighteenth century more instrumental music was published in Italy than in any other country.

Petrucci's 1507 book contains a high proportion of vocal transcriptions, and as the century progressed this proportion increased, most of the originals being madrigals and other secular types. This trend, which differs from English and even French practice, was the result of the tremendous popularity of vocal music in Italy, a popularity which, despite the close association between words and music, did not prevent the latter from being enjoyed in the abstract, as it were, i.e. in a purely instrumental form, although this would be partially compensated by various embellishments not possible in the original. Despite the preponderance of such transcriptions, the most important and, indeed, the most attractive class of lute compositions are the dances. The idea of joining two or more dances together has already been mentioned, but the pavane–salterello–piva arrangement, in which the last two are variations of the first, stemmed from Italy and was first introduced by one of the leading lutanists of the first half of the century,

Joan Ambrosio Dalza [fl. *c.* 1500]. Dalza and his contemporary, Francesco Spinaccino [fl. *c.* 1500], both wrote short pieces consisting of chords and scale passages called 'ricercari' (Italian, *ricerca*='research', hence 'study'—in this case of a technical nature). Although the term appears in their works for the first time, its character soon changed, and in the hands of Francesco Canova da Milano [1497–1543] it became for the first time the instrumental counterpart of the motet, i.e. basically a succession of points or themes each of which is treated imitatively—in other words, a polyphonic 'study'. So far as the lute is concerned, Francesco's ricercari are the finest ever written and exerted a considerable influence on other lute composers, both native and foreign, the latter usually employing the term 'fantasia', as indeed did many Italians during the latter part of the century. Apart from the ricercari and dance movements, Francesco also wrote pieces which are much freer in design, alternating between imitative, chordal, and florid passages, and in some respects anticipating the later toccata (see below, p. 355).

The idea of joining dances together remained popular right through the century and formed the starting-point of what was later to become one of the most popular classes of instrumental composition, the suite. If anyone invented the suite it was Pietro P. Borrono [fl. first half of sixteenth century], who wrote a number of them consisting of a pavana followed by three saltarelli, all in the same key, and who clearly considered this arrangement as an entity. However, the most popular dance grouping during the first half of the century was pavana–gagliarda, and in the latter half the passamezzo–gagliarda, which was sometimes expanded by the addition at the end of a padovana, a dance in quick six-eight time. Many of the dances were constructed on one of five ground basses; the two passamezzo ones were 'passamezzo antico' and 'passamezzo moderno', the other three being 'romanesca', 'folia', and 'ruggiero' (see Chapter 1, p. 264); all of these played an important part in baroque instrumental music.

The number of lute composers was legion, and included some of the leading writers of vocal music, such as Vecchi and Gastoldi, but the most important were, in addition to those already mentioned, Antonio Rotta [fl. *c.* 1550], Giacomo Gorzanis [fl. second half of sixteenth century], Vincenzo

Galilei [1520–1591], father of the great astronomer, Galileo Galilei, Fabritio Caroso [fl. latter half of sixteenth century], Giovanni Antonio Terzi [sixteenth–seventeenth centuries], and Simone Molinaro [b. *c.* 1565]. Terzi and Molinaro brought the lute variation dance suite to its highest peak, and in their passamezzo–gagliarda grouping both dances are divided into sections (usually three, but sometimes as many as ten), each of which are variations on the same basic succession of chords, with the first section of the gagliarda melodically linked to the similar section of the passamezzo. A feeling for climax is shown by the use of progressively shorter note values, and the style is either polyphonic or contrapuntal.

Like instrumental music in general, again excluding that of England, Italian keyboard pieces are mainly vocal transcriptions, but original pieces for stringed keyboard or organ became more common as the century progressed and are, from our point of view, far more interesting and important. The chief of these are the ricercare and the canzona. The first we have already met, and although those by the first significant keyboard composer, Marc Antonio Cavazzoni [*c.* 1490–after 1569], are the earlier improvisational type, they became in the hands of his more important son, Girolamo [b. *c.* 1520], the standard type already described, but expanding this by increasing the number of repeats of each point of imitation. Later composers, of whom the chief were Jacques Buus [d. *c.* 1564], Annibale Padovano [1527–1575], Claudio Merulo [1533–1604], and the two Gabrielis (all of them organists at St. Mark's, Venice), displayed greater virtuosity and increased ornamentation compared to G. Cavazzoni, and Andrea Gabrieli introduced a far-reaching innovation by writing a few ricercari based on a single theme instead of several, this theme being varied and the repeats separated by florid interludes. This monothematic type of ricercare was not favoured nearly so much as the standard polythematic type.

The term 'canzona' first occurs in M. A. Cavazonni's book of keyboard pieces published in 1523, where it is applied to transcriptions of French chansons. One of the characteristics of these is some kind of sectional repetition, e.g. *a b a* or *a a b* (see Chapter 1, p. 240), and in the later purely instrumental canzona repetition schemes became one of the main features compared to the ricercare, the other being a generally lighter, less 'learned' style, cleaner, livelier rhythm, and the frequent occurrence of 𝅗𝅥 ♩ ♩ as an opening motif.

The above-mentioned composers of ricercare also wrote canzone, and the vast majority of their examples are transcriptions of chansons. There were, however, two further types of composition which were nearly always original—the fantasia and the toccata. The keyboard fantasia should not be confused with the lute ricercare–fantasia mentioned on p. 353, for it developed from the practice of testing prospective candidates for the two organists' posts at St. Mark's, Venice, by giving them a theme on which to improvise, and when composers (e.g. A. Gabrieli) actually started writing such pieces, these mostly show their origin by being monothematic (like some of Gabrieli's ricercari), but with little polyphony and much ornamentation. Almost entirely ornamental was the toccata, a term first used in a keyboard piece published in 1536. It comes from the Italian *toccare* (='to touch', i.e. the keys, in contrast to 'sounding' strings and 'singing' voices), and its essentially florid style was retained right up to Bach's day; it is not surprising, therefore, that the first great exponent of this, the most characteristic of all keyboard compositions, was the greatest organ virtuoso of the century, Merulo.

Voluminous and important as Italian lute and keyboard music is, it is less purely instrumental and indeed less attractive than that of English composers, but in the sphere of ensemble music Italy, especially through the genius of Giovanni Gabrieli, produced compositions whose rich colours and spacious designs not only compare favourably with English consort music, but also marked both the end of the Renaissance and the beginning of the baroque. While men like Willaert, Rore, and Andrea Gabrieli all wrote concerted pieces; the actual quantity produced compares unfavourably with that of England, and although Giovanni Gabrieli was the most prolific writer of such music his output is small compared to Byrd's. In his canzone, however, which, like his compatriots, he preferred to all other types of instrumental music when writing for ensembles, Giovanni treads the virtually unexplored territory of pure instrumental colour. Thus in his famous *Sonata pian' e forte* (1597) he combines two 'choruses', one consisting of a cornett and three trombones and the other of a violino (viola) and three more trombones. In general, when only one chorus is playing the music is soft (piano), but when both combine then it is loud (forte). Although Giovanni was the first to include dynamic terms in an ensemble composition, such terms had been used in lute music as early as *c.* 1520. The term 'sonata' too dates back to 1561 at least, and in literary references to 1486.

We do not know who made the first violin, or its near relations the viola and 'cello; all we do know is that it developed from the mediaeval vièle, which, unlike the viol, was placed against the shoulder and bowed in the same way as we now bow the violin, that the strings were tuned in fifths by the early sixteenth century at least, and that the first important violin-makers were the Italians Gasparo Bertolotti [1540–1609]—usually called 'da Salò' from his birthplace—Giovanni Paolo Maggini [1581–1628] who, like da Salò, worked in Brescia, and the brothers Amati, Antonio [*c.* 1555–after 1640] and Hieronymus [*c.* 1556–1630], both of whom worked in Cremona. It was Hieronymus's son Nicola and his pupil, Antonio Stradivarius, who built the most famous violins, but their achievements take us outside this chapter.

Apart from artistic presentations (paintings, etc.), our knowledge of later Renaissance instruments is chiefly obtained, typically enough, from two German works, *Musica instrumentalis deudsch* (1529) by Martin Agricola [1486–1556] and the second volume of *Syntagma musicae* (1618) by Michael Praetorius (see Chapter 5). Other notable books of the period are the *Tratado de glosas* (1553) by Ortiz, which deals with instrumental improvisation and ornamentation, mostly for the viol, *Il Transilvano* (1597 and 1609) by Girolamo Diruta (b. 1561) which is concerned with organ playing and composition, the standard treatise on the Renaissance dance by, again typically, the Frenchman Thoinot Arbeau [1519–1595], the *Orchésographie* (1588), and a number on musical theory and composition in general, including, in addition to Glareanus's *Dodecachordon* (see p. 246), Zarlino's *Institutioni armoniche* (1558), *Dimostrationi armoniche* (1571), and *Sopplimenti musicali* (1588), the *Prattica di musica* (1592 and 1619) by Lodovico Zacconi [1555–1627], and Morley's *A Plaine and Easie Introduction to Practicall Musicke* (1597).

The feeling for colour and richness of sound shown in Giovanni Gabrieli's concerted music and in much of his choral music with instrumental accompaniment is paralleled by the school of painting which flourished in the same city and which is one of the glories of the Renaissance. In Part I, Chapter 6, p. 225, we described the main differences between Florentine and Venetian art, and mentioned the first great painters of the latter school—Giovanni Bellini, Mantegna, Giorgione, and Carpaccio. These were followed by Titian [1485?–1576], Veronese [1528–1588], Tintoretto [1518–1594], and Michelangelo Caravaggio [1573–1610]. The sumptuous, glowing colours of Titian, particularly his reds, the cooler but still rich pigments of Veronese, and the vivid contrasts of light and dark in the works of Tintoretto represent, as does much of Giovanni Gabrieli's work, the full flowering of one aspect of Renaissance art and, in their emotionalism, the advent of the baroque spirit. This is particularly true of Tintoretto and Caravaggio, for the former, an impetuous and passionate man frequently embroiled in bloodshed and violence, is often startlingly dramatic in his choice and treatment of subject-matter, while the latter, rebelling against the superficial imitation of Michelangelo, Raphael, and Titian which flooded Italy during the latter part of the century, depicted individuals and scenes from the lower classes rather than from the aristocracy, and depicted them with a realism unknown before. Caravaggio, in fact, not only carried the realistic element of the Renaissance to its farthest extent, but, through the bold emotionalism of his subjects and his striking use of colour and light, rejuvenated Italian painting and exerted a tremendous influence on foreign artists, especially those of the early baroque.

As in the fifteenth, so in the sixteenth century Italy dominated the artistic sphere, for in addition to her painters she boasted the finest architect and sculptor in Europe, Michelangelo [1475–1564], and an exquisite craftsman in Benvenuto Cellini [1500–1571], whose work has, perhaps, never been surpassed in technical finish. Elsewhere in Europe the only men of comparable artistic stature were the French sculptor, Pilon [1537–1590], the German, Holbein the younger [1497/8–1543], who spent the last twelve years of his life as court painter to Henry VIII and who was one of the few sixteenth-century artists who took an interest in the rising bourgeois element in society, the Flemish painter, Bruegel the elder [*c.* 1520–1569], and lastly, and most strikingly original of them all, including the Italians, the Spaniard El Greco [1541–1614], who, though born in Crete and studying in Italy, is typically Spanish in his intense mysticism and emotionalism, the latter frequently being achieved by distorted forms, violent gestures, and exaggerated expressions. He more than any other artist of his time reflected the new spirit of the baroque; indeed, he was more baroque-like than many of his successors, and the powerful, often startling impact of his pictures is yet another salutary reminder that artistic periods are more conveniences than realities.

In the realm of literature Italy was both more influential and superior to all other countries. Her chief contribution was poetic, and men such as Tasso, Michelangelo, Ariosto, and Tansillo [1510–1568] were only partially matched by Ronsard and the Englishman, Donne [1573–1631], and to a lesser extent by Sidney and Raleigh. In the dramatic sphere, however, she was completely overshadowed by the Spaniards, Lope de Rueda [1510–1560] and Lope de Vega [1562–1635], and, more especially, by the Englishmen, Marlowe [1564–1593], Shakespeare [1564–1616], and Jonson, Marlowe and Shakespeare being the greatest European playwrights of their respective generations.

In Shakespeare's non-historical plays the basic plots and characters are borrowed from the writings of others to a far greater extent than with later dramatists, and so reflect contemporary musical practice, which, particularly in large-scale works, such as the mass, but also to a lesser extent in the motet, madrigal, etc., incorporates previously composed material as a melodic or structural foundation. More important, however, is the sometimes terrifying but always fascinating way in which Shakespeare draws his characters, describing in greater detail and with more accuracy and deeper understanding a larger aspect of human personality than any dramatist before or since. His range and penetration are astonishing and remind one of Leonardo, for while his realm was not man's environment, but the character of man himself, he shows, like Leonardo, the typical enquiring mind of the Renaissance.

In addition to the poets mentioned above, Italy could also boast of such writers as Cellini, whose autobiography gives a vivid and valuable insight into contemporary life, Vasari [1511–1574], who has left us a series of sketches on Italian painters, and the historian, Guicciardini [1483–1540]. Their contemporaries abroad include the great French writer,

Montaigne [1553–1592] and his compatriot, Rabelais [1494?–1553], whose accounts of the adventures of two mythological giants, Gargantua and Pantagruel, have remained classics to this day. Spain also produced a classic, the still popular *Don Quixote*, by Cervantes [1547–1616], and in England the writings of Francis Bacon, Lord Verulam [1561–1626], and the historian, Holinshed [*c.* 1520–1580], contain much of value and interest.

Bacon's chief preoccupation was with the philosophy of science rather than its practice, and while as a result he performed very few experiments himself, he advocated strongly the importance of making detailed investigations of nature and of forming general principles which would explain the facts discovered, an approach that cut right across the traditional one in which the authority of men such as Aristotle and Ptolemy were regarded as infallible, or in which philosophers erected a purely abstract world-system that bore little relation to the world as it is. Bacon's influence was mainly felt in the seventeenth century and hence does not concern us here, but his criticism of the general scientific attitude of his day and the originality of his thought were undoubtedly affected by the experiments and theories of a number of late Renaissance scientists and philosophers, the chief of whom were the Pole, Copernicus [1473–1543], the Italian, Bruno [1548–1600], the Dane, Brahe [1546–1601], and the German, Kepler [1571–1630]. These four men proved or believed that the earth, far from being the centre of the universe, was merely one of many planets revolving round the sun. Copernicus's book, published in the year of his death, aroused no controversy because a Preface by a friend assured the reader that the central idea was purely theoretical, but when thirty years or so later, with the Counter-Reformation in full swing, Bruno constructed a philosophy in which the Copernican system is an integral part, he was not only branded as a heretic by the Catholics, but also by the Calvinists, and from 1579 on he was constantly moving about Europe in order to avoid imprisonment and death, finally and inadvisedly returning to Italy, where he was eventually burnt at the stake.

While Bruno philosophized about the solar system, Brahe observed it systematically, the first astronomer to do so. His instruments and calculations were far more accurate than those of his predecessors, and while he rejected the Copernican system because he could not detect any change in the relative positions of the stars, he evolved one which, although the earth is the centre, is mathematically equivalent to that of Copernicus. In 1600 Kepler became his assistant, and his three famous laws of planetary motion, which still describe accurately the movements and speeds of the planets and which later provided the basis of Newton's laws of gravitation, were largely founded on his master's work, and represent an astonishing feat when one remembers that all observations were made with the naked eye, as the telescope was not invented until 1609, the year Kepler published the first two of his laws.

Copernicus's 'heliocentric' system was the great scientific and philosophic bone of contention in the sixteenth and seventeenth centuries, and was not only officially branded as heresy by the Roman Church in 1616, but rejected by many Protestants, particularly the Calvinists. The Church as a whole, however, was not opposed to science as a study, but only when scientific ideas conflicted with traditional philosophic and Christian beliefs, one of which was that the earth was the most important celestial body. In other departments, therefore, men experimented and theorized with no fear of being burnt alive, and while these men did not then and have not since achieved such fame as the four mentioned above, they contributed much to the advancement of scientific knowledge.

In England, for example, Gilbert [1540–1603] supported Bacon in his insistence on experiments, but, unlike his greater countryman, he practised what he preached and made some remarkable discoveries in electricity and magnetism.

In medicine the German, Paracelsus [1493–1541], although propounding a lot of nonsense, advocated the use of mineral drugs—compounds of mercury, lead, copper, etc.—as well as opium. More important were the painter-sculptor, Michelangelo, his compatriot, Fallopius [1523–1562], and the Belgian, Vesalius [1515–1564], all of whom made detailed dissections of the human body; in fact, Vesalius's description of the structure of the body is remarkably correct considering that he had no microscope (invented *c.* 1610). The advance in anatomical knowledge prompted greater skill in surgery, and the most outstanding surgeon of the century, the Frenchman, Paré [1510–1596], discarded the customary treatment of gun-shot wounds (i.e. the application of boiling oil) and of severe bleeding from amputations (i.e. the use of a hot iron to coagulate the blood), employing ointments for the first and stemming the flow of blood by tying up the blood vessels, a method that had not been practised since the first century A.D. The widespread ravages of syphilis, which frequently disfigured noses, prompted a number of surgeons, some of whom were apparently successful, to repair the damage by skin grafts—in other words, to practise plastic surgery.

Herbs played a large part in mediaeval and Renaissance medicine, but the descriptions and drawings of the plants themselves were merely copies from old manuscripts until the sixteenth century, when three Germans, Brunfels [d. 1534], Bock [1498–1554], and Fuchs [1501–1566], described as accurately as was possible without microscopes, and employed artists to draw in detail, both herbal and other plants. Bock even attempted a general classification. If botany before 1500 was rudimentary, zoology was practically non-existent, as the reliance on ancient authority had largely degenerated into imaginary and improbable stories about beasts. With the Swiss, Gesner [1516–1565], however, a great advance was made, and while he shows a natural uncertainty about animals in distant lands, the bulk of his illustrations and descriptions are taken at first hand.

The enquiring spirit which made some men observe and speculate upon the Universe and the position of our world in it made others venture into the unknown places of the world itself and the voyages of Columbus, Vasco da Gama, Magellan, the Cabots, Cortez, and others were succeeded by Pizarro, who conquered Peru (1532–6), Sir Francis Drake, the second man to circumnavigate the globe (1577–80), and the beginnings of English colonization in Newfoundland (1583), Virginia (1607), and New England (1620), the last founded by the Pilgrim Fathers after their historic voyage in the *Mayflower*. In 1542 the Portuguese landed in Japan, the Spaniards discovered the Solomon Islands (1567) and the New Hebrides (1606), and by the latter part of the century most European countries, especially Spain, Portugal, England, and Holland were regularly sending out expeditions westwards to the Americas or eastwards round the Cape of Good Hope to India (the East India Company was founded in 1600 and its Dutch equivalent two years later). By 1600 the main outlines of South America were known, the north-western shores of North America visited several times, notably by the Frenchman, Cartier [*c.* 1491–1557], and in the early years of the seventeenth century the Spaniards had settled in many parts of the American continent south of Mexico, and the French and English had done likewise further north.

The mass of knowledge acquired by these explorations and those of the fifteenth century showed the world maps of mediaeval geographers, who had relied mainly on Ptolemy, to be hopelessly inaccurate, and great strides were made by a number of cartographers, the most important and influential being the Fleming, Mercator [1512–1594], who produced a map of the world based on a projection which still bears his name and which has been used for nearly all nautical charts from the eighteenth century to the present day. Navigational instruments, too, improved in accuracy, and were supported by the revival of mathematics, particularly algebra and trigonometry, and, in the early seventeenth century, by the increasing use of decimals and the invention of logarithms by the Scotsman, Napier [1550–1617]. These developments naturally affected surveying, and as early as 1533 the principle of triangulation had been described; thirty years later plane tables were in general use, and in 1597 the first national atlas of any country was published in England.

Expeditions to distant lands, then as now, are expensive, and these, but more particularly the political and religious wars of the fifteenth and sixteenth centuries, with their resultant bribes either to obtain support or buy off opposition, together with the widespread havoc caused by outbreaks of plague in both centuries, rendered most of Europe very short of money, the chief exception being Spain, where the conquests of the West Indies, Mexico, and Peru brought the Spanish Treasury enormous wealth. Elsewhere the demand for silver was acute, and as a result mining and metallurgy became more important than ever before. Great advances were made in the construction of pumps that could remove water from deep mines, the smelting of ore, the ventilation of shafts, etc. The man who investigated this aspect of science more thoroughly than any other was the German, Georgius Agricola [1494–1555], who has been called "the father of metallurgy"; some of his processes for extracting metal from ore have remained virtually unchanged to this day.

The intense interest in science during the late Renaissance led to the formation of several academies which were very similar in function and constitution to the artistic ones already mentioned, and, like them, the earliest were founded in Italy—Naples (1560), Florence (1567), and Rome (1600). Although she produced few scientists of eminence, Italy was almost as much the main centre of scientific discussion as she was of musical activity, for many foreign scientists studied at her universities, and just as the galaxy of northern composers who at first dominated the Italian musical scene were followed by men such as Palestrina, Marenzio, and the Gabrielis, so Italy eventually produced one of the most famous scientists of all time, Galileo, but he belongs outside this chapter.

The Renaissance has long been regarded as one of the greatest epochs in the history of man, and rightly so, but whereas later historians have paid glowing tribute to the achievements in the fine arts, literature, and philosophy, and have fully recognized the upsurge of creative ability and desire for knowledge which lay behind these achievements, and behind the exploration of distant lands, and the new scientific attitude of experiment and deduction, they have without exception either merely fleetingly touched on the contribution music made to this period or else omitted mention of it altogether. It must be said in their defence, however, that until comparatively recently very little music of the fifteenth and sixteenth centuries was available in modern editions, and as most historians are neither competent nor have the time to undertake the lengthy and often difficult task of editing early prints and manuscripts, nor the faculty for assessing their aesthetic value, the blame rests largely on their musical contemporaries. Today there is no such excuse, and one who writes a social history of England, for example, and devotes a totally inadequate dozen lines or so to the music that flourished under the Tudors and who, while including Holbein's name, makes no mention of Byrd, is guilty of presenting a picture that is neither accurate nor complete.

Music permeated the whole of Renaissance society to an extent unknown before. Folk-singing and dancing were more widespread than in earlier centuries and art music more intensely cultivated. Although the poorer classes were allowed no opportunity to listen to madrigals or chansons and can only have appreciated to a very slight degree the masses, motets, services, and anthems that they heard in church—so complex compared to their own folk-music—the growing wealth of the bourgeois, the middle merchant class, enabled them to imitate and eventually acquire the tastes of the aristocracy; but while they could afford to pay the piper and hence call the tune, they did not at first demand an art more in keeping with their simple, homely background. Not until the seventeenth century in fact did a 'popular' art music arise, and even then it was largely restricted to one country, Italy, and one type, opera.

PERFORMANCE

The general trend described at the end of Chapter 1 is less strikingly evident in the sacred than in the secular music of the late Renaissance; nevertheless, there is a marked difference in approach between the beginning and end of the period, particularly in the motet, and the same considerations with regard to the performance of secular music in general and of madrigals in particular apply to compositions for both the Catholic and Protestant Churches. It should be noted, however, that throughout the period the Gloria, Credo, and Sanctus of the mass, and their Protestant counterparts, should include variations in speed, as in the fifteenth century (see Part I, Chapter 6, p. 229), but masses in general should be performed in a more restrained manner than motets. This restraint should also apply to the motets of Palestrina compared to those of Lassus, Victoria, or Byrd, or, indeed, most other composers of his generation and later.

Instrumental music too reflects the trend towards greater expressiveness. This is clearly shown by the development of the harpsichord (see p. 341), and most compositions for this instrument, especially those in variation-form or with repeated sections (e.g. dance movements), should make use of the timbres and dynamic contrasts that were possible at the time when the piece was written. Changes of speed may also occur between variations within the limits of tactus=M.M. 60–100. The choice of timbre will largely depend on personal taste, and of speed on the nature of the music, or the descriptive title (if there is one), or both. Many instrumental compositions include signs that indicate some kind of ornament; we do not know which ornaments were meant, and it may well be that the composer only added the signs as a general indication as to which notes should be embellished, leaving the exact choice of ornament to the player. In any case, perfectly satisfactory results can be obtained by simply using upper or lower mordants (depending on the context) and the occasional trill on long notes, particularly at cadences. With regard to speed, dynamics, and timbre, the same considerations apply to the clavichord, lute, and organ as to the harpsichord, except that contrasts in tone-colour are impossible on the clavichord and very limited on the lute. It should be realized, however, that modern harpsichords, clavichords, and lutes approximate much more closely, both in sound and construction, to the Renaissance types than do modern organs; indeed, most organ music composed before the nineteenth century, particularly that of Germany, sounds quite different and distinctly superior when played on the original instruments (or copies) than on the vast majority of modern organs.

3

THE BAROQUE: MUSIC FOR THE STAGE—I

LOOKING back over the previous 1,600 years or so, it is clear that up to this point the history of music is predominantly the history of vocal music, and for two obvious reasons; the first is that the voice is the most natural of all instruments, and the second that during most of this period the church was the main centre of artistic activity and sacred music must obviously be vocal. Even if we leave out sacred music, the predominance of vocal over instrumental music is still overwhelming, as the strong bias towards secular composition which began in the fourteenth century was very much in evidence during the late Renaissance, the madrigal and chanson being more popular and progressive than but not necessarily thereby superior to instrumental and liturgical music, whether Catholic or Protestant. The greater popularity of secular vocal music compared to sacred that has existed ever since received a new impetus in the last two decades of the sixteenth century through the creation of a new kind of music that eventually blossomed into opera, and which continued the supremacy of vocal music during most of the baroque period. Like the madrigal and chanson, opera was not only more popular and progressive than sacred and instrumental music but also exerted a considerable influence on them.

This 'New Music', as Giulio Caccini [*c.* 1545–1618], one of its creators, called it, is a rare instance in the history of any art of theory preceding practice, for it was deliberately modelled on ancient Greek tragedy, which, so Caccini and the group to which he belonged thought, was sung in its entirety. They were wrong in this, as only the choruses were actually sung, but they were right in that Greek tragedy is essentially a lyrical art which, at moments of great emotional stress, cries out for and almost certainly received some kind of instrumental accompaniment.

The men most actively concerned in this 'revival' of classical drama were members of one of the many academies that, as we have seen, sprang up all over Italy during the late Renaissance. This particular one, which began meeting *c.* 1580, is usually known as the Florentine Camerata (‘Society’), and included, in addition to the virtuoso singer Caccini, the noblemen Count Bardi [1534–1612], at whose palace the meetings were first held, and Jacopo Corsi [*c.* 1560–1604], the poet Rinuccini [1562–1612], the singer-composer Jacopo Peri [1561–1633], the composer Emilio de’ Cavalieri [*c.* 1550–1602], the theorist Girolamo Mei [fl. *c.* 1600], who considerably influenced the leading spirit of the Camerata Vincenzo Galilei who was not only a lutanist (see pp. 353–4) but also a composer and theorist of no mean order.

It was Galilei who set the ball rolling with a treatise published in 1581 in which he attacks the elaborate polyphonic imitative style of the Renaissance—a style in which he himself had composed—because it can neither render words clearly nor express with sufficient subtlety or force the emotions of the text. In place of this ‘old music’ he advocates a style which consists fundamentally of a single vocal line that follows closely the natural accents and inflexions of the text, and which is supported by a series of simple instrumental chords. Moreover, the singer is expected to deliver the vocal line with great feeling and, if they are not actually written down, to improvise ornaments on the more important words. Such pieces are called ‘monodies’, and although some of Galilei’s examples (all of them lost) seem to have consisted of a vocal line and a written-out accompaniment for four viols, the earliest surviving monodies have only a voice part and a bass. This last was eventually called ‘basso continuo’ or, in English, ‘thorough-bass’ from ‘through’ or ‘continuous’, and at first was played on the lute, theorbo, or a keyboard instrument; during the first decades of the seventeenth century it became standard practice for the bass line to be doubled by a viola da gamba or ’cello, as in many of the English ayres (see Chapter 1, p. 286). The bass line is sometimes figured—that is, a number or numbers are added above or (more usually) below a note which indicate the chords to be played above that note. For example ‘$^{6}_{3}$’ means that the third and sixth (or their octaves) are to be played, i.e. a first inversion, the intervals being major or minor according to the key signature. As the method of figuring became more generally accepted the insertion of numbers was reduced, ‘6’ implying '$^{6}_{3}$' and no number implying '$^{5}_{3}$', or root position. In some of the earlier examples the bass is entirely unfigured, the composer leaving the choice of chord to the player; but even when figures are given the player was expected to add suspensions, runs, trills, interesting or relevant melodic or rhythmic fragments, etc., at suitable places. Thus in both accompaniment and vocal line improvisation played a larger part than at any time previously. (Unless otherwise qualified, the word 'continuo', here and in the next chapters, will mean a figured or unfigured bass line supporting a series of harmonies either specified by figures or implied, and played on the harpsichord, the bass line being doubled by a gamba or 'cello in recitatives, and elsewhere by two or more of these instruments, sometimes with double basses, the latter usually playing only when the full string band (i.e., violins I and II, violas, and 'cellos) is added to the harpsichord.)

Caccini, in his treatise, *Nuove Musiche* ('New Music'), published in 1602, claims that the embellishment of the vocal line is a new departure and that the ornaments he gives are mostly his own invention. Neither is true, for, as we saw in Chapter 1, the madrigal was sometimes embellished, and many of his ornaments are in fact taken from earlier treatises. Nor is it true, as some later writers have stated, that monody was a complete break with Renaissance composition, for the solo song with lute accompaniment was extremely popular and vocal improvisation well-known in the sixteenth century, and the basso continuo was a natural development from the basso seguente (see pp. 317-18). Moreover, the importance of the text and the stress on a dominant vocal line with a subservient accompaniment were also continuations of Renaissance practice, the latter being apparent in the late sixteenth-century madrigal (see Chapter 1, p. 269), and the former in the care with which Rore, Monte, and Gesualdo matched the moods suggested by the poem, or with which Wert and Marenzio set individual words. The pendulum had swung back again, for from Gregorian chant, where the liturgy was, and is, all-important, music became more and more the dominant partner, reaching its zenith in the fourteenth century; from then on the setting of words became not only more circumspect but, in the late Renaissance, an integral part of composition, reaching its peak in the early baroque monody.

It is important to realize that the Camerata were not anti-Renaissance, but only anti-polyphony; indeed, the very fact that they tried to imitate Greek tragedy is proof of this, as the study and interpretation of classical culture was one of the main pursuits and characteristics of the Renaissance. But polyphony was too firmly established to be overthrown in a day; in fact, it never was overthrown, and while the kind of monody described above began to be written in increasing numbers, hardly any are by composers of the first rank, for the lack of melodic interest and poverty of texture was hardly likely to attract first-rate musical talent (Ex. 16*):

(Sad shores, shady ghastly fields, that have not seen stars or suns, nor ever a flash of lightning.)

The monody, in fact, appeals primarily to the singer, who can show off his skill in expressiveness, diction, and the improvising of embellishments, and it is noteworthy that of the first three leading monodists, Galilei, Peri, and Caccini, the last two were professional singers.

* Adapted from R. Haas, *Musik des Baroks*, p. 36.

But the melodic bent of the Italian genius was too powerful to be satisfied for long with such a limited vocal line, and the madrigals and arias in Caccini's *Nuove Musiche* reveal a more lyrical vocal part and a more interesting bass. The distinction between madrigals and arias is that the former are through-composed (as in Ex. 17: see also *H.A.M.*, 184—miscalled 'aria'), while most of the latter are strophic (see Chapter 5) and although both contain florid passages the arias are, on the whole, simpler, more clear-cut, and frankly tuneful (Ex. 17*):

(Be moved to pity my torment, and where weeping and sighing do not reach you...)

* Melody and bass from *I Classici della Musica Italiana: No. 4, Giulio Caccini*, ed. Perinello.

The three kinds of monody so far mentioned, i.e. the simple type (Ex. 16) and the Caccini madrigal and aria, eventually developed into the operatic 'secco recitative' (see p. 382), 'arioso', and 'aria' respectively. The first two are always through-composed with the emphasis on affective declamation of the words, the arioso being the more lyrical or impassioned of the two, while in the aria the melodic element is the most important.

Before we go any further, it will be as well to define baroque opera as a dramatic spectacle unified in style in which the entire text (libretto) is set to music, and which consists mainly of solos, but which may also include instrumental items (dances, preludes, etc.), and vocal ensembles (choruses, duets, etc.), the voice or voices being accompanied by instruments. Furthermore, by 'opera' we mean the most important and popular type—later called *opera seria*—which is based on a serious, sometimes tragic, and always emotional subject, but which may contain comic episodes, and which almost invariably ends happily. The other types of opera will always be qualified, e.g. ballad opera, *opera buffa*, etc. The word 'opera', incidentally, which literally means '[a] work', was not commonly used in the modern sense until the end of the seventeenth century, and composers and librettists employed a bewildering assortment of labels to describe the new art form, those that occur most often being *Tragedia* [or *Dramma*, or *Opera*] *rappresentata in musica*, *Dramma* [or *Commedia*, or *Opera*] *musicale*, and *Dramma per* [or *in*] *musica*.

Just as monody had its roots in earlier practice, so had opera, these being the French ballets and the Italian 'intermedii' and pastoral plays of the previous century. As we saw in Chapter 1, a few ballets in the late sixteenth century comprised a continuous series of dances based on a definite story and accompanied by instruments. The intermedii consisted of vocal solos, duets, etc., with orchestral accompaniment, together with purely instrumental pieces, and were performed before and after each act of a serious drama, the words of the songs generally being relevant to the action of the play. The pastoral play, because it was essentially lyrical in style and content, lent itself very easily to musical treatment, and from Poliziano's *Orfeo*—the earliest pastoral play and first produced in the 1470s—to Tasso's *Aminta* and Guarini's *Pastor Fido* at the end of the sixteenth century, this type of drama was frequently enhanced by musical settings of parts of the text, these settings being for one or more voices with instrumental accompaniment. Moreover, the structure and subject-matter provided the model for most early opera libretti.

Thus all the main ingredients of opera were already in existence except for a style of composition capable of conveying a story expressively and reasonably quickly. Renaissance polyphony and solo song were unsuitable because they were too complex or too concerned with pure melody, but the monodic style fitted the bill admirably.

It is most unfortunate that the music of the first opera, *Dafne*, composed in 1597 by Peri, with a few numbers by Corsi, to a libretto by Rinuccini, has been lost, apart from two fragments by Corsi. The earliest opera that has survived intact is *La rappresentazione di anima e di corpo*, by Cavalieri, produced in February 1600. This has frequently, but erroneously, been described as the first oratorio because it was first performed in one of Neri's oratories (see Chapter 2), and because it was meant to be morally edifying, being concerned with 'representations' of the 'soul' and 'body' of man, together with other allegorical figures, such as Pleasure, Intellect, Time, the World, etc. In fact, it is a genuine opera, for apart from a spoken Prologue it consists entirely of solos—mostly written in the new monodic style—choruses, dances, and instrumental interludes, and is accompanied by an orchestra. Moreover, in the Preface, as well as explaining how to 'realize' the harmonies from his figured bass and what vocal ornaments should be used, Cavalieri explicitly states that the work should be acted in a hall or theatre and that the actors' costumes should be both attractive and varied. Indeed, the opera is more forward-looking than and artistically superior to those by Peri and Caccini, because although the recitatives are more monotonous than in either Peri's or Caccini's operas, some of the solos are more frankly tuneful and thus, apart from anticipating the later aria, provide a greater degree of contrast, as do the choruses, of which there are an unusually large number for an Italian opera of any period. Furthermore, the work is divided into three acts, four being the normal number until *c.* 1640 on, and Cavalieri suggests that four intermedii be performed before and after each act, an idea that became very popular in the second half of the century (*H.A.M.*, 183).

Most history books state that the first opera to have survived in its entirety is Peri's *Euridice* (libretto by Rinuccini), presumably because, although it was performed after Cavalieri's opera—namely, October 1600—it is based on a secular subject, the famous legend of Orpheus and Euridice. But the subject of an opera is entirely irrelevant to it as an artistic type, and hence Cavalieri's work should take pride of place. *Euridice* was published in 1601, as was Caccini's setting of the same libretto, but this was not performed until 1602. Caccini, who had managed by devious means to insert some of his own music into Peri's opera, clearly took the latter as a model, for both versions are very similar, the chief distinctions being Peri's greater forcefulness in tragic expression, and Caccini's less rigid monotony of the vocal line. There is hardly any purely instrumental music in either opera, and the few choruses, which occur mainly at the ends of scenes, even when not in unison, reveal very elementary part-writing. Occasionally a solo song in regular metre occurs, but the bulk of both operas consists of long stretches of monody which, even allowing for affective declamation and ornamentation by the singer, soon tire the ear by their lack of variety and by the irritatingly frequent perfect cadences (*H.A.M.*, 182, one of the opera's more expressive passages).

None of the composers of opera or monody so far mentioned were of the first rank, and although the monodic style attracted scores of musicians, none possessed the musical and dramatic genius of the first great operatic composer, Monteverdi. He it was who clothed the bare bones of the early opera with the living flesh of strikingly forceful recitative, sensuous melody, boldly dissonant harmony, and a sense of the dramatic rarely if ever surpassed by later baroque composers. He came to monody via the madrigal, and in his fifth book (1605) the last six madrigals have an obligatory as opposed to an optional continuo part. These six and many of the 'normal' madrigals in both the fourth (1603) and fifth books contain dissonances far exceeding anything by his contemporaries, although his use of chromaticism is not quite so daring as Gesualdo's. Having experimented in continuo writing and choral recitatives (see pp. 269-70) Monteverdi produced his first opera, *Orfeo*, in 1607. This, though based on the same legend, is superior in every way to the *Euridice* of Peri or Caccini. To begin with, the story is made more poignant, because whereas in Rinuccini's libretto no conditions are imposed on Orpheus during the journey from Hades, so that he can look back as much as he likes and the pair are happily reunited (as they are in most later operas on this subject), the poem of Alessandro Striggio (the son of the composer mentioned in Chapter 1, p. 271) keeps to the original ending, even though Monteverdi transports Orpheus to Heaven on the wings of Apollo's compassion. To this famous legend the composer set music that not only enhances its dramatic and emotional possibilities, but which is also a virtually complete cross-section of contemporary styles wedded into a completely satisfying art form. Thus, instead of the almost unbroken monodic line of Peri and Caccini, Monteverdi contrasts his recitatives with choruses in two, three, and five parts, both polyphonic (madrigals) and contrapuntal (balletts), duets for solo voices, instrumental interludes and dances, and even two short lyrical songs in A, B, A form, the form that was to become standard for secular and sacred vocal solos during the seventeenth and eighteenth centuries. The recitative passages, which still predominate, are far more expressive than those of Peri, Caccini, or Cavalieri, both in the actual vocal line and in the accompaniment, and the harmonic audacities of the composer's madrigals are turned to vivid dramatic effect—for example, in the scene where a messenger tells Orpheus of Euridice's fate to the accompaniment of sudden chord changes, such as E major to G minor and C minor to E major or A major (see *H.A.M.*, 187). The choruses and solo duets rarely carry on the action, for, as in Greek tragedy, they stand aside, as it were, and comment on what is happening, and so provide the audience with moments of relaxation and the composer with opportunities to show his musical as well as his dramatic skill; these vocal ensembles, while not so strikingly original as his recitatives, do reveal Monteverdi's all-round mastery of composition.

Perhaps the most remarkable thing about *Orfeo* is the way it is constructed. Here is no haphazard succession of unconnected solos, choruses, etc., but a carefully planned series with a far greater degree of unity than any earlier and many later operas. For example, the Prologue, a monody sung by a symbolical character 'Music', consists of five variations on a ground bass, each variation being separated by a ritornello or instrumental refrain, which is also played at the beginning and end of the Prologue. Act I, which is pastoral and gay, is constructed thus:

Monody (Shepherd)
Chorus A (contrapuntal *a*5)
Monody (Nymph)
Chorus B (polyphonic *a*5) and ritornello I
Monody (Shepherd, Orpheus, Euridice)
Chorus B and ritornello I
Chorus A
Monody (Shepherd)

Ritornello II and Chorus (*a*2)
" " " (*a*3)
" " " (*a*2)

Chorus C (contrapuntal-polyphonic *a*5)
Sinfonia

(N.B.—The choruses *a*2 and *a*3 have different vocal parts, but are supported by the same bass. 'Sinfonia' can be defined as an independent instrumental piece, i.e. not connected with a vocal number, which usually occurs at the beginning and/or end of an act or scene.)

Again, in Act II the messenger's first poignant phrases are later repeated by a shepherd, and finally twice taken up by the chorus in a five-part version.

The above are only some of the ways by which Monteverdi welds what might easily have become a hotchpotch into a homogeneous whole, and this factor, together with the quality of the music itself and the, at times, deliberate choice of instruments to underline a particular dramatic episode, make the work the most outstanding first essay in any musical genre by any composer.

Monteverdi's orchestra in *Orfeo* was larger than in any previous dramatic or semi-dramatic work, and was typical of the Renaissance in the high proportion of chord-playing or 'fundamental' instruments compared to the purely melodic kinds. Thus fifteen of the former are required, including two harpsichords, two wood organs (i.e. positives with flute pipes), one regal, and three viole da gamba. The latter class comprises fourteen stringed and thirteen wind instruments, including four violins, four violas, two 'cellos, two contrabass viols (violins), two small violins, five trombones, cornetts, trumpets, and a flute. Not all these instruments played at the same time, and mostly it was left to the musical director to decide which should play when; at certain places, however, Monteverdi specifies the instrumentation exactly, as in the choruses of Act III, when the spirits of Hades sing to the accompaniment of a regal, positive, five trombones, two bass gambas, and a violone, the regal's reedy, bitter timbre and the bass strings providing a sombre background, to which a solemn note is added by the trombones; trombones, indeed, later became traditionally associated with anything 'infernal', as, for example, in Mozart's *Don Giovanni*. In Act III also occurs 'Possente spirito', in which Orpheus pleads with Charon to let him pass; most of the vocal line exists in two forms, one plain and the other highly ornamented, the latter not only showing how elaborate such embellishments could be, but also serving a dramatic function in that Orpheus is here pouring out all the resources of his art in order to soften Charon's heart. The emotional intensity of the arioso is also increased by dividing the vocal part into short phrases and inserting between each florid passages for two violins, then two cornetts, then harp, and finally two violins and gamba. In the last section Orpheus, up till now supported by the continuo only, is accompanied by an orchestra *a*4, probably the first instance of what was later called *recitativo accompagnato* (see p. 45) ; it makes a most moving climax to his song.

Considering Monteverdi's output in general and the greatness of *Orfeo* in particular, the fact that of his twenty-one dramatic compositions only six—two ballets, a dramatic cantata, and three operas—have survived complete is undoubtedly the most shattering loss in the whole history of music. The single surviving fragment from his next opera, *Arianna* (1608), gives further proof of his outstanding genius, for 'Arianna's Lament' ('Lasciatemi morire') moved the entire audience to tears at the first performance, and not only became the most famous monody of the first half of the century, but set such a fashion that hardly any serious opera of the next 150 years omitted a similar lament. ('When I am laid in earth' from Purcell's *Dido and Aeneas* is perhaps the best-known example outside the Continent.) Its fame prompted Monteverdi to include a five-part arrangement of it in his sixth book of madrigals (1614) (see Ex. 12, p. 270) and a setting to sacred words in his *Selva Morale e Spirituale* ('Collection of Moral and Spiritual Songs') (1641) (Ex. 18*, p. 378).

Both *Orfeo* and *Arianna* were produced in Mantua, where Monteverdi was court composer to the Gonzaga family from 1590 to 1612. In the latter year he was inexplicably dismissed, but after a year of unemployment spent at his native city of Cremona he obtained the post of choirmaster at St. Mark's, Venice, a post he retained until his death, and during which he composed the bulk of his dramatic music. Nothing of this remains except a dramatic cantata and two late operas, but before we discuss these we must see what progress had been made elsewhere by other composers.

After Peri and Caccini had each produced their own versions of *Euridice*, Florence declined as an operatic centre, although a few later operas were staged by these two composers and by Marco da Gagliano [*c.* 1575–1642], whose *Dafne*, to the same libretto as Peri's lost work, was produced in 1610, two years after its first performance in Mantua. Rome and Venice—especially the latter—now became the focal points of operatic development. In Rome Cavalieri's *Rappresentazione* was followed by *Eumelio* (1606), by Agostino Agazzari [1578–1640], which also aimed at moral edification, and, in 1620, by the first purely secular opera to be performed in the Holy City, *Aretusa*, by Filippo Vitali [d. 1653]. Neither of these works advanced much on Florentine ideals, but in *La Catena d'Adone* ('The Chain of Adonis') (1626), by Domenico Mazzochi [1592–1665], Roman opera received a new lease of life. In this work the unending recitative of the Florentines is deliberately broken up by the insertion of arias, the characters become almost frivolous instead of statuesque, and the complexity of the plot is accompanied by all kinds of stage trickery—disguises, abrupt transformation scenes, ascents and descents of gods, etc. In plot and fantastic presentation, as in the number of arias and the rapid patter of much of the recitative as opposed to the

* Melody and bass from *Tutte le Opere di Claudio Monteverdi*, XI, ed. Malipiero. The realization is based to some extent on the five-part madrigalian version.

(Let me die; who do you think can comfort me in such sad misfortune, in so great a martyrdom? Let me die.)

expressive declamation of monody, Mazzochi's work anticipates the general trend of later baroque opera, but in the large number of its choruses it differs from subsequent developments and shows its link with the past—namely, Cavalieri's *Rappresentazione.*

A word must be said here about stage settings and machinery, as they played such an important part in baroque opera; our discussion will be limited to public theatres and those privately owned by certain of the nobility, not to the simple platforms with their roughly painted canvas or wood scenery used in market-squares and fair-grounds by wandering bands of actors.

In the Middle Ages and during most of the Renaissance, stage settings were static, the usual plan consisting of a series of 'flats' (wooden frames covered with canvas) placed at the sides or 'wings' of the stage, and so arranged as to form two solid walls on both sides (Ex. 19, *d*) from the front ('proscenium arch'—*a*) to the back ('cyclorama'—*b*), and painted so as to represent the different scenes simultaneously, the only indications of a scene-change being a series of differently designed flats that partially or wholly screened the cyclorama and which were withdrawn, either into the wings or hoisted ('flown') above the stage, or replaced, revealing or obscuring the one behind (*c*):

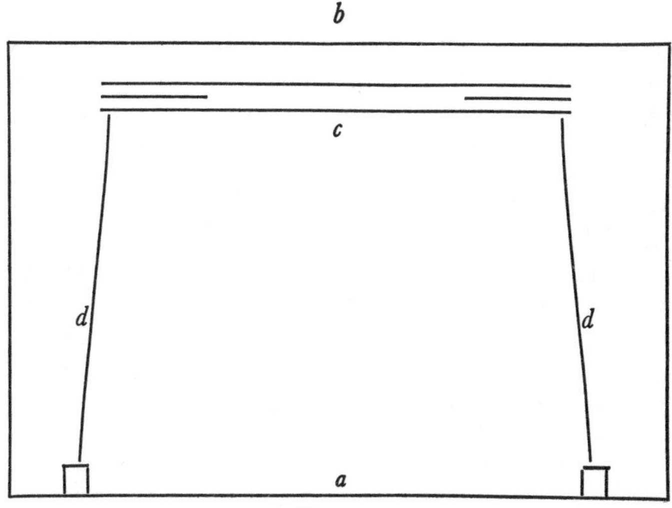

Ex. 19

The combination of the different scenes in the one setting was unrealistic and demanded the imaginative co-operation of the audience, but the realism that, as we have seen, was one of the main characteristics of the Renaissance brought about a change, and in the early years of the sixteenth century an Italian architect, Sebastiano Serlio [1475–1554], applied the then new technique of perspective. Serlio kept the two walls of flats, but painted them so as to represent a single scene, e.g. buildings flanking a street, increasing the natural perspective of the stage as seen from the auditorium by painting the buildings at the cyclorama end smaller than those near the proscenium, thus giving an illusion of greater depth.

The desire for realism brought yet another change, for while Serlio provided designs for three different types of drama—tragedy, comedy, and satire—the static set is less likely to be as realistic as when the scenery changes with the sphere of action. There had been experiments with movable scenery as early as 1530, but it did not become common until the seventeenth century, when public theatres and opera houses found that it was both cheaper and more spectacular than the elaborately painted and constructed static sets. In order to effect scene changes as quickly as possible, the flats were placed parallel to the proscenium and several feet apart, and were either fitted into grooves or else placed on wheeled carriages that ran on rails beneath the stage. In both cases the flats could be quickly withdrawn from or pushed on to the stage (Ex. 20, p. 381). In addition, strips of canvas or cloth ('borders' or 'sky cloths'), painted to match the flats, were suspended across the top of the stage, thus masking the space above the stage (the 'flies'). During the seventeenth and eighteenth centuries the flies housed a number of ropes and pulleys to which were attached not only the borders, which were thus easily raised and lowered to conform to the flats, but also various more or less elaborate 'machines', such as chariots, clouds, bowers, etc. On these one or more characters, usually gods and goddesses, could descend on to or ascend from the stage, or be suspended in mid-air.

Although the spectacular element played such an important part in Mazzochi's *La Catena d'Adone*, this aspect of operatic production was less marked in Rome than elsewhere, probably because it tended to distract the audience's attention from the plot, and the plots of later Roman operas, because of the strong

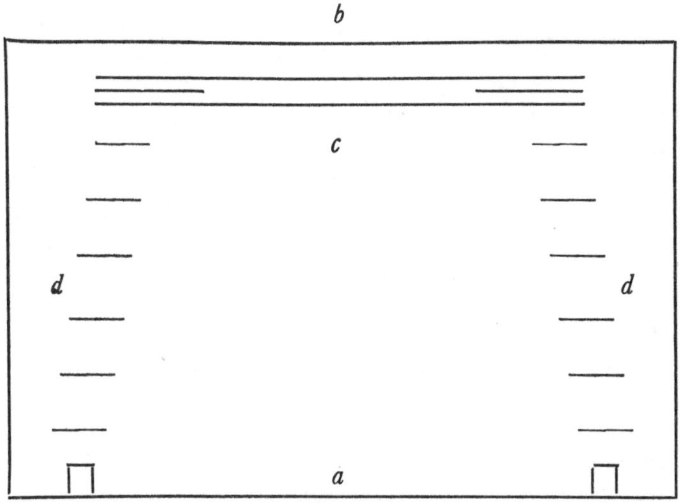

Ex. 20

religious atmosphere and despite the success of Mazzochi's secular opera, were almost invariably moral or religious in tone.

The chief patron of early Roman opera was the Barberini family, particularly Maffeo, who later became Pope Urban VIII [pontificate 1623–1644]. In 1632 the Barberinis built a theatre with a seating capacity of over 3,000, and celebrated its completion with a performance of one of the most important operas of the Roman School, *Sant' Alessio*, by Stefano Landi [*c.* 1590–*c.* 1655]. The libretto, based on the life of St. Alexis [fifth century], is the first to deal with a real flesh and blood individual, and it marked another step along the path of subjective expression, a path that began with Rore, was widened by some of the later madrigalists, notably Gesualdo, and deepened by the Florentine monodists; but whereas the earlier opera composers had been concerned with emotions in general, or had expressed particular ones through legendary or symbolical and therefore universal characters (Orpheus, the Soul of Man, etc.), *Sant' Alessio* is concerned with the emotions of a central figure who actually lived. The other characters, too, are clearly drawn, not from the fifth century, but the seventeenth, and in this and in the inclusion of comic scenes the opera follows the example of *La Catena d'Adone* (*H.A.M.*, 209).

From a purely musical point of view also, *Sant' Alessio* is something of a landmark in that the recitatives are clearly differentiated from the arias, the former approaching the rapid patter or 'secco' ('dry') recitative of later operas, and the latter being more obviously song-like, with occasional use of sequential phrases, and showing at times a definite feeling for form and modern tonality and a striking use of text repetition. This last had been largely rejected by the monodists, but it is a common feature of Renaissance polyphony, where it is employed for musical rather than dramatic ends. Form and tonality from now on become increasingly inseparable, for unity and variety, the twin pillars upon which all musical structures are built, depend more on the relationship and distinction of keys compared to a central key than on anything else. Thus the form A, B, A is not so much a melodic sandwich as a tonal one, because in the middle section the modulations to different keys are usually more striking than are the differences in melody: indeed, melodically B is often a development of A, containing little or no new material; hence variety is achieved largely through the temporary establishment of keys which, while providing a contrast with, also promote a desire to return to the tonic, a desire that is satisfied in the repeat of A, and which also brings a feeling of unity.

Other noteworthy features of Landi's opera are the number of vocal ensembles and choruses, the replacement of viols by violins, and the reduction in numbers and importance of woodwind and brass instruments; the string band is beginning to assume its later function as the backbone of the orchestra, although the harpsichord, lute, theorbo, and harp still play a large part. The theorbo in fact was frequently employed in baroque opera, even as late as Handel, while the harpsichord became the essential instrument of any orchestra, inside or outside the opera house, until after Haydn began to write symphonies.

Some of the instrumental pieces in *Sant' Alessio* are of more than usual interest, particularly the sinfonie that precede the three acts. The sinfonia to Act I consists of a slow chordal section followed by a quicker polyphonic one, an arrangement that became standard in the so-called 'French overture' of Lully and others (see p. 420). The other two sinfonie are in three sections, quick-slow-quick, and anticipate the so-called 'Italian overture' of Alessandro Scarlatti (see Chapter 4, p. 451) (*H.A.M.*, 208).

For over fifty years after *La Catena d'Adone* hardly any serious secular operas, and none of any significance, were produced in Rome. Of the remainder the best is the pastoral opera, *La Galatea* (1639), by the famous castrato, Loreto Vittori [1604–1670], which continues the trend towards clear-cut form through organization of keys in the aria and the rapid patter of secco recitative. (A castrato was a man who, as a boy, had had an exceptionally beautiful treble voice and who was castrated before it broke. This prevented any change in the larynx and resulted in the combination of a voice of great purity and range with the lungs of an adult. Although castrati first appeared in opera in Monteverdi's *Orfeo*, the practice had been common in the sixteenth century, but the importance in opera of the solo singer brought the castrati to the fore, and from *c.* 1650 to *c.* 1750 the more famous of them were sought after by opera-houses as keenly and acclaimed by opera-goers as vociferously as the top-ranking stars of today are by film companies and audiences.) There is, however, one serious secular Roman opera, but it was produced in Paris. In 1644, when Pope Urban VIII died, the Barberinis were forced to emigrate by his successor, Innocent X [pontificate 1644–1655]. They settled in Paris, where Cardinal Mazarin [1602–1661], who had succeeded Cardinal Richelieu [1585–1642] as 'prime minister' of France, made it possible for them to bring many of their musicians. Among these was Luigi Rossi [1598–1653], and his *Orfeo* (1647), while not the first Italian opera to be performed in Paris, was the first to be commissioned and expressly written for the French capital. Dramatically it is a hotchpotch of comedy, tragedy, ballets, and spectacles, but the musical numbers, although as varied as the plot, show more clearly than any other opera hitherto the refinement and sensuousness of melody and harmony which is the hall-mark of Italian music from *c.* 1650 onwards.

In 1653 the Barberinis, having become reconciled to Innocent X, returned to Rome, and to mark the occasion a comic opera with the appropriate title *Dal male il bene* ('Good from Evil') was performed. The music is by Antonio Maria Abbatini [*c.* 1598–1680] and Marco Marazzoli [d. 1662], and the libretto was by a friend of the Barberinis, Giulio Respigliosi [1600–1669], who for the last two years of his life was Pope

Clement IX. This man was virtually the creator of Italian comic opera, for, apart from writing the libretti of several serious operas, including *Sant' Alessio* with its comic scenes, he was the author of the first comic opera text, *Chi soffre, speri*, produced in the Barberini theatre in 1639, with music by Marazzoli and Vergilio Mazzochi [1597–1646], brother of Domenico, and witnessed by a distinguished gathering, including Mazarin and John Milton. The plot is romantic, the comedy being provided by stock characters taken over from the *Commedia dell' Arte* (see Chapter 1, p. 271). Musically it is interesting in that its recitatives follow the rapid patter or secco type already noted in *La Galatea*, but it is less important than *Dal male il bene*, for this work, while continuing the marked distinction between recitative and aria, includes a feature which later became one of the main characteristics of *opera buffa*—namely, the ensembles (i.e. pieces for two or more soloists—duets, trios, etc.—as opposed to the chorus) which occur at the end of each act (see p. 483).

The year 1639 not only saw the birth of comic opera in Rome, but also the production, in December, of Monteverdi's opera, *Adone*, his first to be produced in the first public opera-house in Europe. This had been opened in 1637 through the private enterprise of the famous theorbo-player, Benedetto Ferrari [1597–1681], and the composer, Francesco Manelli [1595–1667], under the name of Teatro di San Cassiano. All operas up to this year and many of them after it were performed in the private theatres of the aristocracy, such as that in the Barberini Palace, and it is an indication of the popularity and importance of Venetian opera that it was in this city, where, as we saw in Chapter 1, the seeds of baroque art found their richest soil, that the most characteristic type of Italian music from the seventeenth century to the present day was first made accessible to the man in the street. But the man in the street has never the same taste and understanding as the aristocratic connoisseur, and as he who pays the piper calls the tune, the tunes and their harmonizations, the libretti, and the productions as a whole underwent a remarkable transformation. Melodies became simpler and eminently singable, except for those virtuosic passages in which the composer gave the singer scope to show off his vocal acrobatics, rhythms became more obvious, and harmonies tended increasingly to crystallize round a firm major or minor centre. This last affected form, which became more clear-cut, because the stronger the tonal centre the greater the effect of modulation away from and back to this centre, unity being achieved through the repetition, often sequential, of melodic-rhythmic motives. The libretti, using the legends of classical antiquity simply as pegs on which to hang some kind of plot, are so constructed as to present a series of rapidly changing scenes in which the characters are either mere symbols of emotions or else provide comic relief.

Naturally, the man in the street was not entirely responsible for this transformation, for we have already seen that developments in Roman opera included more tuneful arias, a clearer sense of tonality and form, and abrupt, often fantastic, changes in scene, but he was unquestionably responsible for the speed at which it took place. Moreover, Venetian opera only reflected, albeit more strikingly than elsewhere, the changing literary and musical tastes of the times. Italian literature, already in decline during the Counter-Reformation, reached its lowest ebb during the seventeenth century. In poetry, prose, and drama there was hardly a writer with a spark of originality or genuine feeling, and, as so often happens, for this lack was substituted an extravagancy and insincerity of expression that but thinly disguises the underlying poverty of invention. The most suitable sphere for such an art was the theatre, where exaggeration, whether of plot, gesture, look, or speech, in order to communicate, is more often both necessary and natural than in either poetry or prose. And here we must make a distinction between 'dramatic' and 'theatrical'; the former, in its colloquial sense, means the occurrence, in any sphere of life, of an unusual, often striking, and always emotionally heightened event or succession of events, either actual in the present or the past, or fictitious, or an idea or succession of ideas (including the products of artistic imagination). Theatrical, also in its colloquial sense, means 'presented in an exaggerated manner', but, in view of what we have said above, it is not, neither should it be, used as a derogatory adjective when applied to the stage. Thus a symphony or a century at Lord's may be dramatic but should never be theatrical, whereas an opera or play should be both.

Theatricality permeated the whole of seventeenth-century Italian culture; it even invaded the Church, where not only the Jesuits (and after them other monastic orders) used the theatre as a means of propagating their religion, but the priest in the pulpit and even the liturgy itself, much of which is inherently dramatic, became affected; so much so that some foreign visitors were scandalized, finding little to choose in atmosphere and presentation between church and stage.

The change in musical taste was the result of the growing desire for greater emotional expression, a desire that, as we noted earlier, began with Rore. So long as polyphony held sway, however, the degree of expressiveness was checked, for polyphony is essentially classical in function in the sense that it tends to promote a balance between the various musical elements (melody, harmony, rhythm), as well as between the individual parts themselves. The declamatory madrigals of the Gabrielis and the chromaticism of Gesualdo stretched polyphony almost to breaking-point, but the desire for greater expression which they represented found complete freedom in the Florentine monody, and the way was open once again for Italian genius to express itself most naturally—that is, through the supremacy of melody. Ever since she had created, virtually single-handed, the magnificent repertoire of Christian chant, Italy had had to contend, so to speak, with part-music, and it is no coincidence that on the three occasions during the reign of polyphony, i.e. from the twelfth to the sixteenth centuries, on which she produced something distinctive her natural bent asserted itself. Thus, compared to the music of other countries, the upper voice or voices of the Ars Nova madrigal and caccia are more prominent and singable, the top part of the late fifteenth- and early sixteenth-century frottola is more clear-cut and 'popular', or else recitative-like with the accompaniment, on at least one occasion, reduced to a few simple chords (see Part I, Chapter 6, p. 210), and lastly the vocal part-music of the late sixteenth century, especially the madrigal, is more sensuous and colourful, with a distinct bias towards high voices. In this connexion, it should be remembered that Italian composers only came to the fore at the very end of the Renaissance; in fact, apart from Palestrina, who, as we have seen, was not fully representative of his time or country, the leading men —Marenzio, the Gabrielis, and Gesualdo—produced most of their work contemporaneously with the monodies of the Florentine Camerata. Furthermore, the amount of frankly popular music, such as carnival songs and balletti, was far greater than elsewhere in Europe, and the madrigal in which the soprano voice predominates was essentially the creation of an Italian—Luzzaschi.

But to return to Venice and Monteverdi. *Adone* was not only his first opera for the first public opera-house, but the first opera by a great composer that the public ever witnessed, and as we know it was a resounding success, it is doubly unfortunate that the music has been lost. However, its popularity prompted Monteverdi to compose three more operas, *Il Ritorno d'Ulisse*, *Le nozze d'Eneo con Lavinia* (music lost), and *L'incoronazione di Poppea*. The first of these was produced at the same theatre as *Adone*—the San Cassiano—in 1641, while the other two appeared in 1641 and 1642 respectively at the Santi Giovanni e Paolo, the second public opera-house in Venice, opened in 1639. This creative activity when the composer was between seventy-two and seventy-five years old inevitably brings to mind his great nineteenth-century compatriot, Verdi, who wrote his last two operas, *Otello* and *Falstaff*, when he was aged seventy-four and eighty.

The two operas that have survived of Monteverdi's last four show a profound difference in style and approach when compared to *Orfeo*, a difference that is more marked in *Ulisse* than in *Poppea*, for the earlier work is more typically Venetian in the rapid succession of scenes—comic, serious, or spectacular—the quick patter of its recitative, which is frequently broken up by short, song-like passages, the infrequency of instrumental numbers, and the way in which every opportunity for emotional expression is seized; as one writer has well said, "one senses the effort to be immediately understood, along with an almost nervous dread of monotony . . .".* Despite some fine musical and dramatic moments, the opera is inferior to *Poppea*, Monteverdi's last essay in this genre. Here the composer's musical taste and dramatic insight largely reject the purely spectacular and the restless succession of scenic contrasts, relying more on the vivid and subtle characterization of the leading figures in the drama, and it was surely no accident that Monteverdi chose an historical plot concerned with the ambitions and emotions of real people. *Poppea*, in fact, is the first great historical opera, foreshadowed by Landi's *Sant' Alessio* and succeeded by a large number on similar themes,

* D. Grout, *A Short History of Opera*, I, p. 87.

but although it was much admired for the brilliance of its characterization, its genuine passion, and the quality of its music, operatic taste, whetted by typical Venetian fare, preferred the sensuousness of pure melody, the excitement of coloratura (virtuoso) singing, and the fascination of gorgeous and variegated spectacles to the more profound, subtle, and hence less easily appreciated (or created) art, wherein music and drama achieve some kind of balance. In most baroque operas, indeed, the characters are treated as symbolical types, not as living flesh-and-blood individuals, the composer being far less concerned with the dramatic situations and characterization than with the purely musical side, and provided that the latter satisfied both its own artistic laws and the audience's love of melody and vocal display, it was quite on the cards that he would write a work that was both excellent of its kind and a 'smash-hit'. Moreover, a second- or third-rate composer with little sense of overall structure or of dramatic situation, but who could write catchy tunes and cater for virtuosity, found it easier to make his mark in serious music than in any other period of history, for at no other time was melody exalted to so high a position.

But we anticipate, because both Monteverdi and his contemporaries maintained some kind of balance between rhythm, melody, and harmony, and between music and drama. In *Poppea* the balance is well-nigh perfect, the music springing directly from the personalities of the characters and their interaction with each other, and revealing a marvellous variety in treatment—secco recitative, arioso, songs in *da capo* aria form (A, B, A), strophic and through-composed songs, songs with ritornelli, and songs supported by a ground bass (see Ex. 21: we shall define a ground, or ground bass, or 'basso ostinato' as a continuous set of variations built on a short recurring motive which is restricted to the lowest part). In order to give some idea of the passion and beauty of the music in this opera, here is the last section of the duet (in A, B, A form) between Poppea and Nero with which the opera ends. In the original the part of Nero was sung by a castrato (soprano), but no violence is done by the substitution of a natural male voice (Ex. 21*, pp. 389, 390).

So long as the music to *Adone* is lost, we cannot tell whether

* Melody, bass, and translation from *Songs and Duets from the Works of Claudio Monteverdi*, No. 3, ed. J. A. Westrup.

Ex.21 The end of the duet Pur ti miro (L'incoronazione di Poppea) (1642)
Monteverdi
(𝅗𝅥 = ♩ = MM.c.72)
Poppea
Pur ti mi - - ro, pur ti mi - - ro, pur ti
I be - hold thee, I be - hold thee, I en-
Nero
Pur ti go - - do, pur ti go - - do,
I en - joy thee, I en - joy — thee,
strin - - - - - - - go, pur ti strin - go, pur t'an-
- fold thee, I en - fold thee, I em-
pur t'an - no - - - - - - - - - - - - - do, pur ti strin - - - -
I em - brace thee, I en - fold
- no - - - - - - - - - - do, Più non pe - - - - no, non
- brace thee, Now I sigh not, I
- - - go, pur ti strin - go, Più non mo - - -
thee, I en - fold thee, Now I die

Ex.21 (contd.)

* The small notes are editorial and are necessary owing to Nero's part being an octave lower than the original.

Monteverdi's style in this opera owed more to public taste than to the work of his gifted pupil, Pietro Francesco Calletti-Bruni [1602–1676], who, as often happened, adopted the name of his patron, Cavalli, and who was the first great popular operatic composer. January 1639, the same year that *Adone* was produced, saw the performance of Cavalli's first opera, *Le nozze di Teti e di Peleo* at the San Cassiano Theatre. This, the first of forty-two operas, two-thirds of which have survived in score, and the first Venetian opera of which the music has been preserved, shows a greater preference, compared with Monteverdi's late operas, for simple, graceful melodies in which the whole consists of well-balanced sections; Cavalli, in fact, ushered in the style known later as *bel canto*, which reached its peak in the late baroque and in which, in marked contrast to recitative patter and monodic affective declamation, melody is all-important—melody typified by smooth-flowing, sensuous lines, sequential patterns, a slowish tempo, and a simplicity of movement that is not destroyed by occasional florid passages. As a result, the character of the bass tends to that of the melody, even to the point of actual imitation, harmony is unobtrusive, with occasional flashes of chromaticism, and rhythm is simple and usually in triple metre, because the melodic flow is naturally smoother in this than in duple metre as the strong accent occurs less frequently. (Quadruple metre is really an extension of duple, for there is a strong secondary accent on the third beat.) Most of these features can be seen in Ex. 22c.

With Cavalli *bel canto* style is not yet an end in itself, but only a means, and although he favoured the aria more than his master, the drama, not the music, is still the backbone, as it were, of his operas, the most famous of which was *Giasone* (1649). Thus, as with Monteverdi, Cavalli selects his musical type—secco recitative, arioso, or aria—according to its dramatic fitness, and not as a result of purely musical considerations (Ex. 22,* pp. 392-4. See also *H.A.M.*, 206).

Like Monteverdi also—indeed, like Venetian opera-composers in general—Cavalli wrote few instrumental numbers and fewer choruses: in fact, none of his operas written between 1644 and 1661, representing the bulk of his total output, contain any choruses at all. The reason for this was the public's preference

* Melody and bass from R. Haas, *Musik des Baroks*, pp. 136–8.

Ex.22(a) Secco recitative Alle ruine (La Didone I.7) (1641)
Cavalli
Hecuba
Al - le ru - - i - - ne del mio Re - - - - gno a - dun - que so - pra -
Thus, by the ru - ins of my king - - - dom, I, an old weak
- vi - vo de-cre - pi - ta, e son giun - ta a ri - pu - tar il pian - to,
wo - man, sur vive, a - las, And I now do be - lieve that tears and weep-ing
te - sti - mon tri - vi - - al de miei do - - lo - - ri.
low - ly wit - - nes - ses are of my deep sor - - row
(etc.)

Ex.22(b) From the arioso - *L'alma fiacca svanì (La Didone I A)*

(𝅗𝅥 = MM.c.54)

Ex.22 (c) Aria - Padre, ferma i passi (La Didone I.1)
(d=d-MM.c.84)
Ascanio
Pa-dre, fer-ma i pas-si e l'ar-mi, non la-
Fa-ther, halt thy steps and wea--pons, This fair
-sciar que-sta ma-gio-ne, non sò dir--ti
house leave not I pray thee, I've no rea--son
al-tra ra--gio---ne, non do--ve--vi ge-ne-
else to gain-say thee, Thou should'st ne--ver have con-
-rar--mi, se vo--le--vi ab-ban-do--nar--mi.
-ceiv'd me If thou e'er de--sir-ed to leave me.
(4 more verses)

for solo singing, and as this meant that the management had to spend a great deal in engaging 'star' performers, and as most of what was left went on scenery in order to satisfy the demand for the spectacular, there was precious little left for the chorus. The orchestra too was much less important than in the earlier part of the century, and its size and constitution had undergone a marked transformation. This had been heralded as early as 1624 in Monteverdi's dramatic cantata, *Il Combattimento di Tancredi e Clorinda* ('The Combat of Tancred and Clorinda'), in which the heterogeneous assortment of instruments called for in *Orfeo* is replaced by a harpsichord and string band. *Il Combattimento* is important not only because it marks the beginning of the modern orchestra in the sense that the strings are the fundamental unit, but also because it increased the dramatic rôle of instrumental accompaniment through the use of, for example, reiterated rhythmic figures to denote a galloping horse, and rapid, repeated notes (tremolo) and plucked strings (pizzicato) to depict the clash and fury of the fight (see *H.A.M.*, 189). The idea of pizzicato seems to have been invented by Monteverdi himself, and he was also the first to use tremolo for dramatic purposes, although the device itself occurs in a few earlier violin pieces. This participation by the orchestra in the drama did not catch on in Venetian opera until later in the century, and during Cavalli's time instruments were entirely subservient to the voice. Even the introductory sinfonia was reduced to a few bars of slow, solemn chords, usually in duple time, that can have done little more than call the audience's attention to the fact that the opera was about to commence. Actually, Cavalli's *Giasone* is something of an exception in that the slow section is followed by a quick one in triple time in which the opening theme is derived from that of the preceding movement.

In the same year and month, but not in the same theatre, that *Giasone* was produced, the first opera, *Orontea*, by Pietro Cesti [1623–1669] was performed at the opening of the fifth public opera-house in Venice. Most writers from the eighteenth century to the present day have replaced 'Pietro' by 'Marc Antonio', this presumably being a corruption of 'Frate Antonio', a title he adopted on his admission to Minor Orders in 1637. Cesti is usually and rightly regarded as a Venetian composer, because although he spent very little of his life in Venice, oscillating between Rome, Innsbruck, and Vienna, and although only a small proportion of his operas were first performed in Venice, his style is typically Venetian. Of the 100 or so operas that Cesti is supposed to have written, only fifteen have survived, including his three most famous, *Orontea*, *La Dori* (Florence, 1661), and *Il pomo d'oro* (Vienna, 1667). In general his operas owe much to those of Cavalli, but in particular he widens the distinction between recitative and aria and carries the *bel canto* style a stage further, applying it to his ensembles (duets, trios, etc.); with Monteverdi and Cavalli these last are still somewhat madrigalian in their use of imitation, but Cesti favours the sensuousness of parallel thirds and sixths.

We have stated earlier in this history that when composers stress any one aspect of music the other aspects tend to be neglected or simplified. This is true of *bel canto* style, and one result is the lack of harmonic variety, compared to Monteverdi or Cavalli, of Cesti's and later Venetian composers' accompaniments; Cesti, indeed, relies to an almost irritating extent at times on tonic, dominant, and subdominant chords, and rarely moves away from closely related keys. With him *bel canto* style became the first real instance of homophony in the history of music, for by homophony we mean a texture in which an all-important melody (sometimes doubled in thirds and sixths) is provided with an essentially chordal accompaniment. Admittedly a number of Renaissance lute songs tend towards homophony, but in the great majority of cases the lute accompaniment is basically contrapuntal or polyphonic, even if it is not in fact an arrangement of the lower voices of a part-song. In real homophony, however, the harmony is conceived as a progression of chords, not as a combination of melodic lines, and hence the movement of the lower parts is quite unimportant, provided, of course, that in ensembles (but by no means necessarily on the harpsichord) consecutive fifths and octaves are avoided (compare the definitions of counterpoint and polyphony in Part I, p. 48). This explains why *bel canto* accompaniments for continuo only were preferred to full orchestra until well into the late baroque, as the former allows the melody greater prominence.

The harmonic restriction of Cesti's *bel canto* style was not only an outcome of letting melody predominate, but also the result of a greater concern for a central tonality. Cesti, in fact, belonged to the generation of composers who marked the watershed, so to speak, between the period when the idea of a central tonality was not yet established and when chromaticism was used for purely emotional ends (as in Monteverdi and Cavalli, e.g. Ex. 22b and c) and the period when the idea had become firmly rooted and chromaticism was used both emotionally and to contrast with or offset the main key without disturbing its central position. The most notable feature of Cesti's chromaticism is his use of the so-called 'Neapolitan sixth' chord, which nearly always occurs in minor keys and which can be described as the first inversion of the flattened supertonic. Thus in Ex. 23b, bar 5, the key is D minor, but the first inversion of B♭ major is treated as the flattened supertonic (Neapolitan sixth) in A minor, for it is followed by the last inversion of the dominant seventh in A (bar 6), and later by a perfect cadence in A (bars 7–8). The same progression occurs in bars 9–12, but a fourth higher, i.e. in D minor. (N.B.—The lowest note of the Neapolitan sixth usually moves up a step to the dominant of the key, e.g. D–E in A minor or G–A in D minor.) (Ex. 23*, pp. 398-9).

The growing concern for a central tonality shown by all composers during the latter half of the seventeenth century is also apparent in the number of pieces (much greater in this period than in the eighteenth century) which are either wholly or mainly built round an ostinato motive. These motives invariably consist of a progression from tonic to dominant and so back to the next statement (Exx. 21 and 23a), or else from tonic to tonic, and were either restricted to the bass (basso ostinato), as in Exx. 21 and 23a, or else occasionally invaded the upper parts (passacaglia). By reiterating the tonic to dominant or tonic to tonic progression, these motives helped to underline the main key, even though the separate notes of the motive were not always harmonized in exactly the same way.

In rhythm and melody, as well as harmony, Cesti shows less variety than Monteverdi or Cavalli, favouring smoother contours and regular, often sequential, patterns. His cadences, too, occur more frequently, and almost invariably comprise the progression subdominant (or supertonic first inversion)–dominant–tonic (IV (or IIA)–V–I) of whatever key he happens

* Melody and bass from *Alte Meister des Bel canto*, ed. Landshoff.

(Come, Alidoro, come, comfort one who is dying!)

to be in. Some of his melodies are long-breathed, but most of them are constructed of short phrases; these last are, in fact, no shorter than those of most individual voice parts in late Renaissance polyphony, but the latter, by overlapping the phrases of the different voices, avoids the frequent 'full stops' of the early *bel canto* style. Harmonic restriction, rhythmic simplicity, and melodic short-windedness are also characteristic of the style that formed the bridge between Bach and Haydn, and when in the works of some late baroque composers and in the Viennese School, polyphony reasserted itself, harmony became more varied, rhythm more subtle and flexible, and melody more sustained. Polyphony, in fact, is and always has been a richer vehicle of expression than homophony, for it not only maintains a balance between the various musical elements, but it also reveals more completely what is perhaps the most unique and wonderful aspect of music—the ability to present distinct and individual ideas (i.e. strands of sound) within an integrated and satisfying whole.

Cesti was probably the most popular operatic composer before Alessandro Scarlatti (see Chapter 4), and the seal was set on his fame by *Il pomo d'oro*, written for the wedding of the Emperor Leopold I of Austria [reigned 1658–1705] with the Infanta Margherita of Spain, and performed in Vienna in 1667. The occasion made this opera something of an exception to the normal Venetian type, and, apart from costing a small fortune to produce with its sixty-seven scenes, forty-eight characters and twenty-four different stage settings (some of them requiring the most elaborate machinery—see Plates XXVII and XXVIII), there are a number of ballets and choruses (one in eight parts) and an unusually large orchestra, including trumpets, trombones, cornetts, bassoons, lutes, and a regal, in addition to the customary string band and harpsichord (see Plate XXVI).

Cesti's operas represent one point at which the swing of the pendulum away from polyphony started to move back (N.B. the part-writing in *H.A.M.*, 221), for his Venetian successors, while cultivating the *bel canto* style as ardently as ever, began to enrich their vocal ensembles and instrumental accompaniments with real part-writing, and hand in hand with this came an expansion of melody, harmony, and form. This development is clearly seen in the works of the three most outstanding opera composers between Cesti and A. Scarlatti, Giovanni Legrenzi [1626–1690], Alessandro Stradella [1642–1682], and Carlo Pallavicino [*c.* 1630–1688]; with them the aria becomes more spacious, with frequent sequential passages (in Pallavicino's operas especially), the orchestra plays a larger part, accompanying the voice more often than in Cavalli's or Cesti's arias (in most of which the harmonic support is provided by the continuo), forms are more varied and include, besides the *da capo*, such types as A, B (binary form) A_1 B_2 B_1, A_1 B_2 B_1 C_2 C_1, etc. (1 = tonic key, 2 = different key(s)), there is a greater variety of harmonic resource and modulation, now set within a firm tonal framework, and the instrumental writing, especially the bass, is more interesting, often anticipating in a short ritornello the main theme of an aria before the voice takes it up. (*H.A.M.*, 241). This last feature, indeed, was sometimes applied to the introductory sinfonia, as, for example, in *Il pomo d'oro*, where the second main theme of the overture reappears later as a chorus. This brings to mind Monteverdi's *Orfeo* (see p. 375), and in some ways, e.g. the greater importance of the orchestra and the less haphazard structure of the whole, mid-baroque opera partially returns to the ideals of the first great operatic composer. In addition, a number of arias begin with a short vocal phrase or 'motto' expressive of the main mood, a feature typical of many of Cesti's arias. (For the full significance of the 'motto' beginning, see Chapter 4, p. 440.)

Side by side with and yet in opposition to this trend towards expansion and enrichment came a pronounced preference for rhythmically simple and melodically catchy songs. Occasionally the two tendencies can be found in a single aria, as when a simple vocal line is supported by a bass that is either florid or else provides scope for a wide range of chords.

The tremendous impact of Italian Renaissance culture overflowed into the baroque era, and the rest of Europe would have followed Italy's lead, for a time at any rate, no matter what kind of music she had produced. Thus the transalpine countries adopted opera, but only with varying degrees of success, and the enthusiasm for this particular art form was and still is more completely natural and spontaneous in the country that gave it birth than any other art form has been in any other country.

That Austria, the southern German states, and Bohemia imported Italian opera before the rest of Europe was only to be expected when one considers their geographical position and remembers the interchange of musicians between the two regions during the Renaissance. Cesti's *Il pomo d'oro* was by no means the first Italian opera to cross the Alps, this distinction, so far as we know, being held by *Andromeda*, by Giralomo Giacobbi (?) [1567–1629], performed in Salzburg in 1618. Other cities followed suit, and performances are recorded at Prague from 1627, Innsbruck from 1655 (where Cesti was employed, though frequently absent, from 1652 to 1666), Regensberg from 1653, and Munich, where the first opera-house was opened in 1657.

The opera produced in Regensberg in 1653 was *L'inganno d'amore*, by Antonio Bertali [1605–1669], who lived in Vienna from *c.* 1623 to his death, was appointed court conductor in 1649, and who first introduced regular performances of Italian opera into the Austrian capital (the first recorded performance took place in 1626). Vienna, for obvious reasons, soon became the main centre of Italian opera outside Italy, and in Antonio Draghi [1635–1700], who resided in the city from *c.* 1658 to his death, she found the most prolific operatic composer of the seventeenth century, whose mature style is similar to that of Legrenzi, Stradella, and Pallavicino.

During the latter half of the century Italian opera spread to most of the other large German cities, among them Dresden, the capital of Saxony, where the Elector held court. Here in 1687 Pallavicino was appointed director of the first permanent opera house, although the first operatic performance dates from 1662. But Dresden is associated with a far greater name than Pallavicino, for Heinrich Schütz [1585–1672], the greatest German composer before Bach and, with Monteverdi, Lully and Purcell, the most outstanding musician of the century, was director of the electoral chapel from 1617 to his death. Although Schütz greatly admired and was considerably influenced by Giovanni Gabrieli, whose pupil he was from 1609 to 1612, and although his enthusiasm for the new Italian music, especially that of Monteverdi, prompted him to cross the Alps a second time in 1628, he never became completely Italianate, as did many of his contemporaries and successors. Thus the delight in expressive polyphony, chromatic harmony, and colourful sonority which he imbibed from Gabrieli, and the dramatic recitative, lyrical melody, and sensuous use of thirds and sixths which he learnt from later Italian composers, were restrained by that meditative, philosophic outlook on life that has always been one of the chief characteristics of his countrymen and which he possessed to a marked degree.

In 1627 Sophia Eleonora, Princess of Saxony, was married in the Saxon town of Torgau, and to mark the occasion Schütz wrote an opera, *Dafne*. The libretto is largely a translation of Rinuccini's text for Peri's opera of 1597, and, like the earlier work, the music is lost. This is doubly unfortunate, because it was Schütz's only opera and the first by a German composer.

The earliest German opera that has survived intact is *Seelewig*, by Sigmund Theophil Staden [1607–1655], produced in Nuremberg in 1644. This is more in the Roman than Venetian tradition, as it is described as a 'spiritual pastorale', and is concerned with the attempts of the 'false deceiver' Trügewalt, aided and abetted by allegorical figures representing Art and the Senses, to capture the 'soul' (Seelewig), but she, with the help of Wisdom and Conscience, evades their evil designs, and virtue ends triumphant. The setting is pastoral, the characters being nymphs, shepherds, and satyrs, while the music consists almost entirely of short, lyrical strophic songs, the through-composed dramatic or impassioned recitatives being conspicuous by their absence, and there are a number of instrumental pieces. The orchestra is remarkable in that there is no part for a harpsichord, theorbo and lute being the only chord-playing instruments, the others consisting of violins, a viola, recorders, flutes, shawms, bassoons, and a horn. Each character or group is associated with a definite instrumental ensemble, e.g. strings and recorders accompany the nymphs, flutes and shawms the shepherds, while the horn is reserved for Trügewalt.

Although the few German operas that are known to have been written during the first seventy-five years of the seventeenth century almost certainly do not constitute the total number actually produced, it is clear that in the south, where Italian influence was strongest, native opera simply could not compete against the constant flow from across the Alps. But even in the north native opera found difficulty in taking root owing to the political and cultural divisions characteristic of the whole country, divisions that were more pronounced than anywhere else in Europe, and which were aggravated by the so-called Thirty Years' War (1618–48). Initially this was an outcome of the Reformation and Counter-Reformation, but it soon developed into a purely political affair. The chief contestants were France and the Habsburg Dynasty, and before it ended two Holy Roman Emperors, Ferdinand II [reigned 1619–1637], and Ferdinand III [reigned 1637–1657], and the Spanish King Philip IV [reigned 1621–1665], three of the most powerful Catholic rulers of their time, were opposed by the Catholic King of France, Louis XIII [reigned 1610–1643], his astute adviser, Cardinal Richelieu, and by the Pope himself, Urban VIII; Richelieu, while he had bitterly persecuted the Huguenots, had no scruples in forming alliances with the Protestant countries of Sweden, Denmark, Holland, and England.

While the Treaty of Westphalia (1648) marked the end of the war and settled the religious frontiers of central Europe, it brought even greater political disunity to the German States, because the homage, however slight, that each State had formerly paid to the Emperor had now gone, as the Treaty recognized the absolute sovereignty of each ruler within his own territory. The war did not affect the States so acutely as is sometimes supposed, for the devastation only visited certain strategic areas and economic stability actually increased during the latter part of the struggle, due in no small part to the founding, in 1619, of the 'Hamburger Bank', which, despite the huge inflation of 1620–3, improved the value of German currency. Hamburg, a flourishing port whose history and tradition of independent government had much in common with Venice, was of all the large German towns the most northerly. She was thus less influenced by Italian music, and it is no coincidence that not only did she build, in 1678, the first public opera house in Europe, apart from those in Venice, but she also became the home of German opera.

The Hamburg opera-house was inaugurated by a performance of *Adam und Eva*, by Johann Theile [1646–1724], a pupil of Schütz; while the music is unfortunately lost, the libretto tells us what we might have guessed anyway, that this is a moral opera. But although a number of similar operas were written during the succeeding years, indicative of the characteristic German seriousness noted earlier, and partially placating that body of Lutheran opinion that inveighed against the worldliness and immorality of the stage, the secular element proved too strong, and plots and translated libretti from the Italian and French theatres soon predominated. In addition, a number of Italian operas were produced in their original language, and sometimes a compromise was reached in which the arias were sung in Italian and the recitatives in the vernacular, a practice that was adopted elsewhere and which has been adversely criticized by some historians, but which is not as absurd as it seems, as we hope to show in the next chapter.

Despite the strength of foreign influence, particularly from

Italy, the actual music of the Hamburg German opera school reveals several independent features, and the leading composers, Johann Georg Conradi [d. *c.* 1694], Johann Wolfgang Franck [*c.* 1641–after 1695], and Johann Sigismund Kusser [1660–1727], all show a less virtuosic vocal line, a preference for long-phrased melodies in contrast to the shorter, snappier tunes of the Italians, and a recitative style that is more akin to the arioso than to the Venetian recitativo secco. In addition, Conradi and Franck wrote most of their arias in simple binary form (i.e. A, B), whereas Kusser, who was the most cosmopolitan of the group, preferred the Italian *da capo* form. Kusser, in fact, is the most important composer of the three, as not only did he probably teach and certainly influence the greatest composer of German operas in the entire baroque period, Reinhard Keiser (see Chapter 4, p. 462), but also profoundly affected the course of German instrumental music during the early years of the eighteenth century. The source of his influence on Keiser was Italy, and on instrumental music France, and it is to the operatic developments in the latter country that we now turn.

Earlier in this chapter we stated that Rossi's *Orfeo*, produced in Paris in 1647, was not the first Italian opera to be performed in the capital; it was in fact preceded by at least three others during the previous two years, all of them under the patronage of Mazarin, who, knowing the French nobility's love of entertainment, used them as means of distracting his opponents from the powerful position he was building up for himself. That he was temporarily unsuccessful and was one of the main causes of the civil war that lasted from 1648 to 1653 is reflected in the fact that the next performance of an Italian opera did not take place until 1654. Only two more performances followed during the ensuing eighteen years, not because Mazarin had lost interest in the art of his native land, or power in the country of his adoption, but because Frenchmen, while admiring the skill and invention that could clothe an entire play with music, were not enthusiastic over the way in which it was done, although naturally enough they enjoyed the ballets which were specially introduced in order to satisfy French taste, and were enthralled by the stage machinery invented by Giacomo Torelli that raised the spectacular element to a pitch never before seen in France.

Although France, unlike Germany and, as we shall see, England, repelled the first invasion of Italian opera, she was sufficiently attracted to try to create her own. The two earliest attempts (the music of both is lost) were *Akebar, roi de Mogol*, by a certain Abbé Mailly, performed at Carpentras (near Avignon) in 1646, and *Le Triomphe de l'Amour sur des bergers et bergères*, by Michel de La Guerre [*c.* 1605–1679], performed at the Louvre, Paris, in 1655, and again before Louis XIV [reigned 1643–1715] in 1657. In a dedicatory letter to the King, La Guerre calls his piece "une Comédie française en Musique", and claims that it is the first of its kind in France ('comédie' meant 'drama', not 'comedy'; see p. 410). Two years later an almost exactly similar claim was made by Robert Cambert [*c.* 1628–1677] for his comédie, *Pastorale* (music lost), produced at Issy (near Paris) in April 1659 and then, at Mazarin's suggestion, at Vincennes before the King. His Majesty was delighted, and, thus encouraged, Cambert and his librettist, Pierre Perrin [*c.* 1620–1675], continued in their collaboration, the next fruits of which were *Ariane, ou le Mariage de Bachus* and *Pomone*. It is almost certain that *Ariane* was completed by 1661, but in that year Mazarin died and performance was indefinitely postponed. Thirteen years later an opera with the same title and with Perrin's libretto was produced in London, but, according to the title-page, with music by Cambert's pupil, Louis Grabu [d. after 1694]. Cambert himself was in London at the time and in charge of the performance, but whether the music is essentially his—Grabu's rôle being restricted to arranging it and possibly supplying additional items—or whether Grabu composed an entirely new setting will never be known until the original score is found.

Mazarin's death caused a temporary hiatus in French opera because no influential person possessed his enthusiasm for this particular form of entertainment, and it was not until 1671 that *Pomone* was staged publicly. It was an immediate success and ran for eight months to packed houses. *Pomone* is the first extant French opera, as it is sung throughout; the same may have been true of *Ariane*, but *Akebar*, *Le Triomphe*, and Cambert's first opera were probably pastorals—that is, plays with songs—for these, modelled on the pastorales of Tasso and Guarini (see p. 266), were much in vogue during the earlier part of the century. Two years before *Pomone* Perrin had obtained a royal privilege that gave him a monopoly of all performances of French opera. In 1670 he and Cambert converted a large building into a theatre, and in the following year founded the 'Académie Royale des Opéra' (the original home of the Paris Opéra), marking the occasion by the performance of *Pomone* mentioned above—the first public presentation of any French opera. Only the libretto and the music to the Prologue, Act I, and parts of Act II have survived (*H.A.M.*, 223), and the same applies to *Les peines et les plaisirs de l'amour*, produced in 1672 with music by Cambert and libretto by Gabriel Gilbert.

The success of these two operas, especially of *Pomone*, was immense, but disaster for Cambert and Perrin was at hand. The latter, a gifted but unstable man, was imprisoned in 1672, and there he was visited by no less a person than Molière [1622–1673], the brilliant actor-dramatist whose comédies are performed as frequently and enjoyed with as much relish today as in his own time. Molière, who had included a certain amount of music and dancing in his comédies from *La Fâcheux* (1661) on, and who clearly saw the possibilities of such entertainments, can have had little difficulty in persuading Perrin to sell the royal privilege. It availed him little, however, for within a few weeks the privilege had become worthless owing to the machinations at court of one of the most outstanding musicians, and certainly the most unscrupulous, in the whole history of French music, Jean-Baptiste Lully [1632–1687].

Lully, an Italian by birth, was brought to France when only a lad of about ten years old. At twenty he so captivated the Dauphin, later Louis XIV, by his violin playing that not only was he appointed to the royal band, the famous Vingt-Quatre Violons du Roi, but in 1656 was permitted by Louis to train sixteen specially selected fiddlers—Les Petits-Violons. This smaller band (which later expanded to twenty-one players) surpassed the larger in both volume and expressiveness, and soon led to Lully's appointment as conductor of the 'King's violins', a body that became internationally famous under his direction. Like other conductors of his time, Lully was expected to provide most of the music for his orchestra, but some years before this, probably in his late 'teens, he had realized that without the ability to play the harpsichord and compose he would never get very far. He accordingly took lessons, and such was his talent for composition that in 1653 he was commissioned to write some music for a ballet de cour.

In Chapter 1 we traced the development of the ballet de cour up to the early years of the seventeenth century. The first notable change occurred *c.* 1605, when the récits, which had formerly been spoken rather than sung, began tentatively, but with increasing sureness, to be set in the Italian monodic style. This change was undoubtedly due to the presence of Caccini at the court of Henry IV in 1604–5, for his dramatic manner of singing made a great impression on the musicians at court, especially Pierre Guédron [1565–1621], who succeeded Claude le Jeune as chief court composer, becoming Maître de la Musique du Roi to Louis XIII, and who, in his numerous ballets written between 1608 and 1620, did much to further the adoption of monody at the expense of part-music. The monodic style also affected the popular air de cour, though indirectly, in that the stress on declamation and the affective rendering of the text soon became all-important, the regular rhythms and simple melodies of the Renaissance type being replaced by the irregular patterns of musique mesurée and by numerous improvised embellishments of the vocal line and accompaniment. Italian influence waxed during the succeeding years, and by 1620 the literary element in the ballet was completely overshadowed by the musical. This resulted in an even greater disregard for dramatic unity than before, and the dances, particularly the ballets à entrées, became a series of virtually unconnected if spectacular tableaux.

This state of affairs persisted until *c.* 1650, when a new lease of life was infused into the ballet de cour by the poet Isaac de Benserade [1612–1691], who reintroduced the feature that had made *Circe* so outstanding—namely, a unified dramatic plot, an example that was followed by the greatest writer of ballets de cour, Molière.

Of the composers who wrote ballet music between *c.* 1608 and *c.* 1650 the two most notable were Guédron and his son-in-law and successor at court, Antoine Boesset [*c.* 1585–1643], who also became Surintendant de la Musique de Roi in 1623. In the next and last important period of the ballet de cour (it had a late brief flowering under Louis XV), when Benserade and Molière raised it to a literary and dramatic level unknown before, the chief composers were Jean-Baptiste Boesset [*c.* 1613–1685], who succeeded his father as Maître and Surintendant to the King, now Louis XIV, and his successors to these titles, Jean de Cambefort [1605–1661] and Lully.

The ballet music Lully wrote in 1653, his first so far as we know, was for Benserade's *La Nuit*, in which the part of 'Le Roi soleil' was so superbly danced by Louis that the title stuck to him for the rest of his life. Other composers also contributed to *La Nuit*, for it had long been the custom to share out the music of a ballet between two or more composers. (This, indeed, applies also to Jacobean and most Caroline masques.) During the next four years Lully contributed music to nine ballets, one of these being inserted into an Italian opera, and all but two by Benserade. In 1658, however, he composed the entire score for Benserade's *Alcidiane*, and its success, together with his dislike for sharing royal or public acclamation, resulted in his never again collaborating with another composer. Between 1658 and 1671 Lully wrote the ballet music for thirty stage works, over half of them by Benserade, the best of which is *Les Muses* (1667); most of the remainder were comédies and comédie-ballets by Molière, beginning with *L'impromptu de Versailles* (1663) and reaching their peak in *Le bourgeois gentilhomme* (1670).

The two chief dancing masters during this period were Beauchamp and Lully himself, and they were the first to advocate a strict professional training for the ballet, which, as we have seen, had been previously performed by men and women who were courtiers first and dancers second. As a result, the Académie Royale de la Danse was founded by Louis in 1661, and in 1672 this was enlarged to the Académie Royale de Musique et de Danse, which still exists, with its headquarters at the Paris Opéra, and which marked the beginning of State ballet with its professional dancers and public performances. Actually the public had first witnessed ballet in the preceding year (1671), when *Pomone* was staged, for in this opera, as in practically all later French operas to the end of the nineteenth century, ballet was a large and important constituent. Only male dancers performed in public at first, but in 1681 the first woman professional solo dancer (ballerina) appeared on the public stage in Lully's *Le Triomphe de l'Amour*, perhaps the most sumptuously staged ballet he ever wrote.

Among the ballets by Benserade for which Lully composed the music were two for the operas, *Serse* (1660) and *Ercole amante* (1662), by Cavalli, whose compositions Lully studied and from them derived his own musico-dramatic style, a style that was fully formed by the time he wrote his first real opera in 1673.

By this date the ballet had become much more than a display of dancing, though naturally dancing was the main attraction, and Lully, apart from writing numerous pieces for the dramatic ballets à entrées and the conventional ballroom types, such as the gaillarde and courante, also made famous a number of newer dances, all of French origin. These were the 'menuet' in stately $\frac{3}{4}$ time, which is said to have been first danced, to Lully's music, by Louis as 'Le Roi soleil' in *La Nuit*; the more animated but still dignified 'gavotte' in $\frac{2}{2}$ or $\frac{4}{4}$; the 'rigaudon' and 'bourée' in quick duple time, the latter appearing for the first time in composition in Lully's ballets and operas, though mentioned considerably earlier in literary sources; the lively, spirited, and very popular 'passepied' in $\frac{3}{8}$ or $\frac{6}{8}$; and finally the 'loure', with its dotted rhythm in $\frac{6}{4}$ time.

But the attention which Lully was bound to pay to the dances in his ballets, because of their popularity with King and court, did not prevent him from extending and developing the part played by both vocal and purely instrumental music. Thus he increased the number of solos and choruses, and adapted the Italian *bel canto* and recitativo secco styles, both of which he had learned from Cavalli. The latter he employed to connect the separate scenes in Molière's comédie-ballets, while the influence of the former is clearly apparent in his récits and airs in both the comédie-ballets and ballets de cour, although the ornamental turns, grace notes, etc., are still very much in the French tradition. When we add to this the fact that he stressed the importance of the orchestra to a far greater extent than any other composer, whether French or foreign, then we can begin to appreciate how richly varied had become the musical element in his ballets, especially the comédie-ballets of Molière, with their dramatic recitatives, affective airs that include both low comedy and tender sentiment, sonorous choruses, striking instrumental pieces, sometimes in five real parts, and dance music that ranges from the vivid characterization of the ballets à entrées to the noble grace of the menuet. It was but a short step from this to opera, and it is to Lully's operas, or 'tragédies-lyriques' as he called them, that we now turn.

Up to 1671 Lully had been contemptuous of Perrin and Cambert's essays in French opera, but the granting of the royal privilege to Perrin, the founding of the Académie Royale des Opéra, and, finally, the enormous success of *Pomone* aroused his jealousy. He executed a rapid *volte-face*, exercised all his influence with the King, and within two months of the production of *Les peines et les plaisirs de l'amour* obtained the privilege for himself. Molière was robbed of his rights, Perrin died in misery three years later, and Cambert, embittered by Lully's deceit, repaired to England, where he became court composer to Charles II until he was mysteriously assassinated. Not content with his ill-gotten power, Lully repeatedly petitioned the King to extend the scope of his privilege; thus in 1673 no theatre was allowed to employ more than two voices and six violins, and in 1684 no opera could be performed without his permission. While his unscrupulousness in achieving his ends irregardless of others can only be condemned, Lully's musical genius matched his lust for power and his dictatorial methods, and he created a type of opera and a style of operatic composition unique to France, and one that lasted for over 100 years; indeed, his third opera, *Thésée* (1675), remained in the repertoire until 1779.

The chief characteristics of Lully's operas and a comparison with those typical of Italy at the time can best be shown as follows:

Lully	*Italian*
1. The libretto is more important than the music.	1. The music is more important than the libretto.
2. As a first result, the recitatives are models of correct declamation, which at times become lyrical, are frequently accompanied by the orchestra, and are of major importance.	2. As a first result, most recitatives are taken at great speed (recitativo secco), are accompanied by a few simple continuo chords and are of minor importance.
3. As a second result, the airs are few, short, melodically simple, and of minor importance.	3. As a second result, the arias are many, extended in form, often very ornate melodically, and of major importance.

Lully	*Italian*
4. The *raison d'être* of the whole is to glorify the king—his person, his realm, his deeds.	4. The *raison d'être* of the whole is to entertain the aristocracy or the populace or both.
5. As a first result (French taste being what it was), the action and music are conventional, never seeking to express violence or passion, and introducing wit rather than broad comedy as light relief.	5. As a first result, composers, in order to satisfy their public, always played on the emotions, and violence and passion are the rule rather than the exception, with broad comedy rather than wit introduced as light relief.
6. As a second result, allegorical scenes abound in which the spectacular element is chiefly used to glorify king and country, which include numerous ballets, and in which the chorus and orchestra play an important part.	6. As a second result, elaborate spectacles involving some of the most complex stage machinery ever devised are common, but there are few ballets. The chorus is hardly ever used and the number of purely orchestral items small.

The importance of the libretto and Lully's insistence that it should make dramatic sense and have some literary distinction falls into line with the traditional French attitude to music mentioned earlier (see p. 273), for whereas composers of opera in the Italian manner did not bother about the quality of the text nor about the probability of the plot, and thus, apart from scenic effects, relied wholly on the impact of their music, Lully made sure that the dramatic and literary sensibilities of his audience were not insulted. It must be remembered in this connexion that in the sphere of literature (including the theatre) France stood head and shoulders above the rest of Europe, and that the so-called 'Classic Age' (*c.* 1660–90), one of the major peaks in her literary history, coincided with the period of Lully's operatic activity. As we saw earlier, Italian literature and drama were at their lowest ebb in the seventeenth century, and this, apart from the Italian temperament, fostered the kind of opera already discussed; similarly in France, where the distinction of such men as Molière, La Fontaine [1621–1695], whose *Contes* and *Fables* reveal him as one of the greatest of French poets, the outstanding playwright, Racine [1639–1699], whose tragedies, particularly his two finest, *Phèdre* (1677) and *Athalie* (1691), display a violence of passion that stepped right outside the aristocratic conventions of his time, and Pierre Corneille [1606–1684], whose *Le Cid* virtually created French classical tragedy, not to mention a number of lesser lights, created a literary standard among the intelligentsia which French opera was bound to reflect to some extent if it was to succeed; that it reflected it to such a large extent was due to Lully, and it is not surprising that he called his operas tragédies-lyriques, for this places the stress on the drama rather than on the music.

Although Lully had provided the music for several of Molière's comédies, he preferred as his regular librettists, both for ballet and opera, men of lesser talent and more docile disposition, the reason undoubtedly being that writers of the calibre of Molière, Racine, and Corneille (the last two also collaborated on occasion) were less likely to abide by his dictates and, moreover, were too distinguished in their own right to permit Lully's star to shine as brightly as he desired, for he wanted no reflected glory. Thus of the nineteen ballets composed between 1658 and 1670 of which he wrote all the music, six are based on texts by anonymous authors, and of the remainder all but one are by the comparatively obscure writer, Benserade.

In November 1672, only eight months after he had obtained the royal privilege, Lully produced *Les Festes de l'Amour et de Bacchus*, a work that stands halfway between his ballets and his operas. His librettists were Benserade, Molière, and Philippe Quinault [1635–1688], and it was the last-named, a dramatist of little significance, who supplied Lully with the libretti of all but two of the thirteen complete operas composed between 1673 and 1686, beginning with *Cadmus et Hermione*, Lully's first opera, and ending with *Armide et Renaud*, his masterpiece, and the first French opera to be performed in Italy (Rome, 1690).

In some ways Lully's operas revive the principles of the early Florentines: in the importance of the text and the insistence on correct and affective declamation, and hence in the preference for the arioso as opposed to the secco recitative so common in contemporary Italian opera. This arioso style—which differs from the Italian in that the voice is often accompanied by violins, and even, at times, the full string band, in addition to the invariable continuo—is clearly shown in Ex. 24, as is the close alliance between the stress and value of notes and syllables which result in fluctuating time-signatures.

(Notice the animated bass line and rapid changes of harmony in the middle of the recitative where the poetic imagery is most intense.) The majority of Lully's airs fall into one of two types, in both of which the underlay is predominantly syllabic, as one would expect from a composer who laid such stress on the importance of the words. The first type stems from the air de cour, and includes most of his serious or sentimental airs, particularly those of a pastoral nature (e.g. the well-known 'Bois épais' from *Amadis de Gaule*, 1684, Lully's most popular opera after *Thésée*.) The second type, characterized by clear-cut rhythms and melodies, is the dance-song, and it is hardly surprising that this occurs more frequently than the first type. The air in Ex. 24 is a typical dance-song, being in fact a gavotte; typical also is the trochaic rhythm of the melismas on '-phez' and '-chai', which so captivated English composers, notably Purcell, and which, via the French overture especially, spread to other European countries north of the Alps (it was too jerky for the Italian *bel canto* style). (Ex. 24,* pp. 415-91. The cross in front of some of the notes indicates an ornament, probably a mordant. See also *H.A.M.*, 225.)

In order to improve his settings of French words and the declamation and acting of his singers, Lully spent much time studying the movements and speech of the greatest actors of his day at the Théâtre Française, but before long the position was reversed, the actors attending the Académie Royale, for Lully's ability to train and discipline, already noted in connexion with the King's orchestra, produced a standard of acting and declamation that was second to none in France, or, indeed, anywhere else, and musicians from all over Europe came to study with him. Even so, it was not the vocal element in Lully's operas that caught on abroad—Italian influence was far too powerful—but the instrumental, a constituent of opera that the Italians treated with comparative neglect.

The importance of the orchestra in Lully's operas was due not only to the enormous quantity of dance music it was called on to play as a result of the numerous ballets, but also to the quality of the music itself. Instead of the rather perfunctory instrumental items of contemporary Italian opera in which only the top and bottom lines mattered, Lully composed pieces of distinction, some of them of considerable length, a number

* Solo and violin parts and bass from the 2nd ed., Paris, 1709, p. 59.

Ex.24 Recitative - *Au généraux Roland* and Air - *Triomphez charmante Reine* (*Roland* I.6) (1688) Lully
(♩= MM.c.96)
Zillante (carrying a bracelet to Angelique)
Au gé-né-raux Ro-land Je dois ma dé-li - - vran - ce, D'un char-me af-
My blest de-li-ve-rance to Ro-land do I owe it, From charms so
- freux Sa va-leur m'a sau - - vé; Il n'a vou - - lu de ma re-con-nois-
dire me he no-bly did save; My gra-ti - - tude he bid me not be- -
- san - - ce, Que ce pré - - - sent qu'il vous a ré-ser - - vé. Je viens pour vous l'of-
stow it, But that this gift thou'd ac-cept he did crave. I bring it from the

Ex. 24 contd.

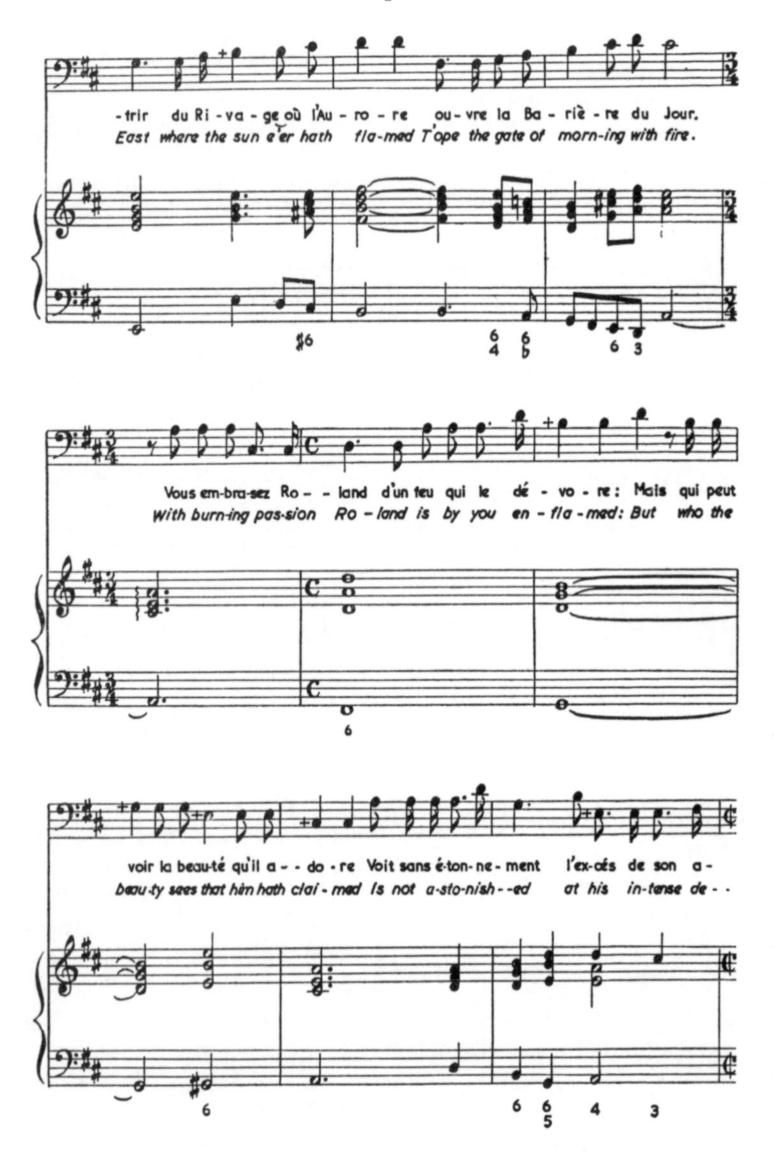
-trir du Ri-va-ge où l'Au-ro-re ou-vre la Ba-riè-re du Jour.
East where the sun e'er hath fla-med T'ope the gate of morn-ing with fire.
#6
6 4
6 b
6
3
Vous em-bra-sez Ro-land d'un feu qui le dé-vo-re: Mais qui peut
With burn-ing pas-sion Ro-land is by you en-fla-med: But who the
6
voir la beau-té qu'il a-do-re Voit sans é-ton-ne-ment l'ex-cès de son a-
beau-ty sees that him hath clai-med Is not a-sto-nish-ed at his in-tense de-
6
6
6 5
4
3

EX. 24 CONTD.

(𝅗𝅥 = MM.c.60)(Violins)
-mour.
-sire.
Tri-om-phez, char-man--te Rei-ne, tri-om--phez des plus grands
Tri-umph thou, O queen al--lur-ing, tri-umph, all great hearts en-
(Ziliante & continuo)
coeurs, tri-om-phez, tri-om--phez,
flame, tri-umph thou, tri-umph thou,
char-man-te Rei-ne, tri-om--phez, tri-om--phez des plus grands
O queen al--lur--ing, tri-umph thou, tri-umph, all great hearts en--
6
6
6
6 5 4 3

Ex. 24 CONTD.

(Fine)
coeurs. Ce n'est qu'aux plus fa-meux Vain-queurs qu'il est per-
flame. 'Tis on-ly he of great-est fame May wear your
-mis de por-ter vô-tre chai
fet-ters of pas-sion en-dur
-ne, ce n'est qu'aux plus fa-meux vain-queurs qu'il est per-mis de por-
-ing, 'tis on-ly he of great-est fame may wear your fet-ters of

Ex. 24 contd.

-ter vô-tre chai - - - - - - - - - - - -
pas - sion en - - dur - - - - - - - - - - - -
- ne, ce n'est qu'aux plus fa-meux vain- -queurs qu'il est per- -mis de por-
- ing, 'tis on-ly he of great-est fame may wear your fet- -ters of
- ter, de por- -ter vô-tre chai - - - - - ne. Tri-om-
pas- -sion, of pas- -sion en- -dur - - - - - ing. Tri-umph
(Dal 𝄋)

of them in five parts, and all of them showing a greater care in the writing of the inner parts; these last were, in fact, often added by his pupils, but only at Lully's command. Here, for example, is part of the fine chaconne (153 bars in length) from Act II of *Phaëton* (1683), an opera so successful that it was nicknamed 'l'opera du peuple'. (We shall define a chaconne as a continuous set of variations on a recurring succession of basic chords which almost invariably lead from tonic to dominant and so back to the tonic again. Thus a chord may not only change its position (e.g. a root may become a first inversion, as in variation (*a*), bar 2, of Ex. 25) and its mode (i.e. major may become minor, as in variation (*b*), bar 2), but it may also be preceded, succeeded, and even replaced by a different chord or chords (as in variation (*a*), bar 3, and (*c*), bar 2), always provided that the route, as it were, from tonic to dominant is recognizably the same: Ex. 25,* p. 421).

Lully's orchestral style, particularly as revealed in his overtures, swept the length and breadth of Europe, penetrating even Italy. The operatic overture in Italy is usually, as we have seen, a rather casual affair, but Lully the violinist and conductor saw in it an opportunity to show off the King's string band as well as to satisfy his royal master's delight in instrumental music. The first distinct example of a Lullian or French overture occurs in the ballet *Alcidiane* (1658); this consists of two movements, a slow, pompous one in a predominantly dotted rhythm, followed by a quick one in duple time which begins in imitative style and is based on a short motive. Lully's ballet music to Cavalli's *Serse* (1660) contains an overture on similar lines, except that the second movement is in triple time; this became standard practice. Some French overtures are concluded by an adagio coda which has been classed as a separate movement by some writers, who, as a result, give the overall plan as slow-quick-slow. This is wrong, so far as Lully's overtures are concerned at any rate, because the final section is not a regular feature, and when it does occur it is simply a broadening out of the concluding bars of the second movement (e.g. *Alceste*, *H.A.M.*, 224). This two-movement plan, slow-quick, was not invented by Lully, as it can be found in a sinfonia in Landi's *Sant' Alessio* (see p. 382), and in a few Venetian operas, such as Cavalli's *Giasone* (see p. 395), as well

* From 3rd ed., Amsterdam [1711], p. 160.

as in the 'ouvertures', as they were called, of a few earlier ballets dating back to at least 1640; indeed, the first movement of some of these ouvertures display the dotted rhythm typical of the Lullian type. That Lully was acquainted with some of these early sinfonie and ouvertures can scarcely be doubted, but he was the first to adopt the slow-quick plan as a standard procedure, and its success, due partly to the admirably contrasted movements, partly to the quality of the actual music, was such that it became the first significant example of orchestral music to achieve independence—in other words, to be composed and played for its own sake without being attached to a stage work.

The country that was most influenced by Lully was England, largely through the enthusiasm of Charles II [reigned 1660–1685], who, after the execution of his father, Charles I, and during the Commonwealth, spent most of his exile in France and became thoroughly enamoured of French music, especially Lully's ballet music. But Charles did not introduce opera into England, for while he may have seen La Guerre's *Le Triomphe* and Cambert's *Pastorale* while in exile, the first English opera, *The Siege of Rhodes*, had already been produced, with great success, four years before he was crowned. This opera is subtitled "A Representation by the Art of Prospective [=perspective] in Scenes, And the Story sung in Recitative Musick". There is no mention of it being a dramatic entertainment, because the Puritans, under their leader, Oliver Cromwell [1599–1658], were strongly opposed to anything that smacked of the traditional theatre; they did not, however, object to music, and so Sir William Davenant or D'Avenant [1606–1668], who, besides being a dramatist and Ben Jonson's successor as Poet Laureate, was also an astute theatrical manager, wrote a play and commissioned a number of composers to set the words in recitative style and to provide songs and instrumental music, none of which unfortunately has survived. (It is worth noting that the performance of this opera marked the first occasion when a woman appeared on the English public stage, i.e. the first professional actress; she was Mrs. Coleman, wife of Edward Coleman [d. 1669], one of the composers engaged by Davenant.)

The Siege of Rhodes was not Davenant's first essay in the musico-dramatic sphere, as he had already written a number of masques for the court of Charles I; nor was the use of recitative the first instance of this style in an English stage work, for as early as 1617 Ben Jonson's masque, *The Vision of Delight*, was partly and his *Lovers make Men* wholly (according to him) "sung after the Italian manner, *stylo recitativo*, by Master Nicholas Lanier . . .". Lanier [1588–1666], of French descent, was Master of the King's Musick to both Charles I and II, and one of a group of composers who sought to adapt Italian monody to English use. This group included Henry Lawes [1596–1662], another contributor to *The Siege of Rhodes*, his brother William [1602–1645], and Simon Ives [1600-1662]. It was William Lawes and Ives who wrote the music for the most elaborate, fantastic, and costly masque ever produced in England, *The Triumph of Peace* (1633), by the popular and prolific dramatist, James Shirley [1596–1666]. This extravaganza was organized in protest against the violent attack on masques and plays contained in *Histriomastic: The Players Scourge*, by William Prynne [1600–1669], and published earlier in the same year. The masque included a procession on horseback from Holborn to Whitechapel of all the characters, and cost the Inns of Court, who commissioned the work, over £21,000 (at least £200,000 in modern money), of which about £1,000 was spent on the music, Lawes and Ives receiving £100 each.

The Triumph of Peace represents, albeit in an extreme form, the general decadence of the Caroline masque, in which realism rather than fantasy was the aim and which, as a result of increasing French influence, relied to a greater extent than did the Jacobean masque on the purely spectacular. It was French influence also, rather than Italian, that was reflected in the English recitative style, a style in which the rhythm of the words is more or less faithfully transmitted to the vocal line, but which lacks the affective nature and harmonic variety of the French and Italian arioso. It was this projection of verbal metre into musical rhythm that prompted Milton, in 1646, to write of Henry Lawes:

> Harry, whose tuneful and well-measured song
> First taught our English music how to span
> Words with just note and accent, not to scan
> With Midas' ears, committing short and long ;
> Thy worth and skill exempt thee from the throng,
> With praise enough for Envy to look wan;
> To after age thou shalt be writ the man,
> That with smooth air couldst humour best our tongue.

Milton was not alone in praising Lawes, but he in particular should have known better, for not only was his father a distinguished enough composer to contribute to *The Triumphs of Oriana*, but he himself had heard Italian opera in Rome (see p. 384). In actual fact Henry's songs are hardly "tuneful" or "smooth"; neither was he the first to set English words "justly", nor are the results superior to those by Lanier, his brother William, and others. Even his fairly well-known setting of Milton's fine masque, *Comus* (1634), owes its distinction to the beauty of the poem, for the music's melodic and harmonic monotony is only occasionally relieved by the comparative tunefulness of such songs as 'Sweet Echo' (*H.A.M.*, 204).

Five years after *Comus* came the last of the court masques, Davenant's *Salmacida Spolia*, but masques for private entertainment continued to be written during the Commonwealth, the most outstanding being Shirley's *Cupid and Death*, presented before the Portuguese Ambassador in 1653, with music presumably by Matthew Locke [*c.* 1630–1677], another contributor to *The Siege of Rhodes*, and Christopher Gibbons [1615–1676], second son of Orlando. We say 'presumably' because the only music to this masque that has come down to us is that for the later performance of 1659 which is unquestionably by Locke and Gibbons. Locke's contributions, which exceed in both quantity and quality those by Gibbons, show a keener sense of drama and a bolder imagination than any previous English composer for the stage. Unlike Henry Lawes and his generation, he is more concerned with the dramatic impact of the whole than with the accurate rendering of speech rhythm, and as a result his vocal lines are more tuneful and flexible, his harmonies more varied, and his part-writing freer. (Ex. 26,* p. 425. Notice the shiver on "cold" the abrupt change of chord on "Bright", and the melismas on the unaccented "a" and "-to" of "into", a breach of verbal rhythm that must have made Henry Lawes shudder, but which arouse a feeling of expectancy for the word following.)

The affective treatment of the words in Ex. 26 shows that Italian influence was beginning to make itself felt in England, an influence that grew as the century progressed. But while Locke's melodies are, in the main, smoother than those of the previous generation of composers, their wayward rhythm and frequent wide leaps still contrast sharply with the simple, often sequential, pattern and melodic curves of the *bel canto*. More important is the comparative lack of feeling for a central tonality, for although there are signs of overall key-planning

* Melody and bass from *Musica Britannica*, II, ed. E. J. Dent, p. 38.

(i.e. within a group of movements) in Locke's music to *Cupid and Death* (and even in that of William Lawes to *The Triumph of Peace*), the chord progressions within a movement, which often lead to a wide variety of keys, lack the single tonal direction that alone can give both greater meaning to such excursions and at the same time a feeling of unity.

Locke never developed a strong tonal sense, even in his later works for the stage. Of these the most important are the incidental music to, and the masque, *Orpheus and Euridice*, that formed part of *The Empress of Morocco* (1673)—a tragedy by the minor playwright, Elkanah Settle [1648–1724], the so-called opera, *Psyche* (1673)—an imitation of Molière's and Lully's comédie-ballet of the same name by the Poet Laureate and successful dramatist, Thomas Shadwell [1642–1692], and incidental music to Shadwell's version of Shakespeare's *The Tempest* (1674). (Adulterated versions of Shakespeare's plays, in which original passages and sometimes whole scenes were omitted and new material and even new characters added, together with songs and dances, became very popular during the Restoration period and later.)

In *Psyche* Locke's vocal line is less angular than in *Cupid and Death*, and his harmony more orthodox, but his instrumental pieces for *The Tempest* contain a number of what the English historian, Charles Burney, called "crudities". Burney's pronouncements are usually sound, but he was prone, like many other critics since his time, to judge an earlier work by later standards, in this case the smooth chord progressions and unerring sense of tonal direction of the late eighteenth century. Locke's harmonic language is undoubtedly sometimes rough and occasionally startling, compared to that of his contemporaries abroad, but to label unorthodoxy as crude is to imply that the composer was incompetent and his ear imperfect. Locke knew perfectly well what he was doing because not only is his harmonic style consistent within a work, but his free use of dissonance nearly always 'comes off'. Indeed, he was but part of that English tradition which stretched back to the Middle Ages, when the comparatively dissonant thirds and sixths were much more favoured than on the Continent. Byrd's use of dissonance is in the same tradition, and so too is Purcell's, as we shall see. In Ex. 27 the dissonant entry in bar 2, the unusual dominant seventh in bar 5, and the false relation in bars 3 and 5 all 'come off' (Ex. 27,* p. 427).

The movement from which Ex. 27 is taken contains the directions "soft" and "lowd", and in the 'Curtain Tune', which is frankly programmatic in that it portrays a 'tempest', occur the expressions "soft", "lowder by degrees", "violent", "lowd", and "soft and slow by degrees", of which the second and last are the most remarkable for the time at which they

* From '*The Tempest*' *Music*, Suite I. ed. W. G. Whittaker.

were written, because while abrupt expression marks, e.g. 'lowd' or 'forte', were uncommon enough before *c.* 1750, graduated ones, such as 'soft and slow by degrees' or 'diminuendo e ritardando', were extremely rare.

Locke's masque, *Orpheus and Euridice*, has been described as "the first surviving example of true operatic writing in England" (Anthony Lewis), for, apart from the fact that, unlike all earlier masques, it contains no spoken passages, the vocal line is very reminiscent of early Italian opera in its occasional use of sequence, its oscillation between arioso and aria styles, and its general smoothness, despite the fondness for iambic rhythm, i.e. ♪ ♩ or ♫, which can be regarded as a fingerprint of late seventeenth-century English vocal writing. It is the first surviving example, because the music to *The Siege of Rhodes* has been lost, as has that to Davenant's two later operas, *The Cruelty of the Spaniards in Peru* (1658) and *The History of Sir Francis Drake* (1659). The notable feature common to all three operas is that they are concerned with what was then recent history. This is obvious enough in the third opera, but the first is based on an actual siege of the city in 1522 by the Turks under Solyman the Magnificent, while the second summarizes the history of Peru from pre-Inca times to the Spanish conquest in 1532, ending with a scene, admitted by the author to be entirely fictitious, in which the Spaniards are expelled by a combined Peruvian-English army. This opera was intended as a kind of lecture-recital, with music, dancing, and scenery to gild the pill, so to speak; in this it was poles removed from the Italian and French conception of opera, which was solely concerned with entertaining, not informing. In complete contrast too are the subjects of Davenant's operas, for, as we have seen, Continental librettists delved mostly into ancient history and classical mythology, even though the characters behaved like seventeenth-century men and women.

Whether Davenant had any intention of founding a school or tradition of English opera we do not know. He was an ambitious man and an opportunist who managed both to evade Puritanical objections and to capture popular appeal with his operas. As early as 1639 he obtained a patent from Charles I which gave him permission to build his own theatre, and to perform in it or other theatres "musical presentments, scenes, dancing, or any others the like . . .". If this meant opera, then he was ahead of the French, but it is more likely that he only had masques in mind, for he could not have seen any opera before his visits to France in the 1640s. Even after the public theatres were reopened in 1660 Davenant produced no new opera, despite the success of his first three. He seems to have clearly understood the nature and purpose of recitative, judging by the speech he puts into the mouth of the Musician, one of the characters in his medley of plays entitled *The Playhouse to Let* (1663):

> Recitative Musick is not compos'd
> Of matter so familiar, as may serve
> For every low occasion of discourse.
> In Tragedy, the language of the Stage
> Is rais'd above the common dialect;
> Our passion rising with the height of Verse;
> And Vocal Musick adds new wings to all
> The flights of Poetry.

By "Recitative Musick" Davenant almost certainly meant something akin to arioso, not the rapid patter of secco recitative, which, in fact, was hardly ever used by English composers before Handel. Perhaps he sensed that opera, while satisfying the lack of public dramatic entertainment during the Commonwealth, could not compete in normal times either with straight drama or with the masque, in which music serves only to heighten, at certain points, the emotional impact or the spectacular element, but which is not used for narrative or conversational purposes; in other words, that a play interspersed with vocal and instrumental numbers was acceptable, but one sung throughout was not. This was certainly Locke's view, for in the Preface to *The English Opera* (1675), which contains his music to *Psyche* and *The Tempest*, he says that the former work "may fitly bear the title of Opera though all the tragedy be not in Musick; for the author prudently consider'd that though Italy is the great Academy of the World for that Science and way of entertainment, England is not: and therefore mix'd it with interlocutions as more proper to our genius".

It seems from the above quotation that Locke would have liked to write a full-scale opera if conditions had been favourable; as it is, however, the first surviving English opera, although it is sub-titled 'A Masque for the Entertainment of the King', is *Venus and Adonis*, by John Blow [1649–1708], composed *c.* 1682. This work has closer affinities to Continental models than Davenant's operas (so far as we can judge the latter from the libretto and contemporary accounts), being a mixture of Italian but more especially French styles and ideas, with a few features peculiar to England added. Thus the overall plan is Lullian in that, unlike Davenant's operas, which were divided into a number of scenes, *Venus and Adonis* consists of a French overture leading straight into a pastoral Prologue and succeeded by three acts. Both French and Italian influence is shown in the fact that the plot is taken from classical mythology, that the libretto is sung throughout, and that the recitatives combine Lully's careful word-setting with the affective line of the Italian arioso; indeed, Venus's outburst of grief when the dying Adonis lies before her reaches a degree of passion unknown before in England and rarely equalled abroad (Ex. 28,* p. 430).

* Melody and bass from *Venus and Adonis*, ed. A. Lewis, p. 89.

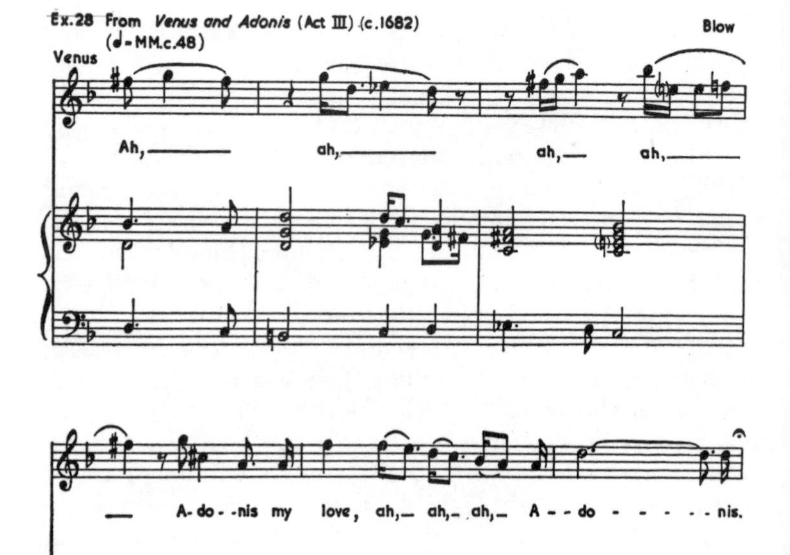

Italian rather than French influence is shown by the preponderance of airs over recitatives, the former being, in the main, not only clearly set off from the latter, but more tuneful and regular in their construction than in any previous English vocal music for the stage. The English features are a certain angularity of line in the recitatives, an uncertainty in tonal direction, and the importance of the chorus, solo ensembles, and instrumental music. This last, to be sure, is also true of Lullian opera, but it undoubtedly stemmed from the masque tradition, as did the inclusion of a large number of choruses (they comprise nearly a quarter of the vocal music) compared to foreign operas. The greater use of the chorus was also due to the amateur and private nature of the performance, in which there were no 'stars' whose talents and temperaments had to be considered (*H.A.M.*, 243).

In its tunefulness, range of mood, and general structure, *Venus and Adonis* represents a considerable advance on what had gone before, even though Blow's grasp of tonality is only slightly superior to Locke's, and it is a pity that he never wrote another work for the stage, particularly as his association with the greatest English composer of the baroque era, Henry Purcell [*c.* 1659–1695], led to a new clarity and simplicity in his melodic and harmonic styles.

Purcell was in fact a pupil of Blow, and the musical relationship between the two was very similar to that between Haydn and Mozart, for both Purcell and Mozart were influenced by and in their turn influenced their older contemporary, and both were the more profound artists. This last is clearly revealed in Purcell's only opera, *Dido and Aeneas* (1689?), for whereas there are sufficient similarities to *Venus and Adonis* to show that Purcell had studied his master's work, the differences are much more striking and significant. The first and most important difference is simply that Purcell's music reveals a far greater skill and imagination. Thus while both Dido's famous lament (*H.A.M.*, 255) and Venus's passionate outburst mentioned above represent the climax of their respective operas (as did 'Arianna's Lament' in Monteverdi's opera), Purcell's air conveys a deeper sense of tragedy which is sustained by a well-nigh perfect fusion of a highly expressive vocal line and poignant harmony supported by a chromatic ground-bass. Again, although Purcell's opera, like Blow's, reveals Italian influence in the number and character of its airs, and French-Italian influence in its arioso-like recitatives, the former are far more 'catchy' and the latter more expressive than in Blow's work. His tonality too is much more assured than the older man's, for although the key structures in *Dido*, both within each Act and as a whole, are only slightly better planned than in *Venus* (but not nearly so well thought out as in the masque from *The Prophetess, or the History of Dioclesian*), his tonal sense within a key is firmer and his modulations smoother. *Dido* also includes, and for the same reasons as *Venus*, a greater number of choruses, ensembles, and instrumental pieces than was common abroad.

Despite the superiority of the music, Purcell's opera is less perfectly constructed than Blow's, the major flaw being the totally inadequate treatment of Aeneas. This is all the more marked because, whereas Venus and Adonis, despite the former's outburst of grief, are presented as dramatic figures roughly equal in stature, though neither are profoundly drawn,

Dido is revealed through two wonderfully expressive airs as a mature and deeply passionate woman, while Aeneas's character is never given a chance to establish itself, as he is only allowed a few recitatives, including an almost perfunctory lover's quarrel with Dido; indeed, Belinda, Dido's sister, is a far more vivid personality. Admittedly the librettist, Nahum Tate [1652–1715], is also to blame, and as the opera was written for a boarding-school for gentlewomen run by a well-known dancing master, Josias Priest, it was natural that the part of Aeneas, which was obviously sung by an imported tenor, should be limited, but not to the extent that it is. Even so, if Purcell had had more operatic experience he would doubtless have insisted that Aeneas be given a larger share in the drama. Actually, however, his experience before *Dido* was limited to providing songs and instrumental music for seven plays, including *Theodosius* (1680), by the minor dramatist, Nathaniel Lee [1649–1692], the composer's first and most popular contribution to the stage, and *Circe* (1685?), by Charles Davenant, son of Sir William, which contains one of Purcell's finest ariosos, 'Pluto arise'. In addition, he almost certainly studied Locke's stage music, and may have seen *Psyche* performed. He may also have been present at the London productions of Perrin and Grabu's (?) *Ariane* in 1674 (see p. 406), and of Cambert's *Pomone* (adapted by Grabu) in the same year, and must have seen *Albion and Albanius* (1685), by John Dryden [1631–1700], the greatest English poet and playwright of his generation, with music by Grabu, and, in the following year, Lully's *Cadmus et Hermione*, given by a visiting French company.

Purcell was probably as impressed by Lully's music as he was appalled by Grabu's, whose songs in *Albion* show an almost laughable unacquaintance with the English language, and the whole revealing a woeful poverty of invention. Why Dryden ever collaborated with him is a mystery, even if we admit that at the time he regarded both Purcell and Blow with disfavour (largely because of their low opinion of Grabu), for he was fully aware of the difficulties in setting English words to music; as he states so admirably in his Preface to the opera, "'Tis no easie Matter in our Language to make Words so smooth, and Numbers so harmonious, that they shall almost set themselves. . . . The chief Secret is in the choice of Words; and by this

Choice I do not here mean Elegancy of Expression; but Propriety of Sound, to be varied according to the Nature of the Subject." Any English musician could have made a better job than Grabu of setting Dryden's libretto, but the complete failure of the opera cannot be laid entirely at the composer's door, as Dryden was also to blame by turning what was originally intended to be only a prologue to a "Tragedy" into a full-blown three-act opera. Dryden's conception of opera was admirable: "An Opera is a Poetical Tale, or Fiction, represented by Vocal and Instrumental Musick, adorn'd with Scenes, Machines and Dancing. The suppos'd Persons of this Musical Drama, are generally Supernatural." He is clear on the distinction between recitative and aria, or what he so delightfully calls "the Songish part", but in the projected tragedy, mentioned above, he shies away from the genuinely operatic, for he says that it would have been "a Tragedy mix'd with Opera; or a Drama written in blank verse, adorn'd with Machines, songs and dances: So that the Fable of it is all spoken and acted . . . the other parts of the Entertainment to be perform'd by . . . Singers and Dancers. . . . It cannot properly be called a Play, because the Action of it is supposed to be conducted sometimes by supernatural Means, or Magick; nor an Opera because the Story of it is not sung."

Even if Dryden's tragedy had materialized and Purcell had written the music it would only have been another semi-opera, like the five that Purcell did in fact write after *Dido*. Of these, two are adaptations from Shakespeare, *The Fairy Queen* (1692) and *The Tempest* (1695?), one an adaptation from Beaumont and Fletcher, *The Prophetess* (1690), and two by Dryden, *King Arthur* (1691) and *The Indian Queen* (1695), the latter being adapted from the play by Dryden and Robert Howard. All these works are characterized by the great importance of the chorus, and abundance of instrumental numbers (ritornelli, dances, preludes, and descriptive pieces), spoken dialogue, very few recitatives (all of the arioso type), elaborate sets and stage machinery, and the fact that none of the principal characters in the drama sing.

The Masque from *Dioclesian* so impressed Dryden (and it has impressed everyone ever since) that, despite the failure of *Albion* and his slight of Purcell, he asked the composer to collaborate in a new play specially designed for musical treatment—*King Arthur*. This, the only semi-opera by Purcell that is not an adaptation of an earlier play, contains the remarkable 'Frost Scene', with its vocal and instrumental 'shivering' tremolandos and its weird harmony, and a host of fine solos, ensembles, and choruses, e.g. 'Fairest Isle' and the superbly extended 'passacaglia'—really a ground—that comprises most of Act IV.

King Arthur loses far more by being presented in a concert version than do any of the other semi-operas, particularly *The Fairy Queen*, which is really a succession of highly spectacular masques with the original text of *A Midsummer Night's Dream* grossly mutilated and used merely as a series of connecting episodes. It is the longest of Purcell's dramatic works, but it is remarkable how very few items there are that strike one as commonplace; indeed, the quality of inspiration is consistently higher than in either of the two earlier works, as, for instance, in such fine songs as 'If love's a sweet passion', 'Hark how all things in one sound rejoice', 'Hark the echoing air', and some delightful fairy music. It also shows more clearly the influence of Italy in the use of coloratura and of the *da capo* aria. (In *Dido*, *Dioclesian*, and *King Arthur* there is only one air in this form—Belinda's 'Pursue thy conquest love'; in *The Fairy Queen* there are four.)

In the three years that elapsed before Purcell's last two semi-operas, he composed incidental music to well over twenty plays, some of them by such well-known authors as Dryden, William Congreve [1670–1729], Thomas D'Urfey [1653–1723], and Thomas Southerne [1660–1746]. Several of the songs from these and earlier plays are among the best he ever wrote—'Nymphs and Shepherds' (*The Libertine*, 1692?), 'Music for a while shall all your cares beguile' (*Oedipus*, 1692), 'Man is for the woman made' (*The Mock Marriage*, 1695)—and reveal an astonishing versatility, ranging as they do from lighthearted amorousness and rustic comedy to passionate declamation and 'mad songs' in which rapid changes of speed and style represent passing fits of insanity. The overtures, dances, and other instrumental pieces, like the songs, are a veritable mine of first-rate music, from hornpipes and jigs to poignantly chromatic adagios.

The experience Purcell gained from all this incidental music bore rich fruit in *The Indian Queen* and *The Tempest*, which are not only the greatest of his works for the stage, but also represent the peak of his entire output. To enumerate the gems they contain would be simply to compile a list of most of the vocal and instrumental numbers; indeed, both works display a technique that accomplishes with ease the dictates of a rich, versatile, and mature imagination, a melodic gift that is universally recognized as being one of the most remarkable in history, a firm sense of tonality that is undisturbed by certain features typical of earlier English compositions, and a style which absorbed but did not submit to French and Italian influences.

The typically English harmonic features mentioned above are essentially a free and (for the time) unorthodox use of dissonance, including false relation, which sprang from a mode of thinking that we can call 'horizontal'. Such a mode of thought had practically ceased in Italy, where melody and bass were all-important and where inner parts, even when written down, were primarily 'fillers-up' of the harmony; the same is largely true of France, for while Lully paid more attention to part-writing than the Italians, the parts themselves have less independence than in English compositions. In England, however, the tradition of polyphonic writing had been maintained right through the seventeenth century in both vocal and instrumental music, and most of Purcell's harmonic quirks, like Byrd's dissonances (see Chapter 2) are the result of this, e.g. his use of false relation, either in passing—often for descriptive reasons, as in the chorus, 'Full fathom five' (*The Tempest*)—or in the so-called 'English cadence' (see Chapter 2), as in 'What ho! thou Genius of the Clime' (*King Arthur*).

Roughly speaking, one can say that in Purcell's music for the stage, particularly that written during the last five years or so of his life, Italian influence is most apparent in the vocal numbers and French influence in the instrumental pieces, although there are examples of the Italian canzona and sinfonia on the one hand and of French dance-songs on the other. Thus the overtures, in the main, follow Lully's pattern, and most of the dances are those popular at the court of Louis XIV, while the songs reveal their author's study of Italian models in their greater regularity of structure, their lyricism, and the range of mood within a single number, apart from an increasing but still comparatively infrequent use of *da capo* form and coloratura. In addition a number of features occur so often in his melodies as to be characteristic, e.g. the rhythm ♩ 𝅗𝅥 | 𝅗𝅥 ♩ in $\frac{3}{4}$ time, successions of trochees, (♩. ♪ ♩. ♪) and the expressive use of iambs (♪♩.), in which the short accented note is usually an appogiatura (i.e. a dissonance) that is often followed by a falling fourth or fifth (see Ex. 28). This last feature was more common in England than in France or Italy, probably because of the more marked accentual nature of the language, but the other two features are typical of Lully's style. Purcell's fondness for repeated motives (ground bass and passacaglia) was also typical of French, and indeed Italian, composition, and it is interesting to note that he used this technique less as his tonal sense developed (see p. 397). What distinguishes Purcell's stage music from that of the Continent is the combination of French-Italian sequential structure with a greater freshness, breadth, and irregularity of phrase, supported by harmonic progressions that are basically orthodox but which include 'odd' dissonances.

Purcell never travelled abroad, and while he almost certainly saw one of Lully's operas (see p. 432) he never saw one by an Italian. His knowledge, therefore, of operatic performances in Italy was acquired at second hand, either from Englishmen, like his teacher, Pelham Humfrey [1647–1674], who had been sent there at the King's expense, and Dryden, or from Italians who, from the Restoration on, visited or settled in England in increasing numbers. These last brought with them a fair quantity of vocal and instrumental music, chiefly cantatas and trio sonatas (see Chapters 5 and 6), and it must have been from these manuscript copies that Purcell's enthusiasm for and knowledge of the Italian style chiefly derived.

In the Preface to *The Fairy Queen*, after defining opera as "a Story sung with proper Action", and praising *The Siege of Rhodes* as "a perfect Opera", except that it lacked "the Ornament of Machines, which they Value themselves so much upon in Italy", the anonymous writer says: "That a few private Persons should venture on so expensive a Work as an Opera [i.e. *The Fairy Queen*] when none but Princes, or States exhibit 'em abroad, I hope is no dishonour to our Nation: And I dare affirm if we had half the Encouragement in England, that they have in other Countries, you might in a short time have as good Dancers in England as they have in France, though I despair of ever having as good Voices among us, as they have in Italy." From this it may be deduced that there would have been some support for full-scale operas in the Italian manner to English libretti, and, judging by the tremendous success of Arne's *Artaxerxes* (1762), it is possible that had Purcell lived another twenty years or so he might well have established a national operatic tradition.

4

THE BAROQUE: MUSIC FOR THE STAGE—II

"... *no Music can support an opera without great and favourite singers.*" (CHARLES BURNEY, *A General History of Music*, 1776, Vol. IV, p. 457.)

ITALIAN opera, or, more precisely, the opera that stemmed from Naples, during the late baroque, (i.e. *c.* 1680–*c.* 1750) has been adversely criticized more widely, consistently, and violently than the music of any other period, country, or type. From the eighteenth century to the twentieth, Englishmen, Frenchmen, Germans, and even Italians have poured contumely if not ridicule on an operatic type that inspired men of the calibre of Alessandro Scarlatti, Handel, and Hasse to write some of their finest music. In recent years, however, a more imaginative approach has been made, and as a result the virtues as well as the vices of Neapolitan opera have been shown in a truer perspective.

Up to *c.* 1680 Venice was the main operatic centre, and even in second-rate Venetian operas, not to mention those by Cavalli, Cesti, and the later generation of Legrenzi, Stradella, and Pallavicino, dramatic integrity and, though to a much lesser degree, musical characterization were important, but not to the same extent as with Monteverdi. As a result, the nature of an individual aria depended on the composer's reaction to the story or the poetic quality of the libretto at that particular point. In Neapolitan opera, musical characterization is almost totally lacking, and dramatic integrity is entirely subservient to musical variety. This last was achieved partly through the alternation of secco recitative and aria (as in late Venetian opera), in which the former is primarily concerned with action (i.e. the unfolding of the drama by means of dialogue), but is musically negligible, while in the latter action is non-existent, the stress being entirely on the music which reveals the emotional response of one character to the preceding events in the drama. Variety was also achieved by ensuring that successive arias were of different types and, less important, that they were sung by different characters.

The chief types of aria were the 'aria cantabile', the most popular type, in slow tempo, sentimental, and providing more opportunities than the other types for displaying the singer's all-round technical mastery; the 'aria di portamento', dignified, and containing many long notes on which the singer could reveal his sustaining powers and beauty of tone; the 'aria parlante' or 'agitata', the most highly emotional type, characterized by syllabic underlay, and sung at a quicker speed and with great intensity of feeling; and lastly the 'aria di bravura' or 'agilita', the singer's show-piece, in which the rapidity, agility, and sometimes the extreme compass of the voice (see p. 461) were abundantly displayed. In addition to being classified as a certain type, each aria was governed by a single mood or 'affection', and this feature, while it was typical of all music during the late baroque, represented the culmination of an aesthetic approach to music known as the 'doctrine of temperaments and affections', and was first fully revealed in the opera aria, particularly of the Neapolitan School.

In the seventeenth and eighteenth centuries the word 'affections' (Italian *affetti*, German *Affekte*) had a far wider meaning than it has today, because it stood for a considerable number of what we may call mental activities. Thus affections included not only general emotions, such as 'pleasure', 'sadness', 'joy', 'anger', but also feelings of association, e.g. 'pastoral', 'warlike', and, especially in instrumental music, abstract mental states impossible to describe accurately in words, but which, nevertheless, were (and are today) clearly recognized and understood. In other words, baroque composers were primarily concerned with "rendering and translating into music the temper, disposition or frame of mind, passions, and mental reactions characteristic of man" (Lang). While this approach bears some resemblance to Plato's equating certain emotions with scales and instruments (see Part I, p. 13)—the latter, in fact, were also classified 'affectively' by some late baroque theorists, the horn being 'pompous', the flute 'modest', the kettledrum 'heroic', etc.—and is a natural development of the Renaissance technique of word-painting, it has much more in common, and indeed can be said to have originated with Rore's mood-expression (see p. 251). Not until the advent of monody, however, did the affections become of paramount importance, although monody, unlike its offspring, the fully-fledged opera aria, was not necessarily governed by a single affection.

The development and fulfilment of the doctrine took place in vocal music because the clearest way of establishing it was through the use of words which alone can impart a precise affection. Moreover, instrumental music, while it certainly added on occasion to the emotions conveyed by the singer, both in the aria and, often with great power, in the *recitativo accompagnato* or *stromentato* (i.e. recitative accompanied by the orchestra), could not by itself express either the intensity or the range of feeling of a well-trained voice. The doctrine reached fulfilment in opera, rather than in the cantata or oratorio, because firstly, from Monteverdi and Cavalli on, opera, to the Italians, was so vital, all-absorbing, and popular that it both reflected more clearly the artistic aims of its time, and also provided a more natural medium for experiment and innovation than any other kind of music. Secondly, only the opera aria was theatrical; in other words, the basic affection was much more easily and naturally 'put across' by the actor whose facial expressions and bodily movements would all contribute.

The basic affection, which, by the late baroque, dominated each independent musical movement, whether of an overture or concerto, or an aria, is always expressed as clearly as possible by means of a distinctive musical idea or motto. Each motto thus represents the quintessence of a basic affection, and while most of them naturally consist of a combination of melody, rhythm, and harmony, the distinctiveness of a motto nearly always lies in the greater importance of one of these elements, quite apart from whether it is in the major or minor mode. Mottoes that are primarily harmonic or rhythmic are first presented, as one would expect, in the opening ritornello, because the solo voice cannot express harmony and is an unsuitable vehicle for pure rhythm, but when melody is the prime feature of a motto it was natural that, with the affection clarified by words, it should be delivered by the voice at the very beginning of an aria. This 'motto beginning', which, as we have seen, became common with Cesti and later

Venetian composers (p. 401), is usually succeeded by a short instrumental ritornello which either imitates the voice (see Ex. 30, p. 450), or else introduces a related or new but always subsidiary and never strongly contrasted figure (for this would disrupt the affective unity) which is used in the course of the aria (see Ex. 34, p. 473).

Motto beginnings are musically artistic and emotionally significant when used with skill and imagination, but they became an empty mannerism in the hands of inferior composers who accepted mechanically the pseudo-scientific classification that took place during the early years of the eighteenth century. This linked affections with mottoes, usually in general terms, but the German theorists Scheibe, Heinichen, and Mattheson (see p. 488) went so far as to equate a particular motto with a specific affection, an absurd belief, for music cannot be so specific; thus in Ex. 31 (p. 453), for instance, the most distinctive falling fifth (the germ of the aria) might imply a number of affections, resignation or sadness, and not until the voice enters do we know it to be 'faithfulness unto death'. Obviously, if the mode becomes major, with or without a quickening of tempo, different affections will be implied. Even before this classification it was taken for granted that performers would recognize and their interpretation be dictated by the basic affection; hence the dearth of expression marks in baroque music. But the reliance placed on performers would have been unthinkable if the doctrine of affections had not been generally accepted and if the performers themselves, especially soloists, had not received a much more all-round musical education than is customary to-day. The performer, moreover, was much more than an interpreter in the modern sense; he was also a co-creator, and both composer and audience expected him to embellish in performance what was written down on paper. This applied with particular force to opera singers, especially the castrati, who were the first real virtuosi in the history of music, and in Neapolitan opera virtuosity was ranked higher than in any other art form before or since.

Operatic embellishments were of two kinds, ornaments and cadenzas. The former decorated the written notes with trills, grace-notes, scales, arpeggios, etc., particularly in the repeat of the first part of a *da capo* aria (the reprise); in the words of Pier Francesco Tosi [1646–1732], one of the greatest singing masters of his time, the first part of an aria needs "nothing but the simplest Ornaments, of a good Taste and few, that the Composition may remain simple, plain, and pure; in the second they [i.e. the audience] expect, that to this Purity some artful Graces be added, by which the Judicious may hear, that the Ability of the Singer is greater; and, in repeating the *Air* [i.e. the reprise], he that does not vary it for the better, is no great Master".* Cadenzas very often occurred on the final vocal cadence in both the first and second sections of the aria, and always in the reprise; they varied from short flourishes to extended passages of considerable virtuosity, and, like the ornamentation, the cadenza in the reprise was the most elaborate. The degree of virtuosity depended on the singer's technical mastery, the affection of the aria, and the aria type—ideally at any rate, though by no means all singers exercised such taste and discretion. The cadenza nearly always occurred on the ante-penultimate tonic $^6_4$ chord, and in the classical concerto as established by Mozart, not only the actual idea of a cadenza for the soloist, but also its position in the movement and its announcement by means of a cadential tonic $^6_4$ chord were taken over directly from the Neapolitan opera aria.

The most famous castrati were Nicola Grimaldi or Nicolini [1673–1732], Antonio Bernacchi [1685–1756], Francesco Bernardi or Senesino [*c.* 1680–*c.* 1750], Gaetano Maiorano or Caffarelli [1703–1783], Giovanni Carestini [*c.* 1705–*c.* 1759], and, the greatest of them all, Carlo Broschi or Farinelli [1705–1782]. Bernacchi was taught at Bologna, where he later founded a famous singing-school of his own; he placed execution before expression, unlike his fellow Bolognese, Senesino, whose voice, in the opinion of many, was purer even than Farinelli's, and whose clarity of diction and sensitive delivery in recitatives was unequalled. The other castrati named above were all trained in one of the Neapolitan conservatories that became world-renowned during the eighteenth century. Caffarelli and Farinelli were pupils of the most outstanding singing-master and one of the most influential teachers of composition of his time, Nicola Porpora [1686–1766], who travelled extensively, was sufficiently esteemed as an opera composer to be invited to rival Handel in London, and who, towards the end of his life,

* *Opionioni de' cantori antiche e moderni*, 1723. Translated by J. E. Galliard as *Observations on the Florid Song*, 1742.

taught young Haydn the fundamentals of composition. As a singing-master, Porpora's aims were those of Bernacchi, and his most famous pupil, Farinelli, after he had received some further instruction from Bernacchi, who defeated him in a contest of vocal virtuosity in 1727, was acknowledged as the most brilliant singer in Europe. Four years later, however, he changed to a much simpler and more expressive style of singing, and such was his art that when, in 1737, he visited Spain, he was able, like David before Saul, to banish the prolonged fits of melancholy suffered by Philip V [1683–1746] which had caused the King to neglect his realm. The Queen, by offering a most handsome salary, persuaded Farinelli to stay, and every night for the next ten years he sang the same four songs to Philip. Naturally, he became a great favourite (but never, as is sometimes stated, Prime Minister), and under Ferdinand VI [1713–1759] enjoyed a position of greater confidence and power than any official of the Crown. When Ferdinand died, Farinelli returned to Italy a very rich man, and spent his remaining years entertaining his many friends, among them noblemen from all over Europe, at his palatial mansion near Bologna. According to Giambattista Mancini [1716–1800], a pupil of Bernacchi and one of the leading singing-masters of his generation, Farinelli's voice "was thought a marvel, because it was so perfect, so powerful, so sonorous and so rich in the extent, both in the high and the low parts of the register, that its equal has never been heard in our times. He was, moreover, endowed with a creative genius which inspired him with embellishments so new and so astonishing that no one was able to imitate him."*

We have dwelt on Farinelli at some length not only because he was the most brilliant singer of his time, but also because his position at the Spanish court reflects, albeit in an extreme form, the enormous popularity, power, and prestige accorded to the castrati in every European country except France. But the vocal accomplishments of these men were not lightly achieved, and from the age of nine or ten until their late 'teens or early twenties they underwent a rigorous education that included acting, elocution, musical theory, and composition in addition to exercises that aimed at producing voices of extraordinary beauty, control, flexibility, and power. These four qualities

* Quoted from *Grove's Dictionary*, III, p. 25.

were not always regarded as of equal importance, and in the Neapolitan conservatories the last three took pride of place, as they are the most natural means whereby virtuosity and embellishment can be displayed.

The exceptional popularity and power of the castrati affected Neapolitan opera in a number of ways. Firstly, the lower male voices were virtually restricted to minor parts, because the chief 'male' characters were always castrati. Secondly, even women found it difficult at times to gain a principal rôle unless they were extremely gifted. The three most famous 'cantatrices' (i.e. virtuoso women singers) were the sopranos Francesca Cuzzoni [1700–1770], noted for purity of tone and intonation, and whose trills were so ravishing that on one occasion an enthusiast from the gallery of a London opera house shouted, "Damn her! she has a nest of nightingales in her belly!", and Faustina Bordoni [1693–1781], wife of Hasse (see p. 460), and who, apart from a charming face, figure, and personality (unlike Cuzzoni) was a most gifted actress, and possessed an unsurpassed agility of voice. The third cantatrice was Vittoria Tesi [1700–1775], whose compass was larger than Cuzzoni's or Bordoni's, but who excelled as a contralto of great power, so much so, in fact, that she became renowned in masculine rôles, an unnatural state of affairs that many less-gifted women singers were forced into by the supremacy of the castrati. Thirdly, the ordinary opera-goer was perfectly prepared to accept the spectacle of a castrato (most of whom, because of their operation, were taller and broader than the normal man) looking magnificently masculine as, say, Hercules draped in a leopard skin, but singing in a soprano voice. Lastly, most composers and librettists, apart from being more concerned with the placing of arias according to the conventions noted on p. 439 than with wedding music to drama or the natural development of the latter, were obliged to alter, replace, or add to what they had originally written if a 'star' singer so required.

Nevertheless, there were a few composers and librettists whose reputations were such that they were not bound to comply with the largely egotistical demands of the virtuoso singer. The two most important librettists were Apostolo Zeno [1668–1750] and Pietro Trapassi or Metastasio [1698–1782]. Zeno, whose first libretto, *Gl'Inganni Felici* (1695), achieved considerable popularity, was a Venetian. From 1718–29 he was court poet and historian to the Emperor Charles VI [reigned 1711–1740] at Vienna, and he effected a notable reform in opera libretti. Influenced by the French dramatists, notably Racine, he introduced a greater degree of unity into his plots (most of which are historical in theme) by largely rejecting comedy, the purely spectacular, and the arbitrary intervention of supernatural beings (except for the final *deus ex machina* which, because all his dramas end happily, was often used to resolve the complicated situation in the last act), and limiting the number of subsidiary plots that had formerly been introduced for spectacular or comic reasons. Each drama is generally divided into three acts, each act being divided into a number of scenes, and each scene into (usually) two parts, the first and by far the larger part unfolding the story by means of dialogue (secco recitative), and the second consisting (usually) of two four-line verses written in a highly polished and unimpassioned style, the first of which was meant to be repeated (A, B, A-aria); the verses express either the reactions of one of the characters to the situation of the moment, or else some more general sentiment, and in any case represent a unity of mood or basic affection.

Zeno's reforms, because they eschewed comedy and the irrelevantly spectacular, resulted in a type of opera known as *opera seria*. These reached their peak, so far as the libretti are concerned, in the hands of Metastasio, who wrote his first full-length libretto, *Didone abbandonata*, in 1723. This Roman poet quickly established a reputation, and in 1730 Zeno recommended him as his successor at Vienna. Metastasio was not only a better poet than Zeno, and a more imaginative dramatist (one of his plots even dared to end tragically), he was also a trained musician, having studied under Porpora at Naples, where he met and began a lifelong friendship with Farinelli. As a result, his verse, while it follows the same pattern as, and is no more impassioned than Zeno's, is more lyrical, its imagery is more alive, its language more conducive to a musical setting. This explains why his libretti were more popular than any other, for not only were they the basis of over a thousand operas in the eighteenth century (some of them, indeed, being set as many as seventy times), but, unlike Zeno's, were published in his lifetime.

Neither Zeno nor Metastasio were Neapolitans, but they restored to Neapolitan opera something of the literary distinction, dramatic integrity, and sincerity of expression of the early Venetian opera, the libretti of which, by Rinuccini and his imitators, were frequently, and sometimes luxuriously, printed, and were taken seriously by opera-goers, many of whom read them during performances. But the libretti of late Venetian opera began to deteriorate, and in Neapolitan opera, excluding those by Zeno, Metastasio, and a few others, the libretti are little more than loosely constructed patchworks of threadbare clichés and stereotyped situations. But it was the music and, more particularly, the way it was sung that mattered most.

The first opera produced in Naples was Monteverdi's *Poppea* in 1651. Three years later came *L'Orontea regina di Egitto*, by Francesco Cirillo [1623–after 1662] who, while a Neapolitan composer, spent most of his life in Rome. The first real Neapolitan composer was Francesco Provenzale [1627?–1704], of whose eight operas only two have survived complete —*Il Schiavo di sua moglie* (1671) and *Difendere l'Offensore* (1678). These display not only a remarkable melodic gift heightened by a most expressive use of chromaticism, but also an intimate connexion between music and drama and considerable variety of form (*H.A.M.*, 222); the era when the *da capo* aria and the castrati dominated opera had yet to come.

In 1684 Provenzale, who was highly esteemed in Naples, both as a teacher and composer, resigned from his position as second chapel-master to the Spanish Viceroy because the senior post, which he naturally expected to get, had been offered to a young musician from Rome, Alessandro Scarlatti [1660–1725]. Scarlatti's work was not unknown in Naples, as his first opera, *Gli equivoci nel sembiante* (Rome, 1679), had been presented in 1680, and three years later a new opera, *Psiche*, was performed for the first time in the city, followed by a revival of *Il Pompeo* (Rome, 1683) only a few weeks before his appointment. During each of the ensuing eighteen years Scarlatti composed at least one opera and sometimes as many as four. The demand for his work and the taste of his public caused him increasing irritation, as he was forced to write in a 'popular' style that offended his artistic standards. Matters came to a head in 1702, when his salary was in arrears and the city was politically disturbed. He asked for and was granted four months' leave, and went to Florence, where he enjoyed the patronage of an ardent music-lover, Prince Ferdinand de' Medici, for whom he composed some operas. The Prince, however, offered him no permanent position, and rather than return to Naples, Scarlatti accepted an inferior post as assistant chapel-master at the Santa Maria Maggiore in Rome. Here he suffered another disappointment, because opera was disapproved of by the Pope on the grounds of morality. To compensate for this, he composed a few operas for Venice and a considerable number for Prince Ferdinand.

In 1709 Scarlatti returned to his former post at Naples. His fame was now at its height and he could compose more or less as he liked ; the result was a series of operas that are a considerable improvement on those he had written earlier for Naples, notably *Tigrane* (1715), his 106th opera. But Rome, the scene of his first successes and later disappointments, was undoubtedly his favourite city, and in 1717, realizing that Papal disapproval had waned and that he had a considerable following there, he left Naples and did not return until 1722 or 1723. In Rome he composed his only comic opera, the delightful *Il Trionfo dell' Onore* (1718), and also his finest work for the stage, *Griselda* (1721), on a libretto by Zeno. This was his 114th opera, and the last of the thirty-six that have survived complete from a total of 115.

Scarlatti's operas reveal not only his development as a composer, but also, up to 1709 at any rate, the influence of the audiences for whom he composed. His earliest attempts display Venetian influence—then all-powerful in Rome—via the works of Stradella and Legrenzi. In these the dramatic situation dictates the musical treatment, aria forms are varied (see p. 400), recitatives are carefully composed, coloratura writing is restrained, ensembles are common, but crowd choruses are rare, though often highly effective in their realistic cries of praise, anger, etc. The music itself is short-phrased, rhythmically clear-cut, and sometimes dance-like, harmonically limited with rather angular and often ostinato basses, the texture is frequently polyphonic or contrapuntal, and is most strikingly revealed in orchestral accompaniments in four real parts none of which double the vocal line (Ex. 29*).

* A. Lorenz, *Alessandro Scarlatti's Jugendoper*, II, p. 28.

(destroys so that he should not escape)

These early operas, of which the only ones to survive are, apart from *Gli equivoci*, *L'honesta ne gli amori* (1680), and *Dal male il bene* (1681), show Scarlatti's fundamentally serious approach to music; they also show his immaturity in melodies that are haphazardly phrased and extended by exact repetition rather than by free or sequential development, and in the curious and occasionally harsh sounds that result from polyphony being unmatched by a sufficiently sure harmonic sense.

In Naples, during what we shall call his first Neapolitan period (1684–96), his technique and style became more polished, as he increasingly tended to work within a narrower field. This tendency may well have been partly self-imposed for artistic reasons, but it was also due to the necessity of satisfying the taste of his viceregal master and his audiences. As a result, the characters and dramatic situations of the libretti that he chose or was asked to set become more and more conventional, with the *da capo* aria prevailing, the importance of the orchestra gradually wanes to the point where most arias are accompanied by the continuo, sometimes with a single violin line added, the full orchestra being restricted to the ritornelli; polyphony and imitation seldom occur, and ensembles decrease in number, being mostly dialogue love-duets—the most popular type of ensemble in all Neapolitan opera. These somewhat negative features are more than balanced by others of a more positive kind. Thus partly because he was working within narrower limits, both formal and dramatic, and partly as a result of his natural musical development, his melodies become more regularly phrased, grateful, and sensuous, their construction less fragmentary, and their extensions less purely repetitive, with sequential passages more prominent. Moreover, the dramatic situations, although more conventional, cover a fairly wide emotional range, but any emotional intensity depended entirely on the composer and the singers, and Scarlatti demonstrates his exceptional gifts by producing an impressive array of arias that vary from grief to skittishness, from tenderness to bellicosity, with accompaniments ranging from continuo to full string band, sometimes with wind instruments added. Particularly striking are the arias in which a solo trumpet concertizes with the voice, a very popular feature in Neapolitan opera, as it enabled the singers, especially the castrati, to display their superior agility. The trumpet was chosen because in the seventeenth century its technique was more advanced than that of any other melodic instrument, and when, in the early eighteenth century, the violin surpassed it in this respect, it was still preferred as it alone could vie with the castrati in power and brilliance (Ex. 30,* p. 450).

Four features from the operas of this first Neapolitan period deserve special mention. First, the scene in which one or two characters express conflicting or changing emotions. For instance, in *La Rosaura* (1690) a lady laments her lover's fickleness in a largo aria, but her maid interrupts in an attempt

* Adapted from A. Lorenz, ibid., II, p. 46.

(Arise, brave warriors, rouse yourselves to arms !)

to cheer her up with a popular allegro tune. This is an extreme example, and the more usual treatment is to present different shades of the same emotion through a mixture of secco recitative, arioso, and aria. In at least one of his later operas—*Attilio Regolo* (1719) (III, 9)—Scarlatti developed the mixed scene into something approaching the strikingly dramatic 'grand scena' of Handel (see p. 478) and Gluck.

The second feature, accompanied recitative, combines the lack of form (i.e. of sectional repetition) and verbal clarity of the secco recitative with the semi-lyricism of the arioso, the resultant vocal line being set within an expressive orchestral framework (otherwise exclusively reserved for the aria) that might consist of sustained notes, rushing scales, tremolos, agitated rhythms, sweeping arpeggios, loud punctuating chords, etc. Admittedly this feature can be found in earlier works, e.g. Monteverdi's *Orfeo* (see p. 376) and Schutz's oratorios (see Chapter 5, p. 522), but Scarlatti was the first to make it operatically significant, beginning with *Olimpia Vendicata* (1685). In his last Roman and Neapolitan operas, accompanied recitatives occur regularly, usually preceding the more important arias, a position that became standard for late baroque vocal compositions, and largely through his example they became one of the emotional highlights of Neapolitan opera.

The third feature is the presence of comic characters (usually two) who enliven the proceedings in often broadly humorous episodes and who frequently round off the first two acts on a note of hilarity with a comic duet distinguished by a rapidity of patter and a vivacity of repartee impossible in the serious sentimental love-duets of the principal characters. It was this vivacity and its position that made the comic duet the starting-point of one of the most distinctive features of *opera buffa*—the end-of-act ensembles (see p. 483).

In 1696 Scarlatti revived *Dal male il bene*, composing new introductory music which established the form and texture of the 'Italian' overture or 'sinfonia', as it was called. This, our last feature, is in three movements, quick-slow-quick, its most significant characteristic being its essentially homophonic texture as compared to the contrapuntal-polyphonic French overture. Scarlatti's opera sinfonia, like his *da capo* aria, was shorter, simpler, and less expressive than the overtures of Lully and his successors. Its popularity, which caused the demise of the latter, *c.* 1750, and its expansion and structural development by later composers led to an entirely independent composition (see Chapter 6, p. 553) and ultimately to the classical symphony (see Part III).

In his second Neapolitan period (1697–1702) Scarlatti was forced to adopt a much more popular style. Polyphony gives way to virtually unrelieved homophony, coloratura passages occur in greater profusion, but are usually not excessive, recitatives are scamped, with the cadential falling fourth, axiomatic in later Neapolitan opera, becoming common, accompaniments are thin, the rôle of the orchestra being much diminished, and melodies grow increasingly facile, repetitive, and limited in expressive range, but more highly polished. Most of these last are either square-cut and strongly rhythmic, following the latest successful fashion in arias set by his younger contemporary, Giovanni Bononcini [1670–1755], or else impart, sometimes to the point of cloyingness, a sense of pathos that is one of the composer's most enduring traits. This is particularly true of his sicilianos, admired and imitated wherever Italian opera held sway, and characterized by a lilting $\frac{12}{8}$ rhythm, minor mode, and the prominence of the Neapolitan-sixth chord (Ex. 31,* p. 453).

This was Scarlatti's worst period, only slightly redeemed by some attractive arias (including Ex. 31, p. 453) and the comic episodes, now usually sung by a soprano and tenor or bass. In the Roman operas, because women were not allowed on the stage, the comic characters were generally an old woman (sung by a tenor—the forebear of the pantomime 'dame') and an old man (bass), and such was the popularity of this incongruous pair that they were not replaced by the more realistic young couple (the ancestors of Papageno and Papagena) until *c.* 1700.

We can only assess the operas Scarlatti wrote for Prince Ferdinand if we assume (and it is a reasonable assumption) that the two surviving ones written for Venice during the same period are similar in style. The better of the two, *Mitridate* (1707), is not only remarkable for its political plot and the fact that hero and heroine are brother and sister, but also for the dignity, sincerity, and at times passion of the music, particularly the accompanied recitative 'O Mitridate mio' and aria 'Cara tomba' sung by Mitridate's sister. For the first time since his early Roman days Scarlatti gave rein to his inherent seriousness. In *Mitridate* polyphony and counterpoint again become significant, incisive and fascinating rhythms abound, melodies are more varied and expressive, and are extended by sequence and motivic development (i.e. the use

* Adapted from A. Lorenz, ibid., II, p. 160. Words omitted.

Ex.31 Opening ritornello from 'Non mi tradir mai più' (*La donna ancora è fidele*, Naples 1698)
(♩. = MM. 36) A. Scarlatti

of short distinctive figures, usually taken from the main affective motto, which permeate and unify the texture and provide the chief means of modulating (see Ex. 34, p. 473), coloratura passages are frequent and sometimes reveal unmistakable instrumental influence in typical violin figurations, but seldom pander to mere virtuosity and are often very effective, the orchestra regains its earlier importance, even at the expense of the harpsichord, the string writing in particular being far more interesting and vivid as a result of the general improvement begun by Corelli (see Chapter 6, p. 551), and aria and even recitative accompaniments are enriched by a wider harmonic vocabulary (including the chords of the diminished seventh and augmented fifth in addition to the Neapolitan sixth) directed by a firmer feeling for tonality. Moreover, a number of arias are more extended than usual through the introduction of mildly contrasting ideas in both sections. Ensembles, while they occur in each opera, are infrequent, and so are solo choruses, i.e. choruses sung by all or most of the soloists; crowd choruses, as in the second Neapolitan period, are non-existent.

The most distinctive features of the operas that Scarlatti composed during the last sixteen years of his life, taken as a whole and compared to those immediately preceding them, are the greater number of accompanied recitatives, the more highly organized internal structure of each section of the aria, the occasional ensemble in which the characters express slightly different emotions or states of mind, and especially the more imaginative handling of the orchestra. Thus, horns, used rather tentatively for the first time in *Tigrane*, are employed more extensively and effectively in *Telemaco* (1718) and in every later opera; string parts show a considerable advance in technique, and the tendency, noted earlier, to treat the strings as a self-contained body, i.e. without the harpsichord, frequently results in a complete reversal of the usual procedure by accompanying the voice with strings alone, the harpsichord being restricted to the ritornelli. In this last period, too, recorders (always called 'flutes' in the baroque period), flutes (always designated as 'flauti traversa' or just 'traversa'), oboes, and bassoons occur more often than in the earlier operas, but, despite a few arias in which they have characteristic solos, their chief function is to sustain notes or double string parts, as in the symphonics of the early classical period. Scarlatti, in fact, in his operas written after 1702, laid the foundation of the Viennese classical style in the polish, sensuousness, expressive range, rhythmic precision, and impeccable phrasing of his melodies, in the motivic development of his arias, in his clear but colourful chromatic harmony, and in the variety of his texture, although his harmonic and textural richness was not imitated by most of his immediate successors.

It has been said that Scarlatti inaugurated the decadent Neapolitan operatic style; even if we admit the adjective, this statement is untrue, because his only 'decadent' operas were those written in his second Neapolitan period, in order to please a taste already formed. That he fostered this taste and, through his outstanding melodic gifts, did more to popularize the 'aria opera' than anyone else, is undeniable, and while we may regret the fact that he lowered his standards for a time, we must also recognize their essential seriousness, and also that they are manifest in a considerable number of operas, none of which can be called decadent and some of which are outstanding; indeed, his last operas contain a wealth of fine music, hardly any of which has been published, e.g. the arias 'Come presto nel porto' (*Griselda*, I, 6) and 'Hò in seno due fiamelle' (ibid., III, 7), and the 'mixed' scene in *Attilio Regolo* already mentioned, where the heroine, suffering nightmare visions of Hades, goes mad (see p. 450). As has been well said, Scarlatti, like J. S. Bach, was "a great man . . . forgotten by his own generation" (E. J. Dent).

But was Neapolitan opera decadent? The answer depends on two things. First, that we judge it not on its libretti, either as drama or as literature, but on its arias, which, as we have seen, were so arranged as to provide an admirable series of musical contrasts. (Such a judgement, incidentally, was, and is, applied to many late eighteenth and nineteenth-century operas, some of which are still popular, e.g. Mozart's *Magic Flute* and Bellini's *Norma*.) Secondly, that we are able, to some extent at any rate, to imagine the effect of these arias in performance, remembering that both composer and audience expected them to be embellished, and that hence what appears undistinguished in cold print would on the stage, even if we discount the atmosphere of the theatre with its lights, costumes, and elaborate scenery, be transformed, in the hands of a skilled singer, into something fascinating and even moving. It is this that is the main difficulty in assessing Neapolitan opera, because it is very doubtful whether sheer vocal virtuosity will ever again rank as high or achieve such brilliance as it did in the late baroque, it is even more doubtful whether the practice of extemporized embellishment will ever again become as important, and it is certain that the peculiar beauty and remarkable power of castrati tone will never again be heard.

If we judge a Neapolitan opera as it was meant to be judged by those who created, sang, and listened to it, and if we can imagine it as it was or might have been performed by the star singers of the day, then even if the libretto is a hotch-potch and the music commonplace, the work, far from being decadent, was vital in that it was partially and spontaneously created through the art of the singers. But if a singer fell below the best that was possible in beauty of tone or technique, and, relying on the tasteless ornamentation of some hack singing-master, failed to impart an air of naturalness and spontaneity to the embellishments, then his or her arias failed dismally, unless (and this happened but rarely, considering the enormous amount that was written) the music was so outstanding that it compensated for the singer's deficiency. This was the price Neapolitan opera had to pay for relying so heavily on the performer, and it explains the seemingly incredible behaviour of Italian opera audiences, who talked, played cards, and generally treated a visit to the opera as a social occasion. Such behaviour usually occurred after the first two or three performances, when those who attended had either been before and so knew which were the best arias and singers, or else had acquired this knowledge from those who had already seen the opera, but even on a first night the audience would soon realize whether an aria or singer was good or not, and, if the latter, would prefer to talk and eat, for Italian opera audiences were, and are, much less tolerant of incompetent singers than the audiences of other countries. The recitatives were seldom listened to because the story was usually well-known or followed conventional lines. To sum up, Neapolitan opera at its best was a brilliantly executed, emotionally varied, and vital work of art; at its worst it was musically and dramatically sterile, a vehicle for vulgar display. Before we condemn what we see in the score we should remember the quotation at the head of this chapter, for Burney was an ardent and serious student of opera, and, moreover, was writing when the supremacy of the castrati was on the wane.

By the early years of the eighteenth century Neapolitan opera dominated, to a greater or lesser extent, the stages of all the principal Italian cities and those of every European country in which opera was important, except France. In Russia, for example, the Empress Anne [1693–1740] founded, in 1734, a permanent opera at the Imperial Court at St. Petersburg (now Leningrad), importing an Italian company under the Neapolitan Francesco Araja [c. 1700–1767]. Araja resigned in 1759 and was succeeded by a long line of Italian composers, including such distinguished men as Galuppi (see p. 484), Traetta, Paisiello, and Cimarosa (see Part III, p. 709). While Russia had no native opera until the late eighteenth century, Spain had a flourishing tradition of comic opera, the 'zarzuela' (see p. 485), and this, plus the powerful religious atmosphere that persisted in circles of authority for most of the seventeenth century, explains why, in spite of the close ties with Italy, the first Italian opera house was not opened until 1738 (Madrid), the inaugural work being Hasse's *Il Demetrio* (see p. 460), although a few Italian operas had been produced earlier in both Madrid and Barcelona.

Every composer of Italian opera, no matter what his nationality, derived his style from that of Scarlatti, and unfortunately most of them took as their models the works of the second Neapolitan period, which, as we have seen, were the worst and least characteristic. Of Scarlatti's contemporaries and successors at Naples the most noteworthy were Leonardo Vinci [1690–1730], Francesco Mancini [1679–1739], Francesco Feo [c. 1685–c. 1745], Leonardo Leo [1694–1744], Francesco Durante [1684–1755], Porpora, Niccolò Jomelli [1714–1774] (see Part III, p. 712), and the Spaniard Davide Perez [1711–c. 1779]. Vinci expanded the Scarlattian aria, often by more strongly contrasting motives within each section, and favoured rhythmically arresting melodies and highly dramatic accompanied recitatives. Feo, Leo and Durante (the last the most outstanding teacher of opera composers of the century) were also notable church composers, and hence employed polyphony more than Vinci. Porpora was the virtuoso singer's composer *par excellence* (as one would expect), and his arias, while often excessively florid, are always extremely well written for the voice.

The most important centre of opera after Naples was Venice, and the leading composers were Carlo Francesco Pollarolo [1653–1722], Francesco Gasparini [1668–1727], Antonio Caldara [1670–1736], Tommaso Albinoni [1674–1745], Antonio Vivaldi [c. 1675–1741], Antonio Lotti [c. 1667–1740], Giovanni Porta [c. 1690–1755], and Giovanna Battista Pescetti [*c.* 1704-1766]. Apart from the more important rôle of the orchestra and the greater stress on the spectacular, Venetian opera was similar to Neapolitan, and the same is roughly true of opera elsewhere in Italy, except that in Rome, always the most conservative of Italian cities from early Christian times, sheer virtuosity was less favoured. Elsewhere in Italy the leading men were Francesco Pistocchi [1659–1726], a well-known castrato and the founder of a famous singing school in Bologna, G. Bononcini and his brother, Antonio Maria [1675–1726], Attilio Ariosti [1666–*c.* 1740], and Francesco Conti [1681–1732]. (Most of the composers mentioned above visited other European countries at least once, and some of them stayed for several years.)

Before we discuss the development of Neapolitan opera in Europe, we must make a distinction between what we shall call southern and northern Neapolitan opera. The former was predominant in Italy and relies entirely or very largely on pure melody and the art of the singer; as a result, the texture is basically homophonic, both in the arias, even when accompanied orchestrally, and in the instrumental numbers, notably the sinfonia. The northern type derived from the late works of Scarlatti, but was first actively cultivated in Germany by both Italian and German composers; compared to the southern type, it reveals Germanic traits in the frequency of contrapuntal textures and in the greater significance of the orchestra. Thus although the arias are still the most important items, they are more frequently accompanied by an orchestra in which the lower parts are more interesting, especially the bass, or by solo 'obbligato' instruments, particularly woodwind and brass, beloved by the Germans for centuries, which concertize with the voice; in addition, ensembles and solo choruses occur more often, and the French overture is preferred.

The main centres of Italian opera outside Italy were Munich, Hanover, Vienna, Dresden, and London. At Munich the chief figure was Agostino Steffani [1654–1728], an extraordinarily gifted and versatile man, and one of the most outstanding composers of the late baroque. Ably supported at first by Johann Kaspar Kerll [1627–1693], one of his teachers and a very accomplished musician, Steffani accentuated the difference between southern and northern Neapolitan opera by combining the German penchant for polyphony and instrumental music, imbibed from Kerll, with his native Italian lyricism and sensuousness. His melodies flow effortlessly, avoiding virtuosic excesses, his basses are interesting in themselves, not merely harmonic supports, ensembles, especially duets (see Chapter 5), are commoner than in the south, and his orchestral accompaniments are imaginative, with 'obbligato' arias particularly prominent, though the majority are accompanied by continuo only. During the last forty years of his life he was mostly at Hanover, first as the Elector's chapel-master and later as his chief diplomatist. His most successful operas were *Servio Tullio* (Munich, 1685), *Henrico Leone* (written for the opening, in 1689, of the Italian opera house at Hanover), *La Superbia d'Alessandro* (Hanover, 1690), and *I Trionfi del Fato* (Hanover, 1695).

Polyphonic texture, orchestral writing, and ensembles are also very apparent in the works of the Viennese composer, Johann Joseph Fux [1660–1741], and, though to a lesser extent, in those of his colleagues, Caldara, the Bononcini brothers, and Conti. Fux, a very learned but very dry and pedantic theorist, was the author of a famous text-book, *Gradus ad Parnassum* (1725), which classified Renaissance polyphony in general and Palestrina's in particular into five 'species', and remained the standard authority on strict modal composition until well into the nineteenth century. The best of his operas, however, while they display his academic skill, are by no means as dull and dry as they are sometimes made out to be, for although they lack the sheer lyricism of the Italian style they are full of noble arias, many of them 'obbligato', and some of them presented as fugues and even canons. He also achieves considerable variety by the frequent insertion of solo ensembles and crowd choruses. The least satisfactory items are the overtures, which in form hark back to the early baroque canzona or church sonata (see Chapter 6, p. 532) and are written in a very muddy, semipolyphonic style. His most famous opera was *Constanza e Fortezza* (1723), written to celebrate the Coronation of Emperor Charles VI as King of Bohemia, and produced on an even more lavish scale than was usual in Vienna.

Although Germany and Austria teemed with Italian composers, the greatest and most famous exponent of the southern Neapolitan type was a German—Johann Adolf Hasse [1699–

1783]. Hasse's first Italian teacher was Porpora, but he quickly changed to Scarlatti, for whom he subsequently entertained a lifelong admiration; later he married Faustina Bordoni, and became the favourite composer of Metastasio (all of whose libretti he set at least once) and the leading figure at Dresden. His operas were performed all over Europe, the best of them being *Il Sesostrate* (Naples, 1726), *Artaserse* (Venice, 1730), *Cleofide* (Dresden, 1731), *Il Demetrio* (Venice, 1732, a revival of which Mozart heard in 1770), *Tito Vespasiano* (Pesaro, 1735, which Mozart also heard in 1770 and which was performed in Moscow in 1742), *Demofoonte* (Dresden, 1748), and *Solimano* (Dresden, 1753); they reveal such an astonishing gift of elegant, exquisitely shaped, and effortless melody supported by smooth, limpid harmonies that the Italians called him *il caro Sassone* ('the beloved Saxon'). His aria style represents the quintessence of what we shall call *stile galante*, which stemmed from Scarlatti and which Burney called 'modern'; it was indeed one of the foundations of the Viennese classical style, lacking only the variety of texture and harmony found in the later operas of Scarlatti.

The Italian *stile galante* should not be confused with the French *style galant* (hence the distinction in language), for although both are completely homophonic in texture and the former derived from the latter, *stile galante* developed typically Italian characteristics (compare the following with p. 486), these are a type of melody that is clear-cut, mildly ornamented, rhythmically simple, constructed of short motives that are often repeated exactly, and are largely an extension, so to speak, of the chords which accompany it, and which is, above all, lyrical and sensuous; the rate of chord change is slower than in baroque style, the same chord often being repeated for several bars, with tonic and dominant pedals common, the chords themselves are less varied, the clarity of root position being much preferred to first inversion, and the individuality of the bass line is supremely unimportant. Compare Ex. 34—mature baroque style—with Ex. 35—early *stile galante*—and the aria on p. 497—fully developed *stile galante*. In Ex. 35, notice the waltz-like bass, the amount of repetition, and the way the three motives, *a*, *b*, *c*, are stuck together rather than joined. On p. 497 notice the purely functional bass line, the simplicity of the chord progressions and their slow rate of change, and the basically chordal nature of the melody when stripped of its *fioritura* (i.e. 'flowering' embellishments). Notice also the similarity to many slow movements in Haydn's and Mozart's piano sonatas.

We use the adjective 'gallant' in describing this style because it reflected the same attitude to life as the eighteenth-century courtier, particularly at the Court of Louis XV (see p. 487), when woman was the centre of a hot-house society in which man existed but to please, to charm, to captivate. Apart from *lèse-majesté*, almost anything was permitted, provided that it did not depart from an accepted code of behaviour that placed control of feeling and polished manners before everything, and provided also that it was expressed in elegant, refined language in which the exquisitely turned phrase, the *bon mot*, was more to be desired and commended than originality or sincerity of thought.

Hasse was more than just a melodist, and although the continuo aria predominates in his earlier operas, his later ones contain very few; indeed, he was superior to all his Italian contemporaries, except possibly Steffani, in his handling of the orchestra, in the greater care with which his secco recitatives are set and the music matched to the dramatic situation (hence his popularity with Metastasio), in the expressiveness of his accompanied recitatives that at times achieve real power and depth of feeling, and in his ability to extend a passage and increase its effect by motivic development instead of mere repetition (compare p. 497 with Ex. 35). To compare the best of Scarlatti with the best of Hasse (e.g. *Griselda* with *Demofoonte*) is most instructive, but we can here only mention a few general points. Apart from the features of *stile galante* mentioned, the arias in *Demofoonte* are longer, with secondary motives more clearly marked, and coloratura passages are more frequent and extended, most of them containing an implied vocal cadenza over a held tonic $^6_4$ chord near the end of the first section, and some of them demanding a truly instrumental agility (e.g. II, 2), and an astonishing range (e.g. *e*–*g″* in I, 13; both arias, incidentally, were composed for Carestini). The harmony, on the other hand, is simpler, with diminished sevenths and Neapolitan sixths (both very common in *Griselda*) rarely used, and the texture, even when strings plus woodwind and brass are employed, is more transparent, owing to the greater amount of doubling. In a number of arias section B is in a different tempo, and/or time signature, and/or key from section A (e.g. I, 5, where A=G major, $\frac{2}{4}$, Allegro di molto, and B=G minor, $\frac{3}{8}$, Un poco lento); this feature was probably copied from Handel, many of whose operas were performed under Hasse in Dresden after their début in London.

Hasse was so enamoured of Italian music that he remained quite unaffected by the music of his own country, though late in life he 'discovered' Keiser's excellence, much to his own astonishment (see below). In this respect he differed from his compatriot George Frederic Handel [1685–1759], the greatest opera composer of the late baroque, for Handel assimilated Italian, German, and French elements into a truly culminatory style. The Italian element we have already discussed; the French can be found in Lully's operas; so it is to the German that we now turn.

The chief centres of German opera were the courts of Brunswick (formerly called Wolfenbüttel) and Weissenfels, and, more especially, the city of Hamburg, where the mantle of Kusser fell on the most gifted composer of late baroque German opera, Reinhard Keiser [1674–1739]. Keiser, a man of flamboyant personality and luxurious tastes, and a musician whose talents aroused the admiration of Steffani, Handel, and (later) Hasse, composed well over a 100 operas (most of which have perished) and inaugurated the last and most brilliant period of Hamburg opera. His works, in the immediate appeal and often frankly popular flavour of the music, reflect the fact that he was writing for the public, not for nobility, and they reveal an extraordinary facility of invention and assimilation of diverse styles. From Italy he borrowed the recitative (secco and accompanied), arioso, and *da capo* aria, which last he often modifies slightly by altering the reprise and in which he ranges from lyrical and emotional *bel canto* to bravura passages of extreme difficulty; indeed, the voice is sometimes treated as a solo instrument with typically violinistic figurations and, in concerto grosso style, pitted against an orchestra that may consist of brass and woodwind. In *Croesus* (1711) he introduced the clarinet, which had recently been developed from the chalumeau (a single-reed, recorder-shaped instrument) by Johann Christian Denner [1655–1707]. Denner added two finger-operated keys and discovered the speaker hole, which enabled a new series of notes to be obtained whose fundamental is a twelfth above the natural fundamental—the distinctive feature of the clarinet. Its tone was more like a deep oboe and reminiscent of a distant trumpet, hence its name (from 'clarion'). French influence, which is apparent in the work of all German composers of German opera in the late baroque, is shown in the dance rhythms of some of his songs, in the number of dances, choruses, and ballets, and in the overtures, while native traits appear in catchy or comical Lieder often, like those of his predecessors (see p. 405), in simple binary form, in the comparatively complex texture of his orchestral accompaniments, and in the unusual depth of expression that he occasionally reveals. His best operas, apart from *Croesus*, are *Die Macht der Tugend* (1700), *Octavia* (1705), *Der Carneval von Venedig* (1707), *Fredegunda* (1715), and the comic opera *Der lächerliche Printz Jodelet* (1726).

But Hamburg opera, brilliant and successful as it was under Kusser and Keiser, was not approved of by all sections of the community (see p. 404), and in that branch of Protestantism known as Pietism, which became powerful *c.* 1700, opera found its bitterest opponent. Like the Calvinists, the Pietists believed in simplicity of worship, which meant the avoidance of both elaborate ceremonial and music that smacked of the concert hall or opera house, this last in particular being quite definitely of the devil; to them the congregational hymn (chorale) was the only acceptable kind of church music. The orthodox Protestant, however, believed that the styles and forms of secular music were not evil in themselves and that they became hallowed when set to sacred words, a view that, in Hamburg at any rate, eventually won the day after much controversy. Nevertheless, the split in the ranks undoubtedly weakened the position of German opera in the city and hastened the deterioration that began in the late 1720s and ended with the closing of the opera-house in 1738 and the extinction of German opera for over fifty years. This deterioration, which even Keiser, let alone his less-gifted successors, Georg Philipp Telemann [1681–1767] and Johann Mattheson [1681–1764], could not stem, was due to two factors, one internal, the other external. The former was the essentially popular nature of the operas in which, because castrati were forbidden to appear, the soprano and alto parts were taken by women, some of whom had doubtful reputations well known to the public. The element of vulgarity they introduced was held in check by Keiser's genius and the excellent libretti of a number of poets, of whom the best and last was Barthold Feind [1678–1721]. Feind was a serious writer with a first-rate dramatic sense, but his successors were not, and, pandering to the lowest taste of their audiences, they produced patchworks of inconsequential scenes which, if not obscene, were vulgar or trivial. This internal deterioration was accelerated by the invasion of Neapolitan opera from southern Germany. At first only a few arias in Italian were introduced, but these, owing to the liquidness of the language compared to German and to the enormously superior tone and technique of the Italian singers (castrati were eventually allowed *c.* 1730), increased in number. The result was bilingual opera, which was not so absurd as might appear because, as the recitatives were in German, the audience had a very good idea what each Italian aria was about, and in any case it was the music and the singing that really mattered. (Keiser's *Circe* (1734) is a good example, with twenty-one German and twenty-three Italian arias, the latter mostly by Vinci, Hasse, and Handel.) By 1739 Italian opera reigned supreme, and in 1741 the opera-house reopened under an all-Italian management.

The failure of German opera at Hamburg was paralleled in other German cities and courts. At Weissenfels not even the total ban on the Italian language prevented the eclipse of native opera in 1736. At Brunswick Italian opera was all the rage by the early 1730s despite the presence of Georg Kaspar Schürmann [*c.* 1672–1751], the most gifted composer of German opera after Keiser, and the only one capable of writing arias in the best Italian manner. By 1740 German opera had capitulated everywhere, and Italian *opera seria* reigned supreme until well into the nineteenth century.

The enormous influence of Italian opera is most clearly demonstrated in the works of Handel, for if anyone could have fought the Italians on their own ground and kept German opera alive it was he. As it was, however, after writing a few works for the Hamburg stage in his native tongue, and even after the success of *Almira* (1705), which made Keiser look to his laurels, he decided that a visit to Italy was imperative. Undoubtedly he learnt much from Keiser, but the sweetness of the

Italian style that he had as yet only half tasted, largely through the music of Steffani, whom he had met and impressed in 1703, was too captivating, and, from 1707–10, he visited Rome, Florence, Venice, and Naples, meeting and being acclaimed by some of the leading men and musicians of the day, including Scarlatti, Corelli, Lotti, and, once again, Steffani, and hearing, studying, and assimilating everything. At first his reputation rested on his keyboard playing, and as a harpsichordist he rivalled Italy's most brilliant virtuoso, Domenico Scarlatti, son of Alessandro (see Chapter 6, p. 554); but it was not long before his creative genius manifested itself, and only six months after his arrival his first Italian opera, *Rodrigo*, was performed in Florence. The following year (1708) he went to Naples, where he composed *Agrippina*, first performed, amidst scenes of wildest enthusiasm, at Venice in 1709. His rising reputation, the great success of *Agrippina*, and the recommendation of Steffani (who was vacating the post) led to the appointment of chapel-master to the Elector of Hanover, whose younger brother met Handel in Venice during the performance of the opera. The English Ambassador also suggested a London visit, an idea that was clearly so full of possibilities, in that London had no resident composer of any standing whatsoever, that Handel accepted his Hanoverian post on condition that he was allowed to visit England almost immediately.

In January 1710 Handel was in Hanover; six months later he was in London, where he found native opera moribund and Italian opera growing in popularity, but lacking a significant composer to really establish it. With his inherent shrewdness and flair for opportunism, he was soon convinced that richer rewards, both financial and artistic, lay in London than in Hanover, a conviction that was supported by the success of *Rinaldo* (1711), even though much of this was filched from earlier compositions and hastily put together. But he was not yet sufficiently sure of his own reputation to neglect his duties at Hanover for too long, and he left London soon after. When he returned in 1712 he knew the esteem in which he was held by the Elector and the extent of his own powers, and hence had no qualms about overstaying his leave.

Before we discuss Handel's operas, we must describe the operatic scene in London from Purcell's death to 1712. It is a dismal one; nothing new appeared until 1705, when Thomas Clayton (*c.* 1670–*c.* 1730] arranged a number of arias that he had brought back from a recent visit to Italy, added some music of his own, chiefly recitatives, adapted this miscellany to an English libretto by a naturalized Frenchman, P. A. Motteaux, and produced the result as *Arsinoë, Queen of Cyprus*. It was a fair success, and was described by Joseph Addison [1672–1719], poet, essayist, and Editor of the *Spectator*, as "the first Opera that gave us a Taste of Italian Musick", for the purpose of making this sweeping and stinging indictment of Italian opera: "That nothing is capable of being well set to Musick that is not nonsense." But while Italian opera was anathema to Addison, he seems to have had visions of founding a national school; unfortunately, he thought Clayton had talent and asked him to set a libretto of his, *Rosamond*. Clayton must have exhausted his stock of Italian arias on *Arsinoë*, and so composed all the music himself, with the result that the opera, produced in 1707, was such a failure that neither librettist nor composer ventured into the operatic field again.

Only two English operas followed: *Prunella* (1708), which directs that some of the tunes be borrowed from *Arsinoë*, *Thomyris*, and A. M. Bononcini's *Il Trionfo di Camilla* (for these last, see below); worthless as an opera *Prunella* is interesting as the earliest example of English intermezzi (see p. 482) and the first operatic satire on Italian opera. The second opera was *Calypso and Telemachus* (1712), by John Ernest Galliard [*c.* 1680–1749] (the translator of Tosi's treatise mentioned on p. 442), a work that Handel admired, and the last English opera until Thomas Augustus Arne [1710–1778] set Addison's *Rosamond* in 1733.

The "Taste of Italian Musick" afforded by *Arsinoë* was sufficiently sweet to encourage the Swiss librettist J. J. Heidegger [1659?–1749], Manager of the newly built Queen's Theatre, Haymarket (later King's Theatre, now Her Majesty's Theatre), to inaugurate, in the same year, a season of Italian opera, beginning with *Gli Amori piacevoli d'Ergasto* ('The Loves of Ergasto' as he called it), specially composed by Jakob Greber [fl. 1700], the first opera in London that was sung in Italian throughout. (The Queen's Theatre, designed by the well-known architect Sir John Vanbrugh [1664–1726], and, after its destruction by fire in 1789, its successor, remained the principal centre of Italian opera in London until after 1847, when the Royal Italian Opera House (now the Covent Garden Theatre was formed.)

From 1705 to 1712 at least one new Italian opera, either adapted or composed specially, was given at the Queen's Theatre, the most notable being by Gasparini, Scarlatti, Mancini, Conti, and the Bononcini brothers. Gasparini's *Ambleto* (Venice, 1705; London, 1712) is the earliest *Hamlet* opera on record, but is not based on Shakespeare's play; Scarlatti's *Pirro e Demetrio* (1708) was arranged by a resident Italian, Nicola Haym [*c.* 1679–1729] (who later wrote several of Handel's libretti), with additions from *La Rosaura*, libretto being translated into English by O. MacSwiney, though some arias were sung in Italian, as the famous castrati Nicolini made his London début in this opera. Nicolini also sang in Mancini's *L'Idaspe fidele* (Naples, 1705; London, 1710), a very successful work sung entirely in Italian. This became customary from 1705 on, owing to the increasing number of Italian singers who visited England; indeed, most of those connected with opera were of foreign extraction and included, in addition to Heidegger, Motteaux, and Haym, the German composers Greber, Galliard, John Christopher Pepusch [1667–1752], and John Frederick Lampe [*c.* 1703–1751], and a host of Italians who, from 1700 on, quickly replaced the French musicians, favourites during the Restoration period. The chief of these were the castrati mentioned on p. 442, together with Angelo Maria Monticelli [*c.* 1710–1764], Gioacchino Conti or Gizziello [1714–1761], and Valentino Urbani or Valentini (London, 1707–15), the women Cuzzoni, Bordoni, Anna Strada del Pò (London, 1729–38), Francesca Margherita de L'Épine [d. 1746], who married Pepusch, and Margherita Durastanti [b. *c.* 1685]; and the basses Antonio Montagnana (London, 1731–after 1738) and Giuseppe Boschi (London, 1710–28), the most celebrated bass of his time. In addition there was the French-born but Italian-trained Elizabeth Duparc ('La Francesina') [d. 1778]. Instrumentalists included the violinists Geminiani, Veracini, Pietro Castrucci [1679–1752] and his brother Prospero [d. 1760], Giacomo Cervetto [1682–1783], the Frenchman Charles Dieupart [d. *c.* 1740], and the Fleming William Defesch (b. *c.* 1758]; 'cellists included Filippo Amadei [b. *c.* 1683] (usually and wrongly called

Mattei), Andrea Caporale [d. *c.* 1756], and Dall'Abaco [1710–1805], while the woodwind players, as we might expect, were mostly Germans, e.g. the flautist Karl Friedrich Weidemann [d. 1782], the oboists Kytsch and Galliard, and the bassoonist Lampe, the only notable exception being the Flemish flautist Jean Baptiste Loeillet [d. 1728]. The only English performers who could compare with this galaxy, none of whom could compete with the best, except the two trumpeters mentioned below, and possibly Beard, were the sopranos Catherine Tofts [d. 1756], Cecilia Young [1711–1789], who married Arne, her sister Maria Susanna [1714–1766], and Anastasia Robinson [*c.* 1695–1755], the basses Richard Leveridge [*c.* 1670–1758], Lewis Ramondon [d. *c.* 1770] and William Savage [1720–1789], the tenor John Beard [*c.* 1717–1791], the violinists John Banister [d. 1735], John Clegg [1714–*c.* 1750], and Matthew Dubourg [1703–1767], the flautist Jack Festing [d. 1772], and the trumpeters John Shore [d. 1752] and Valentine Snow [d. 1770].

The most successful operas before Handel appeared on the scene were, apart from *L'Idaspe fidele*, *Thomyris* (1707), one of the many pasticcios (literally 'pie', i.e. 'medley') so popular in the late baroque, and arranged in this case by Pepusch (who composed the recitatives) from arias by Scarlatti, Steffani, Gasparini, Albinoni, and G. Bononcini to an English libretto by Motteaux, the anonymous *Almahide* (1710) and, finally, A. M. Bononcini's *Il Trionfo di Camilla* (Naples, 1696 ; London, 1706), arranged by Haym to an all-English libretto; later, for reasons already given (see p. 467), many of the arias were sung in Italian, but it was never performed wholly in this language, a fact that largely explains why it was the most successful opera in London during the entire eighteenth century.

When Handel returned to London in 1712 he lost no time in establishing both himself and Italian opera with *Il Pastor Fido*, based on Guarini's pastoral play (see p. 266), and *Teseo* (1713). In 1714 Queen Anne died and Handel's master became George I [d. 1727]. The strained relations between Handel and the King have been exaggerated by many writers, and the Water Music story, charming as it is, has no foundation in fact. What is certain is that George I attended a performance of *Amadigi* in 1715, and shortly afterwards doubled the pension of £200 a year settled on Handel by Queen Anne. In 1719, with the King's support, Handel founded the Royal Academy of Music at the King's Theatre and left England in search of singers, returning with Senesino, Boschi, and Durastanti. As the Academy's Director, Handel invited G. Bonocini and later Ariosti and Heidegger to assist him. Bononcini arrived in 1720 and stayed until 1732; Ariosti arrived in 1722, but was not a success.

The Academy got off to a flying start, both artistically and financially, with performances of Porta's *Numitore* (1720), followed by Handel's *Radamisto*, but almost from the beginning friction began to creep in. Bononcini allowed himself to be set up as a rival by an anti-monarchy group, led by the Prince of Wales, who were jealous of the German's prestige at Court. In 1722 Cuzzoni was engaged, and while she was artistically a great asset, her enormous fee, added to that of Senesino, financially weakened the Academy. It managed to keep going, however, largely through a succession of superb operas by Handel, but the end was hastened by the incredibly tactless engagement of Bordoni in 1725. The strife between the two cantatrices spread to their supporters in the audience and eventually developed into free fights, the culmination being a stage brawl in Bononcini's *Astianatte* (1727). In 1728 the disruption within and the tremendous success of *The Beggar's Opera* without (see p. 479), caused the Academy to collapse bankrupt. Handel, undismayed and hardly affected financially, entered into a contract with Heidegger, visited Italy to obtain new singers, and on his return composed *Lotario* (1729). This was a failure, the public's taste, always tickled by something new, being temporarily but completely captivated by the realism and natural freshness of *The Beggar's Opera* and its successors, the so-called 'ballad operas'. But Handel persisted despite repeated financial failures, recouping some of his losses with revivals of his cantata *Acis and Galatea* (1719) and *Rinaldo*, and the first performance of his first oratorio, *Esther* (1732). Handel's quarrel with Senesino in 1733 and, in the same year, the establishment of a rival Italian opera company (the 'Opera of the Nobility') brought Handel's second operatic venture to a disastrous close in 1734. Heidegger gave up the King's Theatre, and the Opera of the Nobility moved in, with first of all Porpora, later Hasse, as chief composer and the star singers

Farinelli, Senesino, Cuzzoni, and Boschi. Again Handel refused to admit defeat and continued to compose operas, which he presented at Covent Garden until 1737. Exhausted by his creative effort and depressed by his financial failures, he spent some months abroad refreshing both mind and body. On his return Heidegger, who was once more Manager of the King's Theatre, after the Opera of the Nobility had also failed in 1737, commissioned two operas, neither of which were successful, nor was his last opera, *Deidamia* (1741).

Handel was unquestionably the greatest composer of operas in the late baroque, but inevitably, in view of the difficulties in justly appraising them (see p. 455), they have been almost completely overshadowed by his oratorios, particularly in England, where, apart from the question of language, opera has never, until recently, taken root. This is both unfortunate and unfair, because we cannot fully appreciate his genius unless we take into account that considerable part of his creative output which was, after all, his first love, and into which he poured so much of his finest music.

When Handel first went to Italy he already had a fair grasp of the Neapolitan style, and on his visit he undoubtedly acquired the final polish. In *Agrippina* he is already revealed, not only as a melodist of the first water, but also as a complete master of his craft, with an expressive range and harmonic vocabulary as wide as Scarlatti's, and an equal if not superior skill in handling the orchestra. His melody and harmony did not develop greatly from *Agrippina* on, for, like Mozart, he reached maturity at a time when musical style was stabilized, i.e. when there was a common stock of melodic and harmonic 'formulae' from which everyone drew, and one of the things that distinguishes his work from that of his contemporaries is the extraordinary consistency with which he unerringly selects and combines some of these formulae to form melodies that make a direct appeal, are seemingly inevitable, often memorable, and remarkably varied, and which are supported by chord progressions, actual or implied, that, while they sometimes surprise, are always apt. None of his contemporaries possessed this melodic gift, not even Bach, who in any case was less concerned with immediate melodic appeal, for while composers like Hasse and Scarlatti, who most nearly approach him in this respect, wrote a great many flawlessly constructed melodies, the proportion of these to their total output is considerably smaller than in Handel's case.

It is impossible to give here even an adequate summary of the riches to be found in Handel's operas, but we can give some idea of the variety that they contain by analysing *Agrippina* (*A*) and *Rinaldo* (*R*) and mentioning in addition the most notable features of later operas that are not included in these two.

All Handel's overtures are based on the French model, and in that to *Agrippina* the Adagio coda to the second movement, common in both Lully and Handel, takes the form of a most effective oboe cadenza. This is a fine overture scored for strings plus third violins, oboe, and continuo. (By strings we mean first and second violins and violas.) In many of the overtures the second movement is in 4/4, as opposed to Lully's almost invariable 3/4 (see p. 420), and most of them have one and sometimes two extra movements (often dances), e.g. *Rinaldo*, where the overture is really an orchestral Corellian sonata (see Chapter 6, p. 551) in that the fugal second movement is followed by a short Adagio passage ending on the dominant of the relative minor by means of a typically Corellian Phrygian cadence (Ex. 32*):

Ex.32 Phrygian cadence from the overture to *Rinaldo*

and is followed by a 12/8 jig in F (the key of the overture) in A, B form.

The melodic types include the undulating pathetic siciliano *à la* Scarlatti (*A*, I, 17), and others in gently lilting 6/8 or 12/8, the popular song (Ex. 33 p. 472; note the superbly placed top A in bar 8): the *bel canto* (*R*, I, 7), the strongly rhythmic, undoubtedly learnt from G. Bonocini (*A*, II, 1), the florid 'bravura' (*A*, III, 11—all the aria types mentioned on p. 439 can be found in every Handel opera), and the spacious, boldly-arched type. (Ex. 34, p. 473. The ritornello that follows the vocal motto beginning shows one of the commonest of all Handel's

*Exx. 32–35 are taken from the Complete Edition, ed. Chrysander.

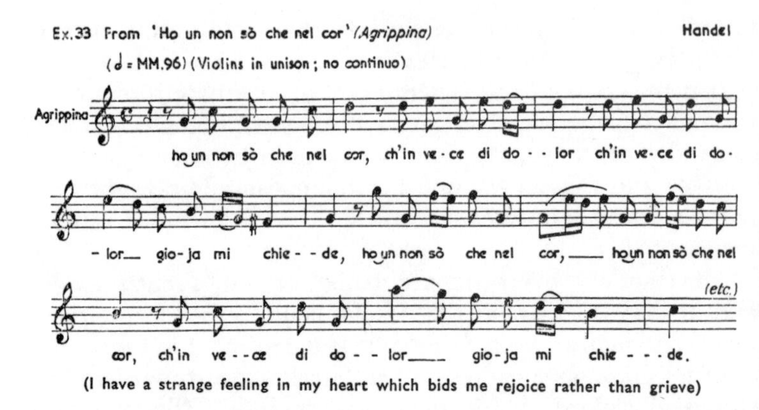

motives, and is a typical example of late baroque expansion through melodic and harmonic sequence.) In addition there are arias based on the popular dances of the day (see Chapter 3, p. 410), such as the bourée (*R*, 'Il Tricerbero'), corrente (*A*, II, 21; see also Ex. 35, p. 278), sarabande (*R*, the well-known 'Lascia ch'io pianga'), and, most common of all, the minuet (*A*, III, 14. There is no gavotte-aria in *A* or *R*, but several occur in his later operas, e.g. *Ottone* (1723), II, 9.) We must also mention the very unusual Ländler-like $\frac{3}{8}$ aria (*A*, III, 10) with its opening rhythmic phrase and its later . It was clearly popular enough for Handel to include in *Rinaldo*, and is typical of his greater rhythmic freedom compared to his contemporaries.

As well as *da capo* arias, which, as we would expect, predominate, there are ariosos (*A*, I, 7) and ariettas, i.e. songs, in one section (*A*, I, 21). The *da capo* arias themselves are remarkably varied in texture, character, accompaniment, and key relationship between the two sections. As regards the last, in arias in the major mode section B ends usually in the mediant minor (e.g. if section A is in C, section B ends in E minor), and in arias in the minor mode B nearly always ends in the dominant minor.

The accompaniments can be divided into three main categories, those for continuo alone or in which strings play only in the ritornelli (*A*, I, 7), those for orchestra and continuo throughout section A (the accompaniment for B frequently differs from A and sometimes is just continuo), and the much

(Today my happy fate comes down upon me from the stars)

rarer class where the continuo plays only in the ritornelli (e.g. Ex. 33, p. 234). In the first category the distinctive feature is usually the character of the bass line, which may consist of an incisive ostinato motive (*A*, III, 2), a persistent dotted rhythm (*A*, II, 16), or running semiquavers (*A*, I, 19), etc.

It is in the second category that Handel's resource in varying his arias is most fully shown. Strings and continuo are the basic group, and these are permuted in all sorts of ways. (Unless otherwise stated, the voice is doubled by an instrument for most or all of the time.) Thus the texture may be homophonic with violins I and II mostly in thirds (*A*, I, 14), contrapuntal (*A*, II, 12), or polyphonic (*A*, I, 13). In this last there are some sudden and, because of their context, most dramatic unison and octave passages with the voice, a technique that Handel used with extraordinary effectiveness, even for a whole aria (e.g. *A*, II, 14). Violins in unison plus continuo were, in fact, a very popular accompaniment in the late baroque, owing to the clear, brilliant, and sometimes striking effect they produce (e.g. *A*, III, 20, where the jagged violin motive that leaps to *e'''* three times punctuates and accompanies a vocal line that is almost as restless. It is worth noting here that unison violin passages occur much more often in the works (vocal and instrumental) of the Italianate Mozart than in those of the more Germanic Haydn). At the other extreme is the contrapuntal texture in five real parts (*A*, III, 8), and imitative polyphony *a*5 and even *a*6 (*A*, II, 5). (In these last two instances the vocal part is quite independent.)

The oboe was the favoured wind instrument, and remained so through most of the century, because, unlike the bassoon, it is a high-melody instrument whose tone, then, could approach both the softness of the recorder and the brilliance of the trumpet; it was thus capable of blending with, but at the same time giving an edge to violin tone, and also of maintaining an independent line more successfully than the recorder or flute. Trumpets and horns could only play successive notes of the diatonic scale in their top register and were usually reserved for hunting, martial, and suchlike arias and choruses, e.g. the magnificent bass aria (*R*, I, 3) scored for two trumpets, tympani (kettledrums), oboe, etc. (i.e. strings and continuo), the 'Battle' music for four trumpets, tympani, two oboes, etc. (*R*, III, 10), and the triumphal opening and closing solo choruses in *Giulio Cesare* (1724) for four horns, two oboes, etc.

Many of the more spacious of Handel's arias are written in the concerto style ('stile concertante'), when one or more solo ('concertino') instruments are set off against an orchestral ('ripieno') body that normally comprises strings and continuo. For example, the concertino group may be violin and bassoon (*R*, I, 9), two trumpets (*R*, III, 9), two trumpets and oboe (*R*, I, 3), or two oboes, two violins, and two 'cellos (*A*, III, 11). Allied to this type of aria are those in which the orchestra is divided into two (*R*, II, 8, where one group consists of violins I and II, oboe, and continuo, the other of violins III, violas, and 'cellos doubled by bassoon; each part is separate and no part doubles the voice; see also pp. 476–7). In this last example, which opens with a poignant, imitative duet between bassoon and oboe, the grief of Armida is underlined by the two groups exchanging the short rhythmic fragment 𝄾♪♩ that later intensifies to 𝄾♬♩—a simple but extraordinarily telling accompaniment. This is an example of mood-painting, which, together with the much rarer word-painting, occurs more frequently and is more imaginatively expressed in Handel's operas than in those by any other late baroque composer, except possibly Rameau. In 'Cade il mondo' ('Let the world fall') (*A*, II, 4), the opening bass phrase in $\frac{6}{8}$ quavers plunges through two octaves (*d'-f-e-d-A-D*), and the whole aria demands the remarkable range of *D-f'*. In 'Vaghe fonti, che mormorando' (*A*, II, 7) the 'murmuring fountain' is delightfully portrayed by two recorders that double muted violins in slow quaver chords in $\frac{3}{4}$ time with a little rippling turn on the third beat, and accompanied by muted violas, pizzicato 'cellos and basses, and no harpsichord. Garden and country scenes never failed to call forth some picturesque music from late baroque composers, and Handel was no exception, the 'Pastoral Symphony' from *Messiah* being the famous but by no means the best example. Instances abound, but we must only give one further reference, the arietta 'Augelletti che cantate' (*R*, I, 6), where 'the birds that sing' are delightfully imitated in a long introductory ritornello, most of it played by a sopranino and two treble recorders accompanied solely by violas, the aria ending with an entrancing five-bar unaccompanied cadenza for the sopranino. The fact that Handel uses the violas (the Cinderellas of the string family) as a support is typical of his imaginative use of instruments and keen ear, for viola tone gives just the right amount of 'weight' to the light-toned recorders and sopranino.

Handel's superior dramatic sense compared to other composers of Italian opera is demonstrated in his accompanied recitatives (e.g. *A*, II, 5, where tremolo strings and shoals of diminished sevenths underline Ottone's shock at being called a traitor), in mixed scenes (*A*, II, 13), and in arias where section B is in marked contrast to A. For example, the aria in the mixed scene referred to begins in $\frac{3}{4}$ Andante, the voice, after a ritornello of broken, restless unison fragments, entering with

'Pensieri voi mi tormentate' ('Thoughts, you torment me') set to a falling phrase echoed by a solo oboe, which later concertizes with the voice on two long melismas to the penultimate syllable of 'tormentate'. (Notice the 'modern' use of the oboe, i.e. as an emotional instrument.) Section B, on the other hand, is in $\frac{4}{4}$ Allegro, and the forcefully syllabic vocal line, accompanied by strings and continuo (but not, be it noted, oboe), impassionately declaims 'Ciel, soccorre a miei disegni' ('Heaven, aid my schemes'). To be sure, most composers would have made some distinction between the two sections, for musical if not dramatic reasons, but none of them at the age of twenty-four created what is in effect a dual-affection aria of such power. Dual-affection arias can, indeed, be found in many of Handel's operas, and also in some ensembles (e.g. *R*, II, 6, and *R*, III, 7); a more striking instance occurs in *Orlando Furioso* (1733) (III, 8), where Angelica sings 'questo pianto e sangue ancor' to a chain of 'sobbing' suspensions, while Orlando sings 'ma non placa il mio giusto rigor' in quick but firm dactyllic rhythm.

If, to the above brief analysis of *Agrippina* and *Rinaldo*, we add two-, three-, and four-part recitatives, trios, quartets, and solo choruses, and purely instrumental pieces, we get some idea of the amazing variety contained in a single opera, a variety typical of all Handel's later operas. Few of these exceed *Agrippina* or *Rinaldo* in this respect, but some of them display individual items that, musically or dramatically, are an advance on or cannot be found in the two earlier operas. A few examples must suffice: in *Orlando* (III, 8) the voice is accompanied by two 'violette marine' (that is, two viole d'amore) played originally by the Castrucci brothers, of whom Pietro was the leader of Handel's opera orchestra; in addition to strings and continuo, we find two horns and two oboes (*Radamisto*, III, 6), two trumpets, two horns, and two oboes (ibid., final solo chorus), two recorders and two oboes (but alternatively, as the same performers played these two instruments, but rarely the flute) (*Alcina* (1735), II, 5), and, finally, the most sumptuously colourful music in Handel's entire output, the seventeen-bar Sinfonia for double orchestra that accompanies the vision of Parnassus, where Virtue, attended by the nine Muses, sits enthroned (*Giulio Cesare*, II, 2); the first orchestra, which plays the first nine bars, consists of strings, 'cellos, oboes (doubling violins I), bassoons (doubling 'cellos), theorbo, viola da gamba (playing two- to four-part chords), and harp (bass doubling 'cellos, treble mostly doubling violins I); in the last eight bars the harp indulges in semiquaver broken-chord figures, and the second orchestra, consisting of strings, oboes (doubling violins I and II), and basses, joins in. There is no harpsichord part.

The importance of the orchestral accompaniment in Handel's operas can be readily appreciated from a casual perusal of the scores. Sometimes the term 'orchestral accompaniment' is positively misleading, because the quality and character of the instrumental parts is as essential to the whole as the vocal part, and it is both amusing and instructive to read that some of Handel's singers objected to the unusual richness and interest of his scoring on the grounds that their thunder was being stolen; nearly 150 years later much the same objections were made against Wagner's music dramas. Nevertheless, it is not so much his skill as an orchestrator as his development in dramatic expression and characterization that distinguishes many of his later operas from *Agrippina* and *Rinaldo*. Again only a few instances must suffice: at the end of the very moving aria 'Stille amare' (*Tolomeo* (1728), III, 4) the dying hero sings 'la morte a chiamar' ('death calls'), and in the final repetition of this phrase Handel, in a stroke of sheer genius, omits the last word as Tolomeo falls lifeless to the ground, ending the vocal line unaccompanied on an implied dominant seventh which the orchestra softly resolves, and, incidentally, anticipating by over a century the final bars of Schumann's *Mondnacht* (see Part IV, pp. 823, 824). Occasionally emotion is intensified by an exceptionally chromatic passage or by unusual chord progressions (e.g. *Rodelinda* (1725), III, 3). In complete contrast to the above are the *stile galante* arias (Ex. 35, p. 478) and those in the racy *buffo* style (see p. 483) that Handel learnt from the operas of Pergolesi and others during his 1733 visit (*Serse* (1738) I, 15). In some of the last operas the solo chorus is replaced by the potentially much more dramatic crowd chorus, especially in *Alcina* which in this respect and in its numerous ballets, was probably influenced by the enormous success of Rameau's *Hippolyte* (1733; see pp. 492-3). Finally, there are the mixed scenes which developed considerably from those in *Agrippina* and *Rinaldo*, and two of these (*Tamerlano*

(1724), III, 10, and *Orlando*, II, 11), because of their length and dramatic impact, are veritable 'grand scenas'; the latter, in fact, is the most powerful scene in Handel's entire output, its most striking aspect being the vivid portrayal of Orlando, here no symbolical type, but a living being in the last stages of mental collapse. In the vast majority of baroque operas neither librettist nor composer was concerned to present the characters as flesh-and-blood figures, and while there are a few exceptions, e.g. Ottone and Ottavia in Monteverdi's *Poppea*, the brother and sister in Scarlatti's *Mitridate*, and Purcell's *Dido*, Handel surpassed all other baroque composers in the extent of his characterization and in the number of occasions in which one feels that he identified himself with the emotions of a particular character. One must not exaggerate this aspect of Handel's operas, for most of his principal figures are treated conventionally enough, but it is possible that his distinction in this respect was influenced by the individualism of English society, so much more marked than on the Continent, and reflected in the detailed observations of ordinary men and women and their affairs portrayed in the largely satirical art of William Hogarth [1697–1764], and more especially in the novels of Samuel Richardson [1689–1761], the founder of the modern novel.

To sum up: Handel, in his operas, drew together a number of different threads, as it were, and wove a musical fabric that is more skilfully constructed, varied, and consistently excellent than the operatic output of any of his contemporaries. Italy gave him the foundations of his style—the supremacy of sensuous melody supported by clear, diatonic, though sometimes richly spiced harmony, and the homophonic *galante* and *buffo* styles, as well as the *da capo* aria and the secco and accompanied recitatives. French influence is revealed in his dance-arias, in his overtures, and his German origin in the frequency with which contrapuntal and polyphonic textures occur. The frankly popular element, the use of non-*da capo* forms, the greater contrast of vocal timbres through the use of natural male voices (favoured by Handel more than any of his contemporaries except the French), and, above all, the delight in instrumental sonority and colour also stem from his native country.

The waning fortunes of Handel's operatic ventures after 1728 were due to a number of causes, of which *The Beggar's Opera* and its successors were but one. This work is another example of a pasticcio, for the poet and dramatist John Gay [1685–1732] selected a number of popular pieces, asked Pepusch to add a bass to those that had none and compose an overture, and strung them on to a story about London's thieves and vagabonds. The result is by no means a ballad opera, because only a few of the tunes are folk-songs, the majority being well-known items by Handel, Lully, Purcell, etc. It was very successful because it was a completely new kind of entertainment in which the Government, particularly the Prime Minister, Walpole, was satirized (always good box-office this) and Italian opera caricatured (but not violently). Moreover, it was performed in English throughout, with spoken dialogue instead of recitative, the story was up-to-date and down-to-earth, and the tunes were both popular and of a high standard. It was neither intended as nor did it become the death-blow of Italian opera (Gay and Pepusch, in fact, were both personal friends of Handel), and the period immediately after its production witnessed not only a host of similar ballad operas, but also the most intensive activity in the field of Italian opera.

Most of the ballad operas were performed at the Lincoln's Inn Fields Theatre, where the actor-dramatist John Rich [1682?–1761] was Manager from 1714 to his death. He is important as the founder of English pantomime (originally, as the word implies, a mime or dumb show), which he developed from the Italian *Commedia dell' Arte* characters, and presented annually from 1716 to 1760. In 1728 he accepted *The Beggar's Opera* (refused by his rival, Colley Cibber [1671–1757], then Manager of the Drury Lane Theatre), and its success, in the words of a contemporary wit, "made Gay rich and Rich gay". In 1730 he opened a subscription list for building the Covent Garden Theatre, which was completed in 1732. The next year, at Lincoln's Inn, he switched from ballad opera to Italian opera (the 'Opera of the Nobility'), a significant fact that helps to place in its right perspective the sometimes exaggerated effect of the former on the latter. Ballad opera, indeed, was only really popular for seven years, during which nearly fifty were produced (further evidence of the passion for novelty), and not until Arne's *Love in a Village* (1762) was there a brief revival. Arne was the only English composer of any distinction during the late baroque and early classical periods, and while he shows the influence of *stile galante* much more than does Handel, he imbued it with a freshness, simplicity, and charm that one can only describe as 'English', and which is best displayed in the numerous songs he wrote for the stage, e.g. 'Blow, blow, thou winter wind' and 'Where the bee sucks'. In 1733 he successfully re-set Addison's *Rosamond*; other operas followed, including *Artaxerxes* (1762), on a translated libretto by Metastasio, in which the music is completely Italianate, but, unlike most native operas of the time, is sung in English throughout (i.e. recitatives, not spoken dialogue). It was a great success, but instead of following it up with another similar one, Arne, like the vast majority of opera composers of his time, must needs emulate the Italians on their own ground; the result, *L'Olimpiade* (1764), on an original Metastasian libretto, was a complete failure.

Apart from Gay, the chief ballad-opera composers were Fielding, Cibber, and the playwright Charles Coffey [d. 1745]. Any success they or other writers had depended primarily on their wit and satire, which, as in *The Beggar's Opera*, was directed mainly at political and social targets, not at Italian opera. Musically they are inferior to their model, and contain, as do all the later ballad operas, a greater number of specially composed pieces mostly by the popular song-and comedy-writer Henry Carey [*c.* 1687–1743], Pepusch, and an obscure musician named Seedo. These satirical operas, once their novelty had worn off, proved much less satisfying to the musical élite than Italian opera, and during the last two seasons of the ballad opera craze, i.e. 1733–5, there were, as we have seen, actually two Italian opera companies, both of which managed to keep going until 1737. Even after this date at least one new Italian opera (not to mention revivals) was produced at the King's Theatre every year, including works by Hasse, Pescetti (both of whom had several successes), Leo, Galuppi, Pergolesi, Jomelli (for these last three, see below), and Gluck, who composed two operas for the Theatre in 1746 (see Part III, p. 715.)

The collapse of 1737 was due partly to the effect of the ballad operas on public taste, partly to the rivalry between the two companies, which naturally reduced the audience potential of each one (far smaller then than now) and which exhausted the supporters of both, and partly to two deliberately aimed satires, Fielding's play *Pasquin* (1736) and Carey's enormously successful *The Dragon of Wantley* (1737), with music by Lampe that burlesques superbly the Italian style. Like *The Beggar's Opera*, it contains a brawl between the two principal female characters (*à la* Cuzzoni-Bordoni), and was inspired by and directly tilts at Handel's *Giustino*, produced earlier in the same year, in which a sea-monster figures prominently.

The failure of Handel's company was also due to his lack of sufficient first-rate singers and to the uneven quality of the music, for the operas composed after his second Italian visit (1733), although they contain much fine music, including some delightful *stile galante* and *buffo* arias, do not, in general, reveal the same consistent quality of inspiration, nor the vigour, spontaneity, and, because of the mixed styles, the unity of the operas from *Agrippina* to *Admeto* (1727). It may be that consciously or unconsciously he was beginning to lose heart, but went on writing operas because he had been writing them all his life and because opera was the only vehicle he knew at the time through which he could express his exceptional dramatic gifts. These two reasons together account for his slowness in exploring the dramatic possibilities of oratorio, even after his ventures into this field had brought him a small fortune.

Although the ballad opera phase was both short and artistically undistinguished, its scheme of set musical numbers interspersed with spoken dialogue became a characteristic of most later English operas. This is also true of the German *Singspiel*, which, in the hands of its first important composer, Johann Adam Hiller [1728–1804], became very popular during the later part of the century. (In the late seventeenth and early eighteenth centuries *Singspiel* meant any opera in German, but after *c.* 1750 it was used in the restricted sense described below.)

The *Singspiel* sprang directly from the English ballad opera, in particular Coffey's *The Devil to Pay* (1731), which, as *Der Teufel ist los*, was frequently performed and imitated from 1743 on, first of all in north Germany, as a reaction against Italian opera, and later in the south. Hiller's entirely new setting of Coffey's text (Leipzig, 1766) established *Singspiel* as a significant art form which, unlike ballad opera, *opéra comique*, and *opera buffa*, was not limited to comic plots. This is particularly evident in the works of Georg Benda [1722–1795] whose two melodramas, *Ariadne auf Naxos* and *Medea* (both 1775), profoundly impressed Mozart. (A melodrama contains, in addition to set musical numbers (arias, etc.), spoken dialogue much or all of which is accompanied orchestrally.)

The roots of *opera buffa* go back to the Renaissance intermedii (see pp. 266–7) which, during the latter part of the seventeenth century, developed into the intermezzi. These were scenes (usually two) of a light and often humorous nature placed 'in between' the normal three acts of a serious opera, partly in order to give the audience their money's worth (people expected far longer entertainments in the seventeenth and eighteenth centuries than they do now), and partly to satisfy that craving for variety already noted. By 1700 the two scenes formed a continuous plot, by 1725 what we call '*buffo* style' was fully fashioned, and by 1740 *opera buffa* was a completely independent art form.

We must make a distinction here between *opera buffa* and comic opera; the latter can be traced back to *Chi soffre speri* (see p. 384), and most opera composers of the early and late

Baroque wrote at least one, the main difference between it and *opera seria* being the nature of the story. In *opera buffa*, however, like ballad opera, the plot is not only humorous and often satirical, but is also concerned with contemporary life. Another distinction is the small number of characters, sometimes only two, as in the comic scenes of Neapolitan *opera seria* (see p. 451). More important is the naturalness of the characters and their doings reflected in arias often vivacious, sometimes sentimental, and always expressing the text in a life-like manner (coloratura passages are rare), in recitatives that are little more than musically inflected conversations, in a completely homophonic style, often in only two real parts, and in the fact that all the voices are natural (i.e. no castrati). The conversational character of the recitatives is also found in the ensembles at the end of each act, these being a direct offshoot from the comic episodes of many Neapolitan operas (see p. 452), and, undoubtedly stimulated by the range of timbre of natural voices, they eventually developed into the most dramatically distinctive feature of *opera buffa*.

Opera buffa was essentially a Neapolitan creation—many of the early libretti, in fact, are in Neapolitan dialect—and, like ballad opera, it represented a partial reaction against the largely stereotyped characters and situations, and the often excessive coloratura of *opera seria*. But, like ballad opera also, it did not oust *opera seria*, for although it was musically more unified and skilfully written than ballad opera, it satisfied neither the love of virtuosity nor the delight in contrasting emotions, occasionally profound, that were possible in *opera seria*; indeed, all composers of *opera buffa* from Pergolesi to Mozart also wrote *opera seria*, and most of them were successful in both fields.

The earliest surviving example of the fully-fledged *buffo* style is Vinci's three-act comic opera in Neapolitan dialect, *Li Zite'n Galera* (1722), but the first genuine, original, and successful *opera buffa* was by Giovanni Battista Pergolesi [1710–1736], a pupil of Durante and Feo. In 1733 he composed two intermezzi entitled *La Serva Padrona*, which he placed between the acts of his *opera seria*, *Il Prigionier Superbo*, and while the former, like his next intermezzi, *La Contadina astuta* (1734—sometimes known as *Livietta e Tracollo*) was much more favourably received than the main work, it did not become famous until after 1738; indeed after 1752, mainly owing to the violent controversy caused by its production in Paris (see p. 495), it became an international smash-hit. In most of the later performances the work was given as a whole, i.e. not as two separated intermezzi, and while a few earlier intermezzi had been similarly presented and hence, to this extent, qualify for the title *opera buffa*, none possesses the vivid characterization, the racy vivacity allied to sincere but never profound sentiment, and the delicate vein of tender pathos that distinguish both *La Serva Padrona* and *La Contadina astuta.*

The success of Pergolesi's *opera buffa* stimulated other composers to follow suit, and it was not long before *buffo* style and even *buffa* characters invaded *opera seria*, as in Handel's *Serse.* Conversely, *opera buffa* itself began to change, and in the late 1740s a much greater degree of sentiment was introduced, the original two acts were expanded to three, and the cast became larger, often consisting of two clearly defined groups, the comedians (usually three men and two women) and a pair of young lovers; in other words *opera buffa* became more conventional, but never to the same extent as *opera seria.*

The leading composers of comic opera, intermezzi, and *opera buffa* were, apart from Pergolesi, the Neapolitans Leo, Nicola Logroscino [1698–after 1765], Niccolò Jomelli [1714–1774], Rinaldo di Capua [b. *c.* 1715], and Tommaso Traetta [1727-1779], and the Venetian Baldassare Galuppi [1706-1785]. Leo, who taught Jomelli and Piccini (see Part III, pp. 711-12), achieved fame with *Amor vuol Sofferenza* (1739); Logroscino was so successful that he was called '*il dio dell' opera buffa*'; Jomelli, one of the first to break away from the rigidity of the *da capo* aria, had an exceptional flair for popular melody; Rinaldo stressed the emotional possibilities of the orchestra, particularly in accompanied recitatives; Traetta was very highly regarded in his time, notably by Burney, and, in his *opera seria*, anticipated Gluck in the importance he attached to the drama; Galuppi, the greatest of them all, wrote *Il filosofo di compagna* (1754), the most popular *opera buffa* after *La Serva Padrona.* Galuppi is important also because he was the first to extend the rather limited finales that then existed, constructing them of five or six linked movements, during which the plot developed. Thus the finale of Act I of *Il mondo alla roversa* (1750) is constructed as follows: (1) C major, $\frac{4}{4}$, Allegro non molto, 56 bars ending in G major; (2) G minor, $\frac{3}{8}$, Allegro, 34 bars ending on the dominant of A minor; (3) C major, $\frac{4}{4}$, Tempo primo, 50 bars partially based on (1) ending in G major; (4) C major, $\frac{6}{8}$, Larghetto, 19 bars ending on the dominant of C; (5) C major, $\frac{4}{4}$, Tempo primo, 19 bars. There is no musical climax in this finale, and the three characters that sing at various times are on the stage all through; there is thus no dramatic climax either, as there is, for example, in the finales of Mozart's *Figaro*.

Galuppi wrote nearly 100 operas, the majority being *opera seria*; of his comic ones most are on libretti by Carlo Goldoni [1707–1793], the most popular Italian playwright of the eighteenth century, whose comedies paralleled *opera buffa* in their delightfully vivid portrayal of lower- and middle-class life, and their satire of the aristocracy. Much the same is true of the Spanish 'tonadilla' which flourished during the last half of the eighteenth century. The tonadilla was preceded by the 'zarzuela', which was very popular during the latter half of the previous century, and which consisted of two acts of spoken dialogue interspersed with solos, ensembles, and choruses (a few were, in fact, sung throughout), and which relied to a considerable extent on scenic effects; it was thus somewhat similar to the Lullian comédie-ballet and the English masque. A tremendous number of zarzuelas were written by the host of fine dramatists whose achievements represent the peak of what is usually called 'the Golden Age of Spanish Literature', and of whom the most outstanding was Pedro Calderón de la Barca [1600–1681], the successor to Lope de Vega (see p. 358). Nevertheless, the popularity and excellence of this native art crumbled during the early eighteenth century before the invasion of Italian opera, although a flicker of the national culture remained in the 'entremés' (intermezzo) performed between the acts of a play. The entremés often concluded with a song or tonadilla, and *c.* 1750 this expanded into a number of separate items linked by a simple plot, eventually, in the hands of Luis Misón [d. 1766], Pablo Esteve y Grimau, and Blas Laserna [1751–1816], becoming sufficiently highly organized and popular to achieve an independent existence.

We turn finally to France, the one country that did not capitulate to Italian opera, though she could hardly escape being influenced to some extent, despite the widespread admiration for Lully's works. Lully's operatic aims, indeed, were partially continued by his pupil, Pascal Colasse [1649–1709], whose *Thétis et Pelée* (1689) remained in the repertory for sixty-five years, but his successors, to a greater or lesser degree, tended towards a conception of opera that, while it maintained the importance of dancing and scenic display, placed charm and elegance of melody and harmony before literary distinction and dramatic integrity. This can be seen in the operas of André Cardinal Destouches [1662–1749], and more particularly in those of André Campra [1660–1744]. Both composers produced a smash-hit in 1697, the former with the opera *Issé*, which remained popular for nearly eighty years, and the latter with a new kind of entertainment, the 'opera-ballet' *L'Europe galante*. In *Issé* the recitatives are Lullian, but the airs are mostly written in *style galant*—that is, a style similar to the Italian *stile galante* (see p. 460) but more profusely ornamented with grace notes, turns, etc. These had been rigorously controlled by Lully, as they would have interfered with the clear enunciation of the text and marred the clarity of his vocal line, but they became an integral part of *style galant*, reflecting the taste of contemporary society which abhorred simplicity and tedium. This delight in ornamentation is also apparent in the painting, architecture, and sculpture of the period and is known as 'rococo art' (from the French *rocaille*, which implied artificially and elaborately decorated rockwork). Thus while both *style galant* and *stile galante* can be defined as a homophonic texture with melody governed by harmony, rococo refers to melody that is highly embellished and, in order to avoid being tedious, short-phrased, and it is the rococo element that chiefly distinguishes the French from the Italian gallant style.

The mood of *Issé* is predominantly pastoral and frivolous, in contrast to the classically statuesque nobility of Lully's tragédies-lyriques. This contrast is even more marked in *L'Europe galante*, the airs being more *galant* and Italianate in their lyricism (Campra, incidentally, was of Italian descent), with coloratura passages commoner and modulations, chromaticism, and discord more freely used; recitatives are less declamatory and more perfunctory, and the orchestra is sometimes most strikingly employed to heighten the drama by means of tremolos, rapid scale passages, etc., as in the Italian *recitativo accompagnato*, all these features serving to adorn a series of loosely connected scenes of great splendour, but of little dramatic or literary merit.

Issé is a finer work than *L'Europe galant*, but the influence of the latter was far greater and led to a host of similar opera-ballets in which the pastoral gaiety and charm of the music, together with an abundance of dances and frequent changes of scene, with the orchestra often providing a highly effective background, satisfied that craving for variety already mentioned more than once in this chapter, a craving that explains the enormous vogue of the *spectacles coupés*, where favourite airs, scenes, and even acts from operas of one or more composers were torn from their contexts and performed as concert pieces. This craving was more intense in France than elsewhere because in the unparalleled sophistication, elegance, superficiality, and sinfulness of the French aristocracy during the Regency [1715–1723], and for most of Louis XV's reign [1723–1774], boredom was the most intolerable of all states, and amusement the only goal worth pursuing. Morally, we can but condemn such a society, but artistically we must recognize its exquisite refinement and, considering the narrow emotional limits that were *de rigeur*, its variety.

Perhaps the most remarkable feature of the entire baroque period is its duality—the way in which strongly contrasted and even opposing trends existed side by side. Thus the period covering the reigns of Louis XIV and XV is commonly called both the 'Age of Absolutism', when the life of every individual was more completely subject to the King than in any other country, and also 'the Enlightenment', when the freedom of thought that originated in the Renaissance received a new impetus through the scientific discoveries of the sixteenth and more particularly the seventeenth century. These discoveries encouraged men to regard as true only what could be tested by direct observation or proved by logical deduction, and to accept the premise of the first great modern philosopher, Descartes, that doubt is the starting-point of philosophy. This attitude struck right at the roots of absolute authority, and it was almost inevitable therefore that, fanned by the *Lettres philosophiques* (1634) of Voltaire [1684–1778], which caused an uproar by implicitly criticizing French society through extolling the personal and political freedom that he experienced in England, the bitterest struggles between absolutism and enlightenment should have taken place in France.

The achievements in science, mathematics, and philosophy in the eighteenth century elevated the power of reason to a position never held before or since, and was strikingly exemplified in France by the group known as the Encyclopaedists. This was formed in 1749 when Denis Diderot [1713–1784], the most original French thinker of the eighteenth century, became Editor of what has been called "the great literary monument of the age of enlightenment"—the *Encyclopédie*, published between 1751 and 1772 in twenty-eight volumes. Diderot gathered about him some of the most distinguished men in France, including the German writer Melchior Grimm [1723–1807], who arrived in Paris in 1749, the mathematician Jean Le Rond d'Alembert [1717–1778], who became co-Editor, and the Swiss Jean Jacques Rousseau [1712–1778], of whom more anon. These men aimed at creating a society entirely governed by reason, and which permitted freedom of thought and speech (hence their rejection of the Church's authority), and so reflected the spirit of their times in which men attempted to classify everything, and in which a subject's status was raised immeasurably if it could be treated in a scientific and philosophic manner. Of all the arts, music was most affected by this rationalist approach, because its raw material (sound) is most readily expressed in mathematical terms (ratios and logarithms), and its affect on man had been recognized ever since Plato. The first type of classification we can call scientific and the second philosophic; the latter has already been partly covered in our discussion of the doctrine of the affections (see pp. 439-41); it reached its peak theoretically in *Der critische Musicus* (1737–40) by Johann Adolf Scheibe [1708–1776], *Der General-Bass* (1738) by Johann David Heinichen [1683-1729], and *Der vollkommene Kapellmeister* by Johann Mattheson [1681-1764] but practically in the operas of the great French composer of the late baroque, Jean-Philippe Rameau [1683–1764].

It is typical of both the man and his period that Rameau first achieved notoriety through his theoretical work, the *Traité de l'harmonie* (1722), which was received with scorn by professional musicians, and which attempts, with some success, to classify music both scientifically and philosophically. As regards the first, Rameau believed that music "depends on reason, nature, and geometry", and that it is "a physico-mathematical science"; he also believed that "melody is born of harmony"—in other words, that every melody implies its own harmonization, which is certainly true of late baroque, especially *galant*, melody. In his *Traité* and later works (see below) Rameau 'proved' that the major triad was the basis of all harmony because it is the only triad in the harmonic series (see pp. 247–8), that $^{6}_{3}$ and $^{6}_{4}$ chords are inversions of a triad, and that the tonic, dominant, and subdominant are the three fundamental chords in any key, these two last propositions being his most important discoveries. The three fundamental chords had, of course, been recognized in practice for some time, but Rameau was the first to classify them and point out their tonal significance. Unfortunately, his desire for a neatly classified system led him into a number of errors, including the assertion that all chords are derived from the three fundamental ones (discords being obtained by adding thirds), and that each chord has what he called a *basse fondamentale*, for the discovery of which he gives quite arbitrary rules; this bass is supposed to link all chords together, but in fact it often makes nonsense of tonality.

Some of the assertions in the *Traité* were corrected or modified in later publications, notably the *Nouveau système de musique théorique* (1726), *Génération harmonique* (1737), *Démonstration du principe de l'harmonie* (1750), and 'new thoughts' on the last in 1752. The errors in the *Traité* were not, however, the cause of its hostile reception, as no musician was sufficiently well versed in the science of music to point them out; the probable reasons were the pedantic and turgid style and the fact that the author was virtually unknown as a composer (apart from a few claveçin (harpsichord) pieces which everyone was turning out, anyway), and in the baroque, especially the late baroque, musical theory and practice were more inseparable than in any previous period. At any rate, the work was not accepted until after Rameau had fully established himself as a creative artist in the late 1730s.

In the philosophic treatment of his art, Rameau was as convinced about the power of music as was Plato. "It is certain", he says in his *Traité*, "that harmony can arouse in us different passions, depending on the particular harmonies that are employed." He then lists in detail the various emotional effects of concords, discords, keys, modulations, chromaticism, and cadences; melody he does not classify, for although he states that it is just as expressive as harmony, it depends more on good taste than anything else; nevertheless, his use of intervals and figures follows conventional practices, some of which go back to the Renaissance.

The importance that Rameau attached to nature was more than scientific-acoustic, for one of the most characteristic features of the Regency-Louis XV period was the way in which all art sought to imitate or portray Nature. But it was Nature idealized, not "red in tooth and claw", Nature limited to superbly ornamental gardens and sunny landscapes with well-trimmed hedges and pleasant, sheep-filled meadows in which elegantly-dressed courtiers wandered, conversed, and flirted in the shade, attended by charming shepherdesses and servile shepherds. The 'back to Nature' movement affected France more than any other country because it was more akin to French taste, which had never subscribed so completely to the emotional full-bloodedness of the early baroque as had other countries, and which, always avid for variety, revelled in a pastoral paradise where courtly manners and morals still obtained, but where the environment provided both the illusion of a new life and fresh scope for the delicately sensual and superficially refined attitude to living.

Although Rameau's treatises are important and alone entitle him to a distinguished place in the history of music, it seems strange to us, who regard him primarily as a creative artist, that all his life he was more sensitive to criticism of his theories than of his compositions, though he fully realized that he could only demonstrate the validity of the former through the latter, which meant in effect composing successfully for the theatre. Three *opéra comiques* appeared in 1723 and 1726, none of them of much merit, but in 1733, at the advanced age of fifty, he wrote his first important dramatic piece, the tragedie, *Hippolyte et Aricie*. At first audiences were stunned, because they never expected a learned theorist to compose such emotional stuff, nor were they prepared for some of the startling dissonances, modulations, and orchestral effects. It was not long, however, before most of the musical élite, headed by Campra, became enthusiastic, while the more reactionary musicians, plus a strong bourgeois element, remained antagonistic, faithful to the glories of the past—Lully's operas. The two rival parties, the Ramistes and the Lullistes, waged a bitter pamphlet war which was aggravated by having to share the only opera-house in Paris, but Rameau himself was much less partisan than his followers, and, as he plainly stated in the Preface to his ballet héroique *Les Indes galantes* (1735), had the greatest respect for his predecessor. The merits of *Les Indes galantes*, the ballet *Les Fêtes d'Hébé* (1739), and, more particularly, the tragédies *Castor et Pollux* (1737, revised 1754) and *Dardanus* (1739) did not convert the Lullistes, but as time went on their numbers waned as Rameau's popularity increased, especially after his appointment at Court in 1745, until by 1750 there was virtually no opposition; he was at the height of his fame.

At sixteen Rameau's father sent him to Italy for three years to study music, and although he was apparently unimpressed by what he saw and heard, Italian influence is clearly apparent in all his stage works; indeed, this was one of the chief criticisms of the Lullistes. Nevertheless, his conception of dramatic entertainment is much more in the Lullian than in the Italian tradition, for his airs, while more Italianate than Lully's, i.e. more sensuous, graceful, and sequential in structure, particularly the ariette type (e.g. 'Venus, que ta gloire réponde', *Castor* (1754), Prologue), are less purely melodic and important than in Italian opera. His recitatives are thoroughly Lullian in their overall importance, rhythmic freedom, careful underlay, and arioso-like style, although on occasion they contain bolder leaps (sevenths and ninths), richer harmony, and more vivid accompaniments. Lullian, too, are the spectacular but usually irrelevant scenes and elaborate ballets, both of which occur in greater profusion, and in the position to which he raised the orchestra Rameau was but accentuating one of Lully's outstanding traits.

The big flaw in Rameau's stage works is the lack of literary distinction and dramatic unity insisted on by Lully. Contemporary Italian opera is superior in this respect, for many libretti, especially those by Zeno and Metastasio, have some literary merit, are dramatically consistent, and avoid superfluous spectacle. Even if the story that he boasted he could set

La Gazette de Holland to music is untrue, it indicates his attitude, for he clearly did not bother about the quality of the language, nor did he care how many absurdities the plot contained, nor how many irrelevant scenes and dances were incorporated. In this he was truly the child of his time and nation, faithfully reflecting the excessive appetite for variety of the French aristocracy, but he was ahead of his time in his use of the orchestra, for, apart from the rarity of solo continuo accompaniments (true also of contemporary Italian opera), the orchestra is considerably more 'affective' than the voice, and even on occasion paints an introductory vignette of a character, e.g. the ritornello before Iphise's first appearance (*Les Fêtes d'Hébé*, II, 1). Compared with Italian opera, the great similarity between recitative and air is underlined by the frequency with which the orchestra accompanied the former and in the more varied orchestration of both, in which woodwind and brass instruments are added to strings and continuo more often. In most of the airs the nature of the accompaniment is orthodox, i.e. it is homophonic, contrapuntal, or polyphonic ('Brillez, astres nouveaux', *Castor* (1754), V, 7; 'Hâtez-vous', *Dardanus*, II, 3; 'Cruelle mère des amours', *Hippolyte*, III, 1, respectively), but in what Rameau called 'récitatif accompagné pathétique' the orchestra becomes sensational, portraying a violent emotion, such as suicidal grief ('Grands Dieux', *Hippolyte*, V, 1), the appearance of a monster (*Dardanus*, IV, 3), an earthquake (*Les Indes galantes*, II, 5), thunder (*Hippolyte*, I, 4), etc., by means of all the devices used in the Italian *recitativo accompagnato* but in a more vivid manner. Moreover, such recitatives occur far more often than their equivalents in Scarlatti, Hasse, or even Handel, and were, in fact, enormously popular, particularly those depicting storms—a direct result of the aim to imitate Nature.

The importance that Rameau attached to the orchestra was not only a reflection of the 'back to Nature' movement, nor merely the continuation of a tradition begun by Lully and continued by Campra; it was also an expression of his belief that harmony is the basis of music, for orchestral harmony can obviously be fuller, richer, and more affective than continuo harmony. This same belief also explains his fondness for ensembles and choruses, and here, as in the vocal line of his recitatives, which are further removed from speech and hence are less 'natural' than secco recitative, the scientific approach overruled the philosophic, for in nature people do not normally speak at the same time, except when they are part of an enthusiastic or angry crowd. Ensembles, in fact, occur far more frequently in Rameau's stage works than in Italian opera, and choruses, virtually non-existent in the latter, are even more common, and contain some of his best music, e.g. the extraordinarily dramatic 'Trio des Parques' (*Hippolyte*, II, 5; see Plate XXV), with its violent orchestral accompaniment, the almost as fine demons' chorus, 'Que l'Averne' (ibid., II, 3), the delicate gaiety of 'Volez, Zephirs' (*Les Indes galantes*, I, 6), the pastoral languor of the musette 'Suivez les lois' (*Les Fêtes d'Hébé*, III, 7), and the unusually long, imitative, almost Handelian 'Que ce rivage retentisse' (*Hippolyte*, III, 8).

The choruses and, more especially, the spectacular scenes and ballets provided the contrast which would otherwise have been lacking owing to the similarity between recitative and air. Indeed, it is generally true that the choruses cover a wider dramatic range more effectively, and the incidental music is on a consistently higher level than the solo vocal numbers. In the choruses, which are mostly contrapuntal with occasional snatches of imitation and even canon, melody is less exposed than in an air or recitative, less ornamental because of the number of voices singing each part, and the short phrases typical of Rameau are made less objectionable by the ejaculatory nature of the text or by the overlapping of one voice with another.

In the purely orchestral pieces, the dance and incidental music, Rameau, unfettered by the lack of accent and prevalence of feminine endings of the French language, produced a wealth of attractive, rhythmically clear-cut melodies in which rococo phrasing is more natural (for all dance music must be sectionalized) and ornamentation more effective (because fingers are nimbler than vocal chords) than in recitative or air. This mass of instrumental music, from which several excellent ballet suites could be culled, includes marches (*Hippolyte*, V, 8), rigaudons (ibid., III, 8), minuets (*Dardanus*, Prologue, 2), tambourins (*Les Fêtes d'Hébé*, III, 7—the well-known one from the 1724 book of claveçin pieces), gavottes (ibid., I, 8), musettes (ibid., III, 7—also adapted from the 1724 book), passepieds (ibid., III, 7), loures (ibid., III, 7—delightfully scored for piccolo and strings), chaconnes (*Les Indes galantes*, IV, 6), etc. Most of these dances were strongly pastoral in character and mood, particularly the tambourin (in duple time) and the musette (in triple time), both of which have a bagpipe-cum-drum flavour by being wholly or largely constructed on a tonic and/or dominant pedal.

In Rameau's later works the pastoral and spectacular elements become even more important, and the tone, with a few exceptions, more frivolous. Thus of the eight stage pieces composed between 1733 and 1740 five are 'tragédies' or 'opéras', but of the twenty-six composed from 1744 to his death only three are so designated, the majority being ballets. Admittedly in Louis de Cahusac, who contributed to at least seven of the later pieces, Rameau found a librettist who to some extent anticipated Gluck's collaborator, Calzabigi (see Part III, pp. 718, 719), by making the ballets and spectacles more an integral part of the story, but in general dramatic and literary considerations mattered even less than formerly.

The best of the later works are the tragédie *Zoroastre* (1749), the tragédie-lyrique *Abaris, ou les Boréades* (1763)—both with libretto by Cahusac—the ballet bouffon *Platée* (1745), and the acte de ballet *Pygmalion* (1748). The overture to *Zoroastre* is interesting because, apart from typifying the breakaway from the Lullian model, its three movements portray (according to the composer's own descriptive notes) a general picture of the whole opera, and it underlines a feature of Rameau's overtures that was exceptional for the time, but was fully in keeping with his views on the expressive powers of music—namely, an association either of mood- or word-painting or of actual music with part or the whole of the rest of the work. For example, the overture to *Zaïs* (1748) paints the chaos of the opening scene, that of *Pygmalion* imitates the chipping of the sculptor's chisel, the first section of the overture to *Hippolyte* is thematically linked with the opening chorus of nymphs, and so is the same section in *Castor* with the 'Entrée des Astres' (V, 7). But remarkable as this feature is, it is not Rameau's overtures to the later works that show him most consistently at his best, though that to *Pygmalion* is delightful; nor is it his airs, though there are a number of fine ones; it is, as in his earlier stage pieces, the choruses and dances that contain the highest proportion of first-rate music, e.g. the battle chorus in *Zoroastre* (V, 4), the choruses 'Douce paix' (ibid., V, 4) and 'Hymen l'Amour t'appelle' (*Platée*, II, 5), the two gavottes in *Abaris* (IV, 4), the two minuets in *Platée* (III), the musette in G (*Zaïs*, IV), the 'gavotte en rondeau' in *Naïs* (1749; IV, 6), and the sarabande in *Pygmalion* (Sc. 4).

Platée was the first and almost the only avowedly comic stage work by Rameau. The plot is appalling, but the music not only contains many excellent numbers, but is also more Italianate in the sense that much of it is melodically and rhythmically simpler than anything written previously. It was performed once as part of the wedding festivities of the Dauphin Louis and Maria-Theresa of Spain, when it aroused no comment, and again in 1749 at the Opéra, when it was favourably received. In 1754 it was revived during the famous battle against Italian *opera buffa* known as the 'Querrelle (or 'Guerre') des Bouffons'. This had been sparked off in 1752 by performances of a visiting Italian troupe of Pergolesi's *La Serva Padrona*, and Paris was divided immediately into two camps. The Lullistes, forgetting their earlier strictures on Rameau's Italianisms, joined forces with the Ramistes and, backed by Louis XV, engaged in a most acrimonious war of words with the pro-Italian group headed by the Encyclopaedists and encouraged by the Queen. *La Serva Padrona* was followed by a number of *buffo* operas by Leo and others which were opposed by revivals of *Platée*, *Pygmalion*, *Les Indes Galantes*, *Les Fêtes d'Hébé*, and *Castor* during the years 1752–4, the performance of *Castor* in the latter year deciding the issue (but only temporarily) in favour of French opera.

Why did the Parisians, who had consistently withstood the invasion of Italian opera and who were completely indifferent to an earlier performance of *La Serva Padrona* in 1746, suddenly become so violently partisan in 1752? There are three reasons. Firstly, the successful public performances of *Platée*, which took place only three years before, prepared the way for *opera buffa* via the ballet's comic character and Italianate style. Indeed, Grimm, who was self-confessedly pro-Italian and prejudiced against French opera, called it "a sublime work", and *Pygmalion* "a ravishing ballet", though he later became one of Rameau's most violent detractors. Rousseau, also pro-Italian and more consistently antagonistic than Grimm, described it as "divine", "Rameau's masterpiece", and "the most excellent piece of music that has been heard as yet upon our stage", while in 1753 d'Alembert wondered "whether *La Serva Padrona* would have pleased so greatly if *Platée* had not accustomed us to that kind of music?" Secondly, many Frenchmen, because of their craving for variety, seized on *La Serva Padrona* which, with its limpid texture, simple harmony, conversational recitative, and catchy tunes, its few characters and straightforward plot, could hardly have contrasted more strongly with Rameau's rich harmonies, complex scoring, and the spectacular irrelevance and unreality of most of his libretti. Thirdly, *La Serva Padrona* was more 'natural' because its arias were less artificial (in the original sense of that much-abused word), its recitatives nearer to speech, and, above all, its situations more lifelike.

The last reason brings us back once more to the 'imitation of Nature', the influence of which, in what we may call its philosophical aspect, became considerable *c.* 1750, partly as a reaction to scientific Rationalism, partly as a result of the Rationalists' rejection of Christianity but acceptance of God as revealed in Nature. This aspect was ardently advocated by Rousseau, the most versatile and inconsistent of the Encyclopaedists. In 1762 he published his *Contrat social*, the main theme of which is that the individual must be completely subservient to the community, and which thus repudiates freedom of thought and speech, but in his *Discours* (1755), *La Nouvelle Heloïse* (written 1756–9, published 1761), *Émile* (1762), and his last works he stresses the individuality of man, whom he regards as essentially good, but corrupted by civilization, and who can only be 'saved' by communion with Nature.

Rousseau expressed his 'back to Nature' philosophy not only in books, but also in music. He had studied the art in Switzerland, and later invented a new system of notation, but his few compositions, which include an opera, *Les Muses galantes* (1747), reveal a poor harmonic sense, for which Rameau duly castigated him. In 1752 he produced, in support of *opera buffa*, his comic opera *Devin du Village*, and followed it up with the now famous *Lettre sur la Musique Française* (1753), the most important musical manifesto of the period. The *Lettre*, apart from its vituperous attacks on Rameau, is sensible and constructive, but the opera reveals the paucity of his talent. Its enormous success was due to its *opera buffa*-like simplicity.

its completely rustic setting, and the greater 'naturalness' of spoken dialogue compared to recitative. This last was an essential feature of the French equivalent of ballad opera—the vaudevilles of the *théâtre de la foire* which, almost entirely due to the brilliant playwright Charles-Simon Favart [1710–1792], had developed from rather primitive and often vulgar comedies interspersed with songs mostly to popular tunes, to polished, witty satires with newly composed vocal solos and ensembles. The success of *Devin* and of Favart's translation of *La Serva Padrona* gave a new lease of life to the *théâtre de la foire*, and with the merging, in the 1760s, of vaudeville and *opera buffa*, *opéra comique* was born.

The beginning of the aria 'Di gli ch'io son fedele' from *Cleofide* (1731), by Hasse, as sung at the first performance by the castrato Porporino (Antonio Uberti) [1697–1783], a pupil of Porpora ; it is in Frederick the Great's own hand.

5

THE BAROQUE: MUSIC IN CHURCH, HALL AND HOME

BY ANTHONY MILNER

AT the beginning of the seventeenth century in Italy the interaction of the developing monodic technique and the declining madrigal proved a fertile source of new forms. The success of the early monodies was not due merely to their simplicity, but also to the presence of features deriving from popular music. Their melodic style continued that of the frottola (see Part I, p. 209) which had, so to speak, survived 'underground' in popular music, occasionally reappearing in the upper parts of the polyphonic villanella and balletto (see Chapter 1, pp. 245 and 272). This similarity between the frottole and the monodies is especially noticeable in the use of straight forward rhythms and sectional repetitions: Ex. 36 provides a simple comparison :

Repetition offered an easy solution of the chief problem facing the monodists—namely, how to provide a formal organization that would not impede the free expansion of the melody while avoiding the formlessness of the primitive operatic monody which quickly became intolerable apart from the drama. Here the monodists were influenced by the new 'continuo madrigals' (see Chapter 1, p. 271), whose instrumental basses frequently used repetition in the form of sequential patterns, or the ostinato melodies traditionally employed in accompanying poetry (see Chapter 1, p. 264, and Part I, p. 209), or strophic variation. The last of these became a favourite device of the later monodists: each stanza of the poem had the same bass, but the melody of the opening was elaborated in subsequent stanzas. Such basses did not possess sufficient individuality to make them ostinati, but the mere fact of repetition provided a simple method of sectional structure. Sometimes the strophes were separated by instrumental ritornelli. The monody *Tempo la cetra* from Monteverdi's 'Seventh Book of Madrigals' (1620) has four strophic variations separated by repeats of a ritornello whose material is taken from an introductory sinfonia. Alessandro Grandi [d. 1630] was apparently the first to describe an aria of this sort as a cantata in his *Cantade et arie a voce sola*, published in the same year as Monteverdi's collection.

The appearance of the *bel canto* style marks the beginning of the typical baroque solo cantata. Consisting of a dramatic or pastoral narrative poem set to a mixture of aria, arioso, and recitative, it offered the music-lover a means of enjoying in his home the kind of music he heard in the opera-house, and thus had much the same place in Italian social life of the seventeenth century that the madrigal had in the sixteenth. Moreover, it served as a training-ground for opera composers, who frequently experimented with new harmonic, melodic and formal features in the cantata before proceeding to their employment in opera. Its popularity may be assessed from the fact that thousands of examples survive, many in still uncatalogued manuscripts.

Luigi Rossi, the first great master of the cantata, composed over 250 works in this form. Some, the simplest, merely repeat an aria for every stanza of the text; others change the middle section while preserving the first as a refrain. The majority, however, and the most interesting, are 'rondo' cantatas, in which a succession of sections in arioso and recitative is interspersed with repetitions of an aria. Strophic variation and ostinato basses are found in these rondo cantatas as also instrumental ritornelli (generally for continuo, but occasionally for violins) which mark the separation of secco recitative and aria.

Some thirty cantatas for two and three voices preserve features of the continuo madrigal, ensemble sections alternating with solo arias. Rossi preferred the AB_1B_2 aria form to the ABA (see *H.A.M.*, 203 for an example of the latter), a preference shared by his contemporary, Giacomo Carissimi [1605–1674].

Compared with Rossi, Carissimi reveals a capacity for longer melodic lines, a closer organization of internal details of form by means of contrapuntal sharing of thematic material between melody and continuo bass, and an increasing tendency to abandon strophic variation for sequential passages in the bass. Cesti, Carissimi's pupil, continued and developed these features of his master's style, bringing to cantata composition all the characteristic technique of his operas (see Chapter 3, pp. 395–400). From Cesti onwards the formal development of the cantata closely parallels that of the opera. Legrenzi and Stradella (who composed 190 cantatas) increased the average overall length of the form by employing a sequence of two contrasted arias, each preceded by a recitative.* They regularly preceded their arias with instumental ritornelli. Although they used the *da capo* aria form more frequently than their predecessors, they by no means neglected the ABB forms, which are to be found even in the cantatas of such late baroque composers as Scarlatti and Handel. A noteworthy feature of many of the later cantatas is the elaborate quasi-virtuoso writing for the continuo bass instrument, which thus becomes the equal partner of the voice.

Rossi and Carissimi designed their solo cantatas in the first instance to please the sophisticated élite of the Roman aristocracy and clergy. The same public also fostered the development of the oratorio, which may be defined as a religious drama presented without stage action. From the beginning of the seventeenth century the Oratorian Church of S. Marcello was a fashionable centre for experimental combinations of quasi-dramatic music, religious services and sermons, especially in Lent, when the opera-houses were closed. Much of the music consisted of 'dialogues': descriptions or narrations by a *testo* (narrator), with comments by a chorus. When Carissimi in 1650 took over the direction of these musical activities, he embarked on a series of Latin oratorios (only sixteen survive) that established the form as a musical entity independent of a

* Cf. *H.A.M.*, 258, for an example of this form by Scarlatti.

liturgical setting. The libretti, composed by an unknown Jesuit, are mostly based on Old Testament subjects, such as the Flood, the judgement of Solomon, and the history of Jonah (see *H.A.M.*, 207). Although the *testo* is retained, its importance is considerably reduced; for example, in Carissimi's masterpiece, *Jepthe*, the narration is confined to the minimum necessary to ensure the continuity of the story: the chorus no longer merely comments, but sometimes takes over the narration, frequently participating in the drama first as the Israelite army and later as the attendants of Jepthah's daughter. Both stylistically and formally, Carissimi's oratorios present a striking contrast to his cantatas. All have features characteristic of the early baroque: the simple triadic harmonies of the choruses, the rapid succession of brief recitative and *arioso* sections, the absence of the ternary aria (though *bel canto* style occasionally appears in the arioso). The instrumental accompaniment consists only of two violin parts and continuo. This deliberate restriction of musical means was probably due to the need to keep each work short (since it was heard in the context of a religious service) and to the desire to emphasize the sacred narrative as strongly as possible, thus fulfilling the original moral and didactic purpose of the oratorio form. Carissimi's importance in the history of oratorio lies chiefly in his choruses, whose massive strength deeply impressed his contemporaries and successors: Handel occasionally 'borrowed' from his works when pressed for time. But generally his oratorio style had few imitators: faced with the competition of the all-dominant opera, composers turned to its religious counterpart, the *oratorio volgare* with Italian text.

Like the Latin type, the Italian oratorio flourished only under princely or prelatical patronage: it never shared the popularity of the opera. It was performed not in theatres, but in large halls or churches before an aristocratic audience, for whom it served either as a Lenten substitute for opera or as a musical garnish on important liturgical feasts. Since it was virtually opera without the stage, the same sort of music that in opera portrayed the anguish and transports of lovers accompanied the penitence of a sinner and the ecstasy of a saint. Thus it is scarcely surprising that some examples were dubbed *oratorii erotici*. In most of the mid-century oratorios the chorus was confined to exclamations and moralizing finales, but later composers restored the chorus to its previous importance and, availing themselves of the growing resources of tonality, wrote for it more and more in contrapuntal style. The chief opera composers of the period were also the leaders in oratorio. Legrenzi's *La Morte del Cor Penitente* is noteworthy for its elaborate fugal choruses that look forward to the Handelian type: Stradella's *S. Giovanni Battista* for the richness of its harmony and the use of obbligato instruments in the arias. Both show the same developments in harmony, tonality and formal expansion to be found in operas by these men (see Chapter 3, p. 400).

Eighteenth-century Italian oratorios are generally not as interesting as the operas: in most of them the chorus is again relegated to a subordinate rôle so that the oratorios, like the operas, become strings of arias and recitatives. Alessandro Scarlatti's works in this form, though full of charming music, are often hampered by utterly undramatic libretti: *La Santissima Trinità* (1715), for example, consists of theological discussions between Faith, Divine Love, Theology, Unbelief, and Time. Two are unusual in presenting the lives of post-Reformation saints: *S. Casimir Re di Polonia* and *S. Filippo Neri*. But they are insufficiently represented in modern publications, and it is very possible that closer acquaintance might perhaps entail reassessment. A new type of subject, the so-called 'secular oratorio', is found in such works as Marcello's *Il pianto e il riso delle quattro stagioni dell' anno* (1731), i.e. "The weeping and the laughter of the four seasons of the year", whose inscription "for the Death, Exaltation, and Coronation of Mary ever Virgin, assumed into Heaven" is perhaps due to an attempt to make the best of two worlds, for the Feast of the Assumption in mid-August was traditionally an occasion for holiday-making and carnival. The secular oratorio is related to the numerous cantatas and serenatas commissioned for occasions of public importance, consisting usually of a mixture of arias and instrumental movements: thus Scarlatti's *Nato è già l'Austriaco sole* (1716), written to celebrate the birth of an Imperial heir (who died in infancy) has the four seasons for *dramatis personae* and thus has close parallels in subject matter with Marcello's work.

Composers of liturgical music in the first decades of the seventeenth century had two methods of composition: the *stile antico* and *stile moderno*. The *stile antico* resulted from the attempts of conservative Roman composers to maintain the tradition of Palestrina (already revered as the supreme master of Catholic church music) on the grounds that it was the most suitable for worship. In fact, under the influence of the new continuo harmony the older technique was misunderstood: it is significant that arrangements of Palestrina's works were published which provided a continuo bass. But the distinction between the two styles endured throughout the baroque period and its influence may still be seen to-day: firstly, in the division of a composer's training into 'strict' and 'free' work,* which begins in the treatises of Berardi, who classified the older contrapuntal techniques in five 'species' a century before the publication of Fux's famous *Gradus ad Parnassum*; and, secondly, in the mistaken notion that certain styles are inherently more suitable than others for church music. All the leading composers of the seventeenth and eighteenth centuries from Monteverdi to Lotti wrote works in *stile antico*.

In 1610, while still in the service of the Duke of Mantua, Monteverdi published a collection of liturgical music which provides a representative cross-section of the changing forms in this field. Its chief work, a parody mass in *stile antico* based on a motet by Gombert, shows the effect of the new vertically-conceived continuo harmony on the melodic movement of ostensibly individual parts: its rhythms are more square-cut than those of late Renaissance polyphony and the harmonies tend to emphasize metrical accents. The remainder of the collection, consisting of Vespers of the Blessed Virgin (responsory, five psalms, hymn and Magnificat) with some other pieces, is designated on the title-page "for use in princely rooms and chapels"; unfortunately, several editors in the present century, ignoring this direction, have attempted to group all together as a vast choral work, despite the facts that the texts of the additional pieces cannot be fitted into the Office of Vespers and that the music is obviously intended for performance by small forces. The several parts of the Vespers are written in the *stile concertato* developed by Giovanni Gabrieli, which blends and contrasts solo, choral, and instrumental

* Which would have been inconceivable in previous centuries. One has only to try to imagine Josquin giving his pupils exercises in the style of Machaut to realize the enormous revolution in musical attitudes involved in this method of study.

groups (see Chapter 2, p. 318). In the psalms Monteverdi changes the manner of musical treatment for each verse and frequently separates the verses by ritornelli. For the most part he retains the psalm-tones as canti firmi, accompanying them with vocal and instrumental counterpoints which in spite of their frequently ornamental style and agitated rhythms are built on very simple harmonies with strongly marked cadences, but he also sets them in *falso-bordone* (derived from fauxbourdon: see Part I, p. 192) reiterated chords under the melody in the rhythm of the words. Passages for two and three voices alternate with sections in six and eight parts; *Nisi Dominus* employs two five-part choirs. The hymn 'Ave Maris Stella' (whose plainsong is heard in a decorated form in the top part throughout) has two four-part choirs for its first and last stanzas, using solo voices and single choir for the remainder; each verse except the last is followed by a ritornello.

Monodic writing appears in the extra-liturgical pieces, either throughout a movement or in sections alternating with choir or solo trio. *Audi coelum*, which begins as an alto monody and concludes with a six-part chorus, shows how the affective ornamentation of the secular music was transferred bodily to religious works: the triumphant scales on 'aurora' in Ex. 37.* closely resembles those in *Orfeo* where the hero overcomes Charon's opposition. The *Sonata sopra Sancta Maria* testifies to the growing importance of instrumental music for church use in the new style. Although not a liturgical work, the elevenfold repetition (at long intervals) of a plainsong intonation by a solo soprano gives it a quasi-liturgical air which is almost completely belied by the independent music for two violins, viola, cornetti, trombones, and organ.

Monteverdi's contemporaries and successors mostly abandoned the use of a cantus firmus in their preoccupation with the affections of the text. In their hands the *concertato* style split into two: the first used only solo voices with or without instruments and came more and more to resemble the secular cantata in its forms and in the use of ritornelli; the second, the 'grand' *concertato*, employed one or more choirs and groups of instruments, but minimized the importance of soloists. Some Roman composers attempted to blend the contrasts implicit in the *concertato* style with the 'imitation' renaissance polyphony

* *Tutti le Opere de Claudio Monteverdi*, ed Malipiero, Vol. XIV.

(Who is she arising that shines like the dawn, that I may bless her?)

of the *stile antico* in polychoral works. These were mainly intended for the newer baroque churches and can be appreciated properly only when heard in this kind of architectural setting. A French viol-player, Andre Maugars [fl. 1600–1640], who visited Rome in 1624, described the manner of performance: "This fairly long and spacious church had two great organs erected on both sides of the main altar with room for choirs around them. Along the nave there were eight more choir lofts, four on each side, elevated on scaffolding eight or nine feet high, and separated by the same distance, but facing each other. In every one of these choir lofts there was a portable organ. . . . The master composer beat the principal measure at the head of the first choir accompanied by the most beautiful voices. In every one of the other choirs there was a man whose only duty was to keep his eyes on the original beat given by the chief *maestro* in order to conform the measure of his choir to it. Thus all choirs sang in the same measure without dragging the movement."* Despite their apparent complexity, the continuo parts by which such compositions were held together reveal a very simple, even banal, harmonic organization. The zenith of this musical gigantism was reached by Orazio Benevoli [1605–1672] whose fifty-three-part Mass for the consecration of Salzburg Cathedral has two eight-part choirs (each supported by continuo, two string ensembles, two of wind instruments, and three of brass).

As the seventeenth century proceeded the operatic forms increasingly influenced those of liturgical music. While in the early baroque solo singing was generally a subordinate part of mass and motet, the rise of the Neapolitan opera saw the introduction of solo arias in full operatic style, commencing in the motet, which by this date could mean any piece of music set to a Latin text (other than those of the mass Ordinary) and often denoted forms which were in fact cantatas of several movements. Eight of Scarlatti's ten masses are in *stile antico*, but his *Concerti Sacri* (*c.* 1710), subtitled 'motets', for one to four solo voices (some with alternating choral sections) accompanied by two violins and continuo, consist mostly of recitatives and *da capo* arias with instrumental ritornelli. In the hands of Leo, Durante, Feo, and other eighteenth-century composers, the mass was expanded into a huge cantata in which independent choruses and arias were combined with instrumental movements. The employment of double choirs and of the contrast between soloists and chorus in individual movement was paralleled by the adoption of the concertino and ripieno structure of the concerto grosso (see Chapter 6, p. 551) for instrumental sections. An overture in French or Italian style frequently served as an introduction to the mass. The liturgical consequences of such music were disastrous: "the liturgy was not only submerged under this ever-growing art but actually suppressed, so that there were festive occasions which might best be described as 'church concerts with liturgical accompaniment'. Even the connexion with a text was taken very ill by music such as this. Texts which could be chosen at random—as was permitted after the elevation—were transferred to other places in the mass. On the other side, the celebrant often tried to continue with the offertory even while the choir was still

* Quoted in Lang, *Music in Western Civilization*, p. 362.

singing the Credo, or to restrict the singing of the Preface and *Pater noster* to the initial words so as to leave the rest for the music and the organ."*

In France the development of church music was largely determined by the requirements of the court, the artistic and cultural centre of the nation. Louis XIV preferred to attend a low mass, i.e., a mass in which the priest, officiating without deacon and subdeacon and thus with greatly reduced ceremonial, recites the text throughout without any admixture of chant. An elaborate setting of the Ordinary could not be used for a low mass, since there was insufficient time: yet music was considered an essential part of a ritual performed in the King's presence. The result was the so-called *messe basse solenelle*, the performance of motets for voices and instruments during certain parts of the service. The development of the baroque French motet commences with the works of Nicolas Formé [1567–1638] and Thomas Gobert [d. 1672], which frequently employ double choirs in the Venetian manner, though their style is rooted in the polyphonic methods of the previous century. Henri Dumont [1610–1684], Superintendent of the Chapelle Royale from 1663 to 1683, reveals the growing influence of the Italian baroque by the inclusion of an organ continuo in his *Cantica Sacra* (1652); his later motets employ the contrast of solo voices with chorus and the typical instrumentation of the contemporary Italian motet. From the middle of the seventeenth century onwards, Italian style and forms dominate French vocal music. In the works of Marc-Antoine Charpentier [1634–1704], a pupil of Carissimi, all the characteristic traits of the *bel canto* are to be found: his numerous church compositions for the Dauphin's private chapel exhibit greater variety than those of his predecessors and also, since the ritual of the chapel was not restricted by Louis XIV's impatience of solemn liturgical functions, a wider range of forms, including masses, motets and *Leçons des Tenèbres*. The latter provided a remarkable example of musical interference in liturgical ceremonial: the Lamentations of Jeremiah which provide the initial group of lessons for Matins ('Tenebrae') in the final days of Holy Week are traditionally chanted by an unaccompanied soloist, but Charpentier and later composers set them as independent cantatas with instrumental accom-

* J. A. Jungmann, *The Mass of the Roman Rite*, p. 149.

paniment, drawing out their length to five or six times that of the chant version, and destroying textual unity by constant repetition of words. In motets intended for festive or other occasions of importance, Charpentier employed a much larger instrumental band than any previous French composer of church music.

Lully brought to the motet the pomp and brilliance of the *tragèdie-lyrique*. His *Miserere* (1664) and *Te Deum* (1687) are scored for full operatic orchestra, including trumpets and drums. Operatic overture, double choirs, solo aria and recitative are blended with instrumental 'symphonies' (i.e. interludes and ritornelli) to produce some of the most elaborately brilliant church music ever written. Michel de la Lande [1657–1726], Du Mont's successor at the Chapelle Royale, continued the style of Lully's motets, extending it to the mass Ordinary, of which he wrote twelve settings, but despite an almost Handelian grandeur his music has a seriousness, an occasional tinge of melancholy, not to be found in Lully. This perhaps is partly due to the fact that his chief works were composed in the last melancholy years of Louis XIV's reign, when *la gloire* of the *Grand Siècle* was out of favour, whereas Lully's appeared at its zenith, but even more to a perception of the religious meaning of his texts and their relevance to the liturgy that is entirely lacking in the older man's approach.

Rococo style is evident in the sprightly dance rhythms of Campra's motets for one to three voices (cf. *H.A.M.*, 257) and in the sensuous ornamentation of the church music of François Couperin Le Grand [1668–1733]. Much of Campra's music is purely decorative, but Couperin's, even when most ornate, always maintains a vital connexion with the text, a feature particularly evident in the subtle, deeply-felt chromatic harmonies of his *Leçons des Tenèbres* (1713–15). Neither Campra nor Couperin wrote for the Church in the massive style of Lully and De la Lande (which became unfashionable simultaneously with the change from *tragèdie-lyrique* to opéra-ballet), confining themselves almost entirely to solo voices accompanied by small instrumental forces.

Charpentier was the first to establish oratorio in France. His libretti, whether French or Latin, are often based on the same subject as those of Carissimi, whose works he made his models. Compared with the older man, Charpentier shows a greater concern for flowing melodic lines and longer sections: moreover, he employs the full harmonic resources of his time combined with a more contrapuntal approach, which reveals itself in the important parts allotted to instruments and concerted numbers for the soloists. Thus, in *Le Reniement de St. Pierre*, the meeting between Mary Magdalen and the risen Christ begins as a dialogue, but develops into a duet with close imitation between the voices (*H.A.M.*, 226). Like his oratorios, Charpentier's cantatas are heavily indebted to Italian models, though he achieved a stylistic compromise by blending *bel canto* melody with French ornamentation. This Italian influence continued throughout the development of the French cantata, reaching its height in the works of Clerambault [d. 1749], which contrast French-style recitatives with Italian-style arias and instrumental 'symphonies'.

English church music was slow to follow the lead of the masque in incorporating the new vocal styles of the Continent. Compared with those of the opening years of the seventeenth century, compositions written for the Anglican liturgy in Charles I's reign have little musical, as distinct from historical interest: that the majority of church musicians preferred the older music may be seen in *The First Book of Selected Music* [1641] of John Barnard [fl. 1600–1650], Canon of St. Paul's, which contains works by all the chief composers of the Elizabethan and Jacobean periods from Tallis to Orlando Gibbons, but none by the younger men. The first experiments occur in verse anthems by William Child [1606–1697], Henry and William Lawes, and Walter Porter [1595–1659], forming the chief contents of a Chapel Royal choirbook of 1635: these show the beginning of a trend towards a more declamatory and 'affective' vocal line, a trend continued in Child's *First Set of Psalmes* (1639) for three solo voices and continuo "newly composed after the Italian way". The Civil War and the establishment of the Cromwellian Protectorate interrupted further development for nearly twenty years, for, while approving in principle of music as an art and pastime (the destruction of organs and music libraries by some extremists were no part of official policy), the Puritans forbade choral services in churches and cathedrals and disbanded the choirs. At the Restoration a fresh start was made: Charles II appointed Henry Cooke [d. 1672], whom the diarist Evelyn [1620–1706] described as "the best singer in the Italian manner", Master of the Chapel Royal, and gave directions about the type of music to be used. Thomas Tudway [d. 1726], who, like all the famous English composers of the next generation (including Pelham Humfrey [1647–1674] and John Blow, both Purcell's teachers), was one of 'Captain Cooke's boys', has left an account of the royal interest in the newer music: "His Majesty, who was a brisk, and Airy Prince comeing to the Crown in the Flow'r, and vigour of his Age was soon if I may say so tyr'd with the grave and solemn wayes And Ordered the Composers of his Chappell to add Symphonys etc. with Instruments to their Anthems; and ther upon Establis'd a Select number of his private Music to play the Symphonys and Ritornellos which he had appointed."* Charles was partial to the French style (his string band was formed in imitation of the famous *Vingt-quatre violons du roi* of Louis XIV's court), and as soon as he observed that Humfrey showed exceptional promise he sent him to study in France and Italy. Humfrey's early death, two years after he succeeded Cooke at the Chapel Royal, robbed English music of a fine composer: his verse anthems show a sensitive and deeply-felt approach to the problems of English word-setting which he imparted to Purcell.

Though both Blow and Purcell wrote magnificent music in the older quasi-polyphonic style (chiefly 'full' anthems and services, but also Latin motets), their most original and striking contributions to church music is found in their verse-anthems with string accompaniment. There were two chief types of such anthems: the first, composed for occasions of great importance, is well exemplified by Purcell's *My heart is inditing* (1685) for the Coronation of James II [reigned 1685–1688]. This commences with a 'symphony' for strings and organ continuo in the slow-quick French overture form; the eight-part choral sections are accompanied by the strings, but the verses for eight soloists only by continuo. Ritornelli appear in the verse-sections, and the symphony is repeated entire in the middle of the work. The shorter type has a single-section symphony, a solo group consisting of counter-tenor, tenor and two basses, and fewer choruses. Blow's *The Lord is my Shepherd* has arias for three of the soloists, reserving the entry of the chorus for the last verse of the psalm; Purcell's *My Beloved Spake*

* Quoted in E. H. Fellowes, *English Cathedral Music*, p. 134.

has two choruses, but only one arioso section. Blow mingles the strings with the solo voices: Purcell alternates them, save in the previously mentioned arioso, where the solo tenor is accompanied by a single violin. The solo writing of both men has all the 'affective' power of their operas, Purcell's in particular having some astonishing pieces for bass designed for the extraordinary compass and agility of the Chapel Royal singer, John Gostling [1650–1733]. Though the contrapuntal writing for large chorus retains much that is reminiscent of the older style, notably in close imitative entries and frequent 'false relations', the secular element dominates the solo writing. Dotted rhythms and lively sections in triple time characteristic of the French style are found equally in the homophonic choruses (e.g. the choral entry, "And the time of the singing of birds", in *My Beloved Spake*) and solos: if Ex. 38 be compared with such well-known tunes of Purcell's dramatic music as 'Let monarchs fight' the vital connexion between sacred and secular is immediately obvious:

Purcell's and Blow's duties as court composers required them to celebrate royal birthdays, marriages, and the monarch's return to the capital from holiday with ceremonial 'odes', i.e. cantatas for solo voices and chorus with four-part strings and continuo, sometimes with added wind instruments and trumpets. Blow's compositions of this sort are uneven and at times downright dull; it may well have been that he disliked the fulsome flattery and habitual doggerel of the texts provided by the court poetasters. Purcell, on the other hand, seems not to have minded, for though there are occasional dull patches in a few of his seventeen 'Welcome' and 'Birthday' odes, they are far fewer than anyone first reading the poems would expect, and each work contrives to transfigure the wretched verse by some excellent music. The last of the six odes that he wrote for Queen Mary's birthdays, *Come, ye sons of Art* (1694) shows Purcell at his most brilliant. It commences with an overture in three sections (previously used in *The Indian Queen*) for oboes, trumpets, and strings, leading to a counter-tenor* solo which is repeated with full harmony by the chorus. A duet for counter-tenors, the well-known 'Sound the trumpet', is followed by another counter-tenor solo, accompanied by two flutes and continuo and concluded with a 'symphony' that is in effect an instrumental repetition of the solo. Next come a bass solo with string accompaniment, repeated by the chorus; a soprano solo with an oboe part that imitates and echoes the vocal line; another bass solo, and finally a duet for soprano and bass which the chorus repeats with the orchestra strengthened by timpani. All the solos are in binary form with repeats; the counter-tenor duet, the first soprano and second bass solos are built on ground basses which modulate.

Purcell's other odes were written for the wider audience of the public concerts that since the Restoration had become an important part of London's musical life. The first series of such concerts was organized in 1672 by a former violinist of the Royal band, John Banister [1630?–1679] at a public house in Whitefriars: concerts "by excellent masters" took place every afternoon at four o'clock, and the price of admission was 1*s*. In 1678 Thomas Britton [1644–1714], a coal-merchant, began a series of weekly concerts at his house in Clerkenwell which continued till his death, becoming very famous for their presentation of well-known artists; admission was at first free, but later an annual subscription of 10*s*. was imposed. Numerous small bodies of amateurs also sponsored concerts, among them

* COUNTER-TENOR (or MALE ALTO) VOICE : a falsetto development of a normal tenor or bass voice.

the Musical Society which in 1683 commenced annual celebrations of St. Cecilia's Day (22nd November), whose main item consisted of a commissioned work to a poem specially written for the occasion. Purcell wrote four odes for the Society and a *Te Deum and Jubilate* (1694). *Welcome to all the Pleasures* (1683) for three soloists, chorus, and strings has the same basic design as a Birthday Ode; *Hail, Bright Cecilia* (1692) for four soloists, chorus and orchestra is a much larger work which may well be considered Purcell's masterpiece. The instrumental and vocal writing is of exceptional brilliance and variety; the choruses, with their occasional quasi-fugal texture, reveal a more highly developed choral style than is to be found elsewhere in his works, and one which anticipates very strikingly some features of Handel's 'English' style in anthem and oratorio. The opening symphony, scored for oboes, trumpets, drums, and strings, has four movements: a slow introduction in dotted rhythms; a canzona, really a double fugue; an adagio in slow triple time with antiphonal writing for the oboes and violins; an allegro built on a trumpet fanfare followed by a slow section without trumpets which in turn leads to a repeat of the allegro. Nowhere in Purcell's work is the 'affective' power of his word-setting more strikingly and movingly evinced: whether it be in the alto solo, ''Tis Nature's voice' (sung by Purcell himself at the first performance "with incredible graces"), with its descriptive ornamentation and passionate chromaticisms, or in the duets with obbligato instruments (especially that for alto and tenor with two recorders, 'In vain the am'rous flute' (which is perhaps the most sensuous and erotic music that Purcell ever wrote), or in the chorus, 'Soul of the world', with its pictorial matching of texture and rhythm to the various images of the text. Over two centuries passed before any English composer wrote a work that combined masterly composition with the same "genius to express the Energy of English Words whereby he mov'd the Passions as well as caus'd Admiration in all his Auditors".* According to the *Gentleman's Journal and Monthly Miscellany* of November 1692, the Ode was performed twice in that month "with universal applause"; it was repeated with similar success in January 1694. Fifteen contemporary manuscript scores, an unusually

* Henry Playford's Preface to the 2nd edition of *Orpheus Britannicus* (1706), a collection of Purcell's songs.

large number for a work of this period, testify to the esteem in which it was held.

Purcell and his contemporaries provided much vocal music for domestic performance by the music-lovers and amateurs of which the new audiences of concert-goers consisted. In his nine chamber cantatas for two or three voices with continuo (several with additional violins and flutes), twenty sacred songs for one or two voices with continuo, forty-two duets, and over a hundred solo songs Purcell displayed an inexhaustible variety of form and content. His works in this field form a body of song second to none in English musical history and one which is still too little known and appreciated by modern audiences.

Handel's first settings of English texts show that he had studied Purcell's music closely. Before the *Birthday Ode* for Queen Anne and the *Utrecht Te Deum and Jubilate* (both written in 1713), his choral music, apart from the early *St. John Passion* (1704), had consisted of Latin psalms and motets for the Catholic liturgy in the choral cantata forms of Scarlatti and other contemporary Italian composers. (The *oratorio volgare*, *La Resurrezione* (1708) only employs the chorus at the end of each of the two acts; otherwise it consists entirely of operatic-style arias which do not reveal Handel at his best, though their accompaniments contain some remarkable orchestration.) Between 1717 and 1720, Handel was resident at Cannons, the seat of the Duke of Chandos, for whose private chapel he wrote the twelve *Chandos Anthems*. These represent a synthesis of the form and style of the late baroque Italian motet and the more massive choral writing of the English tradition: each anthem, like a motet, consists of a succession of choruses, recitatives, arias, and orchestral movements. In the *Chandos Anthems* Handel laid the foundations of his 'English' style and learnt, as far as he ever did learn, how to set English words correctly; he returned to them over and over again as a source from whence he drew material for his oratorios.

Life at Cannons brought Handel into close contact with the leaders of English literary and artistic circles. The poets Gay, Alexander Pope [1688–1744], and John Arbuthnot [1667–1735] were frequent visitors under whose influence Handel turned his thoughts to English music drama. Although the masque as a musical entity had tended to merge with the late seventeenth-century 'semi-opera' (see pp. 432-4), it still had importance as a literary and dramatic form. Gay's libretto for Handel's *Acis and Galatea* (1719), while following closely the structure of its model, *The Judgement of Paris*, by Congreve, has two important changes from the traditional masque: descriptive choruses replace the older scenery and 'machines', and spoken dialogue is absent. The result is one of Handel's happiest creations: the contrast between the idyllic pastoral world of the lovers and the "monster Polypheme" inspired some of his most original choral writing, while the development of the individual characters in successive arias looks forward to the masterly portrayal of dramatic personalities in the last oratorios. *Acis and Galatea* was the first of several works which mingle elements from cantata, masque, ode, opera, and oratorio. *Alexander's Feast* (1736), a setting of Dryden's poem, is noteworthy for the manner in which the solo arias are taken up and expanded in choruses; the *Ode for St. Cecilia's Day* (1739), also to words by Dryden, is full of original and striking illustrations of the words; and *L'Allegro ed Il Penseroso* (1740), partly based on Milton's poems to which a third section (*Il Moderato*), by Charles Jennens [d. 1773] was added (and later omitted), contains some of Handel's most 'Purcellian' music.

Sir John Hawkins relates in his *General History of the Science and Practice of Music* (1776) that Handel "was used to say, that, to an English audience, music joined to poetry was not an entertainment for an evening and that something that had the appearance of a plot or fable was necessary to keep their attention awake".* Another masque, *Haman and Mordecai* (1720), with libretto by Pope, produced at Cannons with costumes and scenery, is a comparatively slight work, but of historical importance, for in 1732 Handel reconstructed it (with an amended libretto) as *Esther*, his first English oratorio, in an attempt to recoup from the financial losses he had sustained in opera. The advertisement in which he announced its forthcoming performance refers to his *Coronation Anthems* for George II [reigned 1727–1760] of five years before, which had proved immensely popular, being the first example of his massive choral style blended with ceremonial brilliance of orchestration to be heard by the general public: "There will be no acting on the stage, but the house will be fitted up in decent manner for the audience. The Musick to be disposed after the

* P. 890 in Novello's edition of 1853.

manner of the Coronation Service." *Esther* is really a pasticcio designed to catch the public ear by the inclusion of sections from two of the *Coronation Anthems* (*Zadok the Priest* and *My heart is inditing*) and the employment of castrati; the remainder of its music is a blend of *Haman* (considerably rewritten) and selections from the *Chandos Anthems*, *La Resurrezione*, and a Latin motet. Its success prompted Handel to try again: *Deborah* (1733), another pasticcio of his own works, made a great impression by reason of its choruses.

Esther and *Deborah* would never have been written but for Handel's pressing need for money; his haste betrays itself in the perfunctory treatment of the characters. *Athaliah*, composed a few months after *Deborah* for performance at Oxford, is a much better work: for the first time in his oratorios, Handel keeps the drama moving, and depicts a convincing protagonist. After *Athaliah* he became absorbed again in his operatic struggles, and it was not till 1738 that he resolved to concentrate mainly on oratorio composition, though he did not abandon opera entirely for another three years. *Saul* and *Israel in Egypt*, both composed in 1739, show him still hesitating over the best way to construct an oratorio, for whereas *Saul* is a true drama (and could be staged today with very little difficulty), *Israel* is a series of choral frescoes in which the solo arias are merely contrasting interludes. *Messiah* (1741), commenced within a fortnight of the failure of his last opera, *Deidamia*, is not a drama at all, but a lyrical narration and meditation; its popularity is probably the greatest single obstacle to the revival of Handel's oratorios today. The typical Handelian oratorio, a heroic drama, appears for the first time in *Samson* (1743). *Joseph and His Brethren* (1744), *Judas Maccabaeus* (1747), *Alexander Balus* (1748), *Joshua* (1748), *Susanna* (1749), *Theodora* (1750), and *Jeptha* (1751) are all cast in this form; *Solomon* (1748) is a choral pageant resembling *Alexander's Feast* more than oratorio; *Semele* (1743) and *Hercules* (1744), 'secular' oratorios in name, are really operas with large parts for chorus, the former having a remarkable dramatic continuity which makes stage presentation not only easy but imperative.

The chief differences between Handel's operas and his oratorios and choral odes lie in the importance, use and style of the choruses. Otherwise all the characteristics of his operatic technique are to be found in the oratorios. Most of the overtures begin with a slow French-style introduction, but the following quick movement is often a fugato in Italian style; *Saul* commences with a complete three-movement sinfonia (or Italian overture: see Chapter 6, p. 552) followed by a minuet, while *Theodora's* overture follows a French opening and Italian allegro with a sarabande and courante. For those who know only *Messiah* the orchestration of the arias in Handel's other oratorios is full of surprises, e.g. 'Breathe soft ye gales' (*Esther*) has flute, two oboes, violins in five parts, bassoons and theorbo; 'Hark, he strikes the golden air' (*Alexander Balus*) has two flutes playing antiphonally with two 'cellos, harp, and mandoline; the appearance of Samuel's ghost in *Saul* is accompanied by counterpoints for two bassoons playing in their lowest register; trombones and flutes alternate antiphonally for the 'Dead March' in *Saul*. Dance rhythms occur equally in arias and choruses, such as the sarabande for 'Mourn, Israel' (*Saul*), minuet in the aria 'From virtue springs' (*Theodora*) and 'alla hornpipe' for the chorus 'Now Love, that everlasting boy' (*Semele*).

Although Handel occasionally used the counter-tenor voice for his young heroes (e.g. David and Joseph) he ceased to write for castrati in oratorios after *Deborah*. "While in Italian opera the tenor and bass voices were still used to portray villians and comic characters, in oratorio Handel made them heroes and patriarchs. His Hebrew leaders thus attained a virility unknown to the more effeminately cultured emperors and princes of the operatic stage."* Nevertheless, he could still write the leading male role for a soprano (but female) voice in as late a work as *Solomon*.

Handel's choral writing forms his most personal and influential contribution to the development of music. Those choruses which maintain complete 'affective' unity (e.g. the fugue 'And with His stripes' in *Messiah*) are a very small proportion of the total number; often a fugue† with a single subject has a subordinate counterpoint of contrasting character to different words (e.g. 'They loathed to drink of the river' in *Israel* has a counterpoint for 'He turned their waters into blood', which, while it never becomes exact enough in its repetitions

* Julian Herbage, 'Handel's Oratorios' (from *Handel: A Symposium*, ed. G. Abraham, p. 104).

† For an explanation of fugal terms, see Chapter 6, p. 533–4.

to constitute a second subject, provides 'affective' variety throughout). Fugal writing occurs most often as part of a larger movement, particularly those in concerto style, where the chorus (single or double) has the same relation to the orchestral tutti as the solo instruments have in a concerto grosso; generally such movements begin with an orchestral ritornello (e.g. 'For unto us a Child is born', *Messiah*), but occasionally the chorus gives out the main theme, as in 'Your harps and cymbals sound' (*Solomon*). Massed chordal harmony used for choral recitatives (e.g. 'And Israel saw that great work', *Israel*) also occurs in the course of 'concerto style' movements, both as a contrast to figuration, and to mark beginnings and ends of sections. The movements that present an unfolding 'narrative' without formal repetitions are unlike anything else in baroque music. In 'The people shall hear and be afraid' (*Israel*) there are four sections, each with its own thematic patterns; the first three are bound together by a continuous dotted rhythm in the orchestra which ceases just before the chorus begins the fourth section: 'They shall be as still as a stone'; the orchestral bass from this point provides a series of pedal points, representing the 'stone', over which the chorus develops its new theme (rising scales) to the words 'till Thy people pass over, O Lord'. Formal variety is matched by widely-ranging contrasts of mood and colour; one has only to think of the splendid evocations of barbaric magnificence in the 'pagan' choruses of *Deborah*, *Belshazzar*, and *Samson* (Handel generally adds horns, trumpets, and drums to the orchestra for such choruses), the oracular power of the Plague Choruses in *Israel*, or the nature-painting of the double choirs in the third act of *Solomon*. No matter how complicated his counterpoint may seem on paper, Handel's basically homophonic and harmonic approach to all techniques of composition produce a feeling of fundamental simplicity; the listener never complains, as he may when listening to Bach, that Handel's music is 'too complicated'. In this Handel showed his understanding of eighteenth-century Englishmen; "what the English like", he told Gluck, "is something they can beat time to, something that hits them straight on the drum of the ear". Sometimes he deliberately played down to their level: the hero of *Judas Maccabaeus* (written after the rebellion of the Young Pretender (1745)) was obviously chosen to represent 'Butcher'

Cumberland, the bombastic character of the music reflecting the triumphant militarism of the London public.

Not all Handel's oratorios were box-office successes in his lifetime: he wrote quickly and consequently sometimes unevenly. Also, he succumbed far too frequently to the temptation to use movements, sections and themes from earlier works. The late Donald Tovey used to remark that "All Handel's works live by taking in one another's washing"; unfortunately, they sometimes take in the washing of other composer's works as well: *Israel in Egypt* uses material from compositions of Stradella and other composers in sixteen out of a total of thirty-five numbers. Such 'borrowings' do not involve stylistic inconsistency but their presence generally indicates a decrease in musical intensity. For example, the chorus 'Egypt was glad when they departed' (*Israel*), which is a note-for-note transcription of an instrumental canzona by Jacob Kerll [1627–1693], sounds very lame after such magnificent numbers as 'The people of Israel sighed'. Nobody in the early eighteenth century would have objected strongly to the practice of pasticcio-making, but it is impossible not to feel that a great deal of Handel's work would have been better without it.

The development of German Protestant music was profoundly influenced by the Lutheran congregational hymn or 'chorale' (see p. 299). Although new texts and tunes continued to be published throughout the seventeenth century, not all of these found a permanent place in the service hymnbooks. The melodies of Johann Crüger [1598–1662] and the poems of Paul Gerhardt [1607–1676] represent the highest achievements of this second period of chorale composition. Side by side with the new tunes the practice of adapting secular and older religious melodies continued: thus the tune of Gerhardt's famous *O Haupt voll Blut undwunden* (a paraphrase of the Catholic hymn, *Salve caput cruentatum*) is that of Hassler's love-song *Mein G'mut ist mir verwirret* (1601). The growth of Pietism (see p. 463) in the latter half of the century produced a great many devotional songbooks (not only by Pietists, but also, in rivalry, by orthodox Lutherans) the style of whose tunes resembled that of the aria and secular Lied (see p. 525) and whose texts were almost invariably sentimental; while very few of these songs became liturgical chorales, their exaggerated emotionalism ultimately permeated all branches of church music and was thus one of the chief causes of the decline of Lutheran church music in the later eighteenth century.

The practice of accompanying congregational chorale singing on the organ began around the turn of the sixteenth century: the first printed example of organ accompaniment is a Hamburg *Songbook* of 1604. Johann Hermann Schein [1586–1630] published the first chorales with figured continuo in his *Cantional* (1627), while Samuel Scheidt [1587–1654] in his *Tabulaturbuch* (1650) provided elaborate accompaniments with quasi-contrapuntal patterns and occasional chromatic harmonies that are second only to Bach's in originality and beauty. The growth of tonality gradually brought about a change in chorale-rhythm from the free unbarred metre of the sixteenth century to the regular one-syllable-to-a-beat style found in works by late baroque composers.

From the beginning of Lutheranism the choir was allotted an important part in the liturgy. Every town regarded its church music as a matter of civic concern, and thus all church musicians were appointed, not by the church elders, but by the town council. Though the larger churches were staffed by paid professional musicians, the small churches were frequently served by enthusiastic amateurs drawn from the numerous *Kantoreien* (singing societies) and *collegia musica* (music clubs) that sprang up all over Germany in the seventeenth century. Apart from the fortunate few who were able to attend the court chapels of those German princes that had weathered the upheavals of the Thirty Years' War, the average music-lover could hear elaborate music only in church and thus supported the expenditure of money and time required to achieve it. Choral music for the Lutheran service included both Gregorian chant (either in Latin or German translation) and motets in *stile antico* (two large collections of such motets by Italian and German composers, published in 1603 and 1613, were reprinted many times), but both of these were of secondary importance compared with compositions based on the chorales. "Consistent with the Lutheran idea of exegesis as the foundation of the liturgy, Protestant church music had the function of interpreting the 'word' of the Gospel. This goal could be achieved in two ways: the word could either be objectively 'presented' by a chorale, the quintessence of the dogma, or subjectively 'interpreted' by a free concertato composition."*

In 1601 Michael Praetorius [1571–1621] commenced the publication of *Musae Sioniae*, a collection in nine volumes of over 1,200 of his compositions based on chorales. These represent the first German experiments in the new baroque styles, including unaccompanied duets, four-part motets with continuo, simple homophonic harmonizations, and works for two, three, and four choirs. In a Preface to the ninth volume, Praetorius described three main methods of treatment: (i) the 'chorale motet', each phrase of the melody being used as a point of imitation in the older polyphonic style; (ii) 'madrigal-fashion', in which the chorale is split into small motifs that are employed in dialogue between groups of voices; (iii) the chorale in long notes forms a canto fermo over which the other parts develop either independent or derived contrapuntal patterns. A later collection, *Polyhymnia caduceatrix* (1619), adopts the Venetian techniques of Gabrieli, setting alternate phrases of a chorale for solo and choral groups, sometimes separating them with short instrumental passages. Though many of them are of uneven quality, Praetorius' works are of importance as the commencement of a development that led ultimately to the Lutheran church cantata.

Schein's *Opella nova* or *Geistliche Konzert* ('Spiritual Concertos') in two books [1618 and 1626] consist of chorale-settings for small groups of voices and instruments that apply the full virtuoso style of solo-singing to be found in the works of Gabrieli and Monteverdi for the purposes of emphasizing and illustrating the meaning and mood of the text; the melody may appear in single phrases accompanied by elaborate ornamental writing in the other voices, or it may be broken down into tiny groups of notes that are passed from one voice to another. Some of the pieces are monodies in which the chorale is transformed into a flexible solo part in the Italian manner, but accompanied by a bass moving in regular rhythms. Scheidt, Mathias Weckmann [d. 1674], Franz Tunder [1614–1667], Andreas Hammerschmidt [1639–1675], and many others continued to develop the treatment of chorales in large compositions along the lines of Schein's works. Scheidt combined the various methods, choral, ensemble, and monodic,

* M. Bukofzer, *Music in the Baroque Era*, p. 79.

in a continuous form, giving each stanza of the text its own distinctive character. Some of Scheidt's works are really a series of variations over a chorale canto fermo which show the influence of organ methods of chorale elaboration (see p. 483). Tunder and Hammerschmidt sometimes abandoned the chorale melody completely while retaining the text.

Schütz seldom employed either chorale melodies or text in his works. This may have been due partly to his Italian training and partly to an inherently dramatic approach to composition (his chief work using chorales, the *Musikalische Exequien* (1636), a polychoral setting of Biblical texts from the Burial Service, is mainly elegiac and meditative). As director of the Elector of Dresden's Court Chapel, one of the largest musical establishments at that time in Central Germany, Schütz had plenty of opportunities for introducing choral works on the very largest scale. The polychoral 'Psalms of David' (1619) achieved a perfect marriage of the rhythms of the German language and the techniques of Gabrieli, being the first settings of the German Bible that rank as supremely great music. In the *Symphoniae Sacrae*, written after his second visit to Italy, Schütz paid homage to Monteverdi without in any way relinquishing his personal style. For example, the concertato motet for bass and four trombones, *Fili mi Absalom*, published in the first volume of the *Symphoniae* (1628), shows a far more elaborate method of accompaniment than is usual with Gabrieli and Monteverdi: the interweaving trombone parts produce a rich harmonic background to the vocal line. The second part of the *Symphoniae* (1647) includes several striking psalm settings for solo voice, two violins, and continuo in which this style of accompaniment is developed further. Ex. 39 is a passage which no Italian composer of Schütz's generation would have written, preferring to hear the elaborate instrumentation in separate ritornelli rather than combined with the voice, yet for all its 'thick' harmonic texture, it remains faithful to baroque principles of word-painting, the doubling by the violins of the soprano line in sixths and thirds evoking the 'crowding multitude' of stars while solemn chords emphasize the contrast of 'what is man'. Though this contrapuntal elaboration of harmony is to be found in all later baroque music, it is more marked in German than in either French or Italian compositions, reaching its

height in the works of Bach. In the' final volume of the *Symphoniae* (1671) Schütz returned to the polychoral forms of his youth in works of profoundly dramatic intensity; *Saul, Saul was verfolgst Du mich?* (*H.A.M.*, 202), scored for six soloists, two four-part choirs, two violins, and organ continuo, is perhaps the crown of his achievement in the concertato style.

The development of German Passion music in the earlier part of the seventeenth century had at first little connection with that of concertato and chorale compositions. The Lutheran church continued the older method of reciting the Passion narrative to a special chant while punctuating it by settings of the 'crowd' portions of the text in polyphony (see Part I, p. 214). In the sixteenth century this was called a 'dramatic' Passion to distinguish it from the less usual 'motet' Passion in which the whole text was rendered by the choir. Later composers developed the 'dramatic' Passion into what may be called the oratorio-Passion by introducing orchestral and organ accompaniment and inserted sections with non-liturgical texts. The *St. John Passion* (1643) of Thomas Selle [1599–1663] alters the orchestration for each character, though a quasi-liturgical recitative is maintained, and divides the text into three parts introduced and separated by large choral and orchestral movements. Christian Flor [fl. 1620–1680], in his *St. Matthew Passion* (1667), breaks up the narrative by frequent arias and orchestral symphonies, while Johann Theile (a pupil of Schütz) introduced chorales in alternation with arias.

Schütz's Passions according to Matthew, Luke, and John [1666] stand apart from those of his contemporaries by reason of their austere, unaccompanied style. His earlier *Seven Words from the Cross* (1645) is a mixture of recitatives, ensembles, and arioso sections introduced and concluded by instrumental and choral movements in the style of the smaller pieces from the *Symphoniae Sacrae*, the words of Christ being emphasized by additional instrumental parts imitating the vocal line in two-part counterpoint. The *Christmas Oratorio* (1664), while continuing the sectional organization of the *Seven Words*, breaks new ground in the recitatives (as Schütz pointed out in his Preface) by abandoning the 'affective' style of the monody. In the Passions he returned to a quasi-Gregorian type of melody whose rhythmic notation indicates only the points of repose, so that the singer is free to vary the rhythm of the reciting tone according to the verbal pronunciation. It seems likely that Schütz adopted this method of recitative in his concern to establish a truly native musical style for German word-setting. Towards the end of his life he warned young composers not to imitate Italian continuo and concertato music until they had a thorough grounding in the old methods of polyphony and experience in native forms. His warning seems justified when the Latin church music of Catholic Southern Germany and Austria is considered; dominated by the compositions of resident and visiting Italians, it never developed any specifically German character. Not until the beginning of the classical period did German Catholic composers produce liturgical works of major importance (see Part III, pp. 607-11).

In the field of secular song German composers concentrated on the new continuo Lied, a strophic form deriving from the various adaptations and imitations of monody and continuo-madrigal by Schein, Scheidt, and others which frequently incorporated ritornelli for one or more instruments. The *Arien* of Heinrich Albert [1604–1657], a cousin and pupil of Schütz, range in style from simple tunes obviously influenced by the chorale to elaborate arias in the Italian manner (*H.A.M.*, 206). Albert's songs were sung all over Germany and inspired a vast body of similar songs which became the chief fare for domestic music-making. Nearly every important city in Northern and Central Germany had its group of song composers whose productions included not only original works, but also parodies of French, English, and Italian songs (Dowland's 'Can she excuse' appears in one collection). The continuo Lied reached its height in the works of Adam Krieger [1634–1666] whose *Arien* for solo or small vocal ensemble with ritornelli for five stringed instruments combine the melodiousness of the *bel canto* with the sturdy rhythms characteristic of German dance-tunes (*H.A.M.*, 228). Some of Krieger's compositions resemble the Italian solo cantata in their contrasts of aria and orioso sections, and thus foreshadow the later decline of the Lied under the growing popularity of Italian opera in Germany.

By the turn of the seventeenth century the styles of the later Italian opera were already exerting a strong influence on German church music. The blending of the various choral forms based on a chorale with the concertato style of Schütz and his pupils had produced a large composite type of composition later described as a church cantata. The cantatas of Dietrich Buxtehude [1637–1707], which the young Sebastian Bach found so impressive, employ arioso, strophic variation, ground basses and canto-fermo treatment of the chorale, while those of Georg Böhm [1661–1733] and Johann Pachelbel [1653–1706] consist of a series of extended variations on the chorale melody. Many composers of the younger generation, deeming these methods antiquated, welcomed the 'reform' of the cantata advocated by Erdmann Neumeister [1571–1676], a Hamburg pastor who in 1700 published the first of three cycles of cantata texts for the liturgical year on avowedly operatic lines. Regarding the cantata as "a fragment of an opera", he discarded all Biblical passages and hymn texts in favour of poetical paraphrases that could be set as secco recitatives and *da capo* arias. In the face of criticism he modified his scheme to include choruses in his second cycle (1708) and some Biblical verses and chorales in his third (1711). One of the first to set Neumeister's texts was the opera composer Philipp Krieger [1649–1725]. Other poets altered Neumeister's layout still further, producing a compromise which enclosed the solo arias and recitatives setting the poem between two stanzas of a chorale. Friedrich Wilhelm Zachau [1663–1712], Handel's teacher, and Johann Kuhnau [1660–1722] preferred to make the setting of the opening chorale stanza a large choral and orchestral movement while treating the second as a simple harmonization. This became the commonest type of cantata employed by later composers.

A similar development took place in Passion music. Keiser's *The bloody and dying Jesus* [1704] was the first of a series of 'opera-Passions' that abandoned the Gospel narrative for a lyrical poem which did not so much present the story as comment on it with a wealth of blood-curdling detail and exaggerated expressions of emotion. The music, apart from a few choruses, consisted entirely of recitatives and *da capo* arias. Handel's *St. John Passion*, written in the same year as Keiser's work to a text by Christian Postel (Keiser's opera librettist), was in much the same style, save that some portions of Scripture were retained. The most famous of Keiser's later Passions, *Jesus, martyred and dying for the sins of the world* (1712), set a libretto by Neumeister's friend, Heinrich Brockes [1680–1747], a Hamburg City Councillor. Brockes' poem became a 'best-seller' within a year of publication and was translated into several languages. All the leading north German composers set it, including Telemann, Mattheson and Handel (1716). The 'opera-Passion' form enjoyed great popularity, not only during the heyday of the Hamburg opera, but for the rest of the century throughout Germany: Telemann, as prolific in church music as he was in opera, wrote forty-four Passions. Another 'best-seller', *Der Tod Jesu* (1755), by Carl Graun [1704–1759], has features derived from the earlier oratorio, such as choral fugues, but is even more sentimental and tearful in style than Keiser's works.

The *Passions* according to St. John (1723) and St. Matthew (1729) by Johann Sebastian Bach [1685–1750] represent a compromise between the earlier 'dramatic' and the new 'opera' forms of Passion composition. Bach retained the complete relevant Gospel portions in both works, adding chorales of his own selection. For the solo arias and accompanied recitatives of *St. John* he drew on Brockes' previously-mentioned text, while for *St. Matthew* he had a libretto written for him by a Leipzig poet, Christian Henrici [1700–1764], better known by his pseudonym of Picander. *St. John* is more obviously dramatic by reason of the fewer lyrical interruptions to the narrative and the extended 'crowd' sections (the largest, 'Let us not divide', has fifty-five bars); *St. Matthew*, though it has dramatic moments, is more meditative and leisurely in its progress. The relative proportions of the constituent movements (apart from the narrative recitative and 'crowd' choruses) is shown in the following table:

	St. John	*St. Matthew*
Solo arias . .	4 (none *da capo*)	10 (7 *da capo*)
Orchestrally-accompanied recitatives	2	11 (one punctuated by a chorale)
Arias with chorus .	2	5 (including one duet)
Chorales . . .	11	13
Chorus movements .	2	5

Bach's characteristic expansion of musical forms appears particularly in the choral and orchestral movements. The opening and concluding choruses of *St. John* are built in *da capo* form; the vast opening of *St. Matthew* has a chorale sung by boys over a double choir and double orchestra developing the thematic material of one of the largest ritornelli that Bach ever wrote. Bach's treatment of the Gospel narrative is peculiarly his own: he abandoned every trace of the old chant 'intonations', substituting a vocal line ostensibly based on the secco recitative, but with a lyrical turn of phrase not to be found there that conformed entirely to the requirements of the German language and to the expressiveness required by the subject. To those of his contemporaries more obviously influenced by the later opera (especially that in *style galant*) Bach's works seemed old-fashioned. The rich accompaniments of his arias, the elaborate quasi-instrumental writing for voice contrapuntally combined with instrumental parts in which he indulged to the full the traditional German love of 'contrapuntalized harmony' (see p., 567) bewildered or bored many musicians. If, like Handel, he had depended on popular approval for his livelihood, he might have imitated more of the newer styles, but since he remained all his life a paid servant of either prince or town council (as nearly all the long line of his musical ancestors had been before him), he was under no urgent compulsion to tickle the public ear. Whereas Handel's music looks outward, every note being designed to make an immediate impression on its audience, Bach's is introspective, full of detail that can only be perceived through careful listening and sympathetic understanding. It was not always appreciated by his employers: when Bach applied for the post of Cantor at St. Thomas's, Leipzig, he obtained it only because Telemann, the Town Council's first choice, had refused it; "since we cannot secure the best", as one councillor put it, "we must take what we can get".

Bach's attitude to composition sprang directly from orthodox Lutheran notions of the value of music and particularly of its importance in church music: he was a church composer for most of his life and his largest single group of works consists of cantatas for the Lutheran liturgy. Like his predecessors, he believed that the greater the art and craftsmanship that went to the making of a work, the better it praised God, and, as he wrote in a student's notebook, "the aim and final reason of all music is none else but the Glory of God and the recreation of the mind. Where this is not observed, there will be no real music but only a devilish hubbub." Consequently, while he used all that his contemporaries had achieved, combined with the best elements of the Italian and French music of his day, he developed it in his own intensely personal manner to a point where he revolutionized it far beyond the understanding of most of his contemporaries and juniors.

To study Bach's cantatas profitably, it is important to remember their intimate connexion with the liturgy: their texts frequently contain quotations from, or reference to, the Epistle and Gospel of the day. The music is full of symbolism, allusion, and word-painting which only become clear when the works are viewed in their liturgical context. There is but one example of the variation cantata (see p. 522) in the 200 odd surviving works in cantata form: *Christ lag in Todesbanden* (no. 4); most of the cantatas commence with a large-scale movement of the type favoured by Kuhnau (see p. 526). Bach frequently gave this opening movement vast size by blending it with the Italian concerto style, but where Handel would have a largely homophonic texture (see p. 518), Bach develops the chorus in elaborate counterpoint, e.g. the Ascension cantata (no. 11). Sometimes this is combined with a chorale canto fermo in the top voice of the chorus (*Wachet auf*, no. 140). The first movement may also be built on a French overture (no. 61) or preceded by it (no. 119); the opening chorus of *Jesu der du meine Seele* (no. 78) has a chaconne bass. Several cantatas use a chorale melody as a thematic basis for all movements, but treated very freely: Ex. 40 shows this principle applied in Cantata 93, where it extends even into the (unquoted) recitatives. Most of those cantatas employing chorale melodies have them only in the first movement (as a canto fermo) and the last (a simple harmonization), though many cantatas use the entire *text* of a chorale. Cantatas having two or more chorales are generally narrative cantatas, e.g. the six constituting the so-called 'Christmas Oratorio'.

A similar variety of style and form is to be found in the solo arias, duets, and trios which form the middle sections of cantatas: ground basses, concerto movements, dances (the arias of Cantata 194 form a dance suite), and even fugue. In Cantata 54 (for solo alto) the second aria is a three-part fugue for voice, violins and violas over a continuo bass in which, inevitably, the voice is treated exactly like an instrument. The movements in which obbligato instruments figure are often those of mystical intensity, such as the two duets in *Wachet auf* for soprano and bass with violin obbligato which portray the love of the Redeemer for mankind in an ecstasy of ornamentation.

The solo items in the Mass in B minor are similar in style to those of the cantatas, some of them actually being adapted from earlier works. The massive choruses of the Kyrie and Gloria reveal Bach at his most magnificent: here both Passion and cantata are eclipsed. In the five-part orchestral and choral fugue of the initial Kyrie eleison, Bach produced both his longest single movement and his richest contrapuntal texture. Neither the Mass (written to gain the title of Court Composer from the Catholic Elector of Saxony) nor the *Magnificat* (1723) were intended for the Catholic liturgy: the first two movements of the Mass were heard at a service welcoming the Elector to Leipzig in 1733, and the *Magnificat* formed part of Christmas Vespers in Bach's first year of office at St. Thomas's.

6

THE BAROQUE: INSTRUMENTAL MUSIC

BY ANTHONY MILNER

WHEREAS in the fifteenth and sixteenth centuries the forms of instrumental music were for the most part derived from those of vocal music, in the baroque era instrumental music gained its complete independence. The works of the Roman organist Girolomo Frescobaldi [1583–1647] represent the final stages of the transition from renaissance to baroque styles. In place of the steady tempo and stylistic homogeneity of the former, Frescobaldi's music is characterized by sudden changes of mood, unprepared dissonances, and rhythmic restlessness, typical of which is the constant succession of short, jerky motifs combined in syncopations and cross-rhythms that are found in his toccatas. The prefatory instructions to his *Fiori Musicali* (1635) bid the performer "find out the affection of the passage before he plays it", vary the tempo, and slow down at cadences. In his keyboard variations (significantly termed 'partite') on traditional melodies with ground basses (*H.A.M.*, 192) he accentuates the differences between them by sharp contrasts of figuration and changes of metre. The same technique occurs in his canzonas, though in some he obtains a fundamental unity by building the sections on modified versions of the same theme. This type of variation-form appears in many of his ricercars: either the theme is altered for each fugal exposition,* or the unaltered theme is combined successively with new counterpoints. The latter form, which he sometimes describes as 'Fuga sopra un soggetto', approximates closely to the later baroque fugue (see p. 534).

The short sections and strong contrasts of Frescobaldi's keyboard works are also typical of the ensemble compositions of his contemporaries, which initiate a new type of ensemble

* FUGAL EXPOSITION: the presentation of a theme ('subject') by a number of 'voices' entering in turn at prescribed intervals: thus if the first begins on the tonic, the second voice ('answer') starts on the dominant, the third on the tonic again, and so forth.

NOTE. "Portions of chapter 6 are based on material from a Ferens Fine Arts lecture *The musical æsthetic of the Baroque* given in the University of Hull, and subsequently published by the University in 1960."

writing by adopting the continuo and hence the emphasis on top part and bass characteristic of the monody. Many ensemble pieces of this sort were dances, often paired and with variations (see p. 354), or ground bass variations for one or more violins, or canzonas with numerous sections. This later form of canzona allied to the continuo was soon known as 'sonata' (which at the beginning of the baroque referred not to the form of the work, but to its style), of which there were two chief kinds: the 'solo' sonata for one violin, continuo instrument (harpsichord or organ), and bass stringed instrument, and the 'trio' sonata for two violins and similar accompaniment. While both maintained the multisectional form of the canzona, the solo sonata tended to concentrate on exploiting the virtuoso possibilities of the violin; double stopping, pizzicato, large leaps, elaborate scale and arpeggio passages, and the use of harmonics are all to be found in the works of Biagio Marini [1600–1660], Giovanni Battista Fontana [d. 1630] and many others. The trio sonata, on the other hand, avoided virtuoso writing and preserved the contrast between chordal and imitative sections of the older canzona far more than did the solo sonata. Salomone Rossi [d. 1633?] in his first set of works for trio ensemble, *Sinfonie e Galiarde* (1607) showed a preference for an initial imitative or 'fugal' section, and for a slow dance-rhythm in a subsequent section.

The next generation of composers gradually abandoned the mixture of dance and contrapuntal sections to establish two different types of trio sonata: 'the sonata da camera' (chamber sonata), which was really a dance suite (see below, pp. 535, 538), and the 'sonata da chiesa' (church sonata), consisting of four or five slow and fast movements in alternation, generally commencing with a slow movement, and whose first quick movement was always in fugal style. The opera composers of northern Italy took the first steps towards this formal differentiation by reducing the number of sections in their canzonas to five (or less), expanding each section till it became a virtually independent movement. Legrenzi's sonata *La Cornara* (published 1655) affords an example of the intermediate stages between the multisectional canzona and the trio sonata.* It begins with an extended fugal allegro movement, but continues with three much shorter sections of which the second is a transitional Adagio leading to a recapitulation of the allegro's first bars.

* Recorded in *History of Music in Sound*, 6.

Larger sections necessitated more highly organized music, and here Legrenzi excelled in inventing themes whose sturdy up-beat patterns and sequences provided plenty of material for subsequent development. The Church of S. Petronio in Bologna, already famous for the instrumental music of its services, became under Maurizio Cazzati [1620–1677], Music Director from 1657, the centre of a distinguished group of composers known as the 'Bologna school'. Cazzati's pupil, Giovanni Battista Vitali [d. 1692] was the first to distinguish clearly between church and chamber sonatas in his publications. His church sonatas of 1667 have the normal four-movement plan (slow-quick-slow-quick) of the late baroque,* but later publications, such as the *Sonate a due, tre, quattro e cinque stromenti* of 1669, exhibit traces of the older canzona structure. *La Graziani*,† after an imitative Vivace, has a largo preceded by a seven-bar link and followed by a longer movement expanding the material of this link. Vitali's works are important for the habitual contrapuntal style of their quick movements which became an accepted feature of the trio sonata henceforward. Many of his sonatas are built on the variation principle of the later canzona whereby all movements employ transformations of the same basic material. All forms of ensemble music were cultivated at Bologna, including the first solo sonatas for 'cello and sonatas for large instrumental groups. The latter became the foundation of the concerto grosso.

The main development of German keyboard music in the opening decades of the seventeenth century was carried out chiefly by Sweelinck's pupils. Sweelinck, as we have seen (Chapter 2, pp. 351-2), blended the figuration technique of the English virginalists with the earlier Italian style of Andrea Gabrieli and Merulo, and, like Frescobaldi, laid the foundation of the fugue. Scheidt's *Tabulatura nova* (1624–6), so called because it was written in the new Italian 'open score' notation instead of the older German tablature, contains fugal pieces, chorale harmonizations, and a large group of variations and fantasias on popular songs and chorales that apply figuration patterns with logical severity, each pattern being used over and over again till its possibilities are exhausted. Although Scheidt's exhaustive elaborations are occasionally a little dull, they are of

* No. 3 is recorded in *History of Music in Sound*, 6
† *H.A.M.*, 245.

great importance in that they showed German composers an economical method of preserving the unity of a piece in the smallest details, and which proved very useful in later fugues for the sections called 'episodes' in which the subject is absent. Scheidt's choral fantasias have the same structure as the chorale motet (p. 521): each phrase of the melody is treated in fugal exposition. Heinrich Scheidemann [1596–1663], Matthias Weckmann [1619–1674], and Tunder relaxed Scheidt's rather rigid contrapuntal treatment of chorales: their chorale fantasias share features in common with the toccata, such as rhapsodic virtuoso passages, and absorb the melody into the general fabric by decorating it with copious ornamentation. In Tunder's hands the fugue received the general shape that has characterised it ever since (e.g. *H.A.M.*, 215): a piece built on a subject presented in contrapuntal exposition which, together with its accompanying counterpoints, forms the material for subsequent expansion in episodes, the episodes being punctuated by statements of the subject in various keys.*

Up to the middle of the century German composers made very little distinction between organ and harpsichord music: the organ was by far the more important of the two instruments and, since the pedals were little used (when they were necessary the composer always indicated the fact in the title), most of its music could be played quite adequately on the harpsichord. The beginning of idiomatic German harpsichord music is closely linked with that of France, which thus requires prior consideration.

In France the lute remained the fashionable solo instrument well into the seventeenth century. Though its repertoire still consisted mainly of dance pieces, the influence of the English Jacobean lutenists brought about important changes of style. The compositions of Jacques Gaultier (Court lutenist in England, 1617–47) and his famous cousin, Denis Gaultier [1603–1673], are far more 'polyphonic' in the implications of their broken-chord patterns than those of previous French lutenists; moreover, they exhibit a great increase in the use of ornamentation (e.g. *H.A.M.*, 211). Denis Gaultier's music was composed for the sophisticated circle of the French Court: it is

* While this definition is quite adequate as far as it goes, it should always be remembered that fugue is not so much a form (in the sense that the classical sonata first movement is) as a technique, a method of musical thinking; one can therefore speak of passages being written 'in fugue'.

essentially intimate music for a favoured minority. Most of it consists of stylized dances (in forms which had nearly all ceased to be danced to), the chief being the allemande, the courante (see p. 538) and the sarabande (a slow triple-time dance with feminine cadences and an accent on the second beat), which Gaultier combined with earlier dances like the pavane and more modern ones like the gigue (see below, p. 538) and canaries in a suite. Sometimes these suites were built on the variation principle, but more usually the only principle of unification was the fact that all its constituent pieces were in the same key. The suite was generally introduced by a prelude written in notes without fixed values which the player strung together in a freely improvised texture of arpeggios and broken chords. Gaultier continued the English practice of giving suggestive titles to his pieces, such as *La Majestueuse* or *La Voluptueuse*; some of his allemandes were called 'tombeaux', i.e. a piece in memory of some dead patron or friend. Many of his courantes were followed by 'doubles': ornamentalized repeats in which the original notes were replaced by broken patterns of notes of half value, thus 'doubling' the number.

When the lute began to yield in popularity to the more sonorous harpsichord (or clavecin) the keyboard composers transferred all the chief aspects of lute style, such as broken chord patterns and continuous ornamentation, to the latter instrument. The works of the chief clavecinists of the seventeenth century, Jacques de Chambonnières [1602–1672], and his two pupils, Louis Couperin [d. 1661] and Jean Henri d'Anglebert [1635–1691], contain many movements marked 'a la luthe' which require the use of the 'lute stop' (p. 341) invented in France at this time. These composers increased the number of keyboard ornaments so much that an elaborate system of signs had to be designed to indicate their positions in the texture. Chambonnières in his *Pièces de Clavecin* (printed 1670, but composed nearly thirty years earlier) provided ornament tables and explanations in notation. These signs were adopted by composers of other countries and still survive (though with altered implications) today. Some of the best pieces of Chambonnières and L. Couperin are pavanes in the older lute tradition, often elaborately polyphonic, with spacious lines and a fundamental grandeur not to be found in their dance suites. These are very similar to Gaultier's lute suites, the individual movements having titles and the customary bipartite dance structure, but the basic order of the movements is more usually fixed as allemande-courante-sarabande, with optional doubles after the courante and any number of other dances after the sarabande. Both composers favoured the lower part of the harpsichord's range, which corresponds to the compass of the lute. This is particularly noticeable in their chaconnes and passecailles (e.g. *H.A.M.*, 212) which, as in nearly all such pieces by French clavecinists, employ rondeau form* instead of the traditional variations. D'Anglebert exploited the full range of the instrument: his style is more clavieristic and his textures richer. Though L. Couperin developed the Gaultier type of prelude into a toccata-like form consisting of two rhapsodic sections flanking a central fugue, D'Anglebert preferred the older form (e.g. *H.A.M.*, 232) since a simple introductory movement provided a stronger contrast to the closely-patterned style of his allemandes. His numerous transcriptions of airs and overtures from Lulli's operas are the first important examples of such arrangements in baroque keyboard music.

Johann Jacob Froberger [1616–1667], a pupil of Frescobaldi and Court organist in Vienna, combines both Italian and French traits in his keyboard works. In his organ compositions he surpasses his master in tonal, melodic, and structural organization, but seldom matches his bold and arresting harmonies. His toccatas are generally divided into three sections of which the second and often the third are in fugal style; each section has distinctive material, though there may be one motif which appears in more than one section, thus unifying the piece (e.g. *H.A.M.*, 217), which has a six-note chromatic-scale motif dominating its second and third sections. His canzonas and ricercars apply the patterned rhythmic figuration of Scheidt and Sweelinck to melodic lines influenced by the operatic *bel canto*. The French influence is to be seen in his most important compositions, the harpsichord suites. Froberger adopted the dance suite's order of movements as he found it in Chambonnières' works, but restricted the number of dances to three or four, the optional movements being the gigue, which he inserted between the courante and sarabande (though, when his suites were published posthumously, the gigues were placed

* Rondeau Form: a 'refrain' section alternating with 'couplets': ABACAD . . . A.

after the sarabandes). Frequently his courantes are variations of the preceding allemande, a 'pairing' of dances similar to that of the Tanz and Nachtanz of the preceding century (see p. 349). Froberger's capacity for blending French and Italian stylistic elements (characteristic of nearly all German composers of the later baroque) is demonstrated in the remarkable variations (*partite*) on the popular song, *Mayerin.* The first presents the theme accompanied by the broken chords typical of the French lutenists (Ex. 41a), but the second employs figuration in the North German style (Ex. 41b); similar figuration is applied to an Italian gigue for variation 3 (Ex. 41c). Variations 4 and 5 dissolve first the melody and then the bass in continuous semiquavers reminiscent of the chorale fantasia, while the sixth is chromatic and intermittently polyphonic in the style of Frescobaldi's ricercar sections. The last three variations are French dances, a courante (Ex. 41d) followed by a double and a sarabande (Ex. 41e), all of which have a 'figured' German texture of scale-patterns:

Some of Froberger's allemandes are *tombeaux*. The beautiful *Lamento* on the death of the Emperor Ferdinand III contains features that are 'programmatic', such as the ascent of the Emperor's soul to Heaven depicted at the close. Froberger was unusual among his contemporaries in that, as Matheson relates, "he could depict whole histories on the clavier, giving a representation of the persons present and taking part in it, with all their natural characters". Matheson mentions a suite (which is now lost) "in which the passage across the Rhine of the Count von Thurn, and the danger he was exposed to from the river, is most clearly set before our eyes and ears in twenty-six little pieces".* The ancestry of such musical narratives can be traced back to the numerous instrumental arrangements of Jannequin's *La Guerre* (p. 240) through imitations, such as Byrd's *Battell* in *My Ladye Nevell's Book*. Froberger started a vogue for them in Germany which continued into the eighteenth century.

The establishment of the suite as a stereotyped form was the work of Froberger's successors; keeping his order for the four main dances† (the gigue being last), they inserted optional dances between the gigue and sarabande which were the newer 'modern' dances of the contemporary French ballet (minuet, bourree, gavotte, etc.) and hence simpler in texture than the older forms. When the Italians adopted the dance-suite in the sonata da camera they varied the order and number fairly frequently; moreover, the Italian courante (*corrente*) and gigue (*giga*) differed markedly in style from the French. The 'corrente' (actually the older form, being found in the *Fitzwilliam Virginal Book*) was in quick $\frac{3}{4}$ or $\frac{3}{8}$ time with quick running figures; the 'courante' was in moderate $\frac{3}{2}$ or $\frac{6}{4}$ with a frequent shift from one to another. Similarly the 'giga', generally in rapid compound duple time, had running rhythms over a straightforward harmonic foundations whereas the 'gigue', in compound triple time, was a little slower (often in fugal style) and had dotted rhythms. Some German composers wrote 'Ouvertures': suites commencing with a French (operatic-style) slow-quick overture followed by several French ballet dances.

German ensemble music at the beginning of the seventeenth century was chiefly influenced by Italian older-type dances

* Quoted in Spitta, *Bach*, I, p. 236.

† Originally each represented a different 'national' style: German (allemande), Italian (courante), Spanish (sarabande) and English (gigue).

and English consort music. Schein's *Banchetto musicale* [1617] shows both coupled with the favourite German scoring for mixed wind and string instruments (*H.A.M.*, 217). The trio sonata was developed by Paul Peuerl [d. 1650?], Johann Vierdanck [1600?–1660], and Johann Rosenmüller [1619–1684], the last of whom amplified the form by adding a slow introduction or 'sinfonia'. All these men composed sonatas for four, five and six instruments which maintained the slow-quick alternation of their Italian models while writing in a considerably more contrapuntal style. The long quasi-fugal themes of Rosenmüller's movements strongly resemble those of contemporary German organ canzonas, but without the strict 'patterning' to be found in Scheidt's contrapuntal writing. In central and southern Germany a school of violinist-composers explored the virtuoso technique of their instrument to the utmost: at a time when Italian violinists had virtually abandoned the earlier baroque experiments in multiple stopping of strings, the Germans had perfected a polyphonic technique of great subtlety by the use of 'scordatura' (i.e. altering the tuning of the strings). The greatest of the group, Heinrich Biber [1644–1704] wrote a cycle of fifteen *Mystery Sonatas* (*c.* 1675), each a meditation on a 'mystery' of the Catholic devotion known as the Rosary, in which every sonata has a different tuning. Biber mingles church and chamber sonata movements with 'arias', ground-bass variations and elaborately rhapsodic preludes in a stylistic synthesis typical of many later German composers. In the MS. the titles are indicated by small pictures placed before each sonata, a device copied from the French lutenists. Some of the sonatas are strongly programmatic: for example, the sixth, *Christ's Agony in the Garden of Gethsemane*, for which the violin is tuned a♭-e♭′-g′-d′, begins with a slow lamento followed by a presto filled with repeated double-stops and rapid semiquavers as the agony increases. The third movement, an andante in triple time, depicts Christ's prayer by a leaping figure for the violin which is filled in with rapid scales as the agony redoubles. A passionate recitativo adagio follows which clearly portrays the petition, "Father, if it be possible, let this chalice pass from me; nevertheless, not as I will, but as Thou wilt". (Ex. 42). The quiet finale suggests Christ's acceptance of His passion.

The use of musical symbols in these and other works is

EX. 42 From Mystery Sonata No. 6 H. I. F. BIBER

closely bound up with the instrumental application of the 'doctrine of the affections' (pp. 439-41) and the monothematic conception of musical composition it involved. Instrumental music approached monothematic form in a different way from vocal. As we have seen, the earliest baroque instrumental pieces were sectional; thematic unity, or figural consistency, within each section was mainly the result of the north German organists' contact with the patterned variation of the English virginalists as applied by Sweelinck to the elaboration of chorales. When joined to the Italian ground bass technique with its repetition of a fixed order of harmonies (p. 562) the variation-cycle provided the first instrumental solution of the problem of overall musical consistency. The development of the fugue from the ricercar is fundamentally the replacement of a sectional form elaborating successive affections by a unified form based on one affection. But whereas in vocal music the affections expressed a mood or notion, specified in the text, their meaning in instrumental composition was not defined: hence a purely abstract art that relied on musical consistency alone. Hence also a tendency to regard instrumental music as inferior to vocal. "An instrumental player or composer must observe the rules which lead to good melody and harmony much more clearly and assiduously than a singer or choral composer, because when singing, the singer is aided by the great clarity of the words, which are always missing in instrumental music" (Mattheson). Biber's sonatas and the French lute and clavecin pieces previously mentioned are examples of the frequent employment of titles, pictures, and emblems to elucidate the affections in instrumental works. Some of the apparently 'abstract' use of figures in instrumental music disappears if it is remembered that many of them held 'affective' values from their use in vocal and dramatic music. When Purcell used a descending chromatic counterpoint in the Allegro of his 7th Trio Sonata he did so well aware of the associations it would have in his hearers' minds: a storehouse of allusive memory would thus be awakened, heightening its poignancy.

By the end of the seventeenth century "the specific formal principle is the statement of the 'basic affection' and its subsequent exploitation by continuous expansion".* This 'basic affection' may be a ground bass with its harmonies, a fugue subject, an aria or concerto ritornello, or a tiny figure that pervades the texture of a dance movement or contrapuntal study. Bach's well-known two-part invention in C major affords a compact illustration. The 'exploitation' of the affection was not, of course, necessarily as strict and exhaustive as this. Handel's Allemande from his first harpsichord suite shows a somewhat similar figure receiving broader treatment in the context of a dance movement. Sometimes it is possible to compare two composers' treatment of the same theme. Johann

* Lang, *Music in Western Civilization*, p. 443.

Caspar Ferdinand Fischer's E major fugue in his *Ariadne Musica** (1715) has the same subject as Bach's 9th fugue in the second book of *The Well-tempered Klavier*. The comparison recalls Tovey's remark: "A theme belongs to the man who knows how to use it."

The selection of the musical formula which is the basic affection of a piece may often have been determined by extra-musical considerations; the theorist Chabanon justified this when he wrote that "music cannot reproduce images for the ear but must always fall back on metaphors contrived by the intelligence". Originality in the invention of themes was not expected: the interest lay in the unfolding and elaboration of the basic material and the composer's individual method of treatment. The figures were regarded as already existing. Composers had fundamentally the same attitude to the notion of 'artistic inspiration' as Locke had to the sources of human knowledge: "All those sublime thoughts which tower above the clouds and reach as high as heaven itself, take their rise and footing here; in all that great extent wherein the mind wanders in those remote speculations it may seem to be elevated with, it stirs not one jot beyond those ideas which sense and reflection have offered for its contemplation."†

During the first quarter of the seventeenth century English instrumental music was second to none. Its excellence was recognized in northern Europe: Roger North [1653–1734] wrote that "the foreigners themselves use to owne that the English in the instrumentall and the Italian in the vocal musick excelled". The influence of English keyboardists on German organ music has already been mentioned; composers such as William Brade [1560–1630] and Thomas Simpson [fl. 1600], most of whose lives were spent in north Germany and Scandinavia, where all their chief works were published, were no less influential in the development of ensemble music. But this supremacy was short-lived: the golden age of keyboard music did not long outlast that of the madrigal. Tomkins was the last great master in both fields. Only in ensemble music did a strong native tradition survive. Composers continued to write polyphonic fantasias and In Nomines up to the Restoration period, the last being those of the twenty-one-year-old Purcell.

* *H.A.M.*, 247.
† Locke, *Essay concerning Human Understanding*, II, i, 24.

The newer instrumental styles of France and Italy made little headway except in Court circles; even in Charles II's time, to quote North again, "the French manner of Instrumental musick did not gather so fast as to make a revolution all at once, but during the greatest part of the King's reign, the old musick was used in the countrys and in many meetings and societys in London".

Whereas Elizabethan chamber music usually employed a consort of viols (the 'broken' consort of viols, wind, and plucked-string instruments being restricted to theatrical or outdoor performances), Jacobean composers preferred to mix violins and viols and to support them with a continuo instrument. Dowland's *Lachrimae* pavans (1604) are written for this new type of 'broken' consort. The continuo instrument could be a lute (as in *Lachrimae*) or harp, but the later Jacobeans and most of the mid-century ensemble composers preferred the chamber organ, except in dances for which the organ was inherently unsuitable. As far as England was concerned, the harpsichord did not become a normal continuo instrument for chamber ensembles before 1680. Some of the Jacobean and Caroline fantasias have the continuo fully written: others merely provide a bass line.

William Lawes, John Jenkins [1592–1678], and Matthew Locke were the most important ensemble composers of the mid-century. Lawes's compositions fall into three main groups: (i) fantasias, pavanes, and In Nomines for five and six parts, designed to cater for the conservative tastes of music-lovers outside the immediate influence of Court society; (ii) fantasias for various combinations from three to seven parts, all with elaborate harp or organ continuo, to please the more 'up-to date' chamber players; (iii) *The Royal Consort*, a collection of sixty-six dances grouped in six suites, which were originally used for Court dancing, first scored for two violins, two bass viols, and two theorboes, but later arranged for the trio sonata ensemble of two violins, bass viol, and continuo. With the exception of the dances, Lawes's works are characterized by frequent large melodic leaps and the typically English use of 'free' dissonance in false relations and abrupt chord changes (cf. Chapter 3, p. 426).

Jenkins, the most prolific English instrumental composer of the century and, as North, his pupil, confirms, regarded as 'the mirrour and wonder of his age', exhibits even greater stylistic variety in his works than does Lawes, reflecting the many changes in taste and society that occurred during his long life. From his first youth he was encouraged by powerful patrons, who probably recommended him to Charles I (himself a proficient viol-player and a pupil of Coperario), whom he served as Court musician from 1625 to 1640. During the Puritan interregnum he had the good fortune to find refuge and employment in country houses far from the capital. Shortly after the Restoration he joined the Court musicians of Charles II. His last years were spent at Kimberley, Norfolk, in the house of the music-loving Wodehouse family. Over a hundred of his fantasias survive, of which those for four parts were nearly all written during the earlier years of Charles I's reign. Their polyphony is as intricate as Lawes's and seems even more complicated by reason of their longer melodic lines. A group of three-part fantasias in the same style written over twenty years later suggests that there was still much demand for this sort of music, though several five- and six-part fantasias and pavanes dating from the same period show the partial influence of newer styles in more homophonic textures and shorter simpler themes. One of these, *The Bell Pavin* for six parts, depicting the mingled evening chimes of Oxford, was perhaps his most famous piece. The largest section of his output consists of several hundred dance suites, the majority dating from the Restoration period; designed for various combinations of two, three, and four instruments (the favourite being the trio sonata ensemble), they contain anything from two to fifteen movements, such as ayres (bipartite pieces in French style), pavanes, allemandes, courantes, sarabandes, and gigues. Pavanes are used as introductory movements (they had long ceased to be danced to), sometimes being replaced by fantasias. Another group of fantasias for trio sonata ensemble composed when Jenkins was over seventy employs forms of short sections reminiscent of the Italian canzona and early sonata. Also dating from the same period are works for one or two bass viols with continuo which demand the utmost skill and dexterity. The bass viol had become a popular solo instrument towards the middle of the century: the *Division-Violist* (1659) of Christopher Simpson [d. 1669] not only provides instruction for beginners, but includes several sets of 'divisions upon a ground' using techniques for improvisation described a century earlier by the Spaniard Ortiz (p. 348) and kept alive in England long after their virtual disappearance elsewhere.

Matthew Locke's 'fantasias' are really four-movement works based on the plan of some of Jenkins's suites. Each consists of a fantasia in polyphonic style, followed by a courante, ayre, and sarabande. The influence of the trio sonatas is evident in the fantasia motifs (up-beat patterns often closely resembling the fugal themes of Vitali) and in the attempt to unify several works by following the sarabande with a short section (often only six to eight bars) which recalls the style of the opening contrapuntal movement. On the other hand, the imitative counterpoint of the fantasia style appears in many of the dance movements. Some works having the same basic plan are named 'consorts': *The Broken Consort*, like Lawes's *Royal Consort*, is a collection of six suites. All Locke's instrumental works exhibit the same harmonic freedom and daring found in his dramatic music.

Purcell wrote nearly all his chamber music during his early twenties. Though the harmonic writing of his fantasias, pavanes, and In Nomines is influenced by that of Locke, all preserve the older contrapuntal style without admixture of dance elements. Their characteristic intensity of expression is combined with complete mastery of the most varied devices of counterpoint. Though he described the first of his two sets of trio sonatas (published in 1683 and 1697) as "a just imitation of the most famed Italian masters" intended "to bring the seriousness and gravity of that sort of Musick into vogue, and reputation among our countrymen", their instrumental style retains considerable traces of the older fantasia polyphony. He studied Vitali's sonatas closely, yet in neither set is he content merely to 'imitate': while he often followed Vitali in the order of the movements, he frequently has five or six instead of the usual Italian four. Some sonatas have their movements arranged in an order utterly unlike the Italian: the fifth of the first set has three slow movements flanked by two quick ones. The sixth sonata of the second set is a chaconne with variations. In the title-page of the first set Purcell designates the continuo instrument as organ or harpsichord.

Thurston Dart has recently demonstrated that the organ is the ideal continuo for the apparently very insufficient figured-bass provided: "simple and slow-moving organ chords form a perfect background for the elaborate harmonies and intricate counterpoints of the strings. It allows the bass viol to take leave of the thorough-bass from time to time, in order to play an independent inner part above it."* Thus Purcell links the older organ continuo style of the later Jacobean fantasia to the newer style of the Italian 'sonata da chiesa'.

Purcell, like Locke, whom he succeeded in 1677 as Court Composer in Ordinary for the Violin, was required to produce dance music for the King's entertainments; all that survives are three Overtures and a suite for strings and continuo which mingle French rhythms with typically Purcellian harmonic and contrapuntal treatment. Large-scale instrumental music in seventeenth-century England existed only in connection with drama or choral music: some of Purcell's best instrumental writing is to be found in the dances and interludes of *The Fairy Queen* and *King Arthur* and in the introductory symphonies to his anthems.

The increasing number of public concerts, the success of the semi-operas, and the Royal patronage of the newer types of instrumental music brought about the gradual eclipse of the older instruments and the chamber music in which they were employed. Thomas Mace deplored their loss and the changing taste in his *Musick's Monument* (1676): "Very little of This so eminent Musick (for viols) do we hear of in These Times, the Lesz the Greater Pity. Then again, we had all Those Choice Consorts, to Equally-Seized Instruments (Rare Chests of Viols) and as Equally Performed: For we would never allow Any Performer to Over-top, or Out-cry another by loud play; but our Great Care was, to have all the Parts Equally Heard; by which means, though we had but sometimes indifferent, or mean Hands to Perform with; yet This Caution made the Musick Lovely, and Very Contentive. But now the Modes and Fashions have cry'd These Things down, and set up a Great Idol in Their Room; observe with what a Wonderful Swiftnesz They now run over Their Brave New Ayres; and with what High-Prized Noise; viz. 10, or 20 violins, etc. to a Some-Single Soul'd Ayre; it may be of two or three Parts, or some Coranto . . . and such like Stuff; seldom any other; which is rather fit to make a Man's Ear Glow, and Fill his Brain full of Frisks, than to Season, and

* Thurston Dart, 'Purcell's Chamber Music'. *Proceedings of the Royal Musical Association*, Session 85.

Sober his Mind, or Elevate his Affection to Goodness." Such complaints are always made when the new supplants the old. The abandonment of the viol consort music would not have mattered at all if Purcell's lead had been followed, tempering the fashion for all things Italian by the continuation of a strong native tradition. The tragedy in the state of affairs described by Mace lay in the virtual cessation after Purcell of anything characteristically English in the instrumental music written by English composers.* Keyboard music had languished after the great Jacobeans: Blow and Purcell produced some attractive trifles, Arne in the following century a few sonatas in the manner of *style galant.* Thomas Roseingrave [1690–1776] was the only Englishman who tried to maintain a 'national' approach; his keyboard works, while showing the influence of his friend Domenico Scarlatti, still preserved the typical freedom in dissonance treatment that had marked English music for over a century. His contemporaries' lack of appreciation is summed up in Burney's judgement: "harsh ungrateful harmony, and extravagant and licentious modulations". Most English composers in the eighteenth century adopted an Italianate style: "rightly recognizing the greatness of Handel's work, they mistakenly set themselves to use it as their model and to imitate its style and character. Thus they fell between two stools, for they failed to achieve success in the Handelian manner, and they warped their own natural gifts."† Even the best works of the period, such as the symphonies of William Boyce [1710–1799] and the violin sonatas of Joseph Gibbs [1699–1788], though competent, polished, and charming, provided nothing of importance for the future development of English music. By the middle of the century, music for the average educated Englishman had become, as Burney defined it, "an innocent luxury, unnecessary, indeed to our existence, but a great improvement and gratification of the sense of hearing . . . a manufacture in Italy, that feeds and enriches a large portion of the people; and it is no more disgraceful to a mercantile country to import it than wine, tea, or any other production of remote parts of the globe".‡

* The corresponding situation in English vocal music did not develop so quickly by reason of the strongly conservative trend in Anglican church music, and thus lies outside the scope of this volume.

† E. E. Fellowes, *English Cathedral Music*, p. 179.

‡ *A General History of Music* (1776), Preface to Vol. I.

The contrast between French and Italian styles of instrumental music (which reflects that between *tragèdie-lyrique* and opera) is of fundamental importance for later baroque music. Each style had its own tradition of performance (not indicated in the written appearance of the music) concerning methods of string bowing, phasing, details of tempi, ornamentation, and alterations or departures from the notated rhythm, the last being especially important in French music. These matters are far too complicated to be discussed here:* suffice to say generally that the French style was more 'mannered' and had a stylized system of ornamentation, whereas the Italian was less sophisticated and added freely extemporized ornamentation to slow movements. A few quotations will serve to show how marked from the listener's standpoint were the general differences between the two.

The Abbé François Raguenet [1660–1722], in his *Parallèle des Italiens et des Français* (1702), compared French music unfavourably with Italian: "As the Italians are naturally much more brisk than the French, so are they more sensible of the passions and consequently express them more lively in all their productions. If a storm or rage is to be described in a symphony, their notes give us so natural an idea of it that our souls can hardly receive a stronger impression from the reality than they do from the description; everything is so brisk and piercing, so impetuous and affecting, that the imagination, the senses, the soul, and the body itself are all betrayed into a general transport; it is impossible not to be borne down with the rapidity of these movements. A symphony of furies shakes the soul; it undermines and overthrows it in spite of all its care; the artist himself, whilst he is performing it, is seized with an unavoidable agony; he tortures his violin; he racks his body; he is no longer master of himself, but is agitated like one possessed with an irresistible motion.

"If, on the other side, the symphony is to express a calm and tranquillity, which requires a quite different style, they however execute it with an equal success. Here the notes descend so low that the soul is swallowed with them in the profound abyss. Every string of the bow is of an infinite length, lingering on a dying sound which decays gradually till at last it absolutely expires. Their symphonies of sleep insensibly steal the soul from

* Cf. Thurston Dart, *The Interpretation of Music* (Hutchinson's University Library), for an admirable summary of the chief points involved.

the body and so suspend its faculties and operations that, being bound up, as it were, in the harmony that entirely possesses and enchants it, it's as dead to everything else as if all its powers were captivated by a real sleep. . . . Their violins are mounted with strings much larger than ours; their bows are longer, and they can make their instruments sound as loud again as we do ours. The first time I heard our band in the Opéra after my return out of Italy, my ears had been so used to the loudness of the Italian violins that I thought ours had all been bridled. . . . Their bass viols are as large again as the French, and all ours put together don't sound so loud in our operas as two or three of those basses do in Italy."*

Raguenet was answered three years later by Jean Laurent le Cerf de la Viéville, Lord of Freueuse, in his *Comparison de la musique italienne et de la musique française* (1705), written in the form of dialogues. The following observations occur in the sixth dialogue in the section entitled "Treatise on good taste":

"I reduce the merit of a player upon an instrument to three things: exactness (*netteté*), delicacy, getting the most out of his instrument . . . exactness is the principal quality, especially for the players of instruments which are played directly by the fingers, without a bow. Count that of five hundred players of the lute, the harpsichord, etc., there will not be one who succeeds in playing as exactly (*nettement*) as one has the right to ask. And without exactness, what is a piece for the lute or the harpsichord? A noise, a jangling of harmonies in which one understands nothing. I would sooner listen to a hurdy-gurdy. After this precious exactness comes delicacy. It is in instruments what neatness (*propreté*) is in singing. . . . Last, to get the most out of the instrument. It is certainly necessary that an instrument should sound (*parle*), and it is true that to make it sound well is an art and a most important talent, but let us not lose sight of the capital maxim, the golden mean. In truth, your Italians carry too far a certain desire to elicit sound from their instruments. My intelligence, my heart, my ears tell me, all at once, that they produce a sound excessively shrill and violent. I am always afraid that the first stroke of the bow will make the violin fly into splinters, they use so much pressure. Besides, you comprehend that the sovereign perfection of an instrumentalist

* From the eighteenth-century translation in Strunk, *Source Readings in Music History*, pp. 478, 486.

would be to ally the three qualities and . . . to combine them in equal proportions. But I think I have observed that they never have all three in equal measure."*

The most important feature of instrumental music of the later baroque, a fully-organized system of tonality, which first appeared in the Neapolitan opera and the instrumental works of the later Bologna composers (p. 533), has already been surveyed in Chapters 3 and 4; we need only consider now its consequences in instrumental composition, which were:

(i) increased range of modulation, because since all the harmonies used (including discords and so-called chromatic chords) were now fully related to a tonic triad and key, so too the degrees of relation of all neighbouring keys were established according to the number of notes each related key had in common with the main key;
(ii) longer movements, because the interior structure of a movement could be organized on a modulatory plan far wider than that of earlier compositions;
(iii) far more elaborate counterpoint by reason of the firm harmonic basis now provided;
(iv) an increasing tendency to unify a movement by employing the same themes, patterns and figuration throughout.

A cadence was now more than ever before a central point in the musical organization, and therefore it had to be approached in a manner that made it sound important and inevitable. A favourite way of achieving this was the sequence: a harmonic,

* Strunk, op. cit., pp. 502-3.

melodic, and rhythmic formula repeated over and over again (generally on a descending bass) till the cadence was reached. Passages like Ex. 43 (p. 550) are typical of late baroque music.

The implications of fully systematized tonality were first realized in the concerto compositions of Archangelo Corelli [1653–1713] and his contemporaries. His concerti grossi (heard in Rome as early as 1682, but not published till 1714) exploit the contrast of smaller and larger instrumental groups within a movement that had been used previously by Gabrieli and the later Venetian composers, particularly Legrenzi. Corelli's treatment differs fundamentally from that of his predecessors, for whereas they had merely detached small groups from a main orchestral body from time to time to vary the texture, he opposes a fixed 'concertino' string trio of two violins and 'cello to a 'ripieno' string band, each group having its own continuo. He makes little or no difference between the two groups either of material or treatment: the soli tutti contrast is his chief concern. He was not an innovator in formal organization, usually following the patterns of the earlier Bolognese church and chamber sonatas in the number and order of the movements: thus the *Concerti da chiesa*, nos. 1–8, have normally five movements (occasionally supplemented by brief linking movements) alternating slow and quick tempi; the *Concerti da camera*, nos. 9–12, consist of a prelude in contrapuntal style and three dances, with either brief links or contrapuntal movements between the dances. In matters of style, however, his works were of fundamental importance for the subsequent development of Italian baroque music. His allegros are characterized by rapid changes of harmony underlining the metrical structure, repeated notes, widely ranging themes, more idiomatic violin writing than any previous composer had used, and above all a mechanically progressive rhythm which, in conjunction with the sequential progressions and strictly organized harmonies mentioned above, gives an impression of inevitable development and relentless progress. In contrapuntal adagios he produces an effect of diversity of parts without thickening the texture by continually crossing the lines of the two violin parts, the apparent polyphonic complexity being heightened by chains of suspensions and seventh chords. His fugues achieve a similar effect by frequent entries of the subject in a texture which shifts rapidly from two- to three- or four-part counterpoint.

Giuseppe Torelli [1650–1708], Corelli's fellow-student at Bologna, distinguished three types of concerto composition: (i) concertos for string orchestra without the concertino-ripieno division, the title referring to the instrumental style; (ii) concerti grossi; (iii) concertos for one or two solo violins and string orchestra. After his first essays in the new style, he dropped the initial slow movement of the Bolognese sonata forms and established the typical three-movement form of quick-slow-quick (very like that of the opera sinfonia) used by all later Italian composers. He distinguished between concertino and ripieno by giving the former virtuoso figuration. In the first movements (and occasionally in the finales) he repeated the opening orchestral tutti in rondo-fashion, though in different keys and with slight variations. This ritornello form* (so named because the return of the tutti was called a ritornello) closely resembles the basic ABA shape of the *da capo* aria in its broad aspects, though each 'section' may contain more repeats (whether partial or complete) of the ritornello than occur in the normal aria. Antonio Vivaldi [1676–1741], the greatest Italian master of the concerto, gave the ritornello an even greater importance in the formal design (especially in his solo concertos), often breaking into the solo sections with a partial repetition of its material. Moreover, he made an important innovation by frequently giving the solo new material which had not appeared in the ritornello. Many of his concertos have titles and programmes: the best-known is the group entitled *Le Stagione* ("The Seasons"), in which each of the four concertos is preceded by a sonnet describing the events and setting depicted. The imitations of birds and other onomatopoeic effects are confined to the solo passages, the formal structure of the concerto being strictly maintained. Vivaldi's themes were much admired by his contemporaries for their simplicity and vigour: their strong rhythmic patterns commencing on an upbeat were imitated by all the leading composers of the day, including Bach and Handel.

Alessandro Scarlatti's concertos closely resemble those of Torelli in their general style while looking back to the earlier Bolognese sonatas in form and number of movements. In his later opera sinfonias, Scarlatti incorporated many elements of the concerto style:† the brilliant violin figuration, the up-beat

* Cf. *H.A.M.*, 246, for an example.

† Cf. *H.A.M.*, 259 and 260, for a comparison of a concerto and *Sinfonia avanti l'opera* by Scarlatti.

rhythmic patterns, and occasional if brief opposition of contrasted instrumental groups. Public performances of concertos encouraged concert repeats of opera sinfonias. About 1730 Pietro Locatelli [1693–1764] and Gian Battista Sammartini [1701–1755] began composing sinfonias intended purely for concert performance: these had the usual allegro-adagio-allegro form, but the individual movements tended to be longer than those of the operatic sinfonia. Such movements contained much important subsidiary material which contrasted strongly with the themes of the ritornello. This type of sinfonia in the hands of later composers led ultimately to the classical symphony (Part III).

In his trio sonatas, Corelli established the four-movement structure used by all Italian composers of the late baroque. His works in this form are noteworthy not only for their rich 'harmonic' counterpoint, but also for the fact that in them the bass instrument participates fully in the contrapuntal texture. While preserving the main differences between the church and chamber sonata, he blended elements of both. Apart from the few that employ the techniques of the variation canzona or the five short movements characteristic of his predecessors, his church sonatas begin with a contrapuntal slow movement that has two imitative parts over a bass moving regularly in quavers; this is followed by an allegro in fugal style and two dance movements, an adagio in stylized sarabande rhythm, and a gigue. The chamber sonatas have a closely knit contrapuntal prelude and two or three largely homophonic dances. In his twelve solo sonatas, six church and six chamber sonatas, the same characteristics are evident,* but the violin is treated in a far more virtuoso style. Many of the adagios in the solo sonatas provide only a simple melodic line for the violin, the player being expected to embellish this according to the Italian conventions of 'gracing' (e.g. *H.A.M.*, 252, for a contemporary written version of such ornamentation). These observations apply equally to the sonatas of Corelli's contemporaries, of whom the chief were Felice Evaristo dall'Abaco [1675–1742], whose trios are far more varied in manner and whose counterpoint is often much more interesting than Corelli's,† Tommaso Vitali [1665-1747], son of G. B. Vitali and the last member of the Bologna school, Geminiani, and Locatelli.

* E.g. *H.A.M.*, 253.
† E.g. *H.A.M.*, 269.

The solo sonatas of Francesco Veracini [1690–1750] represent the end of the true baroque form: they not only virtually abolish the distinction between church and chamber sonata, but include movements in *da capo* aria, ritornello, and French overture forms. Veracini's occasional use of *style galant* bears witness to the continuing influence of the opera on the development of instrumental music. In the trio sonatas of Pergolesi and the solo sonatas of Giuseppe Tartini [1692–1770] this influence appears even more strongly, for the instrumental adaptation of *da capo* aria led to a new type of opening movement which repeats the opening section in the original key. The resulting structure is one of many that led to the classical sonata form at the end of the century.

Italian keyboard music has little of interest or importance after Frescobaldi (save in the works of Bernardo Pasquini [1637-1710], who composed harpsichord sonatas modelled on the forms of the violin sonata) till Domenico Scarlatti [1685–1757], son of Alessandro. Most of his 544 sonatas (really single movements) were written for his employer, Princess Maria Barbara of Portugal, whose service he entered in 1729 when she was betrothed to the Spanish Infante Ferdinand (later Ferdinand VI [1746-1759]) and in which he remained, living in Spain for the rest of his life. Consequently, apart from the thirty published in 1738 under the title *Esercizi per Gravicembalo*, the majority of these pieces were virtually unknown (save for a few MS. collections made by wealthy admirers) till they were published in a complete edition* at the beginning of the present century. The majority have a basic bipartite form whose first section modulates from tonic to dominant with the reverse modulation in the second part, but within this general structure the organization of the material varies considerably. Often the modulation is marked by new material which sometimes contrasts dramatically with the main theme. The second section may begin with a repeat of the main theme in the dominant, or introduce entirely new material in another key which may displace repeats of previous material, or may 'develop' the material of the first section, ending with a condensed reprise of the opening. This bipartite structure and its interior variants derive from the new

* By Alessandro Longo. This, still the only complete edition, contains many editorial additions and inaccuracies, some of which are listed in *Domenico Scarlatti*, by Ralph Kirkpatrick.

aria forms of the Neapolitan *opera buffa*.* Recent research has demonstrated that many of Scarlatti's 'sonatas' were originally paired together to make a two-movement composition, such as occur in the keyboard works of the opera composers, Giuseppe Paganelli [1710–1765], Giovanni Rutini [1730–1797], and Galuppi. These men followed Scarlatti's lead in adopting the simple harmonic basis of the *buffa* aria and *stile galante*, which relied mainly on the primary triads of tonic, dominant, and subdominant, but whereas their harmonic treatment sounds often perfunctory and conventional, Scarlatti's is marked by a highly individual approach, seen in the contraction of conventional cadence formulas, the use of multiple acciaccaturas (which often obscure the fundamental chord completely), unorthodox resolutions of sevenths, and unexpected modulations. His brilliant keyboard writing is unparalleled in its frequent crossing of the hands, the wide skips from one end of the keyboard to the other, the elaborate figuration (often derived from the violin concerto style), and the dazzling use of staccato, as also in its occasional imitations or suggestions of the sounds of guitar, bells, trumpet, and bagpipes. His textures are correspondingly varied: melodies with Alberti bass or other figuration accompaniments, melody and bass in octaves, polyphony more often implied than actually present, and frequent use of broken-chord patterns involving rapid large leaps that require hand and finger movements unknown to previous players.

Although French composers acknowledged the importance of Italian music in the late baroque and yielded in some measure to its influence, their strong native tradition preserved them from being dominated by it. Since the musical stage in both France and Italy provided the chief source of new developments, the considerable differences between *tragèdie-lyrique* and opera of vocal style, conceptions of the dance, and performance had their counterpart in instrumental music. Only two important composers, Jean Aubert [d. 1753] and Jean-Marie Leclair [1697-1764], wrote concertos, and, while they modelled their allegros on those of Vivaldi, their slow movements have much in common with the form and style of the instrumental adaptations of the *air tendre*. The term 'concert' in French music of this period was never used as the equivalent of 'concerto', but always as implying

* A typical example is the duet 'Lo conosco' from Pergolesi's *La serva padrona*, *H.A.M.*, 287.

chamber music: Aubert's *Concerts de symphonie* (1630) are trio sonatas. Moreover, the adoption of *style galant* involved abandoning the broad, formal conceptions of Lully and his followers for shorter phrases and profuse ornamentation, characteristics inimical to any fundamental adoption of Italian forms. The main effects of French interest in Italian music appear in the general adoption of fully-organized tonality and in the works of a small but distinguished group of Parisian composers who wrote in both styles, sometimes in contrasted movements within a work, or, less often, blending elements of both in a single movement.

Marin Marais [d. 1725], a pupil of Lully, is a typically ambivalent composer of this group. His chief works, the accompanied suites for viola da gamba (which continued to be a popular solo instrument in France for longer than elsewhere), are generally conservative save for their sprightly melodies and delicate ornaments, yet he was one of the first French composers to publish works for the trio sonata ensemble. Though the medium of his *Pièces en trio* (1692) is Italian, their style has little in common with that of the sonata; the descriptive titles and programmes reveal their fundamentally national cast. The first composer to attempt to meet the Italians on their own ground was François Couperin [1668–1733]. His seven sonatas written in 1692 and 1695 adopt the basic four-movement plan of the sonata da chiesa and imitate Corelli's contrapuntal style for the first and second movements. But neither form nor style are slavishly followed: No. 3, *La Visionnaire*, follows the two opening movements with a canzona, gigue, and double fugue; No. 7, *La Sultane*, exceptional in requiring two violas da gamba in addition to the normal violins and continuo, has six movements, of which the third is an *air tendre*. In all sonatas the passages and sections employing chromatic harmony are far richer than anything to be found in Corelli, since they preserve something of the English freedom of dissonance as inherited by the French lutenists and developed anew by the clavecinists and organists. When Couperin published these works in 1726, he renamed four, added to each of these a set of dances, and entitled the group *Les Nations*: thus each work consists of a sonata da camera plus a French suite. The general stylistic contrast implied by this division is not strictly followed, however; both French and Italian types of courante and gigue occur and he distinguishes between two kinds of sarabande, *tendre* and *grave*, the second related to the $\frac{3}{2}$ sarabande of the Italian sonata da camera. While Couperin follows the Italians in making the allemande the most extended of the four main dances and in treating it polyphonically, his 'suites' are truly French in their final chaconnes (both in ground-bass and rondeau forms) and ornamentation. The stylistic blending of *Les Nations* is continued in the programme sonatas *Le Parnasse ou L'Apothéose de Corelli* and *L'Apothéose de Lulli* (both published in 1725). In the Lully *Apothéose* (whose Preface enumerates alternative methods of performance, such as two harpsichords or with flutes replacing the violins) forms from the tragèdie lyrique are mingled with the church sonata. It begins with an *Ouverture*, 'Lully in the Elysian fields', followed by theatrical pieces entitled 'The singing shades', 'The Flight of Mercury', 'The descent of Apollo', 'The subterranean noise' of Lully's rivals and 'the tender complaints' of his contemporaries. The Italian style first appears in a canzona, 'Lully taken up to Parnassus' and continued in a largo in which Corelli and the muses welcome Lully, who thanks Apollo in an Italian aria with French ornaments. At Apollo's suggestion of a united French-Italian style, the muses have an *Essai, en forme d'ouverture*, consisting of a section in dotted rhythms followed by a triple-time tune in quaver rhythm. Two *airs légers* follow for the violins unaccompanied (Lully has the tune in the first and Corelli the accompaniment, reversing rôles for the second), leading to a complete sonata da chiesa in the mingled styles. Couperin's two sets of *Concerts royaux* (1722 and 1724) are extended dance suites introduced by a prelude in slow tempo. The mixture of French and Italian styles is emphasized in the title of the second set, *Les Goûts Réünis*, and in its Preface, wherein Couperin observes: "I have always valued works which deserve it without making exceptions of composers or nations." Alternative media of performance are again indicated: either harpsichord, or an ensemble of violin, oboe, viola, and bassoon.

Leclair's trio sonatas represent the complete union of Italian and French chamber-music styles. He keeps the four-movement scheme of the Italian sonata, generally avoids programmes and uses Italian tempo indications, yet his ornamentation and violin-writing are always French. His solo sonatas exhibit a very advanced violin technique (*H.A.M.*, 278) in which multiple stoppings and difficult bowings are combined with highly elaborate ornamentation in some of the most personal and beautiful music of the period. Occasionally he links the movements by common thematic material, thus looking back to the earlier canzona, but the form of his second movements (i.e. of the contrapuntal allegros) has the brief reprise of the main theme that characterizes the later Italian sonata.

Rameau's *Pièces de clavecin en concert* (published 1741, but composed from ten to twenty years earlier) are not trio sonatas: the harpsichord is treated as a virtuoso solo instrument and the other instruments (violin or flute and viola or second violin) are regarded as 'accompanying' the harpsichord. Keyboard works 'with accompaniment' were increasingly common in France from 1730 onwards. The 'accompaniment' was not by any means always subordinate: apart from unison and octave passages, and sections where the harpsichord is supported by harmonic figuration, there are frequent examples of true 'concerted music' where the material is shared equally by all the instruments, as also of the harpsichord accompanying melodic lines in the flute and violin with arpeggios. Rameau afterwards arranged some of these pieces for harpsichord solo, and he orchestrated others as instrumental movements for his operas. *La Livri*, a *tombeau* for Rameau's patron, the Comte de Livri, exists in three versions: concerted, solo harpsichord, and orchestrated as a gavotte in the third act of *Zoroastre*. 'Accompanied' keyboard music of this kind was taken up by the German composers of the mid-eighteenth century. Some of Haydn's 'violin and piano sonatas' are really works of this type, while several of his early piano sonatas exist in an alternative form, with optional violin accompaniments.

French keyboard music, whether for organ or harpsichord, remained a stronghold of the native musical tradition. Couperin's two organ masses,* composed at the age of twenty-one, look back to the older polyphonic tradition in their close, imitative technique and in the frequent use of shifting chromatic progressions only loosely bound to the home key, though these are combined with sections inspired by the style of the ballet dances. Most of the organ music of Couperin's contemporaries, chief of

* Compositions in which solo verses (or, in French parlance, *couplets*) replace alternate sections of the plainsong. The first complete examples were printed in Cavazzoni's *Intravolatura* of 1542 (e.g. *H.A.M.*, 117).

whom were André Raison [fl. 1680–1730?], Louis Marchand [1669–1732], one of the great virtuosi of the period, Jean Dandrieu [1684–1740], and Claude Daquin [1694–1772], is similarly liturgical in form, but increasingly coloured by elements of style deriving from opera, by harpsichord ornamentation, and by broken chord patterns. In their publications they give detailed indications of registration (unusual elsewhere in Europe), professing, as Nicolas-Antoine Lebègue [*c.* 1630–1702] wrote in the Preface to his *Premier livre d'orgue* (1676), to give instruction in "the manner of playing the organ on all stops and particularly on those in little use in the provinces . . . to distant organists who are unable to come to hear the diversities that have been discovered on quantities of stops during the last few years". French baroque organs, while conforming generally to the previous description in p. 351, had generally a higher proportion of mixture and mutation stops than the German or Italian organs.*

Couperin's four books of clavecin pieces, grouped into twenty-seven *ordres*, form the culmination of French harpsichord music. An *ordre* is not a strict formal structure, such as the German suite of four basic dances or the sonata da chiesa, but a loose collection of as many as twenty movements in the same key or closely-related keys. Although Couperin used the conventional dance forms, he did not preserve any fixed order of succession, omitting them and adding other forms as he wished. Each movement has a title, and sometimes directions for performance: he was the first composer to write pieces expressly designated for performance on two manuals. In his tutor, *L'Art de toucher le clavecin* (1716), he prescribes a reformed system of fingering, gives detailed instruction on phrasing and style, provides a table of ornaments with explanations (following the custom of all clavecinist-composers from Chambonnières onwards), and concludes with a group of preludes to illustrate the technical and interpretative matters discussed. The range of style, form, and mood in these works is very wide, being surpassed only by that found in Bach's keyboard compositions. While in the shorter pieces† he avoids the long lines of the earlier clavecinists, substituting the short phrases typical of French rococo style and embroidering them with exceedingly intricate and delicate ornamentation (Fig. 2), in the longer dance pieces his quasi-polyphonic

* Cf. Wilfrid Mellers, *François Couperin*, pp. 326-8, for a detailed description of Couperin's organ at St. Gervais and the effects of the various stops.

† E.g. *H.A.M.*, 265.

textures move in broad paragraphs that are obviously influenced by his intimate understanding of Italian music. Allemandes like *La Raphaele* and sarabandes like *L'Unique* (both

'La Garnier', from *Pièces de Clavecin*, Book I, '2nd Ordre' (1713), by François Couperin Le Grand.

from the 8th Ordre) were closely imitated by Bach in his French suites. Many pieces employ rondeau form, such as the gigantic *Passecaille* in B minor (8th Ordre) and *Les bergeries* (6th Ordre) which Bach included in Anna Magdalena's *Clavierbüchlein*. Dance forms from the French opera ballet appear frequently (including the *air tendre*), but the *ouverture* only once, in the opening movement, *La Visionnaire*, of the 25th Ordre. The chaconne variations *Les Folies françaises* (13th Ordre) and the group of movements, *Les Fastes de la Grande et Ancienne Ménestrandise* (11th Ordre), are both 'programmes' of satirical character sketches.

Rameau's clavecin music is closely related in style and harmonic orientation to the instrumental movements of his operas. Though most of it was written before he began opera composition, the essential connection between the two is shown by the number afterwards orchestrated and included in the operas. After his first book, he abandoned many of the conventional aspects of clavecin procedure, especially the imitation of lute chords and the profuse ornamentation of Couperin. He employed arpeggio figuration and wide skips much more frequently than previous French composers. Certain movements, such as *Les Cyclopes*, demand a virtuoso technique in advance of anything hitherto written in France, approaching in difficulty the most elaborate of Scarlatti's sonatas.

French and Italian styles and forms bulk large in German instrumental music of the late baroque. Many composers deliberately tried to combine them to produce a characteristic 'German' style; thus Johann Quantz [1697–1773], writing in 1752, could say: "When we know how to select with due discrimination from the musical tastes of various peoples what is best in each, there arises a mixed taste which, without overstepping the bounds of modesty, may very well be called the German taste, not only because the Germans were the first to hit on it, but also because, introduced many years ago in various parts of Germany, it still flourishes there."* The chief ingredients combined by the Germans were the orchestral technique of Lully, Couperin's keyboard style and technique, and the forms and styles of the Italian concerto. Lully's pupil, Georg Muffat [d. 1704], published two books of orchestral pieces in the French style entitled *Florilegium* (1695 and 1698), with detailed instructions for correct performance. Later, having studied with Corelli in Rome, he issued a third collection of "instrumental concertos, blending the serious and the gay, entitled 'of a more select harmony' because they contain (in the ballet airs) not only the liveliness and grace drawn intact from the Lullian well, but also certain profound and unusual affects of the Italian manner,† various capricious and artful conceits, and alternations of many sorts. . . . These concertos, suited neither to the church (because of the ballet airs and airs of other sorts which they include) nor for dancing (because of other interwoven conceits, now slow and serious, now gay and nimble, and composed only for the express refreshment of the ear), may be performed most appropriately in connection with entertainments . . . and

* Strunk, op. cit., p. 596.

† Cf. *H.A.M.*, 240, for a passacaglia by Muffat amalgamating French and Italian methods.

assemblies of musical amateurs and virtuosi."* Many composers preferred to devote themselves mainly to one style: the Austrians, among whom Fux was the chief, normally followed the Italian closely, while some North Germans, particularly Johann Kaspar Ferdinand Fischer [1660–1738] devoted their efforts to the thorough assimilation of the French.† The blending of the two styles and their (sometimes profound) modification by the fundamentally polyphonic German approach to composition can be most easily seen in keyboard works because the keyboard was for the Germans the natural medium of polyphonic expression.

The German treatment of ground-basses affords many illuminating examples of stylistic incorporation and adaptation. Ex. 44a shows three common basses whose implied harmonies were normally used by the Italians as a foundation for variations built on arpeggio and scale patterns (Handel's two G major chaconnes are typical of this style). Ex. 44a is the opening of an organ chaconne by Johann Pachelbel [1633–1706] on the first bass: the basic harmonies implied serve as an accompaniment to a graceful melody which is not heard again till the end; the twenty-two intervening variations add to and embellish the harmonic structure, clothing it in many different textures (mostly polyphonic), each variation being but a link in a continuous expansion that is only equalled in the chaconnes of Dietrich Buxtehude [1637–1707] and J. S. Bach. Fischer's treatment of the second bass is characteristically decorated in the French manner (Ex. 44c) and modifies the bass (a device found in Couperin's chaconnes) by diminution in the later variations, yet the patterned motifs of the contrapuntal variations and the chromatic progressions in variations 6 and 8 are nearer to Froberger's adaptations of French technique than to the rococo style of the later clavecinists. Pachelbel's D major chaconne on a modified version of the third bass (Ex. 44d)‡ uses the melody, harmony, and bass of its opening as material for variations, some of which are typically Italian in their harmonic figuration, while others resemble the German chorale variations of the mid-seventeenth century.

* Strunk, op. cit., p. 449.

† Cf. *H.A.M.*, 248, a suite by Fischer.

‡ The complete works are readily available in modern editions: both Pachelbel's chaconnes in the edition of his organ works, published by Bährenreiter, and Fischer's in *Alte Meister des Clavier*, published by Peter.

EX.44

(a) Chaconne Ground basses:

(b) Organ chaconne in F minor J. PACHELBEL

(d) Organ chaconne in D J. PACHELBEL

Similar partial adoption of foreign styles appear in the works of Johann Kuhnau [1660–1722], whose harpsichord sonatas employ the forms of the sonata da chiesa, but whose programme sonatas, based on Biblical incidents (e.g. *H.A.M.*, 261), have very little in them that is French, apart from the use of titles and a few French dances. Buxtehude's harpsichord suites follow Froberger's order of movements and also his combination of dance rhythms with 'patterned' variations, while using French ornamentation and lute-style broken chords. Telemann's *Three Dozen Fantasias* include twelve each in Italian and French style, and another twelve in 'mixed' German style. Telemann's chamber music is nearly all written in *style galant*, though the German conception of this was rather more affected and sentimental than the French. Fux, Christoph Graupner [1683–1760], whose music was much admired by Bach, and the Hamburg organist, Jan Reinken [1623–1722], all wrote trio sonatas in the forms of Corelli, but their strict fugal (often canonic) counterpoint was alien to a truly Italian style.

Buxtehude, Pachebel, and Georg Böhm were the three chief organ composers of the generation immediately preceding Bach. Buxtehude's treatment of the instrument displays originality of a very high order. He was one of the first composers to demand virtuoso technique on the pedals, as may be seen in his toccatas (e.g. *H.A.M.*, 234). In compositions based on chorale melodies, he combined the older variation form with the dance suite, and treated the chorale fantasia very rhapsodically. Pachelbel continued to write counterpoints against a chorale canto fermo while experimenting with patterned variations. Böhm introduced French ornaments and lute-style broken chords. Both he and Buxtehude developed the new chorale prelude in which the melody was heard complete in the treble, often profusely ornamented, accompanied by harmonic patterns or quasi-contrapuntal writing.

Handel's instrumental music is basically Italian, though it includes movements written in French style. His twelve concerti grossi for strings (op. 6) have few movements in the Vivaldi form: at least one movement in each employs Torelli's 'orchestra concerto' form, while those that have the Corelli trio concertino are decidedly conservative in manner. The astonishing variety of forms (including French overture, hornpipe, and *da capa* aria) and outstanding melodic appeal make these works some of the greatest in this genre. The six concertos for woodwind and strings (op. 3) exhibit the same general characteristics (several show marked resemblance to some of his trio sonatas, even sharing common material) as do the organ concertos, though these are marked by an improvisatory character which even extends to leaving entire movements to be extemporized by the soloist. On the other hand, the *al fresco* style of the *Water Music* and *Royal Fireworks Music* shows Handel responding to the English musical situation in a strong individual style analogous to that of the choral writing in his oratorios.

Most of his trios have a basic church-sonata structure, but vary greatly in the number of movements and in additional dances: a few (e.g. op. 5, no. 2) consist of a French overture and suite. His keyboard music (which is unjustly neglected today) includes six 'grand fugues' which are masterpieces of the Italian fugal style, eight suites, chaconnes, and sonatas in concerto forms. The suites are as formally varied as the concertos of op. 12 no. 7, for example, opens with a French overture, continues with the four dances of the sonata da camera, and concludes with a passacaglia; no. 6 has a French prelude and Italian largo, a double fugue, and gigue. Handel assumes that the player knows the different style and the correct methods of ornamentation: the full transcription of ornamental signs into musical notation for the aria of the third suite (Ex. 45a) is exceptional and highly personal in its improvisatory style. Bach's transcription for keyboard of the slow movement from Marcello's oboe concerto shows a more systematic approach to the

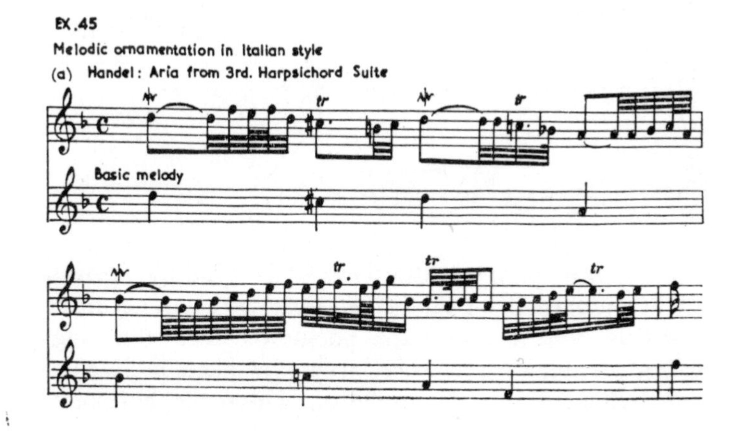

technique of gracing an Italian adagio. The cumulative use of rhythmic division suggested by these bars (Ex. 45b) appears at its height in the second movement of Bach's Italian Concerto, where the subtle thrust and balance of the ornamentation strengthens the long lines of the melody in a manner that, while superficially Italian, is more the result of German habits of melodic decoration learnt in the organ treatment of chorales. The free method of varying a chorale by altering the entire metrical structure of the original tune (as in Ex. 46) permits a greater scope and a broader design than the superimposition of ornaments on a metrically fixed melodic skeleton.

Bach's chorale preludes afford examples of all the forms previously mentioned. He transformed them by choosing the style and texture best suited to the poem to which the chorale melody was originally set. There are many places in his chorale forms (particularly in the preludes) where the harmony or counterpoint cannot be fully understood without reference to the poetical text. In the broad canto fermo pieces, such as *Come, Holy Ghost* from the *Eighteen Chorale Preludes*, he obtains large forms partly by enriching the counterpoint by elements from the concerto style, but mainly by harmonic and contrapuntal textures far richer than those of his contemporaries. This is partly due to the way in which he adds notes which are not part of the fundamental harmony of each beat, but nevertheless blend rather than clash with it, but still more it is due to the nature of his melodic (and therefore contrapuntal) lines, which often imply a two-part or three-part framework. Ex. 47 (a comparatively simple example) shows how a melody can be resolved into two components. When such melodic writing occurs in the individual lines of a fugue the effect is overwhelming in its complexity and yet always immediately compelling. In writing of this sort Bach is unequalled anywhere. "His melodies have the maximum of linear energy, but are at the same time saturated with harmonic implications. His harmonies have the vertical energy of logical chord progressions, but are at the same time linear in all their voices. Hence, whenever Bach writes harmonically the parts also move independently, and whenever he writes polyphonically the parts move also in tonal harmony."*

As a young man Bach acquired his knowledge of French and Italian styles by making copies of other men's compositions and then imitating them. Examples of the first are the early keyboard arrangements of Reinken's trio sonatas and the transcriptions of Vivaldi's and Marcello's concertos for harpsichord; the experience thus gained bore fruit first in such works as the organ fugues on themes by Corelli and Legrenzi, leading later to the better-known orchestra and keyboard suites in French style, the keyboard partitas, containing both French and Italian forms, and the *Concerto in the Italian manner* for harpsichord. The *Brandenburg Concertos* employ the forms of Vivaldi, but are transformed by the German penchant for wind instruments and the fundamentally German contrapuntal approach. In the harpsichord and violin concertos, the sonatas for flute and violin with harpsichord, and the solo sonatas and suites for violin and 'cello, Bach carried the polyphonic instrumental tradition to its conclusion, enriching it always with stylistic elements drawn from French and Italian sources. In organ music he drew little on

* Manfred Bukofzer, *Music in the Baroque Era*, p. 303.

foreign styles, mingling the best of the three 'schools' of German organists (north, central, and southern) into a personal synthesis.

It is still frequently said that Bach wrote *The Well-tempered Clavier* (two books each of twenty-four preludes and fugues in all the major and minor keys) to urge the abandonment of the mean-tone system of tuning (see p. 247) for the method known today as 'equal temperament', which is the accepted basis of modern music. (In this all intervals except the octave are slightly 'out of tune' by the measure of 'just intonation': since all semitones are equal, the fifth is a little flatter, and the fourth a little sharper than they ought to be, and similarly for the other intervals, but as the error in tuning is small and evenly distributed it forms an acceptable compromise.) It is quite true that Bach's

pieces in extreme keys would need to be performed on an instrument tuned in 'equal temperament', and that in his time there was much discussion on methods of tuning and their problems. But similar collections were written by other composers, not so much because of the question of tuning as to satisfy a desire for abstract order in the arrangements of a musical composition. Bach never intended a complete performance of one book of *The Well-tempered Clavier* at a sitting any more than he did of *The Art of Fugue* or *The Musical Offering* (canons, fugues, and a sonata on a theme given to him by Frederick the Great of Prussia). He, like many Germans of his time, found such systematic arrangements logical and intellectually satisfying. This attitude was partly the result of the scientific trend of his age; music was regarded both as an art and a science, and therefore demonstrations of its techniques (as the above-mentioned works are) demanded a 'scientific' presentation. This did not (and does not) mean that such music was 'dry' or 'unemotional'—quite the contrary; the 'intellectual' order of the music was felt to be a reflection of the Divine order of the Universe, "an Hieroglyphical and shadowed lesson of the whole world", and greater pleasure was accordingly derived from it.

INDEX OF MUSIC EXAMPLES

VOLUME II (*c.* 1525–*c.* 1750)

Volume II

GENERAL INDEX